SLA Applied

This singular new textbook is both an introduction to the major theories of second language acquisition and a practical proposal for their application to language-learning courses. In each chapter it explains and evaluates these theories and focuses on recent research that has enriched thinking about the best ways to facilitate communicative effectiveness in an L2. It then suggests practical applications regarding language planning, curriculum development, pedagogy, materials development, teacher development and assessment, thus establishing useful connections between theory and practice.

In addition to focusing on the acquisition of language, *SLA Applied* explores also the roles of such factors as pragmatics, paralinguistic signals, gesture, semiotics, multimodality, embodied language and brain activity in L2 learning and communication.

SLA Applied connects research-based theories to the authors' and students' real-life experiences in the classroom and stimulates reflection and creativity through the inclusion of readers' tasks in every chapter. This engaging and relevant text is suitable for students in Applied Linguistics or TESOL courses, trainee teachers, researchers and practitioners.

Brian Tomlinson (Anaheim University, University of Liverpool) is considered to be one of the world's leading experts on materials development for language learning. He has over a hundred publications and has given conference presentations and run workshops in more than seventy countries. He has worked as a teacher, teacher trainer, curriculum developer, researcher and football coach in nine countries and is the founder and president of MATSDA (the international Materials Development Association). His recent publications include *SLA Research and Materials Development for Language Learning* (Routledge, 2016) and *The Complete Guide to the Theory and Practice of Materials Development for Language Learning* (Tomlinson & Masuhara, Wiley, 2018).

Hitomi Masuhara (University of Liverpool) has worked in Japan, Oman, Singapore and England and is a renowned coursebook and academic author in Japanese and English (e.g. *Materials and Methods in ELT* (McDonough, Shaw & Masuhara, 2013, Wiley) and *The Complete Guide to the Theory and Practice of Materials Development for Language Learning* (Tomlinson & Masuhara, Wiley, 2018)). She is a Higher Education Academy fellow and has won an Innovation and Leadership Chancellor's Award and a Leadership and Teaching Support Network grant for her work *The Cultural Twist*. She has researched the neural-network development process, second language acquisition and materials development, and has given invited presentations in over forty countries.

In a refreshingly innovative look at what actually leads to communicative effectiveness in L2, Tomlinson and Masuhara connect research with practical guidance for teachers and learners of language. This highly accessible textbook should be of keen interest both to researchers, teacher educators, teachers, and writers of curricular materials. The reader is challenged by thought-provoking questions and tasks throughout the book.

Andrew D. Cohen, University of Minnesota

Written in a comprehensive, inclusive and authoritative style, this book provides in-depth coverage of some of the major theories informing SLA research. However, it does so much more than simply cover the theoretical ground. It offers teaching practitioners an informed and insightful means to convert theory into practical application in their own context. It's a volume that every teacher who wishes to be professionally aware will want to have on his or her bookshelf.

Anne Burns, University of New South Wales

The sub-title of the latest book from Brian Tomlinson and Hitomi Masuhara, "Connecting theory and practice" is entirely appropriate. Both authors have collaborated before on several publications aiming to show the mutual interplay of SLA theory and practice, and this volume is another very successful outcome. It presents a comprehensive but accessible overview of the latest SLA research together with a balanced set of relevant pedagogic applications, with many ideas drawn from the authors' own wide experience. It should be on the bookshelf of all second language teachers, trainers, and curriculum specialists as a valuable reference resource.

Chris Kennedy, University of Birmingham

The divide of decades that existed between SLA and the classroom has finally experienced effective bridging! A thought-provoking reference that will especially help undergraduates grasp early in their education, the connections between SLA theory and practice.

Jayakaran Mukundan, Universiti Putra Malaysia

Tomlinson and Masuhara masterfully present SLA theory and showcase its pedagogical applications in this new book. Written in an engaging and approachable style, with abundant real-world examples and up-to-date evidence on how second languages are processed and acquired, this book is sure to meet the needs of both researchers and teachers.

Stephen Fafulas, University of Mississippi

Establishing a lucid connection between theory and practical application is no small task. In this book, Tomlinson and Masuhara succeed in bridging this important gap, illustrating the relevance of SLA theory in the classroom setting. This book is an especially helpful guide to educators seeking to engage more with SLA theory. A valuable contribution to the field.

Michael T. Putnam, Penn State University

SLA Applied
Connecting Theory and Practice

Brian Tomlinson
University of Liverpool

Hitomi Masuhara
University of Liverpool

CAMBRIDGE
UNIVERSITY PRESS

University Printing House, Cambridge CB2 8BS, United Kingdom

One Liberty Plaza, 20th Floor, New York, NY 10006, USA

477 Williamstown Road, Port Melbourne, VIC 3207, Australia

314-321, 3rd Floor, Plot 3, Splendor Forum, Jasola District Centre, New Delhi - 110025, India

103 Penang Road, #05-06/07, Visioncrest Commercial, Singapore 238467

Cambridge University Press is part of the University of Cambridge.

It furthers the University's mission by disseminating knowledge in the pursuit of education, learning and research at the highest international levels of excellence.

www.cambridge.org
Information on this title: www.cambridge.org/9781108471824
DOI: 10.1017/9781108559263

© Brian Tomlinson and Hitomi Masuhara 2021

This publication is in copyright. Subject to statutory exception and to the provisions of relevant collective licensing agreements, no reproduction of any part may take place without the written permission of Cambridge University Press.

First published 2021

A catalogue record for this publication is available from the British Library

Library of Congress Cataloging in Publication data
Names: Tomlinson, Brian, 1943- author. | Masuhara, Hitomi, author.
Title: SLA applied : connecting theory and practice / Brian Tomlinson, University of Liverpool ; Hitomi Masuhara, University of Liverpool.
Other titles: Second language acquitision applied
Description: Cambridge, UK ; New York : Cambridge University Press, 2020. | Includes bibliographical references and index.
Identifiers: LCCN 2020033878 (print) | LCCN 2020033879 (ebook) | ISBN 9781108471824 (hardback) | ISBN 9781108458535 (paperback) | ISBN 9781108559263 (epub)
Subjects: LCSH: Second language acquisition.
Classification: LCC P118.2 .T655 2020 (print) | LCC P118.2 (ebook) | DDC 418.0071–dc23
LC record available at https://lccn.loc.gov/2020033878
LC ebook record available at https://lccn.loc.gov/2020033879

ISBN 978-1-108-47182-4 Hardback
ISBN 978-1-108-45853-5 Paperback

Cambridge University Press has no responsibility for the persistence or accuracy of URLs for external or third-party internet websites referred to in this publication, and does not guarantee that any content on such websites is, or will remain, accurate or appropriate.

Contents

List of Tables, Figures, Diagrams and Boxes	*page* vi
Preface	vii
Introduction	1
1 **Input**	15
2 **Intake Part One – Theory**	66
3 **Intake Part Two – The Application of Theory to Learning**	114
4 **Further Processing, Acquisition and Development**	148
5 **Recognition, Recall, Rehearsal and Retrieval**	191
6 **Comprehension of the L2**	219
7 **Production and Monitoring of the L2**	246
8 **Auto-Input**	282
9 **Some Salient Issues in SLA Research**	298
Summary	342
References	357
Index	407

Tables, Figures, Diagrams and Boxes

Tables

1.1 Selected definitions of input	*page* 23
2.1 Product	68
2.2 Process	68
2.3 Product and process	69
3.1 The learning of English in Betu	122

Figures

1.1 Word cloud of key terms used in the definitions of input	31
1.2 Providers, constituents and receivers of input	38
1.3 Kinds of input	43

Diagrams

2.1	98

Boxes

3.1	125

Preface

We have written this book in order to try to bridge the gap between the research and theories of second language acquisition (SLA) and the practice of second-language learning.

There are many books that provide information about research into what determines SLA as well as information about the theories that have been developed from this research. There are also many books that provide practical guidance for teachers and learners of languages. Unfortunately, there has often been little connection between these two types of publication. The former books are usually written primarily for fellow researchers and for post-graduate students on applied linguistics courses, and sometimes they offer little of practical value for the teacher. The latter books are written primarily for teachers in training and in practice, and often offer little of academic value to researchers. There are some books that have tried to bridge the gap between theory and practice. For example, Ellis and Shintani (2013) focuses on instructed second-language learning, starts each chapter from consideration of the problems faced in a specific area of pedagogic practice and then provides a link to applicable theory. This is different from our book, in that we start from significant findings of SLA research and then consider the value, the feasibility and the ways of applying them to practice. To our knowledge, no other book has as yet tried to relate the major findings of SLA to the practical realities of language learning. That is what we are attempting to do in this book, and what we think makes our book distinctive in the field.

Most of our chapters focus on a specific feature of SLA, with our focus moving gradually, as does the process of acquisition, from input to output to outcome. Each of these chapters (with the deliberate exception of Chapter 2) starts from a description of what the SLA literature says about the focused feature, and then goes on to suggest applications of the SLA findings to such aspects of second-language learning as methodology, materials development, curriculum development, assessment and language planning. In doing so, we keep in mind that not all research findings are directly applicable, that practitioners and learners are often constrained by factors not considered in the original research and that the interaction between theory and practice should be two-way.

In the descriptive parts of our chapters we have been as objective as possible in reporting what the literature has said but, when informed opinions are divided, we have offered our own views based on our experience as researchers and as teachers, teacher trainers, curriculum developers, materials developers and examiners. In addition, in areas that are under-researched we have offered our informed speculation as an impetus to thought and further research. In the application sections we have referred to what little literature there is on the application of SLA theory to practice and have offered our suggestions for implementation, most of which we have tried out in practice. We have also included tasks in both parts of each chapter to stimulate reader thought, discussion and development and we have added suggestions for further reading. We have not provided an answer key or commentary for the tasks, as most of them invite the reader to relate the chapter to their own knowledge, experience and educational environment before coming to their own conclusions.

In reporting the literature on SLA, we have taken a broad view of language acquisition as a multidimensional process involving not just the learning, understanding and production of linguistic items and structures but also the encountering, acquiring and use of language as an element of multimodal, contextualised and purposeful communication. In doing so we have considered how language interacts with visual, auditory, sensory, kinaesthetic and emotive signals to achieve communication and we have referred to literature from the fields, for example, of neurolinguistics, pragmatics, embodied cognition, semiotics, kinaesthetics and communication. In other words, we believe that language acquisition (despite its name) is not just about acquiring language but also about developing the ability to use language accurately, fluently, appropriately and, above all, effectively in conjunction with other means of communication. We do not belong to any particular school of thought or subscribe to any particular -ism but many of our views are similar to those of researchers who consider themselves to be constructivist, humanist, experiential and sociocultural. Put simply, we believe that communication is primarily about human interaction and that human interaction should drive any attempt to teach or learn a language.

Our main aim is to help post-graduate students, teachers in training and in practice, teacher trainers, materials developers, curriculum developers, examiners and language planners to understand what SLA research and theory have to say about the process of learning a second language, to provide them with suggestions for connecting theory and practice and to help them decide for themselves what to apply, and how to apply it, to their own practice. We hope that our book will also be informative, and maybe sometimes provocative, for those students and researchers who specialise in SLA and those who focus on other disciplines in applied linguistics.

Our style we hope is acceptably academic and our approach acceptably rigorous. We have aimed primarily, though, at clarity and impact in our attempt to make SLA accessible to non-specialists in the field, and to do so we have sometimes included personal examples to illustrate and clarify points being made. Our intention is to interact with the reader rather than to lecture or preach. Sometimes we try to achieve this by being informal and personal, sometimes by inviting the reader to think and to connect and sometimes by being provocative.

As we started out as teachers of English as a second or as a foreign language, most (but not all) of our examples are of the learning of English. However, we have worked with teachers of other languages in Belgium, in Luxembourg, in Mauritius, in Singapore and at the then Leeds Metropolitan University, and we are convinced that most of what we say about facilitating SLA is relevant for practitioners involved in the teaching and learning of any language.

We hope you both understand and enjoy our book and find it relevant to your studies, your research and your practice.

Introduction

Our Experience

We both started our careers as teachers of English, Brian in Nigeria and Hitomi in Japan. At that time, we were young and enthusiastic, and focused on keeping our students interested and attentive. Now we are "mature" and enthusiastic, and focused on applying what we know about how languages are best acquired to the practicalities of teaching, teacher training and materials development. This change in focus has been a result of our increased experience, knowledge and awareness, and our determination to bring the theory and the practice of language learning much closer together.

But why do the theory and the practice need bringing together? In our view, second language acquisition (SLA) theory can offer insights and possibilities to practitioners, and language learning in action can inform and enrich SLA research. Many practitioners say that SLA theorists look down on language-learning practitioners, that they publish to enhance their academic reputations rather than to contribute to the improvement of practice, that they write obliquely in SLA jargon to create an exclusive clique, and that much of their research is either devoted to proving what teachers already know or to achieving statistical validation of a theory of little practical value. Many theorists say that second-language practitioners are atheoretical, that they follow unsubstantiated dogma, that they do not make the effort to keep up with research that they could learn from and that they are narrow minded in their adherence to repertoire. There is some truth in what both sides say (see Maley, 2016 for a provocative indictment of SLA research) but not all researchers and practitioners are as separatist as the characterisation above suggests. There have now been many researchers whose presentations and publications are accessible and potentially valuable to practitioners (for example, Anne Burns, Ron Carter, Andrew Cohen, Pauline Dickens, Rod Ellis, Irma Ghosn, Steven Krashen, Michael Long, Mike McCarthy, David Nunan and Jack Richards) and there are many practitioners whose presentations and publications are research-based and of potential value to SLA researchers (for example, Gail Ellis, Jeremy Harmer, Jayakaran Mukundan, Prabhu, Scott Thornbury, Jane Willis and, we hope, ourselves). There is also a group of practitioners whose publications, whilst not making much reference to SLA research, are principled and often informed by research from outside the field of applied linguistics (for example, Rod Bolitho, Alan Maley and Mario Rinvolucri). Most importantly, there are experts now (many of them allocated rather arbitrarily to one of the groups described) who would not consider themselves as exclusively researchers or practitioners. In addition, there is now a rapidly increasing determination to make the findings of SLA research more accessible and useful for language teachers. For example, *The MindBrainEd Think Tanks* is a monthly multimedia magazine published in Japan that aims to make recent SLA-related research in brain studies relevant and accessible to language teachers (see, for example, *Our Favorites in Brain Science and How They Changed Our Teaching*, 2019). The magazine is free and can be subscribed to by sending an e-mail to BRAINSIG+ThinkTankTeam@gmail.com. Another recent initiative is that taken by the journal *Language Learning* in an endeavour to make the findings of SLA research more accessible. See Marsden, Trofimovich and Ellis (2019) for an editorial that introduces this initiative and in which the editors state:

> *Language Learning* is proud to extend its support of open science practices by participating in the OASIS (Open Accessible Summaries in Language Studies) initiative, which aims to make language-related research openly available and easily accessible, both physically and conceptually. As part of the OASIS initiative, *Language Learning* now publishes accessible summaries of all accepted articles, including reviews and syntheses. Written in nontechnical language, accessible summaries provide information about each study's goals, its design and approach, and its results, highlighting findings that may be of interest to those outside academia, such as language educators. (Marsden, Trofimovich & Ellis, 2019, Abstract)

Mackay, Birello and Xerri (2018) is another recent contribution to a growing movement that aims to bridge the much lamented gap between theory and practice in SLA by making research findings more accessible to practitioners, by exploring the application of research to practice and by turning practice into research. The book is a collection of papers covering a number of diverse issues in SLA, such as the value of cooperative learning in the classroom, demotivation and drop-out, memory, pronunciation and teacher questioning of learners. In the Preface, Dörnyei says:

> [R]esearch can be understood in several different ways, but at the most fundamental level it concerns simply *trying to find answers to questions*. If we take this basic definition, the researcher versus classroom practitioner divide disappears, because both groups spend a great deal of their time trying to understand issues and find answers and solutions to questions that are relevant to their profession. (Mackay, Birello & Xerri, 2018, p. 7)

In our book we aim to make the answers that researchers have found more accessible to classroom practitioners, and the answers that practitioners have found more available to researchers.

Providing an accessible introductory overview to the main issues of SLA and suggesting effective applications to classroom practice are also aims of both Benati and Angelovska (2016) and Nava and Pedrazzini (2018). The latter is particularly interesting, as it introduces eight key principles of SLA and then provides the reader with the videoed experience of these principles in action in interaction between teachers and learners in the classroom and with tasks inviting reflection, connection to previous experience and application to practice.

Applicability to classroom practice is also a focus of DeKeyser and Botana (2019) and Lessard-Clouston (2018). DeKeyser and Botana (2019) is a research-based book bringing together studies on instructed language acquisition that all focus on what makes the research relevant to classroom applications. Lessard-Clouston (2018) provides an overview of such significant aspects of SLA as input, output and interaction, as well as the roles of age, anxiety and error correction. It focuses on how research and theory can be applied to classroom practice. It does so in a very accessible style and is written very much to help teachers, and teachers in training, to understand current SLA theory and to make use of it in their methodology and materials. This is a very short book (only forty-nine pages) that is addressed directly to teachers and frequently asks them "Reflective Questions" inviting them to think about information and issues and to connect them with their own experience (for example, "What connections between languages are you aware of that you can share with students? How might you incorporate those in your English teaching?" (Lessard-Clouston, 2018, p. 3).

In addition to a recent determination to make research more accessible to practitioners, there is also a movement of researchers to focus their research less on discrete, tightly controlled laboratory experiments and more on the naturalistic, holistic use of language. For example, Kandylaki and Bornkessel-Schlesewsky (2019, p. 405) state:

> The study of language in the brain has traditionally been undertaken via tightly controlled experimental designs. However, current streams of research have started to challenge the assumption that results from controlled experiments should be expected to generalise to more naturalistic settings. Accordingly, a number of research groups are now actively exploring the use of new designs and methodologies in order to extend our understanding of language processing under ecologically valid conditions. (Kandylaki & Bornkessel-Schlesewsky, 2019, abstract, p. 405)

There is hope, then, of a greater coming together of expertise, excellence and enthusiasm, and this is what we are both working towards and what inspired us to write this book in order to bring theory and practice even closer together.

In our early experience of teaching and of our reading and learning about teaching, we concentrated on the practicalities of getting our students to progress. We used coursebooks that followed a grammar translation approach, then coursebooks that followed a situational approach, then coursebooks that followed a Presentation–Practice–Production (PPP) approach, and then coursebooks that followed a communicative approach. Then we did courses on applied linguistics and discovered the research and the theories of SLA. What struck us both was how fascinating and potentially valuable they were but also how disconnected they were from what typically went on in the coursebooks and classrooms we had experienced. They were disconnected, in that most of the researchers and theorists seemed unaware of such realities as that many teachers were faced with the unattainable task of transforming large classes of unmotivated and often reluctant learners from low level language users into high level language users in two or three hours a week. They were also disconnected in that most language teachers were unaware of SLA research and theory and taught their learners basically in the ways they had been taught themselves.

On our courses, we learned about sociolinguistics, psycholinguistics, discourse analysis, phonetics, error analysis and language acquisition, and when we asked the question, "How can we apply this to language teaching?" we were often told, "That's not my responsibility. That's yours". We also learned about methodology, materials development and assessment, but there was little connection between these practical modules and the theoretical modules that made up the bulk of our courses.

Independently, and many thousand miles apart, we started to think for ourselves and to work out ways of applying what we had learned theoretically to what we were doing practically. We began, for example, to reject the PPP approaches of the coursebooks because they did not match such requirements of language acquisition as rich exposure to language in contextualised use, affective and cognitive engagement, opportunities for learner noticing and discovery and opportunities for authentic communication. We also began to develop our own experiential and humanistic approaches to materials development and to share them with teachers and trainees on courses and in workshops.

When Brian was working as leader of the PKG English Programme in Indonesia in the 1980s (Tomlinson, 1990) he was able to send over thirty teachers to do MA courses at universities in the UK. When these teachers returned to Indonesia, they nearly all said they had enjoyed their courses and had learned a lot about language and about language learning. They also said that they could not see any way of applying what they had learned to the teaching and teacher training they were going to do now they had returned. It was at this point that Brian developed the determination to design and deliver an MA course that combined theory and practice in ways that would benefit the participants in terms of professional development, theoretical awareness and practical application. A few years later, he designed and delivered such a course at the then University of Luton. Hitomi came to the University of Luton to work on her PhD research and contributed to the development and delivery of the MA course. Its focus was on materials development for language learning, and its approach was to start by introducing such topics as materials evaluation, materials adaptation, materials writing and materials use, and then to raise theoretical questions about them in relation to the facilitation of language acquisition. Modules on the usual applied linguistics topics were then introduced, with the emphasis on SLA and with the intention of helping the students to answer the questions raised in the introductory modules on materials development. The topics of these introductory modules were then returned to, and practice and theory were connected by the students prior to their production of a set of innovative language-learning materials supported and driven by a theoretical rationale. This MA was further developed by Brian and Hitomi at the then Leeds Metropolitan University, and was cloned with permission by the International Graduate School of English (IGSE) in Seoul. This is one example of coherent postgraduate courses that are now attempting to break down the barriers between theory and practice and to help their participants to achieve valuable connections. Other courses we have worked on or examined that combine theory and practice in useful ways include MA courses at the now University of Bedfordshire, Bilkent University in Ankara, the New School in New York, the Norwich Institute for Language Education, the University of Liverpool and the University of Portsmouth, as well as an Ed.D course at Anaheim University.

The Literature on the Learning and Teaching of Languages

There is a rich literature on the teaching of languages, but not as many publications on the learning of languages. The publications on the teaching of languages tend to focus on methodology and, in particular, on what the teacher can do in the classroom. This is true for example of Widdowson (1978), Littlewood (1981), Brown and Yule (1983), Stern (1983), Richards (1985), Nunan (1991, 2004), Ur (1996), Jones (1997), Kelly (2000), Carter and Nunan (2001), Richards and Rodgers (2001), Thornbury (2002, 2005), Nuttall (2005), Harmer (2007a, 2007b) and Richards and Schmidt (2010), books which all feature "teacher" or "teaching" in the title. The publications that focus on learning and the learner (and have learning or learner in the title) tend to have been published since around 2005, for example, Hinkel (2005), Mishan (2005), Griffiths (2008), Tomlinson (2008a, 2012), Allwright and Hanks (2009), Coyle, Hood and Marsh (2010) and Shatz and Wilkinson (2010). This is a shift that probably mirrors our eventual success in persuading publishers to allow us to focus on learning in our titles rather than on teaching, as for example, in Tomlinson (2013b, 2016a) and Tomlinson and Masuhara (2010, 2018b) compared to Tomlinson (1998, 2003). It is also a shift, though, that reflects a very noticeable acknowledgement that, whilst teacher procedures and techniques are important, what really matters is the quality of learning that is facilitated. There are still books published with teacher or teaching in the title, but nowadays they tend to focus on aspects of teacher behaviour previously unresearched or on the effect the teacher can have in creating conditions favourable to language acquisition rather than on teacher procedures and techniques. For example, Meddings and Thornbury (2009) focus on Dogme in language teaching and on the replacement of materials with conversation-driven activities, Oxford (2011) focuses on language learning strategies in the teaching of languages, Goh and Burns (2012) focus on an holistic approach to teaching speaking and Agudo (2018) focuses on emotions in second-language teaching. There are also books with both teaching and learning in the title and an objective of linking together the principles of both, for example Nunan (1999), Hedge (2000), Johnson (2001), Byram and Hu (2013) and Cook (2016).

Our stance has always been that it is not teaching techniques and procedures that matter but the promotion of learning, and that the teacher's main role is to generate energy, stimulate learners and provide opportunities for learning. Unfortunately, that has not always been the focus of teacher training or teacher assessment, in which teachers have often been judged on their ability to demonstrate the techniques favoured by the experts at the time. Nor has it always been the focus of the literature on language teaching. Things are changing now though, and the focus is much more on the teacher achieving rapport, empathy and stimulation as well as on the pivotal role of the learners in their own learning, and especially on the learners as agents of their own learning (Larsen-Freeman, 2019; Piccardo & North, 2019). This is a role that is being investigated by SLA research and theory, and it is this that we are particularly interested in. What can learners do mentally and physically, inside the classroom and outside it, to maximise their potential for language acquisition? And what can teachers do to facilitate this process?

In addition to books focusing on teaching and on learning languages, there are also books focusing on materials development for language learning, on digital language learning, on curriculum development, on assessment and on language planning. Some of the publications in these areas include overt connections to SLA research and theory, for example, Garton and Graves (2014), Harwood (2014), Tomlinson (2013b, 2016a) and Tomlinson and Masuhara (2018b) on materials development, Pegrum (2014), González-Lloret and Ortega (2014) and Zou and Thomas (2018) on digital learning, Nation and Macalister (2010) and Richards (2017) on curriculum development, Hughes (2002) and Wolf and Butler (2017) on assessment, and Kennedy and Tomlinson (2013) on language planning.

The Literature on Second Language Acquisition (SLA)

There is a long history of theory- and research-based books on SLA, with the early books that focused specifically on it including Dunkel (1948), Cazden, Cancino, Rosansky and Schumann (1975), Gingras (1978), Hatch (1978b), Richards (1978), Andersen (1981), Krashen (1981, 1982), Bailey, Long and Peak (1983), Ellis (1985), Gass and Madden (1985), Cook (1986), Fletcher and Garman (1986), McLaughlin (1987) and Tarone (1988). These early books focused mainly on linguistic issues, such as transfer from the L1 to the L2, the causes and roles of making errors, teacher feedback, error analysis, the developing learner interlanguage, which was neither the L1 nor the L2 but was influenced by both, the developmental sequence of acquisition, the relative significance of input and of output, and code switching from one language to another. There was also much discussion on the issue of conscious versus subconscious learning, which had been introduced by Krashen's distinction between conscious, deliberate *learning* and subconscious, incidental *acquisition* (1981). Their contributors tended to use evidence derived from analysis of learner language to develop metaphors and conjectures about what happens in the language learner's brain, for example, Krashen's (1981) use of the metaphor of the LAD (Language Acquisition Device) originally posited by Chomsky and Chomsky's use of the theory of universal grammar (1976), "the abstract knowledge of language which children bring to the task of learning their native language" (R. Ellis, 1994, p. 727). Most of these metaphors about the brain have now been discredited as a result of evidence from neurolinguistic research (for example, evidence that there is no one single area of the brain dedicated to language learning) but they were very useful at the time in stimulating thought and enquiry.

Books on SLA continued to be published in the 1990s. They revisited the issues of their predecessors, but gave greater emphasis to the learner when discussing such psycholinguistic issues as language anxiety, language aptitude and learner affect, as well as such sociolinguistic concerns as sociological distance and social interaction, and such issues as learner differences, learner autonomy, learner strategies and variability. These books included Skehan (1989), O'Malley and Chamot (1990), Oxford (1990), Van Patten and Lee (1990), Cook (1991), Larsen-Freeman and Long (1991), Wenden (1991), Johnson (1992), Lightbown and Spada (1993), R. Ellis (1994), Gass and Selinker (1994), Ritchie and Batia (1996) and Skehan (1998).

Books on SLA continue to be published in the twenty-first century, with many of them revisiting the issues of their predecessors and many adding sociolinguistic and/or psycholinguistic issues (for example, Lantolf, 2001; Doughty & Long, 2003; Long, 2006; Norris & Ortega, 2006; Van Patten & Williams, 2007; R. Ellis, 2008; Atkinson, 2010; Gass & Mackey, 2012; Cook & Singleton, 2014; Hummel, 2014; Dörnyei & Ryan, 2015; R. Ellis, 2015; Saville-Troike & Barto, 2017). Some have paid special attention to pragmatic development (e.g. Rose & Kasper, 2001), some have added small sections on implications for L2 learning and teaching (for example, Hummel, 2014; R. Ellis, 2015; Saville-Troike & Barto, 2017) and a few have devoted considerable attention to neurolinguistics perspectives (e.g. Schumann et al., 2004; R. Ellis, 2008; Gass & Mackey, 2012).

The literature on SLA referred to in the paragraphs above is just a small sample of the massive output of SLA researchers so far. Some of the references are to publications on specific aspects of SLA, but many of them are general books covering the main focus of SLA research at the time. Perhaps the most comprehensive and influential general books on SLA have been R. Ellis (1994) and its revised version, R. Ellis (2008), with the most recent comprehensive account of most aspects of SLA probably being Gass and Mackey (2012) and the most concise and accessible discussion of the main issues probably being R. Ellis (2015). The chapter titles of R. Ellis (2015) give a good indication of the current concerns of SLA researchers and are as follows:

1. SLA research: an overview
2. Age and SLA
3. Psychological factors and SLA
4. The development of a second language
5. Variability in learner language
6. The role of the first language
7. Input and interaction: the cognitive-interactionist perspective
8. Cognitive aspects of SLA
9. Social aspects of SLA
10. The role of explicit instruction
11. The role of implicit instruction
12. Understanding and applying SLA

What is noticeably absent from many of the publications listed above is reference to neurolinguistics research investigating what happens in the brain to facilitate or inhibit language acquisition, reference to research on the role of the inner voice and of sensory imagery in language acquisition and reference to research on the role of embodied cognition (i.e. the use of the body to acquire and use a language). There are now, however, some publications that address one or more of these areas directly. For example, Pavlenko (2005), Altarriba and Isurin (2012), Colantoni, Steele and Escudero (2015) and Schütze (2017) focus on brain studies in relation to SLA, Archer (2003), Centeno-Cortes and Jimenez (2004), de Guererro (2005), Paivio (2007), Tomlinson (2011d, 2020a) and Tomlinson and Avila (2007a, 2007b) focus on the roles of inner speech and/or visualisation and Atkinson (2010), McCafferty and Stam (2008), Paradowski (2014) and Rosborough (2014) focus on embodied language and/or cognition, and especially on the way that sensory, affective and motor images interact in the brain. Also some of the mainstream general books on SLA now include sections on, or at least reference to, brain studies (for example, R. Ellis, 2008; Harley, 2008; Gass & Mackey, 2012; Saville-Troike & Barto, 2017).

The Literature on the Application of SLA Theory to Language Learning

Publications that Focus on Practice and Look for Theory to Support or Inform It

One book that has been attempting for a long time to link SLA theory and teaching practice is Cook (2016). Now in its fifth edition, this book looks at the main language-teaching practices, such as the teaching of grammar, the teaching of pronunciation and the teaching of writing, and links them to SLA findings that could be applied in these practices. It is a well-informed book that is interestingly and provocatively self-centred, in that it highlights those theories favoured by Cook. Whilst other SLA researchers might accept many of these theories, there are some theories and applications advocated, for example applications of the theory of universal grammar, which many researchers would now consider to be unsubstantiated and outdated.

Another publication that takes the approach of focusing on pedagogy and then linking it to research and theory is Ellis and Shintani (2013). The authors examine problematic issues in language pedagogy in terms of SLA by focusing on pedagogic proposals in teachers' guides and asking for each if it coincides with what SLA tells us about how languages are acquired. Teaching methods, syllabus design, explicit instruction, comprehension versus production-based instruction, task-based instruction, authentic materials, the role of the first language, error correction and catering for individual differences in the classroom are some of the areas investigated.

Recently, there have been a number of publications and presentations advocating the application of theory to practice. For example, Hanks (2017) is an article on "Integrating research and pedagogy" and Halliday and Webster (2018) is a collection of twenty-first-century publications by Halliday (edited by Webster) in relation to what Halliday calls "appliable linguistics". It contains sixteen entries, including one entitled "Putting linguistic theory to work" and another entitled "Applying linguistic theory: Editor's introduction". "Scott Thornbury on mediation between researchers and practitioners", "Prof. Larsen-Freeman talks about complexity theory its implications for TESOL" and "Professor Holme on Cognitive linguistics and the second language classroom" (published as Holme, 2012) are keynote video talks made available in 2019 on the TESOL Academic website (www.youtube.com/user/TESOLacademic).

Publications that Focus on Research and Suggest Applications to Practice

In recent years, there have been numerous attempts to combine theory and practice by focusing on what has been termed instructed second language acquisition (ISLA). R. Ellis (1990, 2005b, 2012) has led the way and other valuable contributions include Robinson (2002), Van Patten (2004), Houssen and Pierrard (2005), Benati, Laval and Arche (2013), Ellis and Shintani (2013), Loewen (2015), Shintani (2016), Loewen and Sato (2017), Sato and Loewen (2019) and Rokita-Jaskow and M. Ellis (2019). These books focus on research into the effects of types of teacher interventions on learner achievement, with some of the research being into the effects of typical teacher interventions and some of it on the effects of interventions designed to apply principles which derive from SLA theory and research (e.g. Shintani, 2016). For a review of early publications on ISLA see

Schmitt (2008) and for a clear specification of what ISLA involves see Long (2017). There is now also a journal called *ISLA* published by Equinox (https://journals.equinoxpub.com/index.php/isla).

The area that seems to have led the way in suggesting applications of SLA theory to practice is materials development. Tomlinson (1998a) was probably the breakthrough publication. Many of its chapters focus on practical issues of materials development, evaluation and adaptation but some of them are research-informed. For example, Tomlinson (1998b) includes a lengthy section on "SLA research and materials development" (pp. 5–22). In the same publication R. Ellis (1998) makes frequent reference to SLA theory in investigating the evaluation of communicative tasks, Maley (1998) makes reference to a number of SLA researchers (and especially those advocating a research-informed approach to Task-Based Language Teaching (TBLT)) in proposing the development and use of flexi-materials, Hooper Hansen refers to the acquisition theories of Krashen (1981) and Asher (1977) in describing and advocating the Suggestopedia approaches of Lozanov, and Tomlinson (1998c) makes use of the literature on visualisation in language learning and use in his chapter proposing ways of helping learners to visualise when developing their reading skills. This publication has since been revised (with the addition of a research-informed chapter by R. Ellis, 2011 on macro- and micro-evaluations) and published as Tomlinson (2011a). McGrath (2012) was primarily a publication advocating principled procedures for materials development and evaluation but in doing so it made some reference to current research on SLA, as does its revised version which has been published as McGrath (2016). Tomlinson (2003, 2013a), Harwood (2014) and Garton and Graves (2014) include reference to and reports of materials development research. Tomlinson (2013a) and Tomlinson (2016) are books written with the explicit aim of connecting applied linguistics and SLA research with materials development. Tomlinson (2013a) consists of chapters detailing what we know from research about various aspects of communicative performance and comparing this to what is typically done by language learning materials to help learners achieve communicative competence. Tomlinson (2016a) connects SLA research to materials that aim to facilitate the development of, for example, grammatical competence, pragmatic competence, interactive competence, semantic competence, communicative competence and creativity. Most recently Tomlinson and Masuhara (2018b) follows a research-informed approach in discussing all the main aspects of materials development and also contains an extended chapter on materials-development research.

Another area where applications of SLA theory to practice have been advocated is CALL (Computer-Assisted Language Learning). There are many publications promoting the potential benefits of CALL, and of other types of digital delivery such as smart phones, as well as offering practical advice on how to maximise the affordances they offer. There are also a number of publications advocating and/or reporting research on the effectiveness of CALL and digital delivery in facilitating language acquisition. For example:

- Warschauer and Healey (1998) provides an early overview of the effectiveness of computers in promoting language learning;
- Chapelle and Lui (2007) investigates the research on authentic tasks in CALL;
- Kukulska-Hulme and Shield (2008) reports research on mobile assisted language learning;
- Felix (2008) reviews two decades of research on the effectiveness of CALL;
- Hubbard (2009) also reviews research on CALL;
- Thomas (2010) reviews the research on Web 2.0 and second language learning;
- Grgurović, Chapelle and Shelley (2013) is a meta-analysis of effectiveness studies on computer technology-supported language learning;
- Oberg and Daniels (2013) analyses the effect a student-centred mobile learning instructional method has on language acquisition;
- Thomas, Reinders and Warschauer (2013) reviews the research on contemporary CALL;
- Tomlinson and Whittaker (2013) reports case studies of the use of blended learning;
- González-Lloret and Ortega (2014) focuses on researching technology and tasks;
- Pegrum (2014) reviews the research on mobile assisted language learning;
- Carrier, Damerow and Bailey (2017) reports academic studies and practitioner research in the use of digital learning technologies in language classrooms and in online learning. It explores the experience of researchers and practitioners in both formal and informal learning contexts and provides information about current research, theory and practice at classroom and at education system levels.

There are a number of recent publications that focus on research on one particular aspect or application of SLA and then suggest pedagogic applications. For example, Nassaji and Kartchava (2017) brings together current research, analysis and discussion of the role of corrective feedback in second language teaching and learning. It identifies the principles of effective feedback strategies and makes suggestions for how to apply them in classroom practice. This follows on from earlier journal articles reporting research demonstrating the benefits of corrective feedback in the classroom for the acquisition of some language features (for example, Lightbown & Spada, 1990; Lyster, Saito & Sato, 2013). Other recent publications that focus on practical consequences or applications of a specific aspect of SLA include Bao (2014) on the value of silence, Agudo (2018) on emotions in second language teaching and Tomlinson (2020a) on the use of the inner voice. Tomlinson (2020b) investigates the disconnect between SLA theory and materials-development practice and suggests ways of achieving greater connection.

There are also a few publications that consider applications of SLA research to assessment (e.g. Leclercq, Edmonds & Hilton, 2014), to curriculum development (e.g. Richards, 2001; Nation & Macalister, 2010) and to language planning (e.g. Kennedy & Tomlinson, 2013).

Publications that Report Principles Being Applied in Practice

Kormos (2012) is one of the few books we know that investigates the role of cognitive and affective variables in task performance, in our opinion variables that have been insufficiently considered in both research and materials development. In this book, Kormos summarises studies that have been carried out in Hungary using narrative tasks in the teaching of English as a foreign language. The book investigates discourse and psycholinguistic features of narratives and the ways in which different individual responses to narratives influence learner performance. It is in this context that the role of cognitive and affective variables in task performance are investigated, and their impact on linguistic development assessed.

Another publication that reports principles being applied in practice is Widodo, Wood and Gupta (2018), a book that contains chapters reporting on the meeting of theory and practice in Asian English-language classrooms. The editors believe very strongly in the need for practice to be informed by theory, and theory to be grounded in practice, and this principle is reflected in the seventeen chapters contributed by Asian, Australian, New Zealand and British researchers (another example of the widening of applied linguistics away from the exclusivity of the American/British axis).

A very interesting new approach to investigating principles in application is demonstrated by Nava and Pedrazzini (2018). This is a book that, according to its blurb, uses "the interactions of teachers and learners to illustrate eight key second language acquisition principles 'in action', (to guide) students from theory to practice with the help of video recordings, key questions and reflective tasks". It is designed to help readers to explore principles in action in the classroom in relation to:

1 Form, meaning and use
2 Comprehensible input
3 Input noticing and processing
4 Implicit and explicit knowledge
5 Interactive and corrective feedback
6 Output production

The Actual Interface between SLA Theory and Language-Learning Practice

Our recent experience of observing lessons, analysing coursebooks, talking to teachers and teacher trainers, attending conferences and participating in projects in many different countries suggests that it is arguable that, despite recent attempts to suggest applications of SLA theory to language learning, language planners are still planning in similar ways, teachers are still teaching in similar ways, curriculum developers and materials developers are still developing similar curricula and materials, testers are still testing in similar ways and learners are still trying to learn in similar ways. There are some exceptions. For example, a new SLA research-informed primary/secondary-school syllabus is being developed in Singapore; British Council sponsored teachers are researching their own practice in India and in some cases linking it to SLA theory (Tomlinson & Keedwell, 2017); Ministries of Education in Asia are developing SLA-informed task-based syllabuses (though in a weakened form) (Thomas & Reinders, 2015; Tomlinson, 2015); and some computer-assisted materials are being developed that match SLA theory (Thomas, 2010; Thomas, Reinders & Warschauer, 2013; Carrier, Damerow & Bailey, 2017). In addition, some coursebooks are attempting to help learners personalise their materials in accordance with SLA theory (Tomlinson & Masuhara, 2013); the Shanghai Centre for Research in Language education (SCRELE) is currently revising Shanghai secondary-school coursebooks in line with SLA theory and some assessors are developing instruments of assessment designed to offer learning opportunities (Tomlinson, 2005b; Hattie & Clark, 2018). However, it seems that throughout the world, most language planning still focuses on teaching rather than learning (Kennedy & Tomlinson, 2013), most teaching still follows a PPP approach that is not supported by most SLA researchers, most curriculum development still results in syllabuses that are lists of language items and structures to be taught and learned, most commercially published materials still follow a PPP approach (Tomlinson & Masuhara, 2013) and feature closed activities (Freeman, 2014; Tomlinson, 2018b), most assessments still feature closed instruments such as multiple-choice tests, true/false tests, matching tests and substitution tests, and most learners are still trying to learn an L2 through memorising rules, memorising lexis and practising structures. The result is that, for example, foreign and second-language learners have a high rate of failure, international companies in Malaysia have complained that university graduates (after fifteen years of learning English) cannot communicate effectively, and private language schools are booming all over the world (especially in such countries as China, Indonesia, Japan and S. Korea, where, despite Ministry attempts at reform, traditional practices still prevail in public-sector institutions).

Why is this so? Why are greater attempts not being made to expose learners to a rich input of contextualised language in use, to ensure that texts and tasks are meaningful to them, to engage them cognitively and affectively, to help them to make discoveries about language use for themselves, to help them to look out for the target language outside the classroom and to provide them with opportunities for purposeful communication? In other words, why are language-learning practitioners not taking the research-informed actions that we will be recommending in this book? Some of the answers are obvious. Many practitioners simply do not know what SLA research is finding, because they have no access to the literature reporting it, they find the literature impenetrable, they have no time to read the literature or they have no faith that the literature will tell them anything of practical value (Maley, 2016). Some practitioners do know about recent SLA findings; however, some of them do not believe that they are of value, some do not know how to apply them, some are threatened by the findings and are reluctant to lose the power and prestige established by their current expertise, and some are influenced by the prevailing language-learning dogma and believe in the value of what they are doing. Or they would like to apply some of the current SLA theories but are constrained from doing so by the authorities, by parents, by syllabuses, by their colleagues, by examinations and by a perceived lack of time.

R. Ellis (2015) concludes by claiming that "the origins of SLA lay in a wish to improve language pedagogy" (p. 308) but also by warning against the dangers of being prescriptive in applying SLA findings. R. Ellis recommends formulating generalisations about SLA findings for teachers to make use of (something that has been done by Ellis, 2010a; Lightbown, 2000; Tomlinson, 1998, 2003, 2011b, 2013a, 2013b, 2016 and Tomlinson & Masuhara, 2018b), getting practitioners to replicate SLA experiments and take "pedagogic issues as the starting point and then scrutinise them from the perspective of SLA" (p. 310). What we are intending to do with this book is to provide readers with relevant information about the findings and theories of current SLA research so they can decide for themselves what is of potential value. We are also intending to suggest universal applications of theory to practice, and to stimulate readers to come up with their own locally appropriate applications.

1 Input

Part One: Theory

Introduction

The word "input" is used in our everyday conversation to mean something that we put into a system, organisation or device. For example, input can be energy that can be put into an energy-supply circuit, resources that are put into a company or information that is fed to a computer.

How is the term "input" used in the field of language learning? How do scholars in second language acquisition (SLA) define the term "input"? What is the role of input in language acquisition? What kinds of input are there? How does input facilitate language acquisition? How significant is input in language acquisition?

This chapter explores such questions in the first part, and discusses in the second part some ways of applying what we understand about input to language planning, curriculum development, teaching methodology, teacher-development, materials development and assessment.

What is Input?

Historical Background

Input and the Language Acquisition Device

In considering definitions of "input", it may be worthwhile to start with Noam Chomsky's quote from his seminal book originally published in 1965 (republished in a 2014 fiftieth anniversary edition) as it exhibits fundamental concepts and issues that run through influential SLA studies from the 1970s onwards.

Chomsky (1965) describes input in relation to a language acquisition device (LAD) and to output: "Much information can be obtained about both the primary data that constitute the input and the grammar that is the 'output' of such a device, and the theorist has the problem of determining the intrinsic properties of a device capable of mediating this input-output relationship" (ibid., p. 48).

By "device", he is referring to his proposed concept of an LAD (ibid., pp. 33–34) – a hypothetical innate capability with which humans are born. In Chomsky's words (ibid., p. 32), "a language-acquisition device ... is capable of utilizing ... primary linguistic data as the empirical basis for language learning".

In sum, he seems to be using the term "input" to mean something that contains "the linguistic primary data" that language users receive by experiencing the language in use.

Chomsky's notion of LAD and use of the terms "input" and "output" seem to provide evidence of the "mind–computer" analogy that characterised the fields of information processing and cognitive science in the 1950s and 1960s. Such an analogy seems to underlie even our contemporary definitions of input in SLA literature, whether this is explicitly acknowledged or not. Note, also, Chomsky (1965, p. 24) is interested in linguistic "competence" (i.e. "intrinsic knowledge of the idealised native speaker") that underlies well-formed sentences in output, regardless of ill-formed or impoverished input in the incoming "performance" data (i.e. actual utterances that may contain errors as a result of various internal and external constraints, such as distraction, noise or memory limitation).

> **Readers' Tasks**
>
> Chomsky (1965, pp. 59–60) argues that "knowledge of grammar ... cannot arise" from step-by-step inductive operations such as "substitution procedures" and "filling of slots in frames" – popular teaching exercises used in the audiolingual method in the 1960s. Instead, he advocates that we should focus on the innate capability for acquiring languages, which is operationalised within an LAD.
>
> However, more than fifty years later, many materials, teachers and learners seem to assume that language acquisition will happen if they teach/learn linguistic input in an explicit manner through repeated practice and tests (e.g. gap filling, pattern practice).
>
> 1 Do you agree with Chomsky's concept of an LAD i.e. native speakers' innate capability to acquire language from input? If so, why? If not, why not?
> 2 Do you think L2 learners possess an LAD?

Comprehensible Input

Stephen Krashen (1981, 1982, 1985) made a considerable contribution in spurring the development of the field of SLA when he proposed his "theory of language acquisition" and highlighted the central role that input plays in language acquisition.

Krashen (1982, p. 6) points out that Chomsky's transformational generative grammar (TG) and the subsequent theoretical developments provide "a theory of the product, the adult's competence, and not a theory of how the adult got that competence. It is not a theory of the process of language acquisition". He then proposes a "theory of language acquisition" that "attempts to deal with the process of language acquisition, not its product".

Krashen (1985) argues that the single most important source of L2 learning is "comprehensible input" i.e. the language that learners process for meaning and which contains linguistic data slightly above their current level.

Krashen's concept of "comprehensible input" derives from studies in the 1970s in relation to what Krashen (1981) called "simple codes" such as:

- Caretaker speech/child-directed speech (including contributions from other input providers such as siblings)
- Teacher talk (i.e. use of the target language by teachers in their classrooms during explanation, classroom management instructions and interaction with learners)
- Foreigner talk (i.e. L1 user's modified language use in order to communicate with L2 learners/users)
- Interlanguage talk (i.e. L2 learners' use of the target language in peer and group work)

It is interesting to note that, based on a case study of the language learning experience of "S.K.", he mentions interlanguage talk as well as teacher talk to be "extremely useful in attaining initial levels of fluency, in acquiring (as opposed to learning)" (Krashen, 1981, p. 124).

The users of simple codes roughly estimate capabilities and adjust their language according to the interlocutors, who may be struggling to understand or communicate. The sole purpose of using simple codes is to achieve successful communication (i.e. not to teach the target language). And yet learners seem to be able to use experience of these codes in order to acquire their target language.

The typical features of these simple codes include phonological modifications (e.g. slower tempo, loudness, longer pauses at grammatical boundaries, exaggerated intonation, clearer enunciation to make the constituent boundaries more intelligible), restricted vocabulary, simpler clause and sentence structures and a limited range of topics (i.e. the "here-and-now"). These simple codes may also involve use of gestures and contextual clues, as well as provision of extra input through repetition, elaboration and recasts (i.e. a type of feedback in which a correctly reformulated version of the learner's original utterance is implicitly or explicitly provided during communication). See Krashen (1981) and Hatch (1983) for detailed accounts of the role of simple code input in language acquisition.

Krashen (1981) explains the relationship of incoming comprehensible input and the child's language acquisition using the term "$i + 1$":

> Children progress by *understanding* language that is a little beyond them. That is, if a child is at stage i, that child can progress to stage $i + 1$ along the "natural sequence" (where i and $i + 1$ may be a block of structures; more correctly the child who has just acquired the members of i can then acquire a member of $i + 1$) by understanding language containing $i + 1$. The child understands language containing a structure that is a bit beyond him or her with the aid of context. (Krashen, 1981, p. 126)

Krashen elaborates on the importance of roughly tuned input as optimal in language acquisition:

> The caretaker is not consciously aiming at $i + 1$. Rather, the caretaker estimates the child's level of competence via the child's own linguistic output and his or her reactions to caretaker speech, and in attempting to communicate with the child provides input that covers $i + 1$ as well as some structures that the child has already acquired (i, $i - n$) and some that the child has not yet acquired ($i + n$). In other words, the caretaker's speech provides a "net" of structure that generally includes $i + 1$, but contains a bit more ... The caretaker's net may have these advantages: by including some of the $i - n$ and $i + n$ structures, by including more than $i + 1$, it provides built-in anticipation and review, which may be useful. Second, the wider, roughly tuned net guarantees that $i + 1$ will always be covered. Also, a wider net allows more than one child to be helped at one time. On the other hand, the caretaker net is not so wide that the child has difficulty understanding, and "tunes out"... (Krashen, 1981, p. 127)

To put Krashen's use of "input" in a historical perspective, readers may notice that:

- he takes a nativist stance, in line with Chomsky's LAD;
- he seems to focus on acquisition of structures (e.g. morphemes) and the sequence of acquisition of formal aspects of language when he describes "$i + 1$";
- unlike Chomsky, Krashen believes in the primacy of meaning and comprehension (through which forms are acquired without learners being aware of doing so – incidental and implicit learning);
- his speculation on how "$i + 1$" in the input leads to acquisition seems to resonate with the general learning theory in psychology of the zone of proximal development (ZPD), which claims that learning takes place when learners are given achievable challenges while supported by more knowledgeable others (Vygotsky, 1978; Yanitsky, 2012);
- he seems to assume L2 acquisition is the direct extension of L1 acquisition regardless of, for example, L2 learners' ages (Granena & Long, 2013) or individual differences (Dörnyei & Ryan, 2015).

More than three decades after Krashen (1985) we know that SLA researchers invariably acknowledge that comprehensible input is, without doubt, necessary for language acquisition. We also know that Krashen's strong position on comprehensible input being sufficient for language acquisition (1985) has been challenged with convincing counter-evidence, for example, that relying on massive comprehensible input results in fluent but ungrammatical output (as recorded in a case study by Schmidt (1990), who points out the importance of conscious attention to formal aspects of language in what he calls the noticing hypothesis). Other counter-evidence has been provided by extensive studies on children in a French immersion programme in Canada, which provides evidence for the necessity of output (i.e. production) in SLA (see "pushed output" and the comprehensive output hypothesis by Swain, 1985, 2005).

Readers' Tasks

1 List what Krashen describes as ideal conditions that provide comprehensible input to learners.
2 Consider whether typical L2 learning situations provide an environment that contains "comprehensible input".
3 Note down ways of increasing opportunities of providing comprehensible input in L2 teaching situations in terms of curriculum, teaching methodology and materials.

Input and Interaction

While Krashen (1985) argues how comprehensible input leads to acquisition, Hatch (1978b) suggests the sources of acquisition may be in interaction, based on her discourse studies of oral interactions, of caretaker talk and of foreigner talk in studies available at that time. The term "interaction" is defined by Ellis (2015, p. 12) as "the oral exchanges a learner participates in – with native speakers or with other learners – which provide both 'input' and opportunities for 'output' (i.e. use of L2 in production)".

Michael Long, in the late 1970s, investigated how comprehensible input can be supplied in a classroom setting by analysing college-level ESL learners' interactions with L1 pre-service and in-service university ESL teachers. Following his initial version of the interaction hypothesis in the 1980s (Long, 1983a, 1983b) his revised interaction hypothesis (1996) has been stimulating numerous interactionist studies (see Mackey, Abbhul & Gass, 2012 for an overview).

Long (1983b), for example, demonstrates how modifications of the interactional structure of conversation are more extensive and more consistently observed than input modifications. Take, for an example, an episode of negotiation of meaning taking place between an NS (native speaker) and a NNS (non-native speaker):

NS: What's the boy's name?
NNS: Uh?
NS : The boy, what's his name?

(Long, 1983b, p. 127)

In the example above, NS is making an attempt to help NNS understand what was said, by repeating the question but in a modified form, a topic-comment construction. Long's statistical analysis of the NS data reveals a native-speaker preference for encoding topic-initiating moves as questions more often when addressing NNSs than other native speakers.

Ortega (2009) explains the mechanism of how negotiation of meaning during an interaction provides comprehensible input by using an episode reported in Gass and Varonis (1994, p. 296):

Jane: All right now [reading from the script], above the sun place the squirrel. He's right on top of the sun.
Hiroshi: What is . . . the word?
Jane: OK. The sun.
Hiroshi: Yeah, sun, but –
Jane: Do you know what the sun is?
Hiroshi: Yeah, of course. Wh-what's the –
Jane: Squirrel. Do you know what a squirrel is?
Hiroshi: No.
Jane: OK. You've seen them running around the campus. They're little furry animals. They're short and brown and they eat nuts like crazy.

Ortega Comments:

When interlocutors like Jane and Hiroshi work through messages in these ways, engaging in as much (or as little) negotiation for meaning as needed, we might say that they are generating tailor-made comprehensible input, or learner-contingent $i + 1$, at the right level the particular interlocutor needs to understand the message. It was for this reason that Long predicted interactionally modified input would be more beneficial than other kinds of input. For example, it may be better than unmodified or authentic input (as in the listening or reading of authentic texts) but also better than premodified input (as in graded readers), which often means simplifying the language, thus risking the elimination of the +1 in the $i + 1$ equation. Interactional modifications have the potential to bring about comprehension in a more individualized or learner-contingent fashion, with repetitions and redundancies rather than simplification. Thus, an important general benefit of interactional modifications is their contingency, in that learners are potentially engaging in what educational researchers would call just-in-time learning, or learning at the right point of need. (Ortega, 2009, pp. 61–62)

Interactionist studies are furthering our understanding of how input can contribute to language acquisition. We are now aware that:

- implicit learning from experience of the L2 being used for purposeful communication is essential for L2 acquisition;
- different kinds and timing of input during interaction contribute to language acquisition (this will be discussed in the section "Kinds of Input");
- language acquisition also benefits from learners paying conscious and motivated attention to formal aspects of language during meaning-focused interaction (see Schmidt, 1990, 2012);
- output induces negotiation of meaning and other interactional features which contribute to acquisition (see Swain, 1985; Swain & Lapkin, 1995; Swain, 2005; as well as a more detailed discussion in Chapter 7 "Production and Monitoring of the L2" and in Chapter 8 "Auto-Input");
- quantity and quality of input during interaction influence intake and acquisition (this will be discussed in the section "The Significance of Input in SLA" in this chapter; see also Chapter 2 Intake Part One);
- teachers, peers and materials play important roles in facilitating language acquisition, roles which had been somewhat undermined by the proponents of the innate views of language learning (e.g. the monitor hypothesis by Krashen, 1985).

Interactions between NNSs

Those who learn or teach in EFL contexts may be wondering at this point, however, about the feasibility of being able to provide in their classrooms such extensive and individualised interactions involving negotiation of meaning between NSs and NNSs. The majority of EFL classrooms consist of non-native-speaking teachers and a large number of L2 learners who are likely to have little or no opportunity for exposure to the target language being used for communication. Even when native-speaker teachers of target languages are available and the curriculum recommends communicative language teaching involving discussions in small groups and pair work, large class size may mean most of the verbal interactions tend to be between non-native learners rather than with their teacher. Furthermore, non-native EFL teachers and learners may feel apprehensive about the value of non-native interactions in comparison to those that involve native speakers. For example, they may feel unsure if interactions between NNSs afford the same kind and quality of interactions containing comprehensible input that are claimed to facilitate language acquisition.

Long and Porter (1985) review five interlanguage talk studies that compare interactions between NSs + NNSs and NNSs + NNSs. The studies they examine reveal general tendencies of the same or greater occurrence of interactional modifications (e.g. confirmation, clarification checking, meaning negotiation) in interlanguage talk compared to the native-speaker teacher-led classes, in terms of both quantity and quality of interactional meaning negotiations.

Studies of learners working together in groups and pairs provide evidence for:

- a larger quantity of meaning negotiations compared to those found in classroom interactions involving one native teacher and students;
- learner interactions in pairs and groups containing a broader range of language functions;
- the learners showing more initiative and less anxiety in unsupervised peer interactions;
- the accuracy of L2 learners' language use being no different between NSs + NNSs and NNSs + NNSs;
- a higher frequency of other-correction and completions by interlocutors in NNSs + NNSs than in NSs + NNSs;
- a slight advantage in achieving successful modified utterances when the interactions have taken place between mixed levels of learners.

Such observations have been confirmed by a growing number of publications investigating the significance of L2 peer interaction in language acquisition (e.g. García Mayo & Alcón Soler, 2013; Philip, Adams & Iwashita, 2014; Sato & Ballinger, 2016a). For further discussion on peer interactions see "Who provides input? Input Provider 2: L2 Learners" in this chapter.

Readers' Tasks

1 Think of ways of creating opportunities for negotiation of meaning between learners in EFL situations.
2 Long and Porter (1985) call for further studies on optimal classroom management, involving group work and teacher-fronted activities. Compare the potential strengths of group work and teacher-fronted activities in terms of creating opportunities for meaning negotiation rich in comprehensible input.

N.B. Meaning negotiation involves interlocutors collaborating to help each other to express what they want to say.

Definitions of Input in the Current Literature

Having investigated the historical background of input, we would now like to see if we can achieve general agreement for the term "input" by collecting snapshot samples of definitions in recent publications in addition to the ones we have discussed in the Historical Background section (see Table 1.1 below).

Summary of the Definitions of Input and Discussion

We will now attempt to identify general characteristics of input by looking more closely at the definitions in Table 1.1 from the perspectives of providers of input, potential recipients and constituents of input.

We will also add "contemporary issues" as necessary to discuss some emerging factors that do not feature in the list of definitions in Table 1.1.

Table 1.1 Selected definitions of input

Researchers/authors	Source	How the authors describe "input"
Noam Chomsky	Chomsky (1965)	What language users receive that contains "the linguistic primary data"
Stephen Krashen	Krashen (1985)	Comprehensible input: roughly tuned language, which a learner receives for meaning during communication and which contains linguistic data slightly above their current level
Michael H. Long	Long (1983b)	"Input refers to the linguistic forms (morphemes, words, utterances) – the streams of speech in the air – directed at the NNS." (p. 127)
Lourdes Ortega	Ortega (2009)	"linguistic data produced by other competent users of the L2" (p. 59)
Susan Gass and Alison Mackey	Gass and Mackey (2012)	"the language that is available to learners; that is, exposure" (p. 594)
Herschensohn and Young-Scholten	Herschensohn and Young-Scholten (2013)	"samples of the target language to which learners are exposed in their linguistic environment, including multiple varieties of spoken, written, visual (e.g. signs, gestures) and tactile (e.g. Braille, tactile signing) language" (p. 718)
Rod Ellis	R. Ellis (2015)	"The term 'input' refers to the samples of the oral or written language a learner is exposed to. This constitutes the 'data' that learners have to work with to construct their interlanguage". (p. 12)
Muriel Saville-Troike and Karen Barto	Saville-Troike and Barto (2017)	"Whatever sample of L2 learners are exposed to." (p. 212)

Who Provides Input? – Input Providers Noted in Our List of Definitions in Table 1.1

The definitions in the list above generally do not mention who provides the input apart from the definition by Ortega (2009, p. 59) i.e. "other competent users of the L2". The common implicit assumption of "input providers" in Table 1.1 seems to be primarily L1 speakers of the target language. Obviously, there are other providers too, for example L1 writers and L2 speakers, writers and learners.

Input Provider 1: L1 Speakers of the Target Language As we have seen in the "Historical Background" section, L1 studies on "caretaker speech" focused on parent–child interactions in the 1970s (Hatch, 1978a, 1978b; Krashen, 1981, 1982). Likewise, early studies on "teacher talk" and "foreigner talk" assume competent NSs of the target language as input providers who are trying to help less proficient L2 learners understand the message by simplifying what they say according to the interlocutors' responses.

In the early studies by the interactionists in the 1970s and 1980s, native-speaker teachers were considered the main providers of comprehensible input through interactionally modified input during communication (e.g. Long, 1983b).

> **Readers' Tasks**
> 1 List examples of kinds of "teacher talk" from your learning/teaching experience.
> 2 Imagine a scene in an EFL classroom. A teacher is explaining in a target language a certain grammatical point in a grammar work book that uses testing techniques such as gap filling and "true" or "false" in a decontextualised manner. Do you think the teacher is providing comprehensible input for language acquisition?

Input Provider 2: L2 Learners Some studies in the 1980s and 1990s provide empirical evidence that L2 learners' interlanguage talk affords meaning negotiation opportunities for language acquisition, in some cases more so than a native-speaker teacher conducting classroom interactions with L2 learners (e.g. Long & Porter, 1985).

Recent literature that has surveyed L2 peer interaction studies (e.g. García Mayo & Alcón Soler, 2013; Philip, Adams & Iwashita, 2014; Sato & Ballinger, 2016a) seems to indicate the following distinctive benefits of L2 interaction:

- L2 learners' interactionally modified input generally provides quantitatively and qualitatively rich sources of SLA.
- L2 peer interactions allow more informal, mutually supportive and relaxed interactions compared to those of NS vs L2 learners.

- Feedback by L2 learners shows more elicitation types (output prompting) and clarification interactions, whereas feedback by NS tends to provide lexically and grammatically richer reformulation types.
- L2 learners self-correct more in peer interactions.

The studies on peer interactions also indicate optimal combinations of NS and NNS teachers' support and guidance to ensure the quality of peer interactions (Philip, Adams & Iwashita, 2014). The literature also seems to point out the value of pedagogical interventions such as learner training. Sato and Ballinger (2016b) describe the influencing variables on peer interactions such as learner relationships, proficiency level, task types and modality of interaction (e.g. oral vs written; face-to-face vs computer-mediated communication; synchronous vs asynchronous interaction).

Readers' Tasks

1. Do you think that peer interactions are useful in SLA? If so, why? If not, why not?
2. What are the strengths and weaknesses of peer interactions in terms of SLA?

Input Provider 3: Writers of Texts in Non-Digital Format As can be seen in the list of definitions in Table 1.1, the modes of input can be written as well as spoken. The writers of texts in non-digital format that can provide input would include L1 or L2 authors of various genres and formats such as books, magazines, newspapers, academic journals, comics, stories, poems and novels written in the target language (see Krashen, 2004; Maley, 2008; Krashen, 2011).

Readers' Tasks

1. Maley (2008) and Krashen (2011) both strongly recommend extensive reading, especially free, voluntary, pleasure reading, as a great source of language acquisition. What are your views?
2. Is extensive reading systematically supported in educational institutions with which you are familiar? Why do you think this is so?

Who Provides Input? – Contemporary Issues in Relation to Input Providers

Contemporary Input Provider 4 - Target Language Users in Digital Format The Internet provides massive access to textual and multimodal media such as:

- videos (e.g. YouTube)
- blogs (i.e. a regularly updated website or web page, typically belonging to an individual or small group, written in an informal or conversational style)
- vlogs (i.e. video blogs) combining video and blogs
- Twitter
- social media (e.g. Facebook; WhatsApp; WeChat; Instagram)

Krashen (2011) includes recreational genre and Web surfing as potential sources of comprehensible input during free voluntary reading/viewing.

> **Readers' Tasks**
>
> 1 In the teaching/learning environments that you are familiar with, is extensive reading/viewing encouraged? If so, how? If not, why not?
> 2 Do the learners in those environments seek opportunities for digital extensive reading, viewing or listening?

Contemporary Input Provider 5: Teachers Who Speak the Target Language as an L2 Readers may find this entry surprising. In contrast to the amount of literature on input provided by L1 native-speaker teachers, studies on input provision by L2 teachers of the target language do not seem to feature very often, if at all, in SLA studies. In defining "interaction", R. Ellis (2015, p. 12) notes, "the oral exchanges a learner participates in – with native speakers or with other learners". He does not mention interaction with non-native-speaker teachers. His definition is based on available interaction studies, thus providing a testimony to our observation about the paucity of information about the role of non-native-speaker teachers in providing input. This seems incredible when the vast majority of language teachers around the globe are teachers who speak the target language as an L2. Selvi (2011) explains possible reasons for the conspicuous paucity of empirical studies on L2 teachers' contribution to SLA, and attributes it mainly to the fact that "Non-native English-speaking teachers (NNESTs) have tended to be conceptualised within ELT along the same lines as NNS [Non-native Speakers] in general".

Chomsky's (1965, p. 24) theoretical abstraction of an idealised monolingual "native speaker who possesses intrinsic knowledge of linguistic competence" seems to have seeped into the subconscious minds of SLA researchers and stake holders of language teaching. For example, Stern (1983, p. 341) states, "The native 'competence' or 'proficiency' or 'knowledge of the language' is a necessary point of reference for the second language proficiency concept used in language teaching". Cook (1999) explores the notion and examples of the "native speaker" and shows how problematic it is to define so-called NSs in reality. He then argues that SLA research has unfairly compared two distinctive groups, between monolinguals and "Multi-competent Language Users", the term that he argues should replace "Non-native Learners":

> The success and failure of L2 learners are often measured against the native speaker's language use in statements such as the following: "learners often failed initially to produce correct sentences and instead displayed language that was markedly deviant from target language norms" (Ellis, 1994, p. 15). Many SLA research methods, such as grammaticality judgments, obligatory occurrences, and error analysis, involve comparison with the native speaker … (Cook, 1999, p. 189)

Cook (1999) further investigates how the notion of the so-called native speaker has been pervasive in ELT and in materials, demonstrating an ideological bias that has later come to be called "native speakerism" (Holliday, 2006).

Medgyes (1994; revised version, 2017) is given credit as the pioneer in L2 teacher-related research, arguing for the valuable contributions that non-native speaking teachers can make, as do Braine (2005), Moussu and Llurda (2008), Selvi (2011) and Copland, Garton and Mann (2016). It is interesting to note, however, that Medgyes, from his Hungarian perspective, seems to subscribe to the idealised native model, when he (1992) says:

> [N]on-natives cannot turn into natives [because of] the fact that they are, by their very nature, norm-dependent. Their use of English is but an imitation of some form of native use. Just as epigons never becomes genuine artists, NNSs can never be as creative and original as those whom they have learnt to copy. (Medgyes, 1992, p. 343)

But are NNSs just trying to imitate native speakers? Surely NNSs are using English differently and creatively when they are using it (as many of them do for most of the time) with other NNSs. Maybe the problem is that non-native teachers of English are attempting to emulate the native-speaker norms in their textbooks, and their inability to do so contributes to a sense of inadequacy. There are a number of studies that report non-native teachers' strengths, weaknesses and contributions (summarised in Braine, 2005 and in Moussu & Llurda, 2008) and that provide evidence of non-native teachers' perceptions that they feel inadequate or inferior in terms of the linguistic competence and cultural authenticity that "native speakers" are capable of, despite their own qualifications and professional and personal abilities.

Ortega (2019) argues that the field of SLA has unjustifiably not taken into account the multitudes of bilinguals and multilinguals in its mainstream studies:

> In a nutshell, language cannot and should not be reduced to whatever happens to be the ways with words of the educated elites. Language research that is complicit with such purist

and standard ideologies works to the detriment and demise of many multilinguals (and many marginalized monolinguals as well) by contributing to the broader problem of raciolinguistics... Whenever the linguistic repertoires of certain speakers are rejected, their ethnocultural heritages and affiliations are also rejected. Namely, speakers who fall short of normative, monolingual, elitist conceptions of linguistic competence are told (by researchers, teachers, parents, peers, and circulating collective societal discourses) that their language is not (yet) good enough and that all doors will open to them in life once they fix it and appropriate communicative repertoires of the kinds that are valued because they are used by educated speakers. (Ortega, 2019, p. 30)

Kirkpatrick (2016, reported in Garton, Copland & Mann, 2016, p. 241) points out the fact that there are "well over a billion speakers for whom English is an additional language compared to fewer than 400 million native speakers today". He (ibid., p. 241) also argues that "in today's multilingual world, multilinguals with multicultural experience are more likely to prove effective language teachers than monolinguals with little cross-cultural experience".

Research on how non-native, bilingual and multilingual teachers may be facilitating L2 learners' acquisition is sorely needed in SLA classroom research so that it can advise governments around the globe to establish future bilingual and multilingual language teaching and teacher-development policies.

There is another side to L2 teachers' contribution to SLA. So far, all the studies quoted in the discussion above share an assumption that L2 interactions do take place in L2 language classrooms. Recent studies on teacher use of materials in the fields of materials development and in education, however, reveal that the majority of language classes may be conducted in local languages in order to cover the teaching content in the coursebooks in preparation for exams (Masuhara, Mishan & Tomlinson, 2017; Tomlinson & Masuhara, 2018a). This point will be further developed in the Application sections in this chapter.

Readers' Tasks

1 In your experience, do non-native teachers typically use the target language when they teach an L2? Why do you think this is so?
2 When using an L2, do you share the feeling of being inferior to "native speakers" in terms of your target-language competence and your ability to represent target-language cultures? If so, why? If not, why not?

Contemporary Input Provider 6: Users of Global Englishes The users of global Englishes (Kirkpatrick, 2010; Pennycook, 2010; Saraceni, 2015; Jenkins, 2015;

Jenkins, Baker & Dewey, 2018; Jenkins & Leung, 2019) have not featured in the definitions of SLA literature in Table 1.1. In the era of the Internet and global communication, motivated and well-resourced L2 learners are communicating with other users of global Englishes with diverse cultural backgrounds through digital as well as non-digital means.

We are using the term "global Englishes" with a small letter "g" in the sense that there is no particular overall variety that can be identified as "Global English". Our conceptualisation of "global Englishes" is dynamic and variable, depending on the users and contexts in a way similar to "Translingua franca English" (Pennycook, 2010) i.e. all uses of English as a tool of communication in multilingual settings, in which participants use whatever resources are available to them from their repertoires of Englishes.

> **Readers' Tasks**
>
> 1 The features of global Englishes involve diverse linguistic conventions depending on the purposes of communications, the users and the contexts. Do you think learners should be encouraged to seek exposure to varieties of Englishes?
> 2 Saraceni (2015) says:
>
> > Students ... should be helped to develop an awareness that they don't belong to a particular class of "speakers of English" according to their birth-place or ethnic group, both of which involve ideologically constructed boundaries largely outside their own direct control. Learning English need not be seen as a strenuous journey whose ultimate destination is the achievement of "native-like" status or a linguistic "visa" into a special "inner circle". Learning English means, above all, making it easier to take part, actively and critically, in the practices and discourses that (re-)present, (re-)construct and (re-)shape the global and local worlds we live in. Saraceni (2015, p. 187)
>
> If you agree with the above argument, why? If not, why not?

What Constitutes Input?

Constituents Noted in our List of Definitions in Table 1.1

According to the collection of definitions in Table 1.1, input contains "the linguistic primary data"; "roughly tuned language which a learner receives for meaning during communication and which contains linguistic data slightly above their current level"; "the linguistic forms (morphemes, words, utterances) – the streams of speech in the air –"; "linguistic data produced by other competent users of the L2"; "the language that is available to learners"; "samples of the target language to which learners are exposed in their linguistic environment, including multiple varieties of spoken, written, visual (e.g. signs, gestures) and tactile (e.g. Braille, tactile signing) language"; "the samples of the oral or written language a learner is exposed to"; "Whatever sample of L2 learners are exposed to".

Frequent key words (see the word cloud on page 31) are "language", "linguistic", "data", "samples", "exposed" and "learners". In Table 1.1, both Chomsky (1965) and Krashen (1985) differentiate "primary linguistic data" and "comprehensible input" from general input. Long (1983b) further narrows down "comprehensible input" into the linguistic forms directed at the non-native speaker to represent modified input during interactions.

The dominance of "language" and "linguistic" is understandable on the grounds that the field of "second language acquisition" focuses on how language and linguistic data are processed and acquired and that we have vast resources from the linguistic traditions underlying SLA research. However, we have to query whether communicative input only contains linguistic data.

Readers' Tasks

1 List the linguistic constituents of input that you can think of (e.g. vocabulary).
2 Make a brief note on typical input that you receive every day in your L1 and in your L2. Are there any other constituents in the input in addition to the list you created in 1?

What Constitutes Input? Contemporary Issues in Relation to Constituents of Input

The word cloud in Figure 1.1 shows the prevalent frequency of "language" and "linguistic" in the definitions of input in Table 1.1. What is meant by "language" or "linguistic data" seems to us to require some updating and discussion in a wider perspective.

Constituents of Input Contemporary Issue 1: Fields of Linguistics vs Form and Meaning Mapping in Learners' Minds Theoretical endeavour in research often requires division of areas of enquiry for the sake of clear focus and thorough investigation. Real-life phenomena such as communication or learning, on the other hand, are intertwined and holistic. The characteristics of theoretical-enquiry

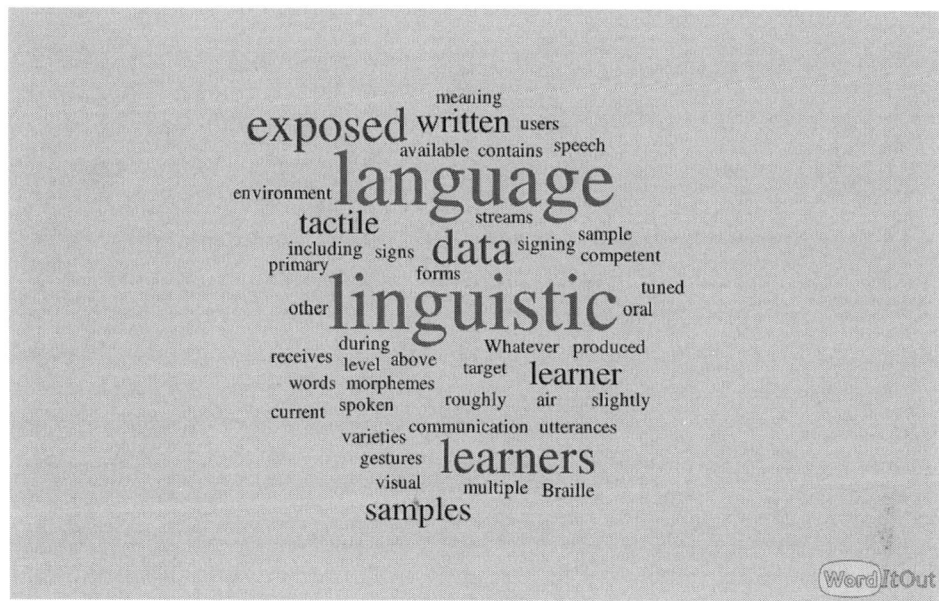

Figure 1.1 Word cloud of key terms used in the definitions of input

procedures might lead to the unintended and unfortunate consequence of theories misguiding exploration of complex real-life phenomena.

For example, researchers of syntax (i.e. study of well-formedness of words and sentences as in Chomsky, 1965) and of semantics (i.e. study of logic and meaning) would have different scope and approaches in their enquiries. The influence of such divisions seems to be still detectable in curricula, teaching and materials in the present day. For example, L2 teachers may say: "We need to teach vocabulary and grammar for the learners to be able to understand a new passage." Those comments may derive from a belief that if we consciously teach key vocabulary and grammar in advance, the students will be able to understand the unfamiliar passage in the textbooks.

In real life, communication is meaning-focused and the interlocutors' purpose is to achieve some kind of real-life outcome through communication. Only when communication breaks down do competent target-language users, be it native speakers, L2 learners or users of global Englishes, choose to provide roughly tuned comprehensible input, possibly in response to overt or covert requests for help from less competent L2 learners. In return, the less competent L2 learners are likely to pay motivated and conscious attention to linguistic features in order to repair unsuccessful communication (not primarily to learn linguistic features). What all the scholars, apart from Chomsky in Table 1.1, emphasise is the primary focus on meaning with the possible consequence of achieving links between meaning and linguistic features in L2 learners' minds during the processing of the input.

In discussing acquisition of linguistic features, we must remember the fact that meaning–form connections and mapping in learners' minds (i.e. their brains) are the most fundamental facilitators of language acquisition. In L1 acquisition, for example, a child may initiate a curiosity-driven, motivated interaction involving a here-and-now referent in a specific context (e.g. whilst pointing to a cat in his garden). In response, caretakers provide comprehensible input that contains linguistic information as rich in quality and quantity as is necessary and wanted. Caretakers' simple codes with typical features of language in context help children segment phonological streams and identify lexical and syntactic boundaries and discourse features while they are attending to the meaning. The diversity and differences may attract L1 learners' conscious attention and lead to cognitive contrasts and the deduction of patterns (Ambridge & Lieven, 2015; Arbib, 2015; Jones & Rowland, 2017; Tatsumi, Ambridge & Pine, 2018).

Corpus studies provide further evidence that there is a tight bond between form and meaning (Sinclair & Carter, 2004). In fact, Sinclair and Carter argue that the frequently occurring combinations of lexis and lexical bundles could be the glue that holds texts together. The developments in investigating neurological correlates of lexis, lexical bundles and lexical chunks (Schütze, 2017) for example, may be pointing to a future in which researchers will be able to integrate linguistic theory, corpus data and direct evidence at the neural level in the brain.

Readers' Tasks

1 When you learned an L2, were there any occasions when your communication in L2 took place in a curiosity-driven way (i.e. you wanted to communicate because ultimately you wanted to find out something about the content)? If your answer is yes to this question, how did it happen?
2 If your answer is no to this question, why not? What was your experience of typical L2 learning?

Constituent of Input Contemporary Issue 2: Written vs Spoken Grammar
Discussion on "well-formedness" in grammar also needs to take into account the differences between spoken and written grammar (Carter & McCarthy, 2006; Carter, McCarthy, Mark & O'Keeffe, 2011; Carter, Hughes & McCarthy, 2011; Carter & McCarthy, 2017). When teachers give corrective feedback to L2 learners during oral interactions, formal corrections often seem to be based on written grammar.

Carter, Hughes and McCarthy (2011) point out that:

> Descriptions of the English language, and of English grammar in particular, have been largely based on written sources and on written examples. ... One consequence of this situation, however, that "correct grammar" has come to mean "correct grammar as represented by the written language" and that many perfectly normal and regularly occurring utterances made by standard English speakers (of whatever variety – not just standard British English) have by omission come to be classified as "ungrammatical". (Carter, Hughes & McCarthy, 2011, p. 78)

In order to illustrate their point, they provide examples of "tails" (*That's just stupid, that* – example from p. 81), which is a prominent feature of the CANCODE data (i.e. the Cambridge and Nottingham Corpus of Discourse in English). Teachers may correct a student, for instance, who says, "It can make you feel very weak it can, flu." and provide a more grammatically better-formed sentence as a recast, "Flu can make you feel very weak". Carter, Hughes and McCarthy (2011, p. 81) argue that "Tails are an important feature of a listener-sensitive, affective grammar and occur frequently in informal contexts of language use". They (ibid., p. 81) explain how "Tails allow speakers to express attitudes, to add emphasis, to evaluate and to provide repetition for listeners".

L1 acquisition takes place in aural–oral spoken modes for at least the first five years of L1 acquisition. Corpus analysis of spoken-language use beyond sentence-level contexts shows extensive examples of flexible use of language. In this sense, rigid corrective feedback during L2 oral interactions based on "well-formedness" in written grammar may result in demotivating L2 learners from attempts to communicate, thus discouraging SLA.

Readers' Tasks

1. Do you agree that spoken grammar and written grammar are different?
2. If you agree, why do you think they are different?
3. If you think spoken and written grammar are the same, or should be the same, why?

Constituent of input Contemporary Issue 3: Beyond Linguistics Multimodality of Input It is interesting to note that multimodal characteristics of input are gradually being incorporated as part of the definition in our list of definitions of input in Table 1.1. Krashen (e.g. 1981) did frequently mention how contextual clues and visuals help comprehension of input but they were not included in his definitions and were treated as extra. In contrast, Herschensohn and Young-Scholten

(2013, p. 718) include in their definition of input "visual (e.g. signs, gestures) and tactile (e.g. Braille, tactile signing) language".

Andrew Cohen (personal communication, 2018) defines input as:

> the oral and written language that learners are exposed to in the environment. In keeping with linguistic landscaping notions, this would include street signs, information on bulletin boards, whatever learners are exposed to on the Internet, instructions accompanying games and devices, and whatever else can be heard and successfully interpreted orally and in written form.

Cohen's examples remind us of the multimodal digital environment that surrounds us in urbanised communities. For example, since the 1990s we have seen a spread of the use of symbols called emoticons that express the sender's emotions in addition to, or in place of, textual messages (e.g. :-) made with a keyboard to indicate a smiley face; pictorial icons used in SMS text messages such as a smiley icon ☺). The definition by Saville-Troike and Barto (2018, p. 212), "Whatever sample of L2 learners are exposed to", is uniquely different from the others in the list of definitions in Table 1.1, in the sense they do not include the words "language" and "linguistic" in their definition.

Multimodality of input does not stop with static visual elements (e.g. iconic signs on the street) available in our environment. When we reflect upon our communication in real life, we realise that we cannot fully understood language functions without understanding the contexts in which language is used. Making requests, for example, could be a sociocultural mine field which requires L2 learners' sensitivity to not only the language but also to multimodal paralinguistic clues in the input, such as tone and pitch of voice, facial expressions and gestures. Beltrán-Planques and Querol-Julián (2018) argue how the centrality of linguistic analysis may lead to a biased understanding of L2 interlanguage pragmatic competence. They provide a Radar chart of paralinguistic measures (e.g. gaze, facial expressions, gestures, head movement) as well as spoken language during complaint sequences and they propose a multimodal analysis of linguistic interactions.

> **Readers' Tasks**
>
> 1 Do you think visuals and paralinguistic features matter in communication?
> 2 If you think so, in what way?
> 3 If you don't think so, why not?

Constituent of Input Contemporary Issue 4: Exemplars for Information and Practice vs Language Utterances in Contextualised Communicative Use Most of the definitions we have explored above seem to assume that exposure to input involves experiencing language in use. But what about exposure to deliberately contrived examples used to illustrate the form and function of structures or the meaning of words, or to provide "input" for practice activities. Are such exemplars considered to be input? Whether it is or is not, there is no doubt in our minds that most learners in classrooms around the world are exposed to contrived exemplars more often than to language in authentic communicative use. And are decontextualised utterances taken from corpora to be considered as input? To a large extent the question of which type of data is considered as input depends upon the researcher's view as to the potential value of the data in facilitating language acquisition, with most researchers, including ourselves, tending to favour language in contextualised and communicative use. It is interesting to go back to Table 1.1 Selected Definitions of Input and decide which researchers include contrived exemplars in their definitions and which do not.

We asked a number of researchers whether or not they would include language provided for practice as input. Andrew Cohen (personal communication: 22/5/2017) replied :

> Most definitely I would see language-practice material as input. In fact, sometimes the best input for intake is that which has been carefully distilled by curriculum experts so that it is more accessible to learners than "language in use". In fact, a concern I have about trying to use corpus data to teach learners pragmatics is that the material is often too complex for learners to intake. Often they do better with material that represents, if you will, idealized versions of how people perform speech acts. What people actually say can be very laborious (even meandering), involving numerous turns.

Pauline Foster (personal communication: 23/5/2017) said, "input is anything read or heard in the TL, so yes, practice material is input. Whether it is the most valuable for SLA, is another question"; and Rod Ellis (personal communication: 22/5/2017) possibly implied the inclusion of language provided for language practice in his definition of input as "oral or written samples of language the learner is exposed to in either meaning focused or form-focused activities."

Related to this issue is the debate about whether the input that learners are provided with should be authentic or contrived. For views on this debate see Gilmore (2007), Tomlinson (2012), Le (2017), Maley and Tomlinson (2017) and Mishan (2017), as well as Chapter 9 in this volume.

Constituent of input Contemporary Issue 5: Information about the L2 So far, our chapter on input has focused exclusively on input as being exemplars or samples of the L2. However, our experience in classrooms around the world indicates that much of many learners' "experience" of their target language consists of information about it. This information could consist of explanations, definitions, rules, generalisations or analyses. Few studies of input actually mention such information, and an unanswered question is whether or not information about a language is considered to be input or not.

One study that does refer to information about the language and to the provision of language for practice (see Contemporary Issue 4) is Nguyen and Franken (2010), which investigates teachers' concepts of input in a Vietnamese university before and after participating in a workshop about input. Most of the teachers in the study considered input to be discrete linguistic elements that have been preselected as teaching points and most of them admitted they used Vietnamese most of the time for explanations and instructions in the classroom, to save time and to help weak students, and also because they were not confident their English was good enough.

If teachers are explaining grammar points to learners in their L1, we doubt if their explanations could be considered as input (see though discussions about the value of teacher provision of explicit knowledge of grammar in R. Ellis, 2006 and Erlam, 2012). However, if teachers are to explain grammar points in the target language their explanations could be considered to be valuable input, as the learners will be exposed to the language in purposeful, contextual and communicative use. The explanations might not help the learners to acquire the teaching point being explained, but the learners might benefit from exposure to the language of the explanations, providing, of course, such input is comprehensible.

Who Are the Recipients of Input?

Input Recipients Noted in Our List of Definitions in Table 1.1

Chomsky (1965) does discuss L2 learning but his interest was mainly in unfolding L1 native speakers' competence in processing and composing well-formed language. Ortega (2009, p. 59) does not mention the recipient in the particular definition listed in Table 1.1. Six scholars out of eight refer to "learners". Long (1983b) specifically mentions "the non-native speaker" as his particular article focused on tutor–learner interaction. The assumptions of "learners" seem to reflect the historical development in a sense that SLA studies stem from L1 acquisition studies in the 1960s and 1970s in which learners meant L1 children. The study of learners in L2 classrooms in the 1970s and 1980s benefited from the foundation of L1 studies.

Contemporary Issues in Relation to What "Learner" May Mean

The meaning of "learners" seems to be changing. From 1970s to the millennium, the common assumption was that "L2 learners" meant those who study face-to-face in classrooms, either in the context of English as a second language in English-speaking countries or of English as a foreign language.

Nowadays, a learner could be anyone, from a very young child to a senior adult. "Learners" may also include L2 users who may or may not choose to enrol in classroom learning. The spread of global Englishes and the development of technology have diversified the characteristics of "learners".

For example, in discussing the European Union's (EU's) visions of Open Learning 2030, Castaño Muñoz, Redecker, Vuorivari and Punie (2013) contrast:

- traditional learning, in which an educational institution enrols, provides content and guidance and conducts assessment before certifying the learners;
- future life-long open learning visions, in which learners select what to learn, how to learn, what guidance to receive in what format and choose the assessment and certification as they wish by establishing through systems that enable different kinds of learning routes (e.g. Massive Open Online Courses (MOOC); blended learning (i.e. combined delivery through face-to-face and various digital modes at a distance).

In elaborating EU visions of Open Learning 2030, Redecker (2014) defines four categories of "learners" along the horizontal axis of learning context (guided to self-guided) and the vertical axis of learning context (externally set to learner-initiated):

1 "Guided journey", in which institutions offer educational content and training (similar to traditional provision)
2 "Self-guided journey", in which learners select institutions to receive targeted educational content, certification and accreditation e.g. MOOCs offered by educational institutions
3 "Guided discovery", in which institutions may offer hubs for individual learners to achieve networks of learning opportunities e.g. community learning facilities
4 "Self-guided discovery", in which autonomous learners self-initiate and direct their learning.

In addition to life-long learning, Redecker (2014) discusses "life-wide learning" i.e. anytime- and anywhere-learning including combined/blended modes of delivery, work-based professional development, community adult education, like-minded communities of people sharing voluntary learning and self-directed learning.

In discussing recipients of input, we need to clarify contexts and learners in our research and in considering implications and applications to pedagogy.

Readers' Tasks

1 Note down the most familiar learning context for you.
2 Consider who receives input in what way in that context.

In sum, providers, constituents and receivers of input may be expressed in a diagram (see Figure 1.2 "Providers, constituents and receivers of input").

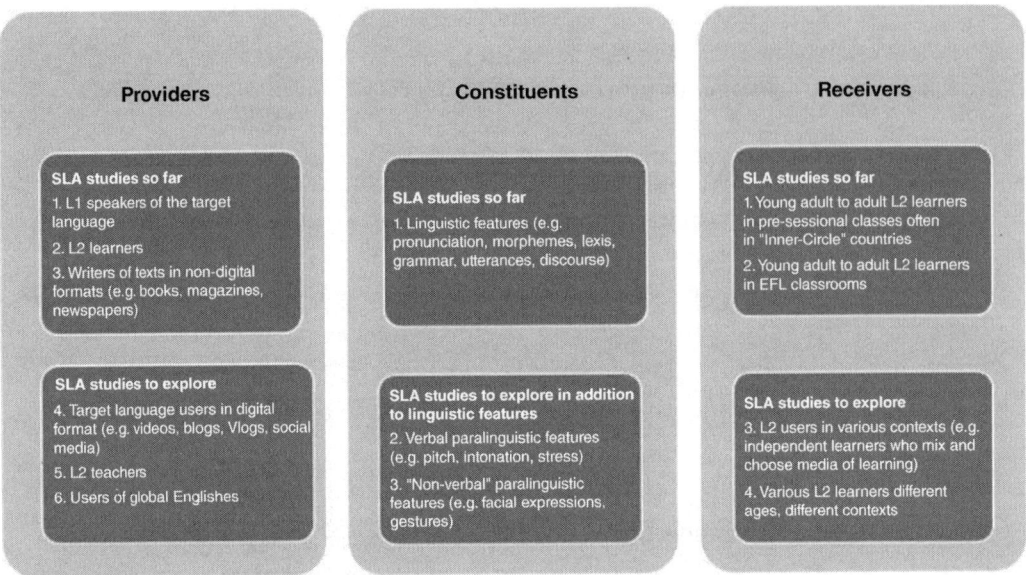

Figure 1.2 Providers, constituents and receivers of input.

Our Definition of Input

We have reviewed what we believe to be representative samples of definitions of input published from the 1960s till the present day in Table 1.1. We have considered providers, constituents and receivers of input in the definitions proposed. We have also discussed contemporary factors that seem to be missing in our selected samples of definitions of providers, constituents and receivers of input in SLA studies (see sections named "SLA studies to explore" in Figure 1.2 "Providers, constituents and receivers of input").

Considering changes in the digital and non-digital environment, the spread of global Englishes and the concept of learners and learning modes available, we feel that the definition of input needs to be updated.

Above all, we feel that past definitions may have had a tendency to overlook the fact that language acquisition takes place during and for the sake of communication. The communication could take place without language (e.g. a nod, eye contact) or with language-plus (e.g. an emoticon together with a linguistic utterance). In this interdisciplinary era, it may be worthwhile to embrace wider perspectives in defining the term "input" as our communication depends as much on paralinguistic and multimodal input as it does on linguistic input. In this sense, we propose the following definition of input to be used throughout this book:

Input means multimodal data that the receiver is exposed to during communication, which could include indicators of meaning and intent that are spoken or written, as well as such vocal and non-vocal paralinguistic features as pitch, intonation, signs, facial expressions, gestures, braille and images.

> **Readers' Task**
>
> If we include paralinguistic and multimodal input, what would be the implications for:
>
> 1) research?
> 2) teaching?
> 3) learning?
> 4) materials?

The Significance of Input in SLA

Nature or Nurture?

The debate between nature or nurture remains controversial.

Chomsky (1965; 2014) hypothesises the existence of an LAD with inbuilt universal grammar (UG), which enables any babies during the developmental stages to identify the grammatical components in the input and put them into slots in the UG parameters genetically equipped in their LAD.

Krashen's input hypothesis (1985), in principle, supports the innateness of language acquisition capability when he argues that implicit and incidental acquisition is necessary and sufficient. The implication of his argument is that the LAD will absorb and integrate language systems as long as learners receive comprehensible input.

Lightfoot (2006), in line with Chomsky, argues that:

> Careful examination of the poverty-of-stimulus problems reveals the genetic factors that must be involved ... In this view, children are internally endowed with certain information, what linguists call universal grammar (UG), and, when exposed to primary linguistic data, they develop a grammar, a mature linguistic capacity, a person's internal language or I-language ... The essential properties of the eventual system are prescribed internally and are present from birth (pp. 9–10)

The "poverty-of-stimulus" argument used in support of UG theorists (e.g. Lightfoot, 2006) is being challenged by recent L1 acquisition studies (Ambridge & Lieven, 2015; Jones & Rowland, 2017; Tatsumi, Ambridge & Pine,

2018). First-language acquisition studies seem to provide considerable evidence of regularities, diversity and richness of input affecting children's acquisition of language systems.

Interactionist theorists (e.g. Long, 1996; Mackey, Abbuhl & Gass, 2012) argue for the value of interactions. Interactions create interactively modified input for learners to process. It seems useful to categorise input so we could navigate our discussion on different kinds of input and on its research and application.

Kinds of Input

Non-interactive Input

In our view, "Non-interactive input" refers to that which has been written or developed by authors, creators and/or producers. It is non-interactive in the sense that listeners/readers/consumers are not directly involved in developing the input or modifying it. Novelists, for instance, may have a vague notion of readership but the main purpose of their writing is likely to be artistic expression.

In digital input, use of hyperlinks allows some degree of interactiveness. Hyperfiction (i.e. a kind of digital literature), for example, allows the readers/viewers/listeners/consumers to select the characters or plot development. Even then, the options have been predesigned and produced in advance. In other words, the operation might be interactive but the texts themselves are non-interactive in the sense that only authors, creators and/or producers have control of the content and expression of the input.

"Non-interactive input" can be further categorised into "unmodified input" and "premodified input".

Unmodified Input

Typical examples of non-interactive unmodified input would include books, magazines, comics, signs, and adverts in print or in digital format. As in line with our definition of input, the text can be multimodal and authors, creators and/or producers can be L2 users of global Englishes as well as L1 users, provided that the input has been produced for communication. The Internet is filled with non-interactive unmodified input.

Discussions about non-interactive unmodified input may require an explanation of the notion of authenticity. The definition and the usefulness of authentic input in language teaching has attracted a lot of discussion (see Gilmore, 2007; Maley & Tomlinson, 2017; Mishan, 2017; Chapter 9 in this book). Authentic input is often associated with issues regarding its compatibility with the receivers in terms of cultures, language use and levels.

As far as "unmodified input" is concerned, our definition of authentic texts would simply be "texts that are produced for communication, not for teaching".

Suitability for readers/listeners/viewers/consumers would be a matter of selection based on appropriateness in terms of objectives, user levels and needs and wants.

Premodified Input
Premodification of input could take place in terms of simplification or of enhancement. In non-interactive premodified input, authors/creators/producers predetermine simplification or enhancement.

Premodified Input: Simplification
A typical example of non-interactive premodified simplification can be seen in *Graded Readers* and publications such as newspapers and magazines. *Graded Readers*, for example, may use a "Readability Formula" to categorise the books into grades. There are well-known readability formulae, such as Flesch's Reading Ease Formula (Flesch, 1948). The rule of thumb underlying various formulae is that the shorter the sentences and words, the easier and faster the reading is going to be (Bailin & Grafstein, 2016). Flesch's formula, for example, calculates reading difficulty of a text based on the ratio of the sentence and word length in a text. Some word-processing and email software can provide readability scores as part of the application. See Wang, Miller, Schmitt and Wen (2013) for an evaluation of a number of readability formulae.

In addition to readability formulae, corpus-based frequency lists of vocabulary may be used to measure readability.

Note here, though, that linguistic simplification could homogenise the writing and affect individual writing styles and authenticity of writing. The *Harry Potter* series, for example, may be rated as "difficult" in the readability test score measurement but multitudes of readers (including learners of English as an L2) seem to enjoy reading them. It seems that such factors as engagement, relevance, topic familiarity and tolerance of ambiguity are also important indicators of readability. An interesting interview article with Dr J. Peter Kincaid, the originator of the Kincaid formula, titled "Readability formulas: Useful or useless?" (McClure, 1987), provides insights into what the formulae can and cannot do.

Premodified Input: Enhancement
Input enhancement was proposed by Sharwood Smith (1993) as a way of drawing learners' attention to linguistic features that otherwise might not be noticed, and thus not taken in for acquisition. The theoretical drive behind input enhancement is the noticing hypothesis (Schmidt, 1990, 2001), which claims a facilitative role for noticing linguistic features in language input.

Input enhancement aims to make the target linguistic features more salient, by flooding or by highlighting. Flooding involves increasing the number of instances of the target features in a text. Highlighting in listening input may manifest in prominent intonation and stress. In reading input, highlighting could take place by using bold, italics or colour for target linguistic features.

Han, Park and Combs (2008) conduct a critical review of twenty-one studies on the efficacy of textual enhancement in language acquisition and find methodological shortcomings and/or inconsistencies that make generalisation difficult. Lee and Huang (2008) conduct meta-analysis of sixteen studies that explore the effect of visual enhancement on grammar learning: "The results indicate that second language readers provided with enhancement-embedded texts barely outperformed those who were exposed to unenhanced texts with the same target forms flooded in them." (p. 307). R. Ellis (2015, p. 152) considers various input enhancement studies and notes, "a trade-off between comprehension and noticing: if learners focus on the top-down processing required for effective comprehension, less noticing occurs and the opposite is true if learners engage in bottom-up processing and attend to the enhanced items in the text."

Despite inconclusive research results and doubts about its benefit, input enhancement features in some coursebooks, especially in relation to vocabulary. Since the 2000s, researchers in vocabulary have highlighted the fact that in order to adequately manage reading and listening, quantity and quality of vocabulary are crucial (Schmitt, 2008; Nation, 2013). They acknowledge the primary importance of incidental and incremental learning during meaning-focused reading and interaction. At the same time, they point out studies that show facilitative values of frequent encounter, exposure and paying conscious attention to linguistic features.

It seems to us that discussion of efficacy of input enhancement should not confuse "reading" with providing learners with reading texts in order to facilitate linguistic features such as vocabulary or grammar. Real-life reading is for enjoyment or utilisation of reading as a form of communication, during which implicit and incidental meaning-form connections in the mind seem to take place for durable learning – i.e. acquisition. Having to process enhanced preselected linguistic features for the sake of noticing might actually disturb the natural reading process. Learners may pay attention to linguistic features themselves, without highlighting as part of problem solving during listening/reading if linguistic features interfere with comprehension. Furthermore, there is no guarantee that learners' problems during the comprehension process coincide with preselected and enhanced features.

We would also like to make the point that for it to be effective, noticing needs to be driven by the learner, by their need, curiosity or interest. Teachers and materials can help create learner need, curiosity and interest but only the learner can actually perform the noticing. Teachers and materials can draw attention to features of the input but only learners can notice them.

> **Readers' Tasks**
>
> 1 Find a coursebook with input highlighted vocabulary. What kinds of effect does the enhanced input have on your reading?
> 2 What do you think of the fact that linguistic features of the text have been preselected for your attention? Does the selection coincide with the words that you think are significant in terms of your objective for reading?

Interactionally Modified Input

Most of our real-life communication involves interactions, be it with ourselves (e.g. using our inner voice) and/or with other beings (e.g. pets, humans). We accommodate each other in communication by modifying input (e.g. content, level and manner of delivery). We would like to discuss three kinds of interactionally modified input (see Figure 1.3).

Learner-Directed Input

In the "Historical Background" section in this chapter, the studies of simple codes in the late 1970s and 1980s were discussed in terms of teacher talk and foreigner talk, as well as "child-directed speech"/motherese/caretaker speech (e.g. Hatch, 1978b; Krashen, 1981; Long, 1981; Hatch, 1983; Long, 1983a, 1983b).

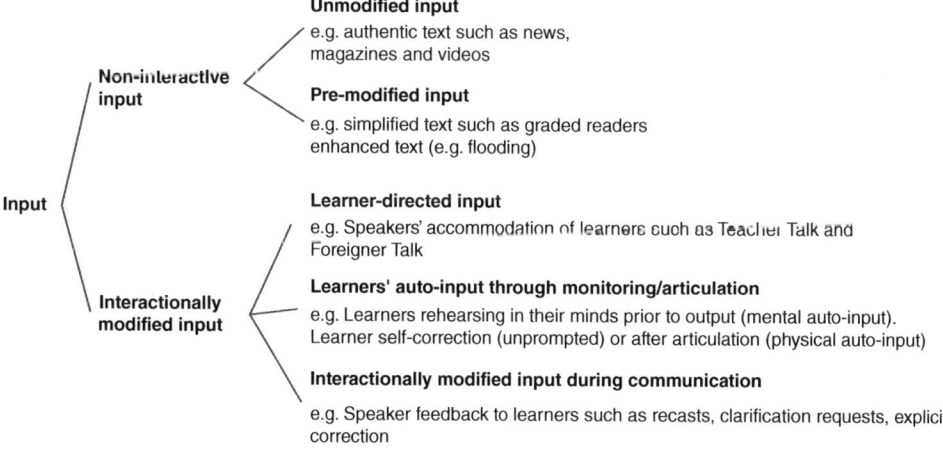

Figure 1.3 Kinds of input

Hatch (1978b, 1983) discusses regularities in child-directed speech in the L1 (e.g. articulation, emphasis, pauses, choice of words, repetition, tempo). Krashen (1981, 1982, 1985) argues for the fundamental contribution to language acquisition made by "comprehensible input" (i.e. the language that learners process for meaning and which contains linguistic data slightly above their current level – $i + 1$).

Long (1983a, 1983b) explores teacher talk and finds a significant number of cases of L1 teachers interactionally modifying their input according to the level and proficiency of the learners. Such accommodation as a result of gauging recipients' comprehension ability seems to be widely observed in child-directed speech, teacher talk and foreigner speech, providing evidence for Krashen's hypothesis of "$i + 1$" and Vygotsky's ZPD facilitated by the "more knowledgeable other" (Van der Veer & Valsiner, 1991; Liu & Matthews, 2005; Yasnitsky, 2012).

In the field of teaching English to young learners (EYL), interactive and intuitive use of simple codes and input enhancement is often observed in extensive listening and shared reading of children's literature. L1 children's literature is rich in word play, rhyming, and creative repetition (Bland, 2015, 2018) and is often written as a result of authors and illustrators interacting with children. The use of L1 children's literature or simplified readers has been reported to result in richer interactions and also in establishing connections between form and multifaceted meaning in various contexts that are believed to contribute to language acquisition (Ghosn, 2013).

Readers' Tasks

1 Look at Figure 1.3. Consider the potential differences in the quality of L2 learners' experience between:
   a) "Non-interactionally premodified input", such as graded readers, which may have been linguistically simplified
   and
   b) "Interactionally modified learner-directed input", as in the case of shared reading of authentic L1 children's literature during which learners talk to each other and to their teacher about what they are reading.
2 Ortega (2009, p. 61) says, interactionally modified input "may be better than unmodified or authentic input (as in the listening or reading of authentic texts) but also better than premodified input (as in graded readers), which often means simplifying the language, thus risking the elimination of the +1 in the $i + 1$ equation." Do you agree with Ortega? If so, why? If not, why not?

Learner's Auto-Input through Production and Monitoring In SLA studies, it is rather rare to find discussion on learners' mental or articulated output functioning as auto-input.

For example, when we speak, we find ourselves mentally rehearsing in our mind prior to articulation by using our inner voice. If the learners are proficient, such mental output could be extensive and it could function as mental auto-input. Likewise, we monitor what we say during interaction. We might self-correct, rephrase or look for better expressions. Such unprompted self-corrections can also work as auto-input. We will discuss auto-input in Chapter 8 in more detail.

Interactionally Modified Input during Communication

Long's interaction hypothesis was discussed in the Historical Background section with a header "Input and interaction".

In sum, the interaction hypothesis (Long, 1983a, 1983b, 1996) claims that:

1 Interactively modified input provides opportunities for more comprehensible input tailored for particular interlocutor learner needs in a specific context, thus facilitating language acquisition.
2 Interaction provides incidental opportunities for negotiation of meaning, which could trigger linguistic adjustment of forms in a meaningful context while learners pay conscious attention to linguistic constituents in utterances (i.e. focus on form).
3 Interaction provides learners with positive or negative evidence of acceptable language use.

R. Ellis (2015, p. 16) summarises how consequent SLA research verified these claims in that

> Overall, ... there is clear evidence that negotiation results in more input and more comprehensible input. However, it is not entirely clear whether it is the modifications themselves that facilitate comprehension or the additional time for processing input that results when negotiation occurs. Ellis and He (1999) found that when the amount of time allocated to the premodified and interactionally modified input was the same, no advantage for negotiation was seen.

R. Ellis (2015, pp. 149–150) also provides a useful summary and description of various feedback strategies:

> Negotiation ... strategies are of two basic kinds. Output prompting strategies – for example, requests for clarification and elicitation – push learners to modify their problematic utterances. Input-providing strategies – for example, recasts and explicit correction – help to solve problems by supplying learners with the correct target language-form. These strategies also differ in terms of how implicit – i.e. they are not overtly corrective - or explicit – i.e. they are more clearly corrective – they are.

SUMMARY

It seems from our reading of the research and our experience as learners and teachers that learners:

- need large amounts of input that is authentic, rich, contextualised, multimodal and comprehensible;
- also need input that is specifically produced in order to be meaningful to them;
- need opportunities to interact for communication in ways that facilitate collaborative output and negotiation of meaning.

> **Readers' Task**
>
> Evaluate the following text as a source of input for sixteen-year-old B1-level learners of English in Spain.
>
> 1 How useful as a source of input do you think it would be if the learners just read it?
> Which elements of it do you think are likely to provide useful input and which elements do you think are unlikely to be useful?
>
> Jim and I both started school on the same day at Claremont Infants School. I can only remember being bullied by a much bigger boy and peeing in my pants when I was too scared to ask the teacher if I could go to the toilet. The bully kept punching me in my side but denied it when I told Miss Mott. Jim claims to remember falling in love with a girl called Janet on that first day at school, a girl I later fell in love with too. It was our mutual interest in Janet which eventually brought us together, that and our passions for steam locomotives and football.
>
> We were in the same class at Infants School but we sat on opposite sides of the room. I had my playground mates and he had his. I walked to school one way and he walked another. We both appeared in the same school nativity play but never spoke to each other either in rehearsals or in performance. I can't remember what small part I played but I remember feeling really nervous and discovering that I couldn't sing. I still can't sing – though I did bellow out "We are the Champions" in Istanbul on the night when Liverpool won the European Champions Cup. I'm no longer nervous though on stage and I love to address audiences of a thousand or more.
>
> 2 What activities do you think you could ask the learners to do to increase the potential value of the text as a source of input?

Part Two: Application of Theory to Practice

Application to Language Policy and Planning (LPP)

LPP requires consideration of various factors, including the intended future directions of countries and their governments' strategic plans. It also needs to consider how policies can be implemented in terms of teacher development and resources.

Recommendation 1: Set up Coherent Specifications Regarding Objectives and Outcomes

We find some interesting reports on language-education policies from different parts of the world (e.g. Euromonitor International, 2012 on eight Middle Eastern countries; The British Council, 2014 on EU language education; Kirkpatrick & Liddicoat, 2017 on East and Southeast Asian countries with specific focus on those that belong to the "ASEAN + 3" forum).

What comes through from these reports are the following tendencies:

- There is a strong drive for global Englishes from pragmatic points of view such as international economic advancement at the national level and personal-career benefits for the people and the nation.
- More and more countries seem to be introducing English at a younger age, even though SLA researchers question the validity of doing so based on research findings (Long, 2013; Ortega, 2019).
- What seems to be currently attracting a lot of attention is English as a medium of instruction (EMI) at the university level, in comparison with English as an object of instruction, as has been widely practised in primary or secondary institutions in many EFL countries.

Note that EMI is somewhat similar to content and language integrated learning (CLIL) in the sense that the subject teaching is done in English. EMI is different from CLIL, however, in that there are no explicit language-learning aims (see The British Council, 2014; Walkinshaw, Fenton-Smith & Humphreys, 2017) in comparison with CLIL, which aims to increase both the learners' subject knowledge and their language proficiency.

Interesting and informative as these reports are, however, it is difficult for us to find specific information about objectives, targets of English education or how their intentions will be realised in the respective language-education systems.

If the objective is to achieve basic communication skills, for example, then the prevalent syllabuses based on linguistic specifications of vocabulary and grammar will be in conflict with this objective. Capability-based syllabuses with appropriate methodologies would be more appropriate.

Language plans are typically written at a very general level, but there is a case for consideration of such specifics as the input that is likely to be available to the learners governed by the plans and the optimum input that needs to be provided for successful realisation of the plans. If a plan targets the achievement of communicative competence in English for international communication then the following questions might need to be answered in the plan:

1. Are the teachers sufficiently proficient in the use of English to be able to provide their learners with rich input through interaction with them? If they are not, then how could the teachers' communicative competence be improved?
2. Are there opportunities for the learners to receive rich and comprehensible input from other writers and speakers of English? If not, then what resources are needed to provide such input?
3. Do the learners have opportunities to experience English being used for international communication (e.g. between users of English who are not native speakers and do not share the same L1s)? If not, how could such opportunities be provided?
4. Does the syllabus currently in use focus on the learning and practice of discrete language items and structures or does it encourage rich exposure to English in contextualised communicative use? How could the syllabus be made more suitable for the implementation of the language plan?
5. Do the examinations assess the learning and reproduction of language items from the syllabus or do they assess the learners' abilities to communicate in order to achieve intended effects? How could the examinations be revised to encourage communicative development rather than explicit teaching, learning and assessment?

Recommendation 2: Provide a Clear Implementation Plan

Answering such questions as those in Recommendation 1 above should help the development of a clear implementation plan.

Knagg (2014, p. 24) describes, "the 'policy is practice' fallacy" in relation to EMI, that "if a national or institutional authority states that a certain context is EMI in policy statements and publicity material, then that is actually the case. This equation of policy and practice is far from reality". For example, Masuhara, Mishan and Tomlinson (2017) contains reports from the Sultanate of Oman (Tasseron, 2017) and from Egypt (Abdel Latif, 2017), which show how the teachers' main concern is to prepare students for exams by direct teaching of discrete knowledge of grammar, despite the fact the materials they are provided with are based on communicative approaches. Similar tendencies are reported from China (Zheng & Borg, 2014), Iran

(Baleghizadeh, Goldouz & Mehrdad, 2016) and Singapore (Loh & Renandya, 2015). In a clear implementation plan, ways of modifying these tendencies would be detailed and would probably include ongoing teacher development and changes in the syllabus and the examinations.

Recommendation 3: Carefully Designed Pre-service and In-service Teacher-Development Programmes Need to be Delivered

Nguyen and Franken (2010) report a very interesting multi-method case study of six Vietnamese EFL university teachers' conceptions of input before and after a workshop. Their findings include that the majority of teachers:

- thought that "input" meant discrete linguistic knowledge
- were concerned about time pressure, perceived students' low proficiency and students' ability to comprehend and therefore used mainly L1, as well as limiting the use of L2 to make the teaching more "comprehensible" (a possible misunderstanding of Krashen's term "comprehensible input").

Such misconceptions would obviously work against a language plan aimed at learners achieving communicative competence and the changes needed in the teachers' conceptions and behaviour would need ongoing teacher-development programmes such as the in-on service programmes of the PKG English Programme in Indonesia. This was a programme that provided teachers with the hands on experience of facilitating the development of communicative competence, both on development courses and in their own classrooms, and that emphasised the need for rich and comprehensible input in English through extensive reading, extensive listening and interaction (see Tomlinson, 1990).

Application to Curriculum Development

The prevailing type of syllabus around the globe seems to be based on linguistic specification and sequencing (e.g. pronunciation, vocabulary, grammar), and in many countries the Ministry of Education may distribute discrete-item-focused textbooks and set discrete-item-testing examinations. Such a focus on linguistic items signals to teachers that:

1 coverage of the linguistic items in the syllabus is what really matters
2 the content of the syllabus will be tested in examinations rather than the learners' communicative competence (thus ensuring a negative exam backwash, which will strongly influence how teachers teach).

In our view, most learners need a syllabus that provides a rich and varied exposure to language in use, that promotes regular recycling of the input provided, that gives learners frequent opportunities to experience interactive input from teachers, peers and themselves, and that encourages learners to seek out-of-class experience of the target language in use.

An example of such a syllabus is a CLIL syllabus (Mehisto, Marsh & Frigols, 2008; Marsh, Coyle & Hood, 2010; Llinares & Morton, 2017) in which subject content (e.g. biology, geometry, music, tourism) or skills content (e.g. playing the saxophone, pottery, football, dancing) is specified and the content and the L2 language needed in learning about, in discussing and in reporting on the content are learned together. The syllabus typically specifies the details of the content to be learned or the skills to be developed, and the language syllabus derives from it. Such a syllabus is potentially rich, recycled and relevant and is delivered through experience of authentic language in use rather than through the explicit teaching of predetermined language items. In the United States, this approach is usually referred to as CBI (Brinton, 2003).

Another example of a rich, experiential syllabus is the text-driven syllabus (Tomlinson, 2013d; Tomlinson & Masuhara, 2018b) in which potentially engaging written, spoken and multimedia texts are selected from a variety of genres and text types and are then used to drive meaningful activities involving experience and production of language in communicative use, learner discovery of features of the language in their input and the seeking of opportunities for out-of-class exposure to language in use. Such a syllabus consists primarily of a menu of potentially engaging texts for teachers (and hopefully learners) to choose from, but could also include an inventory of activity types that can be selected from, in order to exploit a chosen text. An example of a textbook that operationalises a text-driven syllabus is *Openings* (Tomlinson, 1994a). This is a book which provides over fifty extracts from contemporary world literature for teachers and learners to choose from, and a menu of meaning-focused activities for each extract. See Chapter 3 for a detailed discussion and exemplification of the text-driven approach.

A project-based approach also offers the possibility of rich exposure to language in use. A project-based syllabus specifies a number of enquiry-based or problem-based projects for learners to choose from. The projects are normally conducted in small groups and typically involve the learners going out of the classroom to gather information, opinions and ideas before basing a presentation on what they find out. There is great potential in this approach for the elicitation of authentic and relevant input from books, from magazines, from newspapers, from the Internet, from teachers, from peers and from L2 users, as well as multiple opportunities for exposure to interactive input when discussing and preparing to present, and from participating in other groups' presentations. See Stoller (2002, 2006) for information about project-based approaches.

Task-based syllabuses (e.g. Van den Branden, 2006; Long, 2015), in which communication tasks are listed, ideally for teachers and learners to choose from, also have great potential for generating rich input. The learners, usually in groups, are given a non-linguistic outcome to achieve (e.g. designing an advertisement, arranging a meeting, gaining financial support for a project) and they then have to collaborate by sharing their existing resources to achieve the specified outcome. This usually results in valuable interaction in which learners help each other to achieve clarification, modification and elaboration of each other's output as well as in gaining scaffolded input from teachers when the learners seek their help.

A noticeable feature of the syllabuses described above is that they are all meaning-focused, and they typically generate form-focused activity in which learners respond primarily to the content of their input but focus on form when meaning or expression is problematic or significant, as opposed to forms-focused activities in which predetermined language points are taught and practised.

Application to L2 Methodology

Mishan (2013a, p. 269) provides a comprehensive survey of "currently influential language pedagogies, outlining their basis in second language acquisition (SLA) theory" (though she does not include CLIL, text-driven or project-based approaches). Some current approaches are input-rich, in the sense that they expose learners to comprehensible input in contextual use and/or they encourage the generation and modification of input through interaction. Other approaches are, in our view, input-poor, in that they focus on the provision of input as exemplification of predetermined teaching points and tend to generate peer-to-peer practice rather than communicative interaction. In this section we are going to focus on those approaches with the greatest potential to provide and to generate rich input.

Task-Based Language Teaching (TBLT)

TBLT in its strong form encourages learners to make use of their own and fellow learners' existing linguistic resources in order to achieve successful completion of a communicative task with a specified outcome (e.g. designing an appealing poster for an upcoming local event). Whilst collaborating on the task, learners will solicit language they need from each other and from their teacher and after task completion they will gain feedback from other peers and their teacher on the effectiveness of their use of the L2. This is a form-focused in meaning-focused approach, in which the learners sometimes focus on form, not in order to learn prescribed language points but in order to aid their successful completion of the task. The input is generated mainly by the learners themselves whilst engaged on the task and when presenting their product to the class or another group, but input is also provided by other groups' presentations and by the teachers' stimulus, support and feedback. Unfortunately, in many classrooms and in many task-based materials (especially in countries where the coursebooks and examinations are driven by strict and prescriptive syllabuses) the TBLT approach has been weakened into a forms-focused approach in which tasks are selected to practise predetermined language items or features, which are even sometimes pre-taught before the task is introduced. For information about the theory and application of TBLT, see Long (2015), Mackey, Ziegler and Bryfonski (2016), Tomlinson (2015), Tomlinson and Masuhara (2018b) and, especially, Van den Branden (2006) and Van den Branden, Bygate and Norris (2009). For accounts of how TBLT approaches are being used in different international contexts see Lambert and Oliver (2020), and for accounts of how they have been weakened (sometimes into task-supported approaches) in order to achieve face validity and to prepare students for examinations, see Masuhara (2015), Thomas and Reinders (2015) and Tomlinson (2015). For a concise overview of the literature on TBLT, see Moore (2018), and for accounts of recent research on the effectiveness of TBLT see Samuda, Van den Branden and Bygate (2018). For both a comprehensive overview and a review of recent research on the effectiveness of TBLT see Ellis, Skehan, Shintani and Lambert (2019), a book that also focuses on syllabus design, the methodology of task-based teaching and task-based assessment.

Our main criticism of TBLT is that an opportunity to provide rich input is missed if the tasks (as is usual practice) are given to the learners out of the blue rather than being stimulated by a potentially engaging text. We are not advocating starting with a text exemplifying language that could be used in the task (as is sometimes done in weak forms of TBLT). We are advocating using texts as a stimulus for, and as driver of, tasks. For further discussion and an exemplification of a task-based text-driven approach see Tomlinson (2018c) and Chapter 3 in this book.

Readers' Tasks

1 Find a potentially engaging text that you think would appeal to a particular level of class in an institution you are familiar with.
2 Design a task that is driven by the text. Your task should involve the learners returning to the text in order for them to respond to a challenge (e.g. designing a vehicle, inventing a device, solving a problem).

Problem-Based Teaching (PBT)

Another type of task-based approach is PBT, in which the tasks involve pooling existing linguistic resources in order to find and present solutions to problems. Learners are often then led to reflect on their discussions and presentations and sometimes to re-think and re-present. The processes of solving, presenting and reflecting typically generate learner output that is often modified through clarification and elaboration and becomes valuable input for the interactants, especially if they are challenged and engaged by the task. Input can also be provided by a teacher, either taking part as a participant in the task or being available as a linguistic resource and by a text that stimulates the problem-solving task. For example, learners read an extract from the comic novel *Salmon Fishing in the Yemen* (Torday, 2007), or watch the scene from the film, in which a British civil servant is tasked with finding a way of getting salmon up dried-up rivers to spawn in the dry season in the Yemen; and then in groups, they solve the problem and write to the civil servant with their solution.

See Ansarian and Teoh (2018) for a survey of the literature on problem-based approaches and for suggestions for the classroom implementation of the approaches.

Text-Driven Approaches (TDA)

A text-driven approach is a learner-centred, experiential approach in which a core authentic text is selected for its potential to engage, and which then drives the activities in the classroom, rather than a syllabus or a predetermined language- or skills-teaching point. A principled, flexible framework for a text-driven approach is described, justified and exemplified in Tomlinson (2013d) and in Tomlinson and Masuhara (2018b). In this framework, a readiness activity (e.g. the learners visualising and talking to themselves about their experience of travelling by train) precedes the core text and activates the learners' minds in relation to it. The learners are then given a mental task to perform (e.g. visualising the train journey being described) whilst reading, listening to or viewing the text. After experiencing the text, the learners answer personal-response questions designed to facilitate the development and articulation of their representation and/or interpretation of the text (e.g. drawing a scene from the journey described in the text, or giving their explanation for the way the passengers behaved). Then the learners write a continuation of the text individually or in groups. Before this text is handed in, the learners go back to the original text and make discoveries about how a particular language feature is used (e.g. the passive voice) and then make any revisions they want to their text.

TDAs are input-rich. The learners are provided with input by the core text, by themselves in the readiness activity, by peers during various interactions and by the teacher when responding to requests for assistance. They are also principled, in that they are based on such SLA criteria as comprehensible exposure to the L2 in rich and recycled use, affective engagement, cognitive engagement, learner discovery and opportunities to use the L2 to achieve intended outcomes. See Chapter 2 and Tomlinson (2016a) for detailed discussion of these principles.

> **Readers' Task**
>
> Use the same text as in the previous Readers' Task in order to design a text-driven lesson for a particular class of learners.

CLIL Approaches

CLIL approaches involve learners gaining content knowledge and skills from input and activities in the L2. Columbian learners could, for example, be learning about the history of Europe in English, French or Italian, and South Korean learners could be learning to dance through the medium of English or Spanish. The theory is that learners will acquire communicative competence from regular and recycled experience of purposeful and relevant use of the L2. It is predominantly a meaning-focused approach, but most CLIL courses also take a form-focused approach, in which language forms are paid attention to when they are significant or problematic in relation to learners' understanding or use.

All CLIL courses share a basic focus on acquisition from immersion and use, but actual pedagogic procedures vary from course to course. Some courses might pre-teach language and skills prior to encountering texts and activities, some might encourage responsive teaching when teacher assistance is requested, some might have follow-up language phases responding to discovered needs during content-based activities and some might rely entirely on immersion. All CLIL courses, though, are input-rich in quantity and quality, in the sense that the focus is on the meaning of the language being used to achieve relevant communicative outcomes, and in the varied provision of comprehensible input from texts, from teachers and from peers.

See Coyle, Hood and Marsh (2010) and Lasagabaster and Ruiz de Zarobe (2010) for more information about CLIL, and see Sylven (2019) for a research study of the effects of CLIL as used in secondary schools in Sweden.

Project-Based Approaches

Project-based approaches, in which learners collaborate in groups to prepare for, carry out and report on a project, have great potential for providing rich input. They are meaning-focused, form-focused approaches in which the learners' main objective is to communicate meaningful content. However, before achieving this, they need to carry out research that will expose them to relevant language in use in written, spoken and multimodal texts as well as in interaction with informants and with each other. For example, they might be carrying out a project related to a planned demolition and redevelopment of an area of historical value. This will involve them in reading newspaper reports, listening to and watching the news, interviewing local people, administrators and planners, and attending meetings. This will provide multiple opportunities for exposure to rich input, as will interaction with each other in discussions and in the drafting and presentation of a report, interaction with a teacher when seeking help, and listening to and/or reading other groups' reports on their projects.

For discussion of the underlying principles of project-based approaches as well as suggestions for operationalising the approaches, see Wicks (2000) and Stoller (2002, 2006).

> **Readers' Tasks**
>
> 1 Develop a project which learners in a particular institution could carry out locally in order to gain more opportunities for exposure to rich input.
> 2 Build into each stage of the project an activity that could promote rich and comprehensible input.

Extensive Reading/Listening/Viewing

Extensive reading, listening and viewing of audio-visual materials can provide input that is rich in quantity, quality and variety, that is recycled naturally, that is meaningful (especially when chosen by the learner) and that is authentic, in the sense that it is contextualised, that it contains implicit information about pragmatic use as well as semantic meaning and linguistic form and that the meaning is conveyed through extra-linguistic as well as linguistic means (see Maley & Tomlinson, 2017). Of course, this is not always the case, as there are many extensive reading, listening and viewing materials that have been linguistically graded and reinforced with language-practice activities and have then been imposed on learners rather than selected by them. For research-based arguments for the power of the interaction with rich input provided by extensive reading, see Elley and Mangubhai (1981), Davies (1995), Day and Bamford (1998), Krashen (2004), Maley (2008) and Fenton-Smith (2010) and the Extensive Reading Foundation website (www.erfoundation.org).

Total Physical Response (TPR) Plus

TPR Plus is an input-rich approach successfully trialled on the PKG English Programme in Indonesia (Tomlinson, 1990, 1995) as a development of TPR, an approach pioneered by Asher (1981) in which the teacher gives instructions in the target language (e.g. "Put your left hand on your head") and the learners respond physically. We tried using TPR on the PKG with twelve-year-old beginners but found the students got a little bored after a while just following instructions (even though we made them as bizarre as possible). So we developed TPR Plus, an approach in which the teacher gave extended input and the students responded physically to achieve a purpose (Tomlinson, 1994b). For example, the teacher would narrate a dramatic or humorous story and as she did so the students would act out in mime all the actions in the story (e.g. "The people on the beach were very scared. They tried to hide."); or the teacher gave instructions on how to prepare and cook a meal and the students followed them; or the teacher suggested what the students should paint on a wall and the students painted it. This proved very popular with the students in our experimental classes (one in the First Year of almost every secondary school in Indonesia), we were able to achieve implicit "cover" of a six-year syllabus on our six-week pre-production course and our experimental students outperformed the others on a traditional end-of-year exam. What we found was that focusing the first six weeks on rich, communicative, meaningful and engaging input led in most cases to fairly effective communicative ability once the learners started to speak and write.

Teacher Talk

Teacher talk is often considered to be a problem by language-teaching methodologists and teacher trainers, and trainee teachers are often advised to reduce it. The argument is that when the teacher is talking, the learners are not, and that this deprives them of the opportunities to practise the language that they need in order to learn it. Our argument is that for many learners the teacher is the only available source of authentic input, and without such input the learners are not going to acquire communicative competence in the language. It is not a question of quantity of teacher talk but of quality, with the best quality consisting of input that is comprehensible, meaningful to the learners, engaging and humanistic. This can be provided by teachers chatting to the learners, telling jokes, anecdotes and stories, making personal and humorous responses and also when engaged in providing feedback or in explicit teaching. It can also be provided by teachers interacting with learners during plenary discussion, when monitoring group work and in one-to-one tutorials. For discussion and exemplification of how teachers can use quality talk to aid learner acquisition see Tomlinson (2014b).

Task-Free Activities

One initiative we have found in which teacher talk is extremely valuable is the teacher providing learners with a task-free activity at the beginning of every lesson. What happens is the teacher starts every lesson by telling a joke, anecdote or story, reading a poem or an extract from a novel or play, acting out a scene from a play or singing a song. There are no comprehension questions or follow-up activities, just a brief silence whilst the learners reflect on what they have listened to. The teacher reminds the learners that copies of the text will be available for them to take at the end of the lesson if they want to, and that they should put the text into their loose-leaf file if it has engaged them. Sometimes in a subsequent lesson, learners will ask the teacher to clarify something they did not understand in a text, but the teacher does not interrogate the learners about the texts nor embark on unrequested explanations.

This approach massively increases the learners' exposure to contextualised and potentially engaging input, and has proved very popular with learners all over the world who we and our post-graduate students have tried it with. Also popular has been ending each lesson with a riddle (e.g. "Where do fish keep their money?"), another approach that has increased the learners' exposure to stimulating input.

Looking Out for the L2

No classroom-based course can really provide enough input (Barker, 2010a, 2010b) so it is vital that learners are encouraged to look out for their target language in use outside the classroom. This could involve looking out for the language in advertisements, in notices, on signs, on shopfronts and on t-shirts. It could involve reading books, magazines and newspapers and watching films, TV programmes, TV advertisements and videos. It could involve interacting with speakers of the target language and with fellow learners of it. And, of course, it could involve using smart phones, iPads and laptops to surf the Web, to use a search engine to look for information, to watch videos or to interact with speakers and learners of the target language.

We once visited a primary school in Guangzhou and the only three students who could hold a conversation with us in English from a class who had answered all the teachers' questions accurately were a boy who visited Foreigners' Corner every Friday, a boy who subscribed to *World Soccer* (a magazine aimed at adult native speakers of English) and a boy who went on his computer every night looking for English.

For discussion and demonstration of ways of getting learners to look out for their L2 see Benson and Reinders (2011), Cooker (2008, 2010), Nunan and Richards (2015), Pinnard (2016) and Tomlinson (2010c, 2011b, 2014a).

Learners Talking to Themselves

In the L1 we talk to ourselves all the time using our inner voice. We do so to make decisions, to decide on a stance, to amuse ourselves, to vent our spleen, to be creative, to make plans and preparations, to help us to understand what we have read or heard, to prepare for outer speech and to help us to control what we say to other people. We do all this in a highly efficient, restricted code that features simple tenses, the active voice, a basic vocabulary, ellipsis, incomplete utterances and utterances completed by visual imagery. Yet research shows that L2 learners rarely use L2 inner speech until they attain a high level of communicative competence, thus depriving themselves of opportunities to generate communicative output that can become valuable auto-input.

For discussion of the potential roles of inner speech in the use and learning of an L2, and for suggestions as to how the teacher can help learners to use L2 inner speech (e.g. setting inner speech monologue and dialogue activities), see Tomlinson and Avila (2007a, 2007b) and Tomlinson (2020a).

Responsive Teaching

We believe that learners learn best what they need and want to learn when they need and want to learn it. Very often these needs and wants become apparent during learner production activities, and the need for informative input and modification of output can be met in collaborative groups by peers and in any activity other than a test by requesting teacher assistance in the form of responsive teaching. Such teacher-supplied input not only responds to a need but provides information about communicative interaction as well as about form, function and meaning.

Provision of Supplementary Input

Most researchers and teachers would agree that coursebooks and classroom lessons cannot provide enough input, and that it is necessary for supplementary input to be provided for learners to experience outside the classroom. Ideally, this is provided in self-access centres but only really well-resourced institutions can afford them. Some institutions can afford class or school libraries, and all institutions could display initiative and develop simple, cheap ways in which supplementary input can be provided for learners (e.g. subscribing to comics, magazines and newspapers), in which teachers could develop libraries of supplementary materials to select from and in which learners could help themselves (e.g. learners giving presentations, learners presenting video clips, learners "building" their own class library). See Chapter 3 for examples of learner provision of supplementary input and for suggestions as to how the teacher can promote supplementary interaction.

One of the many things that all the above approaches have in common is the provision of authentic input. Whether or not authentic input is more likely to facilitate acquisition than contrived or simplified input is a matter of debate between SLA researchers (see Chapter 9). One thing for sure though is that (providing it is comprehensible and meaningful to the learner) it is much richer in information about how the target language is used than contrived materials. It is likely to contain information, not just about grammar, lexis, pronunciation or spelling, but also about the interaction between context and expression, about pragmatic function, about the significance of paralinguistic and extra-linguistic signals (e.g. intonation, gesture), about ways of achieving intended outcomes and about language variation. There is also considerable evidence that texts in coursebooks often present input that does not represent how language is typically used. Gilmore (2015, p. 10), for example, says:

> For a wide range of discourse features (including lexicogrammatical items, speech acts, generic structure, and interactional features of contingent talk), ELT textbooks often provide learners with distorted or partial representations of the target language to work from, and these are likely to impact negatively on students' developing communicative competence.

For discussion about the value of authentic input see Gilmore (2007, 2015), Mishan (2005), Maley and Tomlinson (2017), Tomlinson and Masuhara (2018b) and Chapter 9 in this book.

Readers' Tasks

1 Come up with suggestions for how teachers in a particular institution you are familiar with could usefully increase the input that their learners are exposed to.
2 Come up with suggestions for how learners in a particular institution you are familiar with could usefully increase the input that they are exposed to.

There are many popular approaches to language teaching and learning that we are not going to consider in this chapter, either because they are valuable approaches but do not specifically promote exposure to rich input (e.g. discovery approaches, consciousness-raising approaches, data-driven approaches) or because we feel that they limit the learners' exposure to decontextualised exemplars of predetermined, discrete language items or features and/or they only expose learners to short, simplified written and spoken texts and provide very few opportunities for communicative interaction (e.g. Presentation/Practice/Production (PPP)). Some of these approaches, are discussed in Chapter 3.

Application to Materials Development

In our experience, an analysis of almost any two coursebooks at an equivalent level, whether they be global coursebooks from a major commercial publisher, local ministry of education coursebooks or institutional coursebooks, will reveal that exposure to the target language in use is very limited and that the available input is restricted to sentences exemplifying a language point, to explanations of language features and to brief (and often contrived) written and spoken texts.

We have just analysed two pages turned to at random from Unit 4 Friends and Strangers of *Global Intermediate* (Clandfield & Robb Benne, 2011) and two pages turned to at random from *The Big Picture* (Goldstein, 2012). This is what we found:

Pages 46–47 of *Global Intermediate*

- There is only one extended text, a fifteen-turn conversation from a film, which is used both for a listening and a reading activity.
- The only other continuous text consists of two sentences of information on Patricia Highsmith and one sentence on Alfred Hitchcock, plus two bullet points on Guy Haines and two on Bruno Anthony.
- Other input comes from a vocabulary panel focusing on the differences between "stranger" and "foreigner", from comprehension questions, from sentences to respond to, from a matching exercise and from four sentence completion activities.
- There are three "work in pairs" activities that might generate peer interaction and therefore peer and auto-input.

Pages 60–61 of *The Big Picture*.

- There is a forty-three-word written description of Berlin, drawing attention to its cultural and ethnic diversity.
- There are three written texts about the Karneval der Kulturen in Brazil. Each text is about eighty to ninety words long and written to entice readers to visit the festival.
- There is a short, spoken text providing four opinions about the festival.
- There is another short, spoken text in which Eva talks about a festival.
- There are six activities involving the students answering questions about the language in the texts.
- There are three sentence completion activities, a summary completion activity and a clause-matching activity.
- There is a grammar panel with a long explanation and examples of the use of sentences with *If* in "Real situations".
- There is a short explanation of the use of "a must".
- There is a pair-expression-practising activity and two group-discussion activities.

For this level of learner (i.e. intermediate) our view, based on our research, our reading of SLA research and our classroom experience around the world, is that in the samples from both books there is not enough exposure to the target language in communicative use and too much time spent practising or being tested. But then you cannot blame the authors, because this focus on the discrete, on explicit teaching, on short texts chosen to exemplify teaching points, on controlled practice and on testing what has just been taught is what is expected (or even required) by publishers and users around the world (see Tomlinson, 2020b). And there are methodologists, materials developers and even SLA researchers who believe that this facilitates language acquisition (see Chapter 2 and Chapter 3 for references to proponents of Skill Acquisition Theory and of PPP – Presentation/Practice/ Production).

What we would recommend in relation to the provision and generation of input in materials for language learning is that:

- the materials should be text-rich in terms of quantity, quality and variety of genre and text type (even at lower levels);
- there should be written, spoken, visual, audio-visual and multimodal texts;
- the texts should be authentic, in the sense of not being written for teaching purposes, in having intended outcomes, in being contextualised and in containing linguistic, paralinguistic and extra-linguistic indicators of meaning;
- the texts should vary in styles, in genres and in varieties of the target language;
- the materials should encourage the teacher to talk with (not at) the learners;
- the activities in the materials should be mainly open-ended activities that stimulate peer interaction and the generation of peer and auto-input.

There are some examples of coursebooks that provide and generate such input as that advocated here. For example, there is a series of coursebooks for teacher-language improvement, published in Ethiopia (Tomlinson, 2004), a coursebook for university students published in Japan (Tomlinson & Masuhara, 1994), a coursebook for young secondary-school teenagers, published in Namibia (*On Target*, 1995), a very aesthetic coursebook for secondary-school teenagers featuring literature and art, published in Norway (Fenner & Nordal Pedersen, 1999, 2006) and coursebooks for secondary school teenagers published in Singapore (Tomlinson, Hill & Masuhara, 2000). All of these publications feature longer than usual authentic written, spoken and visual texts and they all use open-ended activities to stimulate peer interaction.

There are many examples of digital materials that provide potentially engaging, multimodal and authentic input (e.g. Keddie, 2009, 2014; LearnEnglish (http://learnenglish.britishcouncil.org/en); Lessonstream by Jamie Keddie (http://lessonstream.org/video-lessonplans/); Onestopenglish (www.onestopenglish.com)). However, because most of them are targeted at self-access learners and also because of a perceived need to establish face validity and to provide feedback on performance, many of them focus on traditional, closed activities such as filling in the blanks, matching, and sentence completion, which are unlikely to stimulate peer interaction if they are used in a classroom or to generate rich intake (see Chapter 2 in this book).

So far, we have not referred to digital materials in a separate section. This is because we think that our recommended principles of SLA, and our recommendations in relation to materials, apply equally to all materials regardless of their medium, channel or modality. There has quite rightly been a lot of attention paid to the potential value of digital materials (Hockly, 2013; Kiddle, 2013; Motteram, 2013; Carrier, Damerow & Bailey, 2017; Tomlinson & Masuhara, 2018b) and we certainly recognise the affordances they can offer. For example, they can offer:

- the provision of multimodal and embodied input;
- choice of text, task, approach and focus for the learner;
- ease of return for repetition or revision;
- motivation to learners who are comfortable and competent with using digital technology;
- flexibility and mobility of use;
- the potential for interaction not only with the programme being used but with other users of it;
- opportunities to add to, supplement and adapt materials;
- localised and even individualised versions of materials;
- opportunities for combining with face-to-face learning to provide an optimum blend of the two modalities (see Mishan, 2013b and Tomlinson and Whittaker, 2013 for indications of how to achieve this optimum blend when developing blended-learning materials).

We also recognise that digital materials do not magically create acquisition just because they are delivered digitally. They need to satisfy the criteria for facilitating acquisition and, unfortunately, many of them do not.

Digital materials do not in themselves constitute a methodology or a pedagogic approach, and in fact all those we know follow a methodology or approach that has previously been used in paper materials. A blended-learning course, for example, could follow a PPP approach or a task-based approach, or it could follow a different approach in the face-to-face sections from in the digitally delivered sections (e.g. an explicit teaching of language–form approach and a project-based or problem-solving approach). What is distinctive about digital materials is their mode of delivery and the affordances that they offer. Many digital courses take advantage of these affordances in creative ways that have the potential to facilitate acquisition, and many do not. For an evaluation of digital materials when measured against SLA principles see Tomlinson and Masuhara (2018b).

Application to L2 Assessment

One of the biggest problems we have had with assessment is that examinations, tests and teachers tend to assess the learners' achievement in learning the input they have been provided with by a syllabus and/or coursebook, rather than in assessing what learners are able to do with what they have taken in from all the input they have experienced. This, of course, leads teachers to neglect communicative activities in the classroom and to focus on imparting prescribed input. It also leads to learners focusing on learning the discrete items focused on by their teacher and their coursebook, and then revising them for tests and examinations. The result is often that learners get high marks but cannot communicate, or they struggle to learn input that seems remote and unengaging and get low marks. Or it could be that learners have gained communicative competence from engaged experience of authentic input provided by a chatty teacher, by exposure to engaging texts, by interaction with their peers and by engagement with input they have found for themselves outside the classroom, and yet get low marks when assessed. We once participated in writing a young-learners' coursebook for China that featured input-rich texts, which the learners responded to holistically. We are told that the book was popular with the learners. Unfortunately though, many teachers tested the learners on all the lexical items in the texts, the learners' marks went down and teachers and parents were displeased.

Our advice is to ignore prescribed input when assessing learners and instead assess the learners on their ability to make use of what they have acquired from all the input they have experienced. We will say much more about assessing learner capabilities rather than learner knowledge of imposed input in Chapter 3 and in other subsequent chapters. We will also provide references to publications that are critical of prevailing practices of assessment and to those which advocate assessment for learning (AFL), an approach to assessment that makes use of focused feedback to help learners to improve their communicative competence.

Implications for L2 Teacher Development

Awareness and understanding of the applications of SLA theory and practice as outlined above should be an important goal of development courses for language teachers. This could be achieved by following a problem-solving approach in which the participants are confronted with problems caused by, for example, input impoverishment, and then challenged to come up with practical solutions that are both principled and achievable. The participants could be referred to relevant SLA research and theory, not in order to answer questions on it in examinations but in order to apply it when developing and operationalising their solutions. They could also be guided to conduct mini-research projects (or enquiries, as Maley, 2016 prefers to call them) in which they investigate the effects of both existing materials and approaches and of principled, innovative materials and approaches they have developed themselves.

> **Readers' Tasks**
>
> 1 Take any coursebook.
> Analyse a unit from the coursebook to discover:
>
> - how many of the types of input described in this chapter are included;
> - how many of the types of input advocated in this chapter are made use of.
>
> Suggest ways of modifying and supplementing the input in an adaptation of the unit designed to maximise its potential for acquisition.
>
> 2 Evaluate two of the following approaches in relation to their ability to provide input which is likely to facilitate acquisition:
>   - PPP
>   - Task-based teaching (TBT)
>   - CLIL
>   - The text-driven approach (TDA)
>
> For descriptions of these approaches, see the Application to Methodology section in this chapter as well as Richards and Rodgers (2014) and Chapter 8 of Tomlinson and Masuhara (2018b).

CONCLUSION

The most obvious application of the research related to input is that learners need exposure to communicative input that is rich in quality and quantity, and that it is the responsibility of language planners, curriculum developers, material developers, teachers and teacher trainers that opportunities to experience rich input are made available. Unfortunately, in our experience input is often impoverished as a result of an excessive focus on the explicit teaching of discrete items of grammar, by prescriptive syllabuses that preselect input regardless of learner needs and wants, by an unsubstantiated belief that restricting input to short, simplified texts and sample sentences makes learning the target language easier, and by teachers teaching the L2 in the L1 or restricting their communicative use of the L2 to a minimum either on the advice of their teacher trainers or from feeling inadequate in their ability to communicate in the L2 they are teaching.

FURTHER READING

Ellis, R. (2010). Second language acquisition, teacher education, and language pedagogy. *Language Teaching. 43*(2), 182–201.

(2015). *Understanding second language acquisition* (2nd ed.). Oxford: Oxford University Press.

Ellis, R. & Shintani, N. (2013). *Exploring language pedagogy through second language acquisition research.* New York: Routledge.

Shintani, N. (2016). *Input-based tasks in foreign language instruction for young learners.* Amsterdam: John Benjamins.

Tomlinson, B. (2016). Achieving a match between SLA research and materials development. In B. Tomlinson (Ed.), *SLA research and materials development for language learning* (pp. 3–22). New York: Routledge.

Tomlinson, B. & Masuhara, H. (2018b). Developing materials for the acquisition of language. In B. Tomlinson & H. Masuhara, *The complete guide to the theory and practice of materials development for language learning* (pp. 189–219). Hoboken, NJ: Wiley-Blackwell.

2 Intake Part One
Theory

Introduction

In this chapter, we will report on research and theories relating to intake from the literature on second language acquisition that we consider relevant and applicable to the learning of an L2, both for learners and for practitioners. As you will discover, some of the findings of the research are controversial, even contradictory, and some would not be easy to apply, given the political, cultural and practical constraints faced by many learners and practitioners. Here, we are going to focus mainly on those findings and theories for which there is a general consensus of acceptance and which we have found to offer potential for application to many actual contexts of learning. However, as intake is both a mental process and a mental product, we are also going to make reference to research findings and theories from neurolinguistics, in which such procedures as functional magnetic resonance imaging (fMRI) and electrophysiology have been used to find indicative evidence of neurolinguistic processing during language activity. "fMRI detects the magnetic signals resulting from blood oxygenation and flow that occur in response to neural activity" (Wong, Yin & O'Brien, 2016, p. 4). It has been used, for example, to identify the areas of the brain that are active during the processing and use of language, and has produced "compelling evidence for a 'universal' language network of the human brain" (Wong, Yin & O'Brien, 2016, p. 5). Electrophysiology is "a technique for recording electrical voltage potentials produced by cellular activity" in the brain during language processing (Morgan-Short, 2014, p. 15). It has been found, for example, that "L2 neurocognitive processing changes qualitatively with time" (Morgan-Short, 2014, p. 15) and that processing is easier for features that are similar in the L1 and the L2, or are unique to the L2. It has also been shown that it is more difficult for features that the two languages share but that are instantiated differently, and that implicit language training is more likely to lead to native-like processing of syntactic structures than explicit language training (Morgan-Short, 2014, p. 31).

In Chapter 3 we will review the literature on the application of the research and theories relating to intake, and offer our own suggestions for application based on our experience in teaching, teacher training, curriculum development, materials development and assessment.

What is Intake?

Definitions in the Literature
There are many differing definitions of "intake" in the literature, a point made by Chi (2016) in his useful overview of "Intake in Second Language Acquisition". Chi stresses the need to define how "intake" is being used in each context of its use, and utilises Reinders' (2012) categories of product, process and a combination of product and process to review prominent definitions in the literature. We are first going to report definitions of intake according to these three categories, summarise these definitions in a table and then add other definitions that do not belong to any of these categories.

Intake as a Product
Definitions that view intake as a product see it as the result of the processing of selected input. For example Chi (2016, p. 77) refers to Ying's (1995) claim that "intake is a subset of input which has been internalized by learners after processing", to Van Patten's (2002) definition of intake as "the linguistic data actually processed from the input and held in working memory for further processing" (p. 757), to Sharwood-Smith's (1993) view of intake as the "part of input which has actually been processed by the learner and turned into knowledge of some kind" (p. 167) and to Beebe's (1985) belief that "learners are active in deciding what parts/aspects of input will be processed to become intake" (Chi 2016, p. 77). Intake as a product is summarised in Table 2.1.

Intake as a Process
In his section on definitions that view intake as a process, Chi (2016, p. 77) refers to Chaudron's (1985) description of intake as "referring not to a single event or product, but to a complex phenomenon of information processing that involves several stages" (p. 2) and as "the mediating process between the target language available to learners as input and the learners' internalised set of L2 rules and strategies for second language development" (p. 1). Chi also refers to Leow's (1993) definition of intake as "an intermediate process between the exposure to input and actual language acquisition" (p. 334), a definition that makes for us the important point that intake is not the final stage in the process of language acquisition. Intake as a process is summarised in Table 2.2.

Intake as a Combination of Product and Process
Chi (2016, pp. 77–78) introduces his section on intake as a combination of product and process by referring to Alcon's (1998) suggestion of viewing intake as "both the part of the input that learners attend to and process as well as the product gained after processing is complete". He also refers to Reinders' (2012, p. 28) definition of intake as "a subset of the detected input (comprehended or not), held in short-term memory, from which connections with long-term memory are potentially created or strengthened". Chi

is critical of "the lack of precision in discussions of intake" (p. 78) and considers that "one way to introduce more clarity is to posit two types of intake defined as preliminary and final intake (Chaudron, 1983, 1985)" (p. 78). According to Chi, Chaudron argues that input processing creates intake and he sees preliminary intake as the initial stage of perception of input and final intake as the stage in which learners form and test hypotheses about L2 rules. Chi also refers to other researchers who share Chaudron's view of intake as a continuum from perception to generalisation (e.g. Leow, 1993; Batstone, 1996; Alcon, 1998; Reinders, 2012). We share this view, but think Chaudron's term "final intake" is misleading, as we believe that intake continues both as a process and as a changeable product even after acquisition has taken place (see Chapter 4). Intake as both product and process is summarised in Table 2.3.

Summary of the Definitions of Intake

Table 2.1 Product

Researchers/authors	Source	How the authors describe intake
Ying (1995)	Cited in Chi (2016, p. 77)	Intake is a subset of input that has been internalised by learners after processing.
Van Patten (2002)	p. 757	The linguistic data actually processed from the input and held in working memory for further processing.
Sharwood-Smith (1993)	p. 167	Part of the input that has actually been processed by the learner and turned into knowledge of some kind.
Beebe (1985)	Cited in Chi (2016, p. 77)	Learners are active in deciding what parts/aspects of input will be processed to become intake.

Table 2.2 Process

Researchers/authors	Source	How the authors describe intake
Chaudron (1985)	p. 1	The mediating process between the target language available to learners as input and the learners' internalised set of L2 rules and strategies for second language development.
	p. 2	Referring not to a single event or product but to a complex phenomenon of information processing that involves several stages.
Leow (1993)	p. 334	An intermediate process between the exposure to input and actual language acquisition.

What is Intake?

Table 2.3 Product and Process

Researchers/authors	Source	How the authors describe intake
Alcon (1998)	Cited in Chi (2016, pp. 77–78)	Both the part of the input that learners attend to and process as well as the product gained after processing is complete.
Beebe (1985)	Cited in Chi (2016, p. 77)	Learners are active in deciding what parts/aspects of input will be processed to become intake.
Reinders (2012)	p. 28	A subset of the detected input (comprehended or not), held in short-term memory, from which connections with long-term memory are potentially created or strengthened.
Chi (2016)	p. 78	Intake as a continuum from perception to generalisation (e.g. Chaudron, 1983, 1985; Leow, 1993; Batstone, 1996; Alcon, 1998; Reinders, 2012).

Other Definitions of Intake

Other definitions of intake include:

"Intake is the input that is comprehended and that impacts the learner's developing linguistics system" (https://coerll.utexas.edu/methods/modules/technology/04/).

"The subset of input that becomes available to the learner" (Garcia Mayo & Alcón Soler, 2013, p. 209).

"The subset of input that has been attended to and processed such that it becomes available to the learner's developing linguistic system for further processing, which may lead to restructuring of the system" (Herschensohn & Young-Scholten, 2013, p. 718).

"Intake is that portion of the input that learners notice and therefore process in their working memory. Intake may subsequently be accommodated in the learner's interlanguage system – i.e. become part of long term memory" (R. Ellis, 2015, p. 318).

"Elements in the input that are noticed and processed in working memory either subconsciously or consciously; learners intake formal elements from the input and the meanings associated with them (i.e. they create form-meaning mappings). Elements that become intake may or may not enter the learner's interlanguage (i.e. long term memory)" (Rod Ellis – personal communication, 22 May 2017).

"The oral and written language that learners actually attend to enough so that it is processed in their minds, if only briefly. Whether this material becomes part of long-term storage is another issue. That is why over the years I have been concerned about mnemonic devices, for example. New vocabulary words may be intake at the moment, but are not available even an hour later – whether at the receptive or at the productive levels" (Andrew Cohen – personal communication 22 May 2017).

"Intake is input which is supposed to have more than a passing journey through the learner's mind. It is engaged somehow (noticed, consolidated with other knowledge, even reflected upon) and this contributes to TL development" (Pauline Foster – personal communication, 23 May 2017).

For a detailed discussion of definitions of intake, see Reinders (2012).

Although the definitions above vary considerably, most of them share the assumptions that intake is selected from input, that it involves or results from attention, that it is much smaller than input, that it is temporary and that it can, but does not necessarily, result in eventual storage in long-term memory. All the definitions focus narrowly on the intake of language, whereas, as we will see later in this chapter, the intake needed for the acquisition of communicative competence in a language includes not just linguistic items and structures but the body language, gestures, facial expressions, modulations of voice (i.e. extra-linguistic information), sensory and motor images, affective responses, intended and actual communicative effects and contextual references (i.e. nonlinguistic information) that accompany them. For example, the expression "Not now, John" read in isolation communicates very little but, when said by somebody whose voice as well as bodily and facial gestures indicate annoyance to somebody who is making a request, the words can convey a mild refusal of the request with a slight possibility of it eventually being granted, as in the following exchange.

> "Dad, come and play football with me."
> "Not now, John, I'm reading the paper."
> "OK. I'll play by myself then."

The context, gestures, facial expressions, voice modulations and intended and actual effects are all part of the input for somebody listening to the above exchange and are potentially part of any intake too.

We would also take issue with the many definitions that state or imply that intake is made available to the learner. This suggests that the learner plays a passive rather than an agentive role in the process of acquisition. It also implies that languages can be taught to learners, whereas we believe that teachers can only help learners to learn. We would say that input is made available to learners but that intake is achieved by learners. The teachers' role is to make relevant and meaningful input available to learners and to engage learners in interaction with the available input in ways likely to facilitate intake.

Interestingly, some publications on SLA make little or no reference to intake. For example, Saville-Troike and Barto (2017) include in the index forty references to input but none at all to intake, Colantoni, Steele and Escudero (2017) have in the index seven references to input but none at all to intake, and so does Ortega (2009). Long (2015) has seventy references for input and none for intake. Herschensohn and Young-Scholten (2013) have thirteen references to intake but over two hundred page references to input. Is this apparent neglect of intake because SLA researchers do not consider intake to be important? Or is it because in the SLA literature it is a rather nebulous and ill-defined concept, because researchers are subsuming intake into their concept of input (because intake, being a mental process and/or product, is not easily observable or specifiable), or is it because there are brief references to "intake" in these publications but they are not extensive enough to make the index, for example, Saville-Troike and Barto (2017). It could also be that many researchers prefer to use such terms as "input processing", as used, for example, by Barcroft and Wong (2013) and "language processing", as used, for example, by Foucart and Frenk-Mestre (2013), as these terms could be considered usefully more specific and precise.

Our Definition

We are going to use the term intake to refer to *language and the accompanying nonlinguistic and extra-linguistic features from the learner's input that have been taken into the brain for comprehension and for potential further processing*. This could be a new language feature that is taken in for the first time for potential processing, or one that has been encountered before and is taken in to contribute to ongoing processing. This use of the term intake is similar to Herschensohn and Young-Scholten's (2013, p. 718) definition of a "subset of input that has been attended to and processed such that it becomes available to the learner's developing linguistic system for further processing", and it is in many ways equivalent to Chaudron's first two stages of intake. We are also going to use the term intake to refer to the process of constituting and delivering the product specified above. We see intake as a stage in a lengthy procedure that progresses from input to intake to further processing to acquisition to development (see Chapter 4). In this procedure, progress to the next stage is not automatic and the first three stages need to be activated many times. For example, the lexical item "utilise" might be encountered in a written text and taken in because it is salient and recycled in the text, because it is paid attention to, and because the experience of reading the text was cognitively engaging. But the item might not be further processed and acquired because there was no opportunity to make use of it and it was not encountered again. However, six months later, the item might be encountered again, made use of and recycled at spaced intervals, and the by now weak record of the item might be strengthened into a candidate for further processing and eventual acquisition. But this is not going to happen for every item or feature that is taken in. Many will not be re-encountered, not be further processed and not be eventually acquired. Also, many acts of intake will be impoverished because the input and/or what is taken from it will not contain enough contextual and extra-linguistic information to achieve rich comprehension or strong connections, and it will therefore not justify maintenance.

We are going to attempt to give more precision to our definition of intake by specifying three stages of intake. Intake 1 (Perception) refers to the initial processing of language from the input, in which an utterance (be it a sentence, phrase or word) and its accompanying extra- and non-linguistic information is mentally perceived and held very briefly for potential further processing. Intake 2 (Transfer) refers to the temporary storing of a language item or feature "selected" from the perceived utterance for potential processing. Intake 3 (Integration) refers to the initial processing and storage of the language item or feature as a potential candidate for eventual acquisition. Progress from Intake 1 to Intake 3 involves interaction and integration with other items and features and with nonlinguistic and extra-linguistic information as well as with items and features already acquired. As products, Intake 1 is extremely vulnerable and is easily lost, Intake 2 is vulnerable and quite easily lost and Intake 3 is quite vulnerable and can be lost or become dormant. All three need strengthening and maintaining by subsequent encounters and connections. As products, Input is much larger than Intake 1, which is much larger than Intake 2, which is much larger than Intake 3. One obvious implication is that learners cannot learn everything that teachers teach. Each learner's intake will be less than the teacher's input. Another implication is that learners need a rich and massive amount of input both inside and outside of their course in order to successfully acquire an L2.

We are responsible for specifying and naming our three stages of intake, but we have done so as a result of our reading of the research conducted so far on what happens in the brain in between encountering a language feature in input and the acquisition of that feature for use in communication, as reported, for example, in Baddeley (2007), Morgan-Short and Ullman (2012), Field (2014) and Schütze (2017).

Some SLA researchers might relate our three stages to the progress from short-term memory to working memory to long-term memory (for example, "Intake is that portion of the input that learners notice and therefore process in their working memory. Intake may subsequently be accommodated in the learner's interlanguage system – i.e. become part of long term memory", R. Ellis, 2015, p. 18). Others might see short-term memory as the same as working memory. There are many differing definitions of short-term memory, but the essential feature of all of them, and therefore our definition, is that it is a temporary store of new intake that can hold information for between five seconds and one minute. Jackson (2016, p. 27) defines working memory as "a system of temporary storage and attentional control" and refers to the differing models of working memory developed and most recently elaborated on by Engle (2002), Cowan (2005) and Baddely (2012). We would define working memory as *the learner's ephemeral version of perceived input being held and processed for potential transfer to long-term memory*. The processing involves the executive control in the brain, attention (conscious and/or subconscious) by the learner and interaction with the short-term and long-term memory (see Schütze (2017, p. 27) for a description of the activities of the working memory). Long-term memory also has many differing definitions, but the essential feature of all of them is that it is a store that can hold information for a long time and that can be made use of for retrieval during attempts at communication and also for interacting with new information in the working memory. So, what we are saying is that features of attended input are held very briefly in the short-term memory, some of these features are held for a short period in the working memory for potential transfer and some of these features are then held in the long-term memory for use in attempted communication and the intake of new features. Some of the features in long-term memory are acquired and can be used effectively.

Having defined the three types of memory, we would now prefer to avoid the term memory in a book focusing on application of theory to practice, as many practitioners could associate memory with memorising language and with explicit recall. For the same reason, we will be very careful when using the term knowledge. We accept the SLA researchers' categorisation of declarative knowledge (i.e. knowledge about) and procedural knowledge (i.e. knowledge of how to) but are aware of many practitioners' associations of knowledge with something that can be explicitly taught, consciously learned and explicitly recalled. What we make use of in the brain (or as many SLA researchers would say, in the long-term memory) for language acquisition and language use is obviously much more than the conventional meaning of "knowledge" and it is acquired both explicitly and implicitly.

Another way of describing the process of language acquisition would be to make use of research in neurolinguistics to describe what is thought to happen in the brain during this process. For example, Schütze (2017, p. 25) describes "three stages of word processing: coding, storage, and retrieval" and stresses the importance of the working memory in prolonging "the duration of time our brain has to rehearse a word in order to identify its phonemes and lexeme", thus increasing "the likelihood that the brain will create a record of the word that is then stored near the hippocampus in an area called the non-mesial region". As Schütze says, "If a record is created the word can be recalled at a later time".

Schütze refers the reader to Baddeley (2007) for a more detailed account of this process but does himself elaborate further when describing on p. 27 how "when we first encounter a word, the phonemes of the word are rehearsed subvocally in the phonological loop ... These phonemes are then matched to a lexeme in Wernike's area of speech comprehension". If a match is found, the word "– that is the combination of the phonemes to the lexeme – is then forwarded to the hippocampus ... where the record of the word, which consists of linguistic and nonlinguistic information is created". As we will see, the nonlinguistic, extra-linguistic and para-linguistic information (which "is transmitted by the senses to the hippocampus") is a very important component in the process of language acquisition and plays an important role in determining whether the word is recorded, stored and subsequently made available for retrieval.

To rephrase our definition of intake in neurolinguistic terms we could say that *intake is both the process and the product of the coding (Intake 1– Perception), recording (Intake 2 – Transfer) and initial storage (Intake 3 – Integration) stages of language acquisition.*

The progress from input to Intake 1 to Intake 2 to Intake 3 can involve:

1. the executive control in the dorsolateral prefrontal part of the brain directing attention to an utterance in the input (usually a meaningful chunk) – Intake 1 – Perception;
2. the executive control in the dorsolateral prefrontal part of the brain directing attention to a language item or feature – Intake 1 – Perception;
3. the language item or feature being rehearsed in the phonological loop in the left prefrontal cortex – Intake 2 – Transfer;
4. the language item or feature being temporally stored in the left side of the parietal lobe – Intake 2 – Transfer;
5. the nonlinguistic information associated with the language item or feature (e.g. visual images) being processed by what has been called the "visuo-spatial sketch pad" – Intake 2 – Transfer;
6. emotional associations of the encounter with the language item or feature being processed in the amygdala in the mesial temporal lobe (see Mates and Joaquin, 2013) – Intake 2 – Transfer;
7. "information" about 3, 4 and 5 above being passed onto the hippocampus in the mesial temporal lobe for records to be created – Intake 3 – Integration;
8. the passing on of these records for storage (for example, for lexical items to the non-mesial region in the non-mesial temporal lobe) – Intake 3 – Integration.

As we have seen, stages 1 and 2 contribute to Intake 1 (Perception), stages 3–6 to Intake 2 (Transfer) and stages 7 and 8 to Intake 3 (Integration).

Information is transmitted and exchanged through the creation and firing of neurons ("Information is transmitted within the brain by the discharge of a chemical across a synapse (a gap between neurons), which causes a change in the receiving neuron" (Field, 2014, p. 43). For more details about this and the processes referred to above, see Baddeley (2007), Morgan-Short and Ullman (2012), Field, (2014) and Schütze (2017).

What Is Processing?

You might have noticed that many of the definitions above (including ours) make frequent reference to "process" or "processing" but do not clarify what they mean by the term(s). This seems to be true of SLA publications in general, in that they seem to assume that the reader will know what is meant by the terms "process" and "processing". An exception is Van Patten (2002, 2004, 2012) who offers his own rather distinctive definition that, "Processing refers to making a connection between form and meaning/function" (Van Patten, 2012, p. 269).

Dictionary definitions of "process" include:

- "a systematic series of actions directed to some end; a continuous action, operation, or series of changes taking place in a definite manner" – Dictionary.com www.dictionary.com/browse/processing
- "continuous series of actions meant to accomplish some result" – Thesaurus.com www.thesaurus.com/browse/processing
- "A series of actions or steps taken in order to achieve a particular end" – Oxford Dictionaries https://en.oxforddictionaries.com/definition/process
- "a series of actions that you take in order to achieve a result:" the Cambridge English Dictionary *dictionary.cambridge.org/dictionary/english/process*
- a continuous action, operation, or series of changes taking place in a definite manner: Dictionary.com www.dictionary.com/browse/process
- "a series of actions that produce something or that lead to a particular result : a series of changes that happen naturally" – Merriam Webster www.merriam-webster.com/dictionary/process

What all these definitions have in common is that "processing" is continuous rather than instantaneous and that it is a phenomenon aimed at, and resulting in, change through action. Language processing seems to be a continuing (but not necessarily continuous) series of mental actions that converts spoken or written utterances into something else in the brain. It seems to us that the "something else" can differ, and that it is important that it is made clear, when talking about processing in language acquisition, what is being changed and what it is being changed into. The processing of language can refer, for example, to the following macro-processes as well as to the micro-processes involved in each one:

1. the initial representing of an utterance in the brain, which can include both an auditory and a visual representation of the words in the utterance as well as sensory images, extra-linguistic information and affective associations stimulated by the utterance;

2 the retaining of sensory images and affective associations after the representations of the actual words of the utterance have disappeared (usually after about ten seconds);
3 the comprehending of the utterance;
4 the internal recording of linguistic items and features from the utterance;
5 the connecting of stored linguistic items and features to other stored items and features;
6 the connecting of stored linguistic items and features to stored lexical, grammatical and pragmatic generalisations;
7 the generalising of linguistic items and features into hypotheses;
8 the testing of hypotheses;
9 the revising of generalisations;
10 the utilising of generalisations in language use;
11 the acquiring of linguistic items and features;
12 the further developing of the ability to use acquired language items and features.

The listing of stages of processing above does not mean that the stages are distinctively separate and sequential. They can overlap or be simultaneous.

In our definition of intake above we are using the term "intake" to refer to stages 1–6. A linguistic item or feature in an actual utterance might not even proceed to stage 1; it might not be heard or read, or it might be misrepresented. If an item or feature makes it to stage 4, it might not make it any further and might disappear or possibly remain latent. We are concerned in this chapter with how an item or feature makes it to stage 6 (i.e. how it becomes intake) and we will discuss what determines its progress to other stages in subsequent chapters.

For a clear neurolinguistic account of the processing of lexical items in language acquisition, see Schütze (2017, pp. 25–46), an account that does not require prior knowledge of neuroscientific research to understand, and which we will refer to when considering the determiners of intake later in this chapter and when describing other stages of the language acquisition process in subsequent chapters. See also Syerett and Arunachalam (2018) for a collection of papers reporting research on the role of intake in the acquisition of semantics.

This section has so far given the impression that processing is an exclusively mental activity. In our view, processing does take place in the brain but we would agree with Van Lier (2014) and with socioculturists such as Lantolf, Thorne and Poehner (2015) that social interaction plays a crucial part in triggering, informing, strengthening and maintaining language processing.

> **Readers' Tasks**
>
> These tasks are not intended as tests but as a means of facilitating comprehension. Feel free to go back to the text and to talk with other people to help you to answer the questions.
>
> 1. From what you have read so far:
>   a) What's the difference between input and intake?
>   b) What's the difference between extra-linguistic information in the input and non-linguistic information in the input?
>   c) What is required for intake to take place?
>   d) What is required for intake to be retained?
> 2. Which of the following are vital for intake to take place?
>   a) The learners are provided with meaningful intake by their teachers.
>   b) The learners are provided with rich input by their teachers.
>   c) Their input is successfully perceived by the learners.
>   d) Integration is achieved within a minute of initial intake.
> 3. From what you have read so far, would you say that the coursebooks you have used as a learner and/or teacher contain input likely to promote effective intake? How could the input in coursebooks be improved?

What Are the Significant Characteristics of Intake?

Intake Is Relatively Small

Intake is always much smaller than input. Not all the input that is available to learners becomes intake. Much of it is disregarded by the learner (i.e. the learner does not pay attention to it, either consciously or subconsciously), either because it is not looked at or listened to, not perceived as familiar, not recognised, not understood, not perceived as significant or not perceived as interesting. This is true not only for input encountered experientially in contexts of communication but also for input encountered in class from course materials and during teacher instruction.

Not All Intake Is Retained

A language feature might be taken in and recorded because of the impact it makes when encountered, but it will only be retained for further processing and for potential eventual acquisition if it is subsequently encountered on numerous occasions and if it continues to meet other conditions for intake during those encounters.

Intake Is Initially Auditory
Intake is initially auditory, regardless of whether the input it derives from is spoken or written. In order for the brain to take in language, graphic signals are translated into auditory signals and passed on for rehearsal in a phonological loop and then to Wernicke's area for comprehension. Or, as Schütze (2017, p. 27) says: "If we see a word, it must be transcribed into a phonological code before it can be rehearsed", (though he does add that the visual code can assist the brain). In other words, what is often referred to as the inner voice (see Tomlinson & Avila, 2007a, Tomlinson, 2020a) plays an essential role in processing language in the input into potential intake, a role it cannot play if utterances in written input cannot be pronounced subvocally or if utterances in spoken input cannot be identified or subvocally rehearsed. The rehearsal in the phonological loop and the comprehension that is achieved in Wernicke's area do not ensure acquisition, but most SLA researchers (though not all, e.g. Reinders, 2012) would agree that they are both essential for the process to be activated further.

Intake Includes Extra-Linguistic and Nonlinguistic Information
Intake does not consist only of linguistic signals. Language is typically taken in in association with extra-linguistic features (e.g. a rising intonation), other modalities (e.g. an illustration of somebody slipping), mental images (e.g. a visual representation of a school created by a combination of previous personal experience and a description in the input), contextual associations (e.g. an informal conversation between intimates), emotions (e.g. amusement, anger, excitement), attitudes (e.g. positivity), facial gestures (e.g. a scowl) and body language (e.g. a gesture of annoyance). Schütze (2017) refers to research by Jones and Plass (2002) and Kim and Gilman (2008) that shows that "non-linguistic information … plays a key role when processing a new word" (p. 11) and he asserts that "the likelihood of a strong word record is higher when a corresponding image is processed". Schütze gives the example of falling off your bicycle "while vacationing in the Rhine Valley" (p. 12) and then being able to easily remember the German word for "to hurt". Another example of the importance of nonlinguistic information would be Brian's ability to remember that "*Mobil Cuci Air Panas*" means car wash with hot water in Bahasa Indonesia, from frequently seeing this on a roadside sign in Jakarta, working out the meaning of "*cuci*" from seeing it above wash basins in restaurants, working out the meaning of "*air*" from seeing it on the labels of bottled water and working out the meaning of "*panas*" from a conversation with a waitress about whether he wanted food that was hot in temperature or in spiciness, and then finally confirming his interpretation when noticing steam coming off cars near the notice. And this also helps him to "remember" that adjectives follow nouns in Bahasa Indonesia. The nonlinguistic information that is processed together with linguistic input does not necessarily derive from the context in which the input is encountered. It could be created mentally from a

combination of sensory imaging and the use of inner speech, as when Brian said to himself "Ringo Starr" and saw a mental image of Ringo when first encountering the Japanese word "*ringo*" (= apple). See Tomlinson and Avila (2007a) for a review of studies of the roles of visual imaging and of inner speech in language learning and use, and see Piazzoli (2018) for suggestions for how to make use of extra-linguistic information to embody language in language education.

The crucial point is that intake is both a multidimensional process and a multidimensional product (see Tomlinson, 2000a; Masuhara, 2005; 2007) and that approaches to teaching and learning that are unidimensional (e.g. memorising lists of words) are unlikely to facilitate Intake 3 – Integration.

Intake Is Variable

Intake is determined by many different factors and is different for each individual learner depending on their previous experience, their needs and wants, their learning objectives, their motivation, their engagement in the learning experience, their confidence, their attitudes towards the target language, their attitudes towards their experience of learning the language, their current level of acquisition and their language-learning aptitude. Forty learners receiving the same input in a language lesson would each achieve a different intake. See R. Ellis (2015, pp. 97–116) for discussion of variability in learner language and Gass and Mackey (2012, pp. 379–522) for detailed discussions of the factors contributing to learner differences. See also Chapter 9 in this volume.

Readers' Task

What implications do you think the fact that intake varies from individual to individual should have for:

1 curriculum development?
2 materials development?
3 assessment?

Not All Intake Is New

Obviously, most of a beginner's intake is likely to be new, in the sense that it has never been taken in before. When the intake is new, it has the potential for the creation of a new record for transmission to storage. Equally obviously, at higher levels much of the intake will be of features previously taken in. In such cases, the intake has the potential for strengthening records and for contributing to the confirmation or revision of hypotheses.

Processing for Comprehension Is Different from Processing for Acquisition

Processing for comprehension is normally of a meaningful chunk of language encountered while reading, listening or interacting. The meaningful chunk of language will normally consist of language features already acquired, of features that are in the process of being acquired, of features that have been previously taken in but not retained and of features that have not previously been encountered. Processing for acquisition is normally of a linguistic item or feature that was part of a meaningful chunk of language that has been processed for comprehension, though many researchers (e.g. R. Ellis, 2015) believe that beginners initially acquire short, meaningful chunks as a whole.

Intake from Interaction Is Different from Intake from Instruction

When interacting with other people or with a written or spoken text, what we initially intake (i.e. Intake 1- Perception) is an utterance plus information about its cotext (i.e. the other language before and after it) as well as its context (i.e. the situation in which it is used). We also take in sensory information generated by our mental images of the utterance. When receiving instruction, what we take in is sometimes restricted to an example of a language feature with a very limited cotext and without a context at all. Intake from interaction is potentially richer and more informative, whereas intake from instruction is arguably easier to attend to (see Noticing in "What are the Determiners of Intake?").

Intake Is Primarily Meaning-Focused

Although teacher input is often forms-focused, learner intake from interactional input is primarily focused on pragmatic meaning (i.e. the achievement of intended communicative effect).

The opportunity to focus on pragmatic meaning is important for a number of reasons:

1. In the eyes of many theorists (e.g., Prabhu, 1987; Long, 1996), only when learners are engaged in decoding and encoding messages in the context of actual acts of communication are the conditions created for acquisition to take place.
2. To develop true fluency in an L2, learners must have opportunities to create pragmatic meaning (DeKeyser, 1998).

(R. Ellis, 2005a, p. 212)

Van Patten (2004; 2012) is another researcher who is insistent that learners naturally focus on meaning. He has put forward "the primacy of meaning principle", which asserts that learners attend to meaning before they attend to form, and claims that "learners process content words before they process anything else" (Van Patten, 2012, p. 271). Barcroft and Wong (2013) provide a concise summary of Van Patten's principles and sub-principles and of research that supports it and Long (1996), R. Ellis (2008) and N. Ellis (2011) demonstrate how learners are more likely to acquire form if their initial focus is on meaning rather than on forms. Sato (1986; 1988) refers to a process of gradual syntacticisation in which learners move gradually from an exclusive focus on meaning when beginners to an increasing focus on form as advanced learners of a language.

Intake Can Be Erroneous as a Result of Mishearing, Misreading or Misrepresenting

If an utterance is misheard, misread or misrepresented then elements of it can be erroneously represented in a learner's intake and then even erroneously acquired through further misperceptions and through communicative use without feedback. For example, Brian took in the Japanese adjective "*mazui*" from exposure to such utterances as "*Kono ebi wa mazui desu*" (This prawn's not very nice). Somehow that was later misheard as "*masui*", misrepresented graphically and acquired. Only now after frequent feedback is "*masui*" being revised to "*mazui*".

See Colantoni, Steele and Escudero (2015) for a very interesting account of the acquisition of L2 pronunciation and for evidence (pp. 38–40) of how an allophone in the target language, which is similar to but essentially different from an allophone in the L1, is initially perceived as being the same as the L1 allophone.

Intake Does Not Equal Acquisition

Just because a linguistic feature has been taught or encountered, has been taken in for processing and can in the short term be recalled does not mean it has been acquired. Intake is only the initial stage of a lengthy process. It is essential but never sufficient.

Readers' Task

According to what you have just read about the characteristics of intake, which of the following are true? Try to answer first without going back to the text, but then go back to the text to check your answers.

Intake:

a) is bigger than input
b) consists of and is facilitated by more than just linguistic information
c) is typically facilitated by attention to language forms rather than to meaning
d) which is derived from written text, is achieved through auditory processing
e) is retained if the input which triggered it is repeated
f) is sometimes faulty as a result of faulty perception of input
g) should be the same for all the learners in a class.

What Are the Determiners of Intake?

Linguistic Determiners

Intelligibility

Learners cannot take in what they do not perceive. If they do not hear or see a feature properly in their input, it cannot be taken in. It could, for example, be that particular phonemes are not heard (e.g. those in unstressed syllables) or recognised (e.g. those not used in the L1), that a significant intonation pattern is not detected, that a spelling is so unfamiliar in both the L1 and the L2 that the learner ignores the word or that a multisyllabic, unknown word is ignored because of its excessive processing demands (see Tomlinson, 2007a; Schütze, 2017). It could be that what a speaker says is unintelligible because the speaker lacks fluency, speaks very quickly or speaks with a strong regional accent. It could be that what a writer writes is unintelligible because of poor handwriting, careless typing or lack of coherence. Often though, unintelligibility of input is simply because, at the current proficiency level of the learner, familiar language is prioritised even at the initial stage of perception.

The result of the unintelligibility of one or more components of an utterance can be that the utterance is not taken in at all, or is only partially taken in. Often nonlinguistic and extra-linguistic features of redundancy can make unintelligible utterances comprehensible, but the linguistic components are still unlikely to achieve intake unless they become retrospectively intelligible as a result of the perceived meaning triggering retrieval of words already acquired. We both find this sometimes happens when conversing in English (Hitomi is bilingual). We initially do not completely hear what the other said, request a repetition but then work out the beginning of the utterance from cotextual and contextual clues before the repetition is made. For example, Brian hears "xxxx xxxx at two" and says, "Sorry?" but then remembers he was expecting a phone call from Alan in the early afternoon before Hitomi can repeat, "Alan rang at two". In foreign- and second- language conversations, the listener often assumes listening failure and does not attempt to recreate the utterance from clues.

Perception failure could be a partial explanation for why many learners of English as an L2 do not initially intake common morphemes such as the -ed ending of verbs used in the simple past or the -s ending of verbs used in the third-person singular simple present. As well as often being redundant and semantically irrelevant, these morphemes in continuous speech are often hardly perceptible (even to acoustic instruments of measurement) and thus fail to make it even into Intake 1 – Perception.

For a detailed discussion of the difference between the input and the learner's perception of it, see Badger (2018). He sees it as a difference between input and intake and makes a distinction "between input, what the teachers say to their learners, and intake, what the learners hear", (Badger, 2018, p. 1073). Despite this terminological difference he does, however, make similar points to ours, and provides a comprehensive literature review of the issue.

Input that is initially unintelligible can become intelligible if repeated immediately, if immediately subsequent input triggers retrospective recognition and if the input is encountered again in an environment in which it is recognisable.

Comprehensibility

Most researchers (e.g. Krashen, 1985) would agree that language needs to be comprehended in order for it to become a candidate for processing (i.e. to progress from Intake 1– Perception to Intake 3 – Integration). They would also agree that it does not have to be fully understood, and that sufficient understanding to make it meaningful to the receiver could be enough to effect further processing. For example, an L2 learner of English who is interested in cinema might grasp that the director and the producer play important roles in the production of a film, but might not have fully grasped the difference between them at the initial intake stage.

Some researchers argue, though, that an item does not have to have been comprehended in order to be taken in (e.g. R. Ellis, 2008; Reinders, 2012; Mishan, 2016) and some argue that apprehension is sufficient to effect intake and that comprehension comes at a later stage ("apprehension (concrete experience) and comprehension (abstract conceptualisation)" (Baker, Jensen & Kolb, 2002, p. 3). See also Kolb and Kolb (2001) for more information about apprehension and how it precedes comprehension in experiential learning.

There is little doubt that beginners "use" comprehensibility as a criterion for intake, and that they take in content words rather than function words, and roots rather than suffixes, even in classroom settings in which their teacher is focusing on high-frequency function words such as determiners and common prepositions.

From the evidence available, our view is that learners need to apprehend language input to achieve Intake 1, to apprehend the language item or feature selected from the input to achieve Intake 2 and to manage at least partial comprehension of it to achieve Intake 3 – Integration. Of course, apprehension and comprehension can be conscious or subconscious, or even both conscious and subconscious.

Salience

A linguistic item or feature, which stands out because of its prominence at the beginning or end of an utterance (see Tomlinson, 2007a), because of being stressed, because it dominates a short utterance, because type size, colour or font has been chosen to get it to stand out (in, for example, a notice or advert) or because it has been highlighted in one of many other ways, is more likely to be taken in than items or features that are not prominent. For example, we can remember that the Bahasa

Indonesian word "*awas*" means "caution" or "beware" from seeing it as "AWAS" on road signs in Indonesia. Obviously, "AWAS" was perceived, apprehended and taken in for processing because of its salience. It was subsequently comprehended as indicating some sort of warning and stored. Subsequent encounters confirmed, reinforced and refined our comprehension and the lexical item was eventually acquired. There are many ways in which materials and teachers can make language items and features salient (e.g. highlighting lexical items in a reading passage in bold; flooding a text with extra examples of a structural feature; recasting a learner's utterance during meaning-focused communication, Lyster, 2007). Our problem with many of the artificial aids to prominence is that highlighting or flooding, for example, can isolate the item or feature from its cotext and context and thus impoverish the learner's intake. Recasting (i.e. rephrasing a speaker's utterance), however, can be more natural and is similar to what mothers and siblings do in L1 acquisition. It is also more meaningful, as it can help the learner to improve the effectiveness of their communication without drawing attention to their inadequacy (providing that they consciously and/or subconsciously notice that a recast has been made). See Tomlinson (2007b) for a critical review of studies of recasting and for a report of an experiment in which Chinese trainee teachers were influenced to use the contrastive "but" during a series of recasts of their oral utterances in a team competition, in a written activity after a short delay and in a written activity a week later.

Significance

We are using significance to mean of semantic or pragmatic importance in an utterance. Obviously, content words are more significant than function words (e.g. Van Patten, 2012), and words that are repeated or referred back to by the speaker or writer are likely to be significant. If an item or feature is both salient and significant in an utterance, then it is likely to be a strong candidate for Intake 3 – Integration.

Redundancy

By redundancy, we mean indicating a meaning or function in more than one way, as for example in "After about three miles I was so exhausted I had to sit down for a rest". Redundancy can be an important contributor to effective communication and to language acquisition. In the utterance, "Last week I walked all the way from Tarragona to Sitges", the item "last" is more likely to progress to Intake 3 – Integration as a marker of past time than the redundant feature "-ed", especially as "last" is salient and significant whereas "-ed" is neither stressed nor prominent. Redundancy in which already acquired language contributes to comprehension of "new" language, however, is a potential facilitator of intake. For example, the lexical item "delighted" is more likely to be taken in from the utterance "I'm delighted. That's great news" than from the utterance "I'm delighted".

Redundancy is often achieved through extra-linguistic indicators such as an increase in volume of voice to indicate urgency, an exclamation mark to indicate annoyance and speech marks to indicate somebody was speaking.

In applied linguistics literature, the redundancy principle is often interpreted as referring to presenting meaning through more than one medium (e.g. telling a story orally while illustrating it on screen with pictures and text). For example, Samur (2012, E166) says, "Therefore, the underlying hypothesis of this study is that when the students are exposed to the material in multiple ways ... the learning and the retention will have better results in foreign language learning". However, in information theory, redundancy is considered to be the expression of the same content in multiple ways and is seen as a vital ingredient for successful communication, especially when there is a danger of entropy (e.g. interference from noise, distractions, topic unfamiliarity, low level of language proficiency). We consider it to be a very important feature of input for lower-level learners and when simplifying a text or communicating with learners we would add redundancy rather than attempt to simplify through reduction. See Shannon (1948) and Shannon and Weaver (1949) for a model of communication that is still influential today and that focuses on context-relevant redundancy of message as a crucial element of successful communication and learning.

Readers' Tasks

1 Add redundancy to the following examples taken from page 8 of Clare and Wilson (2012) to make them more comprehensible. Try to keep the sentences as authentic as possible.
   a) Have you inherited any family characteristics?
   b) Where did your ancestors come from?
   c) Quite a lot. My parents told me a lot of stories about my background.
   d) No, there are no celebrities in the family.
   e) My mother. We look alike and we have similar characters.
2 Compare a number of utterances in a coursebook to a number of authentic utterances taken from a newspaper, magazine or novel. Do the coursebook utterances contain enough redundancy to aid comprehension and acquisition?
3 Look at a page of a graded reader. Do you think there is enough redundancy to facilitate comprehensibility?

Simplicity

Intake is a process that places huge demands on the brain's processing energy. Therefore, the simpler an item or feature is to perceive, apprehend, rehearse, comprehend and store, the more likely it is to progress to Intake 3 – Integration, provided that it is also significant and meaningful. So "big" is more likely to achieve Intake 3 – Integration than "enormous" for a beginner, just as the simple present is more likely to achieve Intake 3 – Integration than the present perfect continuous. Brian watched a television programme last night about art in daily life in Japan. He can still remember that the Japanese word "*ma*" refers to the aesthetic concepts of space, pause or silence, mainly because such a simple word represents such a complex concept but also because of the many illustrations of "*ma*" shown in the program, because the word was both salient and significant in the commentary and the interviews, because it was repeated many times and because it was meaningful to Brian because of an upcoming trip to Japan. See Tomlinson (2007a) for more examples of how simplicity of an item or feature facilitates intake at lower levels of proficiency.

Pointing out that simple items and features are likely candidates for intake does not provide support for such pedagogic strategies as simplifying the input by reducing it to short simple sentences, "simplifying" the learning process by focusing on one teaching point at a time or simplifying the cognitive level of the content. Such strategies risk impoverishing the input, removing redundancy and authenticity and eliminating such determiners of intake as meaningfulness, affective engagement and cognitive engagement. Language acquisition is not just about storing items and features ready for retrieval but about developing the ability to make use of stored items and features for communication.

Recycling

The more frequently an item or feature is encountered in different and ideally spaced inputs, the more likely it is to achieve Intake 3, especially if it is simple, salient and significant in many of those encounters. One way of helping learners to achieve this is to use an item or feature from a text in a meaningful question about the text. This ensures that the item or feature is encountered at least three times if the teacher subsequently asks learners for their answers to the question, and maybe even more if the learners answer the question in groups or pairs. For example, if in the text Jean says, "I'm really concerned about Joe", the question could be, "Why do you think that Jean was so concerned about Joe?". Another way is to ensure that learners "have increasingly spaced, repeated opportunity to give attention to wanted items in a variety of contexts" (Nation & McCallister, 2010, p. 43). See Schütze (2015, 2017) and Nation and McCallister (2010) for reference to research evidence of the importance of spaced repetition in the acquisition of lexis and of the need for at least eight or nine spaced encounters with an item for it to be acquired. Such research evidence does not support the meaningless drills or immediate repetitions still used by many language teachers, as such repetitions are neither spaced nor meaningful. It does, however, explain why Brian can still remember that the

Japanese word "*ikebana*" refers to the art form of flower arranging. In the television programme referred to in the section on Simplicity, "*ikebana*" was repeated at intervals at least nine times in different contexts to a visual background of different Japanese experts arranging flowers aesthetically.

Richness

Providing that the input is accessible to the learners, rich input is likely to lead to more, and to more effective, intake than impoverished input. By rich, we mean plentiful, in context and varied in genre, text type, topic and language. Such input respects the reality that different learners will achieve different intake from the same input, because the learners will differ in needs, interests, aptitude, readiness and prior experience.

For discussion of the value of rich input see Krashen (1994), Nation (2007) and Tomlinson (2016a).

Authenticity

For many years there has been a heated debate about whether authentic or simplified/contrived language best facilitates language acquisition. Tomlinson and Masuhara (2018b, p. 31) say:

> It has been argued that explicit teaching of language through contrived examples and texts helps the learners by focussing their processing energies on the target feature, and this, in our experience, is what most coursebooks typically do. However, many second language acquisition researchers (and teachers) argue that this over-protects the learners, that it contradicts what is known about how languages are acquired and that it does not prepare them for the reality of language use outside the classroom.

Our position is that authentic texts "can provide the rich and meaningful exposure to language in use which is a prerequisite for language acquisition" (Tomlinson and Masuhara, 2018b, p. 31) but that they can also be too culturally, cognitively and linguistically difficult for learners to access. Simplified and contrived texts can help the learner pay comprehended attention to their input, but they can also be providers of impoverished input lacking in richness, engagement, redundancy, context and extra-linguistic information. Without any exposure to authentic input learners are likely to achieve only weak acquisition and to lack the ability to communicate effectively in the target language. For discussion of the pros and cons of authenticity see Mishan (2005), Gilmore (2007), Rilling and Dantas-Whitney (2009), Tomlinson (2016a) and Tomlinson and Masuhara (2018b).

In relation to intake, our view is that authentic input has a greater potential for progress to Intake 3 – Integration, providing that it is intelligible and comprehensible. It is more likely (but not guaranteed) to engage the learners cognitively and affectively, to be richer in communicative information and to be more meaningful to the learners.

Bizarreness

It seems that the more bizarre comprehensible input is, the more memorable it is too. For example, the sentence "The dog danced with the cat" is more likely to be memorable than the sentence "John danced with Mary", the instruction "Run up the wall" is more likely to be memorable than "Touch the wall" and a story about a three-legged alien is more likely to be memorable than a newspaper report of a routine marathon. They are also more likely to achieve impact and, if they stimulate visualisation and engagement, to aid the progress of intake possibly as far as Intake 3 – Integration.

Much of the research on what has become known as the bizarreness effect has been related to the apparently superior memorability and recall of bizarre sentences and images compared to "common" sentences and images. For example, Geraci, McDaniel, Miller and Hughes (2013, p. 1235) found that:

> [R]etrieval processes operating when common and bizarre items are combined in the retrieval set play a unique and important role in mediating the bizarreness effect. Given that in mixed-list designs the retrieval set combines common and bizarre items, it appears that retrieval dynamics are sufficient to produce the oft-reported bizarreness advantage in these designs.

We have recently been in touch with a teacher in Thailand who despairs of the boredom created by the culturally irrelevant coursebooks he has been asked to use and is developing his own video-based materials. We told him about the research on the bizarreness effect and he replied:

> Thanks for the info about the Bizarreness Theory. I checked it out and yes my whole approach is essentially based around that kind of experience for the students. At the beginning of every video there will be a strange sound. Neuroscience suggest this wakes the brain up instinctively. And the videos will be as funny as possible because again from neuroscience people learn better when their brain is predominantly in Theta waves ... (Ajarn Lucky – personal communication 21/7/2019)

For research on the bizarreness effect and its value in stimulating recall and retrieval see, for example, Richman (1994), McDaniel, DeLosh and Merritt (2000), Geraci and Rajaram (2004) and McDaniel and Geraci (2006).

Notice that although the determiners of intake in this section are categorised as linguistic their impact will vary from individual to individual in a group of learners receiving the same input (e.g. a newspaper article). One learner might understand the lexical item "sympathetic" in the utterance "I'm extremely sympathetic towards her ideas" whereas another learner might not, one learner's attention might be drawn to the item whereas another learner's might not, one learner might perceive the item to be significant in the text and of potential significance to their use of English whereas another might not and one learner might have experienced the item before whereas another might not.

> **Readers' Task**
>
> Of all the linguistic determiners of intake listed, which would you say are the three most important?
>
> How could you make sure that these determiners are essential features of your:
>
> a) classroom teaching?
> b) own materials?
> c) use of published materials?
> d) advice to learners about out of class acquisition of their target language?

Psycholinguistic Determiners

We are using this term to refer to determiners that involve activation of the learners' brains.

Attention

It is essential that learners pay some attention to the input in order for an utterance to be taken in to Intake 1 – Perception. This attention could be conscious or subconscious, and needs to persist if language items and features are to progress into Intake 2 – Transfer and Intake 3 – Integration. A learner who is thinking about something else while listening to or reading texts in the L2 or is distracted by other inputs (e.g. loud music or a friend talking in the L1) is unlikely to take much in from the L2 input. This is true also if the learner is faced with new L2 input before having time to process the previous input.

See Robinson, Mackey, Gass and Schmidt (2012) for a detailed discussion of the role of attention in second language acquisition.

Aptitude

Using a longitudinal (pre-test/post-test) design Linck and Weiss (2015, p. 8) claim to have found evidence that learners with greater working memory (WM) "resources were more likely to succeed in learning their L2" and that the results of their study "indicate that measures of WM are likely to improve the predictive utility of tests of language aptitude". This study was located in a classroom setting and the pre test and post-test consisted of a grammar and vocabulary knowledge test. Whether they would find similar results in an immersion situation, or with tests of communicative competence, is open to question though, as are many assumptions about intake based exclusively on controlled research in language classrooms that feature narrow assessment.

Whether or not greater WM is a predictor of language-learning success, there is no doubt that aptitude varies from learner to learner and can play a significant role in intake success. Saville-Troike and Barto (2017, p. 91) say that "[t]he finding that aptitude is an important predictor of differential success in L2 learning holds for both naturalistic contexts and for formal classroom instruction" and they outline the four main components identified by Carroll (1965) as underlying aptitude:

- Phonemic-coding ability
- Inductive-language-learning ability
- Grammatical sensitivity
- Associative-memory capacity

Of the above components, phonemic-coding ability is especially important for intake as "if the hearer cannot analyse the incoming stream of speech into phonemes in order to recognize morphemes, input may not result in intake" (Saville-Troike & Barto, 2017, p. 91).

See also Skehan (2002; 2012), Robinson (2005b) and Ortega (2009, pp. 145–167) for discussions of the significance of aptitude in language acquisition.

Motivation

The more motivated a learner is to learn the L2, the more likely they are to pay and maintain attention when exposed to L2 input. Likewise, the more motivated they are by a particular text and/or activity the more likely they are to intake utterances. They are also more likely to intake items and features when motivated, provided that the items and features are salient and significant in the input as well as meaningful to the learner.

It is generally considered that both instrumental and integrative motivation are major determiners of success or failure in the learning of an L2, but there does not seem to be much research on their impact on intake. In our experience, most L2 learners in educational institutions are variably motivated, are certainly not highly motivated all the time but are amenable to being motivated by stimulating teachers, engaging texts and achievably challenging tasks. Their motivation seems to be dependent on such factors as their relationship with a particular teacher, their self-perception of aptitude, apparent communicative success and the accumulative effect of achieving a high degree of affective and/or cognitive engagement with a succession of particular texts and/or tasks. When Brian succeeded in taking in "*ma*" and "*ikebana*" (as reported above) he was highly motivated to do so because the programme he was watching was engaging and because he was participating in writing a chapter about intake. This motivated him to pay attention to items in the input (another one was "*daiku*", meaning carpenter), to notice how they were used, to associate them with visual images and to rehearse them with the inner voice.

Notice that "motivate" is always followed by "to" as opposed to "interest", which is always followed by "in". A learner can be interested in a text or task but not actually motivated to do anything that facilitates intake.

See Dörnyei (2009a, 2009b) and Dörnyei and Ushioda (2013) for detailed information about the role of motivation in language acquisition.

Affective Engagement

There is very convincing evidence that the emotions, associated with encounters with utterances in the input, play a significant role in determining intake. The stronger the emotion, whether it be positive or negative, the more likely it is that an utterance will achieve Intake 1 and that items and features from it will achieve Intake 3. "It seems that being moved to feel amused, angry, disturbed, entertained, exhilarated, empathetic, sad, sympathetic, or any other emotion ... is a powerful facilitator of language acquisition." (Tomlinson, 2016a, p. 8). The likelihood of intake is even greater if the L2 learner is engaged by the text encountered, and it makes affective connections with their prior experience of life. For example, the lexical item "sublime" in the utterance "I was overwhelmed by the sublime beauty of the mountains" is more likely to be taken in if the learner is moved by a disturbing novel in which she reads it, than if she encounters it in a decontextualised sentence in a coursebook exercise. With such engagement, though, the learner is more likely to intake lexical items than function words or structures, as the engagement is likely to reinforce the learner's tendency to prioritise meaning over form.

"Other aspects of affect include self-esteem and positive attitudes and they can be powerful determiners' of intake too" (Tomlinson, 2016a, p. 8). These aspects of affect can be influenced by a teacher who is supportive, interesting, creative and empathetic, by the social cohesion created when a class of learners get on with and encourage each other, and by an appealing learning environment.

See Immordino-Yang and Damasio (2007) for evidence of how feeling controls attention and memory, and Schumann (1997), Arnold (1999), Pavlenko (2005), Braten (2006), Mates and Joaquin (2013) and Masuhara (2016) for discussion and evidence of the importance of affect in SLA. See Hinijosa, Moreno, and Ferre (2019) for evidence that suggests "that emotion is represented in the brain as a set of semantic features in a distributed sensory, motor, language and affective network" and that "emotion interacts with a number of lexical, semantic and syntactic features in different brain regions and timings" (Hinijosa et al., 2019, Abstract).

Cognitive Engagement

There is also evidence that focused thinking about the content of an utterance is likely to determine the intake of the utterance, and probably of items and features from it too, especially if the thinking is challenging or problematic and stimulates connections to prior experience. The challenges, and the connections stimulated by them, are likely to increase the amount of significant nonlinguistic information associated and stored with the linguistic intake and thus to strengthen its record. It is likely, though, that semantic items and features will be prioritised over grammatical items and features, as they are likely to be more salient in the resolution of the problem.

See Robinson (2005a) for claims that cognitive complexity can, for example, push learners to greater accuracy, promote interaction and help learners to achieve longer term retention of input; and see Mishan (2016) for discussion of the power of cognitive engagement.

> **Readers' Task**
>
> What advice would you give to the teacher of each of the following students?
>
> > Learner A: Not really interested in learning Spanish and has no need to or interest in visiting a Spanish speaking country. Hasn't succeeded in learning any second or foreign languages and has low expectations of ever doing so. Doesn't do anything out of class to contribute to learning Spanish and doesn't seem to pay much attention in class. Doesn't get on with the other learners in the group he's been assigned to and has requested a change. Is very interested in Spanish football and watches La Liga games on TV.
> > Learner B: Wants to learn English so she can read novels and watch films in the original. Intrinsically motivated but frustrated by her apparent lack of progress. Like other members of her group she is bored by the short, simple and shallow texts in the coursebook and by the overtly forms-focused and closed activities she is asked to do.
> > Learner C: Wants to learn Japanese to increase his career prospects, and has taken a year off work to go to Japan to try to do so. Gets on well with his fellow learners but dislikes his teachers' attempts to help him with frequent correction and direct teaching, and the triviality of the texts and tasks in the coursebook. He's very interested in Japanese culture, history, politics and current affairs, but finds he can't manage to understand the newspapers he tries to read and the television programmes he tries to watch.

Meaningfulness

If an utterance is meaningful to the learner, it is likely to be taken in. As Craik (2002: cited in Mishan, 2016, p. 173) says: "More meaningful processing is usually associated with higher levels of recollection". By meaningful, we mean that it is significant, relevant, consequential, valid or worthwhile to the learner and therefore likely to stimulate connections in the brain. This is most likely to be achieved if the content of the intake is proximate to the learner, in the sense of matching their cognitive maturity and immediate needs (see Bouziri, 2017 for discussion of the concept of proximity). Meaningfulness is certainly a major determiner of intake and is likely to stimulate progress from Intake 1 – Perception to Intake 3 – Integration and beyond. In Chapter 3 we will be looking at ways in which the learner can achieve meaningfulness. Can you think of any ways in which learners can be helped to achieve this if they are using a global coursebook that has been written to cater for learners all over the world?

Sensory Imaging

When we perceive utterances in spoken or written texts in our L1, we represent them initially in graphic or phonological form and then through sensory imaging, that is, we convert the utterances into visual, auditory, tactile, olfactory and gustatory representations of them. The stronger these representations are (especially the visual images) the more likely the utterance and some of its items and features are to be taken in. In an experiment in Japan, Tomlinson (2011b) found that the few L2 students who were able to recall many utterances from the poem they had read reported that they had visualised the poem and were able to recall utterances by first recalling the images they had created. Tomlinson and Avila (2007a) report many studies demonstrating that most L2 learners who do habitually visualise in their L1 rarely visualise when reading and listening in an L2, unless they are highly proficient or are encouraged to do so. This could be a significant cause of inadequate intake for many learners of an L2.

It would seem that when using our L1 we all visualise to some extent, but when using an L2 most learners, though capable of visualising L2 utterances, make little use of visualisation until they reach an advanced level (Tomlinson, 2011b). Successful L2 users often seem to visualise both the graphic representation of utterances they hear or see, and representational images of them.

See also Esrock (1994), Sadoski and Paivio (1994), Tomlinson (1997) and Paivio (2007) for more information about the roles of visualisation in the learning and use of languages.

Psychological Distance

If a learner feels uncomfortable with the language being learned, or emotionally remote from the language and the cultures it represents, then this could inhibit intake, especially if the learner considers the target language to be superior or inferior to his or her L1. The more comfortably positive a learner feels about the target language, what it represents and where and how it is being learned, the more likely it is that input will be converted into intake. See Schumann (1978) and R. Ellis (2008) for discussion of the effects of psychological distance.

Anxiety

Learners who suffer from language anxiety, either permanently or in specific input situations, are likely to achieve less intake than those who do not. Krashen (1979) claimed that there was an affective filter that, when raised by anxiety, prevented intake and, when lowered by relaxation, facilitated it. Although Krashen was using a metaphor and did not substantiate his claim with empirical evidence, what he said mirrors what seems to happen in the brain, and subsequent studies have substantiated his claim. For example, Dewaele (2013, p. 170) refers to research by Liebermann and Rosenthal (2001) that demonstrates how "[s]tress releases extra dopamine, which might push individuals over the narrow range of optimal innervation in the dorsolateral prefrontal cortex and impair attentional and WM processes". See also Dulay, Burt and Krashen (1982) and Oxford (1999) for reference to research demonstrating how anxiety inhibits acquisition and how being relaxed and comfortable can accelerate language learning, and see Sato and Ballinger (2016a) for discussion of the facilitative value of relaxed social cohesion in language acquisition. Certainly, Brian suffered language anxiety when trying to learn French with a teacher who demanded and then ridiculed his contribution, and we suffered language anxiety together when failing to learn Bahasa Melayu from a teach-yourself book.

Developmental Readiness

It is commonly agreed that there is a set sequence of items and features that are taken in during the early stages of acquisition. This natural sequence is similar regardless of whether the language is being acquired as an L1 or an L2, or whether it is being acquired naturally or from instruction. It is a sequence that is meaning-focused and determined by significance and simplicity. Nouns are typically acquired first, then verbs, then adjectives, then adverbs and then simple tenses of verbs. Morphemes are also acquired in a similar order in the L1 and L2, with, for example, the progressive -ing being first in the L1 and third in the L2 (Dulay & Burt, 1974; Saville-Troike & Barto, 2017).

These sequences are very much influenced by the learners' prioritising of meaning over form, an understandable preference given their usual desire to understand and to communicate. Interestingly though, the sequence is very different from that of the typical coursebook, which often prioritises forms over meaning, and focuses on morpheme accuracy and on such function words as articles and pronouns much earlier than learners would do naturally. Maybe this explains why many beginners make a lot of errors at the beginning of their course, and why many of them become demotivated by their inability to say anything meaningful in their new language.

Psychological Readiness

It seems that learners only process input to Intake 3 if they really need or want to. The need or want could be related to their objectives in learning the L2 (e.g. for an academic or professional purpose) or it could be created by an engaging activity in which it is necessary to understand and/or use language items or features not yet acquired. It could also be created by discovery activities in which the learners focus on the use of an item or feature in a text by which they have been engaged. Such a need does not magically ensure acquisition, but it is likely to facilitate intake and to alert the learner to the presence of the items or features in subsequent input. Psychological readiness cannot change developmental readiness, but it can promote the eventual acquisition of variational features (i.e. those not normally acquired in any predetermined sequence).

See Meisel, Clahsen and Pienemann (1981) for discussion of their multidimensional model, in which "learners must have achieved readiness in order to learn developmental features ... but can make themselves ready at any time to learn variational features" (Tomlinson, 2011b, pp. 12–13). See Pienemann (1985) for discussion of his claim that instruction can be effective if it coincides with learner readiness and for his assertion (which we support from our experience) that premature instruction can cause learner error and avoidance, and see R. Ellis (1990, 2008, 2015) for detailed discussions of both variational and developmental readiness.

For detailed discussion of psychological determiners of intake see R. Ellis (2015), Gass and Mackey (2012) and Saville-Troike and Barto (2017).

Readers' Tasks

1 As you'll have realised by now by now, there are very many determiners of intake (all of which are important and remind us that you cannot just acquire a language by being told about it and memorising rules and lexical items). You could pause for a while and think back over what you've read so far about determiners of intake.

Which determiners of intake can you remember?
Make a note of the determiners you can remember, and then go back and check which determiners, if any, you have forgotten about.

2 From your experience as a language learner and/or a language teacher:
  a) Which three linguistic determiners of those listed would you say were the most important for facilitating intake?
  b) Which three psychological determiners of those listed would you say were the most important for facilitating intake?
3 Can you think of any linguistic or psychological determiners that are not outlined?
4 Take any L2 textbook and turn at random to a page.
  a) See if you can find any evidence on this page of the six determiners you listed in 1 a) and b) being taken into consideration when writing these materials.
  b) Think of ways in which you could cater for your six determiners if you were using this page of materials with a class.

Sociolinguistic Determiners

We are using this term to refer to determiners which involve interaction between the learner and the learning environment. Such determiners include:

Peer Input

There is evidence that input provided by peers is likely to be taken in, provided, of course, that it is intelligible, comprehensible and meaningful, and especially if it solves a problem or satisfies a need. In fact, some researchers (and many learners) would say that it is more likely to be taken in than input provided by teachers.

See Barker (2010b), Philip, Adams and Iwashita (2014) and Sato and Ballinger (2016a) for comprehensive surveys of studies of the effects of peer interaction.

Interaction

Interaction can be a fruitful facilitator of intake, as the input encountered is likely to be intelligible, comprehensible and meaningful, provided the learner is skilled in seeking clarification and confirmation and in ensuring relevance. The input in interaction is also likely to be repeated and made salient by the interlocutor(s). Saville-Troike and Barto (2017, p. 116) list the following intake-facilitating modifications that are likely to be made by native speakers when interacting with non-native speakers:

- repetition
- paraphrase
- expansion and elaboration
- sentence completion
- comprehension check and request for clarification

We would argue that such modifications are also likely to be made by non-native teachers of an L2, by learners at a higher level of proficiency in the L2 than their interlocutor and by interactants using an L2 as a lingua franca (see Jepson, 2005) for evidence of such modifications between L2 speakers in synchronous computer interaction and Sato and Ballinger (2016a, 2016b) for research evidence in support of our argument and, in particular, in support of the value of peer interaction as a facilitator of intake). According to Sato and Ballinger, and to our experience, learners are more likely to be relaxed, to be creative and to take risks when interacting with fellow learners in a socially cohesive group than when interacting with a teacher or a native speaker.

Saville-Troike and Barto (2017, p. 118) also point out the value of feedback during interaction and report the claims of advocates of the interaction hypothesis (Long, 1996) that "the modifications and collaborative efforts that take place in social interaction facilitate SLA because they contribute to the accessibility of input for mental processing". For detailed and persuasive accounts of the theoretical underpinnings of the interaction approach, see Mackey, Abbul and Gass (2012) and Mackey, Ziegler and Bryfonski (2016).

Scaffolding

Scaffolding typically occurs in interaction between learners and "experts" (e.g. children and mothers, learners and teachers, learners and more proficient learners) and often consists of the "expert" providing chunks of language for the learner to use to achieve communication that would be unachievable without such assistance. It also occurs "when peers collaborate in constructing language which exceeds the competence of any individual among them" (Saville-Troike & Barto, 2017, p. 119). Other means of providing scaffolding are mentioned in the following definition by Ovando, Collier and Combs (2003, p. 345):

> Scaffolding refers to providing contextual supports for meaning through the use of simplified language, teacher modeling, visuals and graphics, cooperative learning and hands-on learning.

See Gibbons (2002) for a detailed consideration of the value of scaffolding in language learning, a value that certainly includes increasing the potential for intake of items and features from the scaffolded input.

Sociological Distance

This concept relates to the extent to which individual learners can identify themselves with or feel comfortable with speakers of the target language and are willing to achieve contact with them. Lack of such identity could reduce the amount of intake from the available input.

We have found when travelling in China, Japan and South Korea, for example, that many non-native speakers of English feel uncomfortable interacting with native speakers and try to avoid such interaction. For example, in a Japanese bank a clerk gave up trying to communicate with Brian and ran away and, in Shanghai recently, we found waiters avoiding us or passing us on to other waiters, to avoid attempting communication. Such embarrassment is understandable, but deprives learners of opportunities for meaningful input and interaction. On the other hand, we have both experienced in the three countries mentioned that some non-native speakers felt comfortable and confident enough to approach us, apologise for their poor English and then ask if they could sit and talk to us to "practise my English". Such learners can benefit considerably from increased opportunities for input and interaction. This is what happened to an MA student of ours at the University of Liverpool. He arrived in Liverpool from Sudan feeling confident about the level of his proficiency in English, but soon suffered a crisis of confidence when he failed to open a bank account and to complete other service transactions and had to ask for a translator. At first, he withdrew from contact with native speakers, but then made a decision to seek out interaction. Although he is a Muslim and does not drink alcohol, he joined a group called Philosophers in the Pub, and also went to his local pub most nights to meet people. He also joined other clubs where he was the only non-native speaker. As a result, he reduced the sociological distance, gained confidence and considerably improved his communicative competence. Now he advises immigrant communities in Liverpool and gives conference lectures on how to improve English through interaction.

See Schumann (1976, 1978) and R. Ellis (2008, 2015) for discussions of the inhibiting effects of sociological distance.

See Lantolf, Thorne and Poehner (2015) for detailed discussion of sociological factors in language development.

> **Readers' Task**
>
> Try to complete the Diagram 2.1 from your reading of this chapter so far and from your predictions of what is still to come in the chapter. When you have finished the chapter come back to this diagram, revise your completions and add extra determiners to each category.

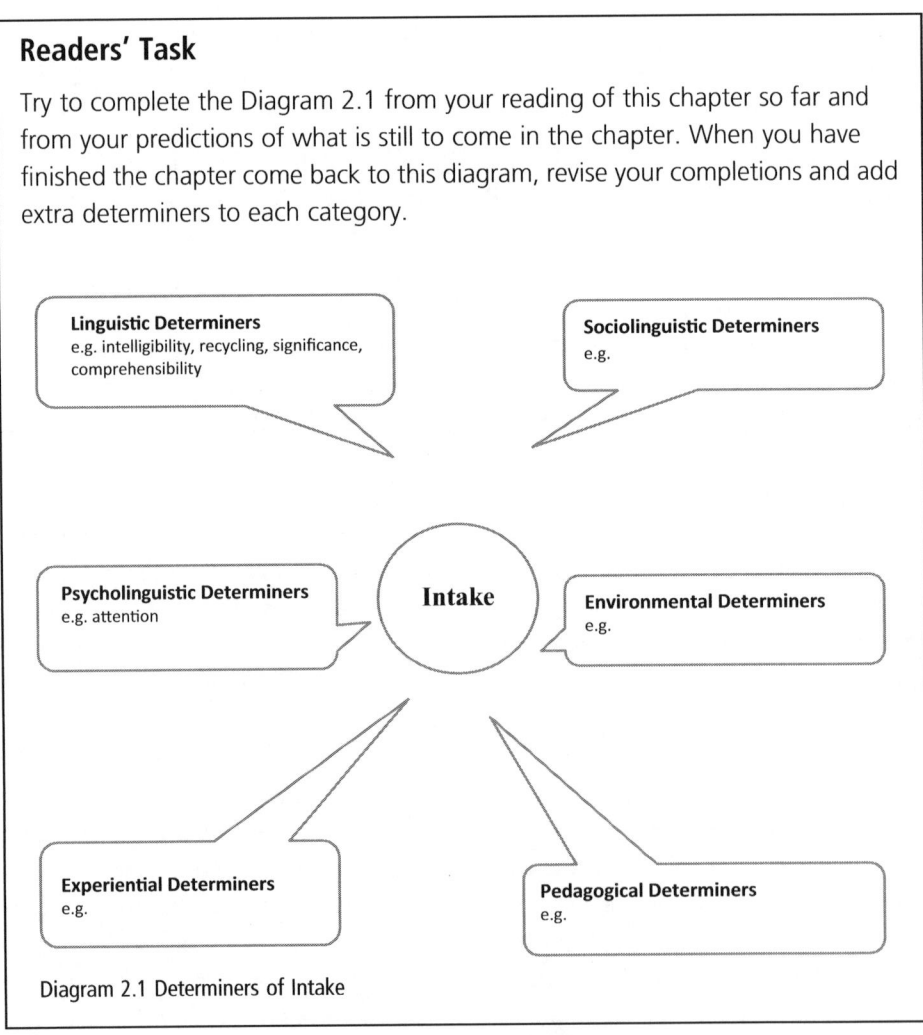

Diagram 2.1 Determiners of Intake

Environmental Determiners

We are using this term to refer to factors in the learning environment that might influence what learners intake. Such factors could include:

- Language input displayed in a classroom, for example wallcharts recycling vocabulary introduced in class. There is research evidence that such displays can positively influence intake, especially if they are changed and recycled so as not to become inconspicuous (e.g. Shoba, 2017).
- Opportunities for meaningful encounters with input outside the classroom (for example with signs, advertisements, newspapers, films, L2 speakers, the Internet, etc.) (Tomlinson, 2014a; Pinnard, 2016). We can remember, for example, from an experience with signs on a station in Barcelona, that in Spanish "*Salida*" means exit and "*Entrada*" means entrance.
- Peer interaction in the L2 as the norm. Barker (2010a, 2010b), for example, reports the positive effects of students at a Japanese university joining an English Club in which all the members agreed to talk to each other in English whenever and wherever they met.
- Teacher talk in the L2 that is informal, interactive and meaningful to the learners. Tomlinson (2013d) reported how a class of elementary learners picked up a lot of the language used interactively by their teacher but very little of the language she taught.

Experiential Determiners

We are using this term to refer to what learners do during a specific experience of input that might influence what they intake.

> **Readers' Tasks**
>
> 1 Before reading the following outlines of experiential determiners, try listing what you think learners can do for themselves mentally in order to facilitate intake from their experience of input.
> 2 How does the following list compare to yours? Does this list, or your list, miss anything out?
> Noticing
> Detecting Significance
> Imaging

> Using the Inner Voice
> Connecting
> Tolerating Ambiguity
> Cotextual Awareness
> Contextual Awareness
> Retrieval
> Using the Language
> Translating
> Using the L1
> Memorising
> Noting

Noticing

Schmidt (1990, 1994, 2001) was one of the first applied linguists to point out that intelligible and comprehensible input was necessary but not sufficient. He claimed that noticing features of the input was necessary for intake to be achieved, and many researchers have since validated his claims (e.g. Robinson, 1995; Mackey, 2006). Noticing involves paying attention to features of the input, becoming aware of how they are being used to create meaning, and also becoming aware of the gap between the learner's use of the item and that of proficient users of the target language. Although Schmidt focused on conscious noticing, neurolinguistic research and research into natural and immersion acquisition indicate that noticing can be explicit or implicit and it can be achieved with or without instruction and with or without conscious attention ("intake = elements in the input that are noticed and processed in working memory either subconsciously or consciously" – Rod Ellis – personal communication 22/5/2017). If we had to pay conscious attention to every language item and feature in order to acquire it, we would never achieve communicative competence. So, as R. Ellis (2005a, p. 214) says "instruction should be predominantly directed at developing implicit knowledge of the L2 whilst not neglecting explicit knowledge". It does, however, seem that conscious noticing of grammatical items and features in use is likely to facilitate their intake, especially if the items and features are unlikely ever to be salient or communicatively significant in authentic input (e.g. function words such as determiners, morphemes such as -s and -ed, which are nearly always semantically redundant).

In our experience, one of the most effective ways of getting learners to achieve noticing is through language-awareness activities that get learners to make discoveries about a language item or feature in a text that has already engaged them. The discovery process does not guarantee acquisition, but it does increase the likelihood of noticing the item or feature again in subsequent input (see Tomlinson, 1994c, 2007c, 2017).

Saville-Troike and Barto (2017, p. 79) make the strong claim that input "is not available for processing unless learners actually notice it: i.e. pay attention to it. Then it can become **intake**". They also refer to Schmidt's (1990) list of "contributors to the degree of noticing or awareness":

- Frequency of encounters with items
- Perceptual saliency of items
- Instructional strategies that can structure learner attention
- Individuals' processing ability (a component of **aptitude**)
- Readiness to notice particular items (related to hierarchies of complexity)
- Task demands, or the nature of activity the learner is engaged in

While we would agree that noticing is a significant contributor to intake, we would not accept that noticing is the same as paying attention, or that noticing is the same as awareness. In our experience, paying attention to a language item or feature is the first stage of noticing but is of little value as a facilitator of intake unless the learner is also "curious" about how the item or feature is used. In our view, noticing differs from awareness in that noticing is a process and awareness is its intended product.

One aspect of noticing, which does not always get attention in the literature, is noticing by the learner of significant extra-linguistic and nonlinguistic information in the input. This could include, for example, volume of utterance, facial gestures, hand gestures, degree of proximity, hesitation and pause. Such information is often of semantic and pragmatic importance in communication and, if experienced and noticed, is likely to be stored together with associated linguistic information. See McCafferty (2004), McCafferty and Stam (2008) and Lutzker (2016) for discussion of the significance of extra-linguistic and nonlinguistic information in language acquisition.

Detecting Significance

Successful language learners seem to be able to detect which utterances are significant for comprehension and which items and features in these utterances are significant for learning. They can do this implicitly and explicitly by detecting such signifiers of significance as position in the utterance, stress, intonation, repetition and highlighting. Being goal-orientated will help learners to detect significance, but instruction and practice can help.

Imaging

As discussed above sensory imaging plays a key role in facilitating intake. This can be achieved subconsciously, as in natural acquisition, or consciously, as a strategy in a classroom situation. Tomlinson (1997, 2011d) and Tomlinson and Avila (2007a, 2007b), for example, found that learners can be trained to visualise, and that this can have a positive effect on comprehension and on intake. See also Weiskopf (2010) and Zwaan and Madden (2005) for discussions of embodied language, an approach to language processing that "includes a number of psychological theories proposing that words are understood through 'perceptual simulation' or activation of sensorimotor representations of concepts". (Hoedemaker & Gordon, 2014, p. 914). We are great believers in this approach, and think it accords with our experience of language learning. For example, Hitomi sees a yellow fruit, feels its roughness and experiences a sour taste when she encounters the word "lemon", and Brian sees and hears a football coach shouting at his players to keep trying when he encounters the Japanese word "*gambatte*".

Using the Inner Voice

Research (see, for example, de Guerrero, 2005; Tomlinson & Avila, 2007a; Harley, 2008 and Schütze, 2017); Tomlinson (2020a) shows that in the L1 we use the inner voice to convert graphic signals into acoustic signals for entry into the phonological loop, to hold an utterance in the mind for twice as long, to repeat and therefore personalise and make meaningful what we read and listen to, to talk to ourselves about what the input means to us and as a preparation for production. Research also shows that when learning an L2, our inner voice is often inhibited by anxiety or by devoting all the brain's processing energy to low-level decoding (Tomlinson & Avila, 2007a). This can have a negative effect on the amount and quality of intake and in particular on the progress of an item or feature from Intake 1 – Perception to Intake 3 – Integration. The good news, though, is that learners can be trained to make greater and more effective use of their inner voice, both in their L1 and in the L2 (Tomlinson, 2000b; Tomlinson & Avila, 2007b). Hitomi once kept an inner voice diary and found herself code switching between Japanese and English according to which language the topic was first encountered in, or which language was more salient to her in relation to this topic. For example, she tended to talk to herself about her family in Japanese and about applied linguistics in English.

Connecting

In addition to making connections between form and meaning/function, one of the most significant of all determiners of intake is the learners' ability to make connections between the input and previous experience. These could be linguistic connections (i.e. recognising a similar grammatical pattern, noticing a similarity to a word in the L1), sensory connections (e.g. connecting an image created by the input to an image evoked from the life experience of the learner), emotive connections, conceptual connections or topic connections. They can be conscious connections, or subconscious connections made automatically by the brain. Of course, connections are only likely to be made if the input is perceived to be significant and meaningful. Brian remembers, for example, learning the word for soya beans in Japanese (*edamame*) by connecting it to one of his favourite cheeses (edam) and one of his favourite dramatists (Mamet).

Connections are made by forming synapses between neurons. All connections will strengthen the record of the new intake, but connections promoted by emotional associations are particularly powerful. Emotions release chemicals in the brain, which can promote and strengthen connections (Immordino-Yang & Damasio, 2007). If new intake "is connected to an emotional experience at the time it is learned, the heightened sensory information adds to the strength of the synapse" (Schütze, 2017, p. 64).

Tolerating Ambiguity

Learners who panic when they encounter something they do not understand in the input are likely to get left behind when listening and delayed when reading. They are likely to experience language anxiety and thus intake very little from that and subsequent input in the text. Those learners who accept that they are not going to understand everything they listen to or read, and who continue unperturbed when they encounter meaning problems, are likely to intake more of the subsequent input, and might even intake the problematic input if it is clarified by contiguous text or by subsequent repetition(s). This is what happened to Brian recently when he compared trying to understand a narrative text in a French advanced textbook by focusing on words he did not know with reading another page in the same book when not worrying about words he did not know. The first reading was painfully slow and he could not remember what he had read, whereas the second reading was faster, more relaxed and ironically more meaningful.

Cotextual Awareness

The more aware the learner is of the cotext of an item or feature, the more this will aid successful intake. For example, "Give him the keys" is likely to be perceived as an instruction for someone to pass on the keys. But awareness of the cotext will enrich the potential intake. For example, awareness of "Here. . . . Give him the keys. Let him drive it" will clarify the specific meaning of "keys" as well as alerting the learner to the attitudinal significance of placing "Here" just before an imperative.

Contextual Awareness

The more the learner is aware of the context of an utterance, the more this will aid successful intake of the utterance and the potential progress of items and features from the utterance from Intake 1– Perception to Intake 3 – Integration. For example, knowing that the speaker of "Give him the keys. Let him drive it" in the novel *The*

Graduate (Webb, 1963) is a recent graduate, who does not want to go to the graduation party organised for him by his father and certainly does not want to take his father's influential lawyer friend for a ride in his new car, affects awareness of how the imperative can have the surface function of instruction and the deep function of expressing annoyance and refusal.

Retrieval

As we have seen, spaced encounters with an item or feature can facilitate and maintain Intake 3. Spaced attempts at retrieval are important facilitators of maintenance too. As Schütze (2017, p. 65) says, "every time we access a memory a chemical process triggers and updates the synapse. If the synapse is not triggered or updated, it eventually dissipates" and "the memory is no longer available". "Retrieval can be receptive or productive and involves recalling the meaning or part of the meaning of a form when the written or spoken form is met (receptive retrieval) or recalling the written or spoken form in order to express a meaning (productive retrieval)" (Nation, 2013, p. 353).

Using the Language

Learner use of language has been shown to be a determiner of intake, especially if the learner is pushed to use language not yet acquired, and if the learner has to negotiate meaning with an interlocutor. Opportunities for intake come from the learner's output (see Chapter 8 on auto-input), from having to pay attention to and notice items and features needed for use and from the input from interlocutor(s) that is intelligible, comprehensible and meaningful. See Swain (1985, 2005) and Mackey, Abbuhl and Gass (2012) for details of research evidence in support of the value of pushed output and negotiation of meaning.

Note that it is language use and not language practice that is a significant determiner of intake. We are using the term language use to refer to language production that challenges the learner to achieve communicative intents and the term language practice to production that is focused on a particular item or feature to be learned and that is scripted, elicited or guided by a teacher or by language-learning materials. Such production does not offer the same opportunities for strengthening synapses through connection and retrieval, and, while the repetition might seem to facilitate intake, it is usually insufficiently spaced and meaningful to do so.

Translating

Many learners translate into the L1 what they read and hear in the L2. This seems to be an inevitable process in the early stages of language learning (Cook, 2010) and follows the basic principle of connecting the new to the familiar. It helps beginners to understand and recollect, but it also delays or even prevents the use of sensory imaging and of the L2 inner voice and it encourages micro- rather than macro-processing of text. Translation can reassure the learner and provide a comforting illusion of learning, but it can also slow down the reading process, halt the listening process, and inhibit interaction. It can also lead to weak, partial or erroneous intake. In our teaching, we train learners to gradually start using visualisation and their inner L2 voice instead of translating when listening, reading and interacting. However, we have found getting learners in groups to read an L1 text, turn it over and then write an L2 version of it can be very useful, as it encourages sensory imaging, the use and pooling of existing resources and the seeking of responsive teaching.

For discussion of the value of translation and for ideas for classroom activities see Cook (2010) and Kerr (2015).

Using the L1

There is much heated debate about the value of the use of the L1 during the learning of an L2, but very little of it relates directly to the facilitation of intake. Our position is that at lower levels, learner use of the L1 can aid comprehension, noticing, confidence and communication in the L2 and therefore facilitate Intake 1 – Perception and, through meaningful repetition and recycling, Intake 3 – Integration. We would recommend allowing lower-level learners to use the L1 when responding to an L2 spoken or written text, when trying to discover how the L2 is used and when preparing for pair or group production. We would also recommend allowing code switching during early attempts at oral interaction. Although teacher use of the L1 when giving explanations and instructions might seem to help the learners, we would not recommend it as it denies the learners the vital exposure to the communicative use of the L2, which is a prerequisite for language acquisition.

See Cook (2001), Turnbull (2001) and Kerr (2015) and Chapter 9 of this volume for discussions of the pros and cons of teacher and learner use of the L1 in the language-learning classroom and for suggested uses and activities.

Memorising

Memorising appears to have the great benefit of outer repetition and inner rehearsal, and can facilitate intake, provided that what is being memorised is meaningful and the memorisation is repeated at spaced intervals to facilitate intake through maintenance and strengthening (Nation, 2013). Hitomi, for example, remembers memorising Beatles songs when she was in primary school and of subsequently using expressions from the songs when communicating in English. On the other hand, Brian remembers learning meaningless Latin texts for reproduction in exams but subsequently not being able to use any of the language from the texts when attempting written or spoken production.

Noting

Many students take notes as they listen to their teacher, or as they are using their coursebook, or even when reading and listening extensively. While this habit induces attention and contributes to Intake 1 – Perception, the slowing down of comprehension, the cognitive demands of the extra task, the typical lack of context, engagement, salience and meaningfulness mean it is unlikely to facilitate progress to Intake 3 – Integration. While being quite common learner behaviour, noting is rarely commented on by SLA researchers, though Saville-Troike and Barto (2017, p. 123) do include it as a form of "intrapersonal activity".

Notice that all the above experiential determiners of intake can only be activated by learners. Teachers can advise, influence and guide, but they cannot do the noticing, connecting or imaging for the learners.

Pedagogical Determiners

> **Readers' Tasks**
>
> 1 List things that you think teachers can do to facilitate learner intake.
> 2 What are your answers to the following questions? Do you think that:
>   a) giving learners knowledge about the language facilitates learner intake? Why?
>   b) helping learners to make discoveries about how the language is used facilitates learner intake? Why?
>   c) having informal conversations with the learners facilitates learner intake? Why?

Explicit Teaching

There has been considerable debate within the field of second language acquisition about the value of explicit teaching, with some researchers claiming that it is of little value (e.g. Krashen, 1981), some considering it to be of value (e.g. N. Ellis, 2005, 2015) and some considering it to be essential (e.g. deKeyser, 1998, 2007b, 2015; Nation, 2013). Krashen (1981) claimed that comprehensible input was a necessary and sufficient determiner of language acquisition, though he did accept that explicit teaching could help learners when they had time to retrieve the declarative knowledge they had gained before communicating. N. Ellis (2005) said that explicit learning can aid language use provided that there is sufficient time available and that it can contribute to acquisition by making taught items and features more likely to be noticed in subsequent input. DeKeyser (2015) asserted that explicit teaching followed by practice can lead to implicit knowledge and acquisition and Nation (2013, p. 351) insisted that "deliberate vocabulary learning results directly in implicit knowledge which is needed for normal language use". With regard to intake, the consensus seems to be that explicit teaching can facilitate it because it draws attention to language items and features, but with regard to further processing and to acquisition there is considerable disagreement about the value of teacher instruction. Our own experience is that responsive teaching, in which the teacher provides instruction in response to and at the time of a discovered learner need is the most likely type of instruction to facilitate Intake 3 – Integration, as it is likely to be salient, significant and meaningful.

For discussion of the value of explicit teaching see Chapter 9 and, for example, Rebuschat (2015).

Explicit Learning

Although the literature often seems to treat them as synonymous, explicit learning and explicit teaching are not the same phenomenon. It is possible for explicit teaching to achieve varying degrees of explicit learning for different individuals in a class of learners, or for it to result in no explicit learning at all for some learners. It depends on such determiners as salience, meaningfulness, significance, relevance and recycling, as well as on the clarity and impact of the instruction and the credibility and rapport achieved by the teacher. And, of course, it is possible for explicit teaching to result in faulty explicit learning as a result, for example, of mishearing, misunderstanding and partial attention, and in particular of teacher and/or textbook over-simplification (e.g. that "some" is used in affirmative sentences and "any" in negative or interrogative sentences). In relation to grammar, explicit learning from instruction could be learning from a prescriptive grammar telling learners what is correct, from a pedagogic grammar telling learners what to learn or from a descriptive grammar telling learners how the language is actually used. In relation to the achievement of valuable intake, learning from a descriptive grammar is arguably the more valuable, though learning from a pedagogic grammar is undeniably easier.

Explicit learning can also be achieved without a teacher as a result of a learner's deliberate and conscious efforts to learn about the target language with the aid, for example, of a dictionary, a grammar book, an online thesaurus, a corpus, a native-speaker informant or of peers engaged in negotiation of meaning during a group activity. It could also result from noticing an item or feature in the input and/or from a deliberate attempt to discover how an item or feature is used. The intake from such learning is arguably more likely to achieve Intake 3 – Integration, because it results from learner needs and wants and might help to solve a communication problem.

Teacher Talk

Teacher talk is often criticised for being teacher-centred and for taking up valuable learner talking time. This could be true if the teacher is taking up sparse and potentially valuable classroom time lecturing boringly, or even incomprehensibly, about the target language. However, if the teacher is chatting to the learners about topics that concern or interest them, she could be providing rich, meaningful and comprehensible input in a situation in which the learners are relaxed and engaged. For many learners, this could be their only opportunity for exposure to language in use and in this situation we would encourage teachers to talk more rather than less. What matters is the quality of teacher talking time rather than the quantity.

Brian remembers a teacher at a college in England, where he was Director of Studies, who chatted conversationally with her students about what they had been doing and what they were interested in. Her lessons were videoed for a lengthy period and it was discovered that the students used very little of the language she taught them but a lot of the language she had used when chatting to them.

Corrective Feedback

There is much debate about the value of corrective feedback. Most SLA researchers would agree that frequent explicit correction of learner errors of form can be frustrating and deflating for learners (it certainly was for Brian when he tried to learn Bahasa Indonesia and Japanese, and for Hitomi when she tried to learn Spanish). It might achieve Intake 1 – Perception and instantaneous self-repair but it is unlikely to achieve Intake 2 – Transfer and Intake 3 – Integration, because it is likely to lack engagement, contextualisation and nonlinguistic and extra-linguistic information. However, there are some forms of feedback that have been demonstrated to have the potential for achieving Intake 3 – Integration, for example recasting (i.e. reformulation of a learner utterance in a more effective way), seeking clarification of meaning, inviting revision of a contextualised utterance rather than of an isolated form and responding to learner need and invitation during interaction or production.

For detailed discussion of the role and value of corrective feedback, see Mackey (2012), R. Ellis (2015), Gass and Mackey (2015), Loewen (2017) and Saville-Troike and Barto (2017). See also Chapter 9 in this volume.

Implicit Learning

There is no doubt that intake can be achieved implicitly, without any deliberate or conscious effort, as a result of exposure to input that matches many of the determiners outlined above.

We would agree with R. Ellis (2005a, p. 215) that "instruction needs to be directed at developing both implicit and explicit knowledge, giving priority to the former". We would also agree with R. Ellis (2016a, p. 204) that:

1. Acquiring an L2 primarily involves the development of implicit knowledge.
2. Explicit knowledge of an L2 can play a role in both L2 use and acquisition.
3. Acquisition of implicit knowledge of an L2 takes place incidentally and involves attention to form.
4. Acquisition of explicit knowledge is mainly dependent on intentional language learning.

For discussion of the value of implicit learning see Chapter 9 and Rebuschat (2015).

Declarative Knowledge

Declarative knowledge is knowledge about the language, about its grammar, its lexis, its phonology, its orthography, its pragmatic norms. It is gained primarily from explicit learning and can be articulated by the learner. However, it could be argued that such invariant norms as the subject preceding the verb in affirmative utterances in English could be learned implicitly as a result of massive exposure and then articulated explicitly if required.

Procedural Knowledge

Procedural knowledge is knowledge of how to use the language. Such knowledge facilitates spontaneous and automatic use. Some theorists (e.g. DeKeyser, 1998) argue that declarative knowledge can become procedural knowledge through practice but most theorists (e.g. R. Ellis, 2016b) would argue that it is gained implicitly from meaningful experience of the language in use.

Most neuroscientists are convinced that the declarative memory system and the procedural memory system are distinctively separate systems, but there is some disagreement about whether declarative knowledge can also become procedural knowledge (see Morgan-Short & Ullman, 2012). In the SLA literature, theorists talk about the no-interface position (i.e. declarative knowledge cannot become procedural knowledge), the strong-interface position (i.e. declarative knowledge can become procedural knowledge) and the weak-interface position (i.e. declarative knowledge cannot become procedural knowledge but it can facilitate its acquisition). See Robinson, Mackey, Gass and Schmidt (2012) for discussions of these three positions.

Forms-Focused Approaches

Forms-focused approaches are those that follow an inventory of forms to teach in a predetermined order. Our view is that such an inflexible approach disregards learner needs and readiness and that the artificial focus on one form can distort the texts and activities used to illustrate and practise the form. Any intake ensuing is therefore unlikely to be valuable in relation to the development of communicative competence.

Form-Focused Approaches

Form-focused approaches are those in which form is focused on during or after its use (Long, 2015; R. Ellis, 2016b), especially if it is perceived to be problematic, significant or meaningful. The focus is not predetermined but is decided on by learners needing help and by teachers becoming aware of learner need. This could, for example, be during or after a task, project or group discussion. Such an approach responds to learner needs and wants and can match the intake determiners of salience, significance, meaningfulness and recycling.

Meaning-Focused Approaches

Meaning-focused approaches pay no attention to form and and they focus on implicit learning from meaningful experience of receiving and/or producing language (e.g. extensive reading, listening and viewing approaches, immersion approaches and project approaches). Intake can be facilitated from the rich input and the interaction, but can also be restricted by a lack of noticing.

Form-Focused in Meaning-Focused Approaches

Form-focused in meaning-focused approaches place the primary focus on meaning, but also provide opportunities to stop and focus on forms discovered to be significant, meaningful, problematic or necessary. This could happen, for example, when a learner who is writing a story asks the teacher for help when attempting reported speech or when a group in a project are struggling with interrogative forms in compiling a questionnaire. Such an approach, in our view, is the most likely to facilitate Intake 3 – Integration.

See Nassaji and Fotos (2007) for a concise summary of the four approaches mentioned above and Long (2015) for detailed discussion.

Ellis (2005) provides a concise summary of research in relation to the pedagogical determiners discussed above, and Fotos and Nassaji (2007), Ortega (2009), Ellis and Shintani (2013), R. Ellis (2016b) and Long (2015) provide detailed discussion.

Readers' Task

Complete the following table so that it becomes a summary of twenty of the main determiners of intake. Try to find an extra reference for each determiner that is not referred to in the chapter.

When you have finished, try to compare your list with somebody else's who has read this chapter.

SUMMARY OF SOME OF THE DETERMINERS OF INTAKE

Determiners	Main Point	References
1 Intelligibility	Learners need to recognise what they hear and see in order to potentialise intake.	Schütze, 2015
2 Comprehensibility	Input that learners achieve sufficient understanding of has greater potential to become intake.	Krashen, 1985
3 Salience	Input that stands out or attracts attention has greater potential to become intake.	Tomlinson, 2007a
4 Significance	Input that is of meaning and value to the learner has greater potential to become intake.	Van Patten, 2012
5 Redundancy	An utterance in which the message is communicated in more than one way is more likely to achieve intake than one that relies on understanding one way.	Gordon, 2019.
6 Simplicity	The simpler an item is to perceive, rehearse, comprehend and recall the more likely it is to achieve intake.	Tomlinson, 2007a
7 Recycling	The more frequently an item or feature is encountered in different and ideally spaced inputs the more likely it is to achieve intake.	
8 Richness		
9		
10		
11		
12		
13		
14		
15		
16		
17		
18		
19		
20		

CONCLUSION

From our listing of determiners of intake in this chapter, it should be obvious that the progress from input to intake is complex and demanding of time and effort, especially in the seeking out and exploitation of experiences of the target language in embodied action. We would like to stress that, although we have separated the determiners for the sake of clarity, they do not operate in isolation but are only effective in conjunction. For example, motivation is of little value to the learner if that learner is not exposed to language in use, and exposure to language use is of little value if it does not involve affective and cognitive engagement, if it is not meaningful to the learner, if it is restricted to linguistic exemplars and if the learner is not encouraged to pay attention to features of the exposure and to make use of the target language for communication. We would also like to stress that, although all the determiners listed are of value to all learners, every learning context, and also every learner, is different and can achieve intake through a combination of different determiners.

We would like to end this chapter by considering how one learner thinks she managed to achieve effective intake from the input available to her.

Hitomi is a non-native speaker of English, who learned the language at school and at university in Japan. She is now basically bilingual and lectures, publishes and gives conference presentations in English. How did she achieve this?

Hitomi thinks that the vital starting point was her love for Beatles songs when she was at primary school. She played these songs over and over again (motivated and engaged exposure to language in use, recycling), she memorised and sang the songs, she studied and made use of expressions in the songs (noticing, explicit learning), she found herself using expressions from the songs that she had not learned (implicit learning) and she developed a positive attitude to English and to learning it (reduction of psychological and sociological distance). At secondary school, she was motivated intrinsically by her love of the Beatles and her developing affinity with English, and extrinsically by her intention to write an impressive letter to John Lennon. She paid particular attention in English lessons (explicit learning) and she watched all the Beatles films and read stories in English (implicit learning). Hitomi won a scholarship to go to the United States, and attended a senior high school in Wisconsin. At first she found that the English she had learned at school did not help her to interact with native speakers in the United States, so she sought out interaction with peers and with adult members of her host family and eventually gained communicative competence (interaction, pushed output, instrumental motivation, confidence, lack of distance, positivity). At university back in Japan, she benefited from an English-only environment and sought out interaction with other learners (motivated and engaged exposure to language in use, interaction). She also studied by herself, and learned and used useful expressions (explicit learning). When she became an English teacher, she joined research groups where English was used for interaction and she continued to do this when she became a university lecturer (engaged and motivated exposure, interaction). She also continued to read English literature and to listen to songs in English. Hitomi won scholarships to do an MA at the University of Reading and later a PhD at the then University of Luton. During the periods of these studies, she was immersed in English academically, socially and recreationally.

In summary, it seems that what helped Hitomi to become bilingual was instrumental and integrative motivation, engaged exposure, immersion, lack of sociological and psychological distance, confidence, positivity and self-study. Interestingly, she failed to acquire other languages she tried to learn because of a lack of similar motivation, exposure, interaction and immersion.

> **Readers' Tasks**
>
> 1 Without going back to the text, what is your understanding of Intake1, Intake 2 and Intake 3?
> 2 Now go back to the text and check to see if your understanding of the three stages of intake coincides with what we have said in the text so far.
> 3 What do you think of our definitions of the three stages of intake? Can you suggest ways of improving them?
> 4 What main criticism would you make of a syllabus, a coursebook and an examination that you are familiar with?
> 5 What suggestions would you make for revisions to the syllabus, the coursebook and the examination so that they are more likely to facilitate progress from input to Intake 3 – Integration.

FURTHER READING

Ellis, R. (2015). *Understanding second language acquisition* (2nd edn.). Oxford: Oxford University Press.

Saville-Troike, M. & Barto, K. (2017). *Introducing second language acquisition* (3rd edn.). Cambridge: Cambridge University Press.

Schütze, U. (2017). *Language learning and the brain*. Cambridge: Cambridge University Press.

3 Intake Part Two
The Application of Theory to Learning

Introduction

In this chapter we will discuss the potential application of the theories on intake reported in Chapter 2 by reference to the literature as well as to our and other people's experience of applying the theories. We will also offer our own principled suggestions for application.

Some of the content of this chapter is repeated from sections of Chapter 1, which are equally relevant to the application of second language acquisition (SLA) theories of intake to practice. However, there is also a substantial amount of new content, as well as elaboration and supplementation of the repeated content.

Application to L2 Language Policy and Planning (LPP)

Some writers (e.g. Tolefson & Pérez-Milans, 2018) make a distinction between language policy as a statement of intent and language planning as the process of implementation. In this book we are going to use the term LPP to refer to "the process of formulating a language policy, drawing up a plan and implementing and evaluating it" (Kennedy & Tomlinson, 2013).

Language planners are often senior civil servants and politicians, and may not be experts on the theory and practice of language learning. If this is the case, they will need advice on how to maximise the learners' opportunities for intake when making such decisions as:

- the language to use as the medium of instruction in language lessons
- the language to use as the medium of instruction in other subject lessons
- the objectives of language learning
- the importance given to language learning
- the number of hours per week allocated to language lessons
- the size of language classes
- the examinations for which to enter learners

- the in-class resources allocated to language learning (e.g. textbooks, reference books, computers, televisions, visual aids, class libraries)
- the out-of-class resources that support language learning (e.g. libraries, self-access centres, clubs, school exchanges)
- the training of language educators (teachers, head teachers, inspectors, trainers)
- the objectives of the curriculum
- the methodology of the teaching

Unfortunately, not many researchers and writers on LPP pay much attention to language acquisition, and very little seems to have been written on the direct application of SLA principles to language planning (Liddicoat, 2004 being one exception) or even on the implementation of language planning in schools. Tolefson and Pérez-Milan's (2018) work is an excellent handbook on LPP and deservedly won the BAAL Book Prize for 2019. However, it is focused very much on political, economic, sociological and educational research and theory rather than on the application of language acquisition research and theory.

Kennedy and Tomlinson (2013) review the literature on the implementation of language planning as well as measuring the match between language-planning ideals and what learners are asked to do in international and national published materials. In doing so, they reveal that there is often a mismatch between the ideals of the planning policy and its implementation in reality. They refer, for example, to: mismatches in China and Malaysia; to the phenomenon they have experienced of officials in Ministries of Education being knowledgeable about and more sympathetic to the old policy and curriculum than to the new ones they have been tasked with implementing; and to the common problem, as reported, for example, by Le (2011, p. xi) of policy decisions being unrealistic and of the "need to align the underlying political, educational and cultural forces towards on-site textbook users' needs, interests and circumstances".

Kennedy and Tomlinson (2013) also refer to Baldauf, Kaplan and Kamwangamalu's (2011, p. 432) list of policy questions to be asked in primary-school projects, which include such principled pragmatic questions as:

- Is the amount of time dedicated to language learning adequate?
- Are available educational materials sufficient and appropriate?
- Are available methodology models appropriate?
- Are system resources adequate to the task?
- Is the education system sufficiently committed to providing primary-school English in terms of resources, spaces and a prospect for continuity?
- Are children in primary school prepared to undertake early language instruction?

We do not know of any publication that focuses on considerations of how to facilitate intake in language planning, but our advice to language planners would be to:

- allocate as much classroom (and out-of-classroom) time as possible to learning the target language
- ensure that rich, comprehensible, recycled and meaningful input is provided, both by classroom resources (e.g. textbooks, extensive readers, CALL courses, access to the web) and out-of-class resources (e.g. self-access centres, libraries, computer laboratories)
- encourage and resource interaction in the target language in the school (e.g. clubs, film shows, language days, school publications) and outside the school (e.g. inter-school projects, visits to theatres, lectures, etc.)
- encourage the development and use of local materials that focus on providing input that is both meaningful to the learners and connects them to a wider world (an objective aimed at in the development of the Namibian secondary school coursebook *On Target*, 1995, as reported in Tomlinson, 1995)
- ensure that the teachers of the target language are confident and competent enough in their use of that language to encourage them to use it to talk to their learners and to develop institution-specific materials for them
- ensure that teachers are aware of the main agreed theories of SLA and of ways in which they could apply them to their practice
- ensure that teachers develop regional and institution-specific materials to supplement the coursebooks used
- develop a pedagogical policy that emphasises a focus on meaning, on affective and cognitive engagement and on the development of communication and thinking skills rather than on the teaching of linguistic forms (see Kennedy & Tomlinson, 2013 for suggestions, and see Tomlinson, 1995 for reference to such a policy in Namibia)
- insist on a match between assessment procedures and the pedagogic principles of the planning policy (a match vital to ensuring that teachers actually try to follow the principles)
- reduce the practical constraints that inhibit the application of SLA theory to practice, such as excessively large curricula and classes; excessively frequent testing of learners; excessive amounts of time spent on such administrative tasks as lesson plans and records of work; unrealistic expectations of learner progress; insufficient classroom time; excessively demanding teacher timetables; insufficient time spent on teacher development; and insufficient encouragement to experiment

We have found that in most countries we have worked in or visited, the advice we have given above is very rarely followed. For example, in Indonesia, Singapore and Vietnam, and in many other countries, the curriculum development and assessment sections of the Ministry of Education were physically and ideologically separated, with the result that many teachers taught to the examination syllabus rather than following the principles of new curricula. In Singapore, we developed a new coursebook (Tomlinson, Hill & Masuhara, 2000) following the introduction of a new and radically different curriculum, but some of the advisers in the Ministry of Education gave feedback in relation to the previous curriculum. In Malaysia, partial English medium instruction was introduced in primary schools but primary-school teachers were not given courses in language improvement. And in many Asian countries, task-based approaches were introduced without teacher-development courses and without any change in the instruments of summative testing (see Thomas & Reinders, 2015). However, we have experienced some positive matches between SLA theory, curriculum planning and its implementation. For example, in Vanuatu, a task-based curriculum was implemented in the primary schools, the school-leaving examination was changed to a task-based examination and teachers came together in workshops to develop a series of tasks that could be used both in the classroom and in the examination (Tomlinson, 1981). In Indonesia, the PKG English Programme encouraged and trained teachers to develop communicative methodologies and materials to implement the national syllabus (Tomlinson, 1990). In Namibia, the Ministry of Education introduced a new skills-based curriculum and brought together thirty teachers to develop a new coursebook to implement its principles (Tomlinson, 1995), and in Ethiopia the Ministry of Education commissioned a communicative coursebook for primary-teacher language improvement, which aimed at both improving the teachers' communicative competence and familiarising them with types of communicative activity (Tomlinson, 2004).

Kennedy and Tomlinson (2013, p. 265) conclude their chapter, as we are concluding this section, by advocating that "language learning experts are involved in the drafting of the policies so that they are compatible not only with political, social and educational ideals but with language acquisition theory and language learning practice too".

Application to L2 Curriculum Development

Although a curriculum is normally viewed in the educational literature as both an educational programme and a syllabus (Richards, 2001; Finney, 2002; Richards, 2017), in many countries and institutions a language curriculum consists mainly of a syllabus, which is little more than an inventory of items to be taught (usually grammatical, syntactical and phonological). Even when there is a curriculum that describes (or prescribes) an overall approach, the accompanying inventory of items to be taught in the syllabus is often given priority by textbook writers, examiners and teachers, even when it contradicts the approach specified in the curriculum and even when the inventory is so unrealistically large that the teachers' main objective is to cover the syllabus rather than to facilitate learner acquisition of the L2. We have been in situations, for example, where a task-based approach was officially endorsed in the curriculum but was considerably weakened by a syllabus that prescribed which lexical items and grammatical structures should be taught and when they should be taught, and an examination that assessed how successful the learners were in learning the language items they had been taught (Tomlinson, 2015). Such an approach seems to assume that all input should become intake, something no learner of a language has ever achieved. Instead of making this impossible assumption, it would make more sense to accept the reality of intake being inevitably less than input and to ensure that the input is rich and varied, that learners are given choices, that the syllabus is neither prescriptive nor mandatory and that the curriculum encourages and facilitates multiple encounters with items and features in meaningful ways.

The most useful approach to curriculum development is one that accepts not only that each learner will intake a very small percentage of their input but also that intake will be different for each learner. Such an approach would also be based on the reality that in language acquisition what matters is what the learners can do with their L2 rather than what they know about it. If there is a syllabus at all in this approach it could be:

- a communication-skills-based syllabus, ideally encouraging and facilitating the development of language skills that are important for communication, while at the same time facilitating the acquisition of language through meaningful exposure and use
- a skills-for-life-based syllabus that aims to help learners develop such important life skills as analysis, criticality and creativity through learning a language and at the same time using these developing skills to help the learners to acquire the target language (for example, the Namibian secondary school syllabus on which *On Target*, 1995 was based)
- a competency-based syllabus, in which specific competencies are listed as potential objectives (for example, "Can give persuasive reasons justifying a proposed course of action"). The Common European Framework (Council of Europe, 2011), while not itself a syllabus, has been used in many different countries to inform syllabuses listing those competencies determined to be significant for the target learners. Unfortunately, this sometimes leads to the prescribing of language items and features that it is thought need to be learned in order to achieve a specific competency and the danger of assuming that taught input will become learner intake. It has also led to competencies, specified

originally as being important for adult migrants, to be imposed on primary-school learners who do not need to develop those competencies
- a task-based syllabus (e.g. Van den Branden, 2006; Long, 2015), in which communication tasks are listed, ideally for teachers and learners to choose from
- a project-based syllabus in which meaningful engagement in purposeful communication exposes learners to rich and varied inputs and maximises their opportunities for intake (Stoller, 2002; 2006)
- a Content and Language Integrated Learning (CLIL) syllabus (Mehisto, Marsh & Frigols, 2008; Marsh, Coyle & Hood, 2010; Llinares & Morton, 2017) in which subject content (e.g. the First World War, the Great Depression, the Second World War; percentages, algebra, geometry) is specified, and the content and language needed in learning about, discussing and reporting on the content are "taught" together. In the United States, this approach is usually referred to as Content-Based Instruction (CBI) (Brinton, 2003)
- a text-driven approach (TDA) (Tomlinson, 2013d; Tomlinson & Masuhara, 2018b), in which potentially engaging written, spoken and audio-visual texts from a variety of genres and text types drive meaningful activities

Our own favoured type of syllabus is a TDA, because we have found it to be the most likely facilitator of intake with the potential for further processing. In Namibia, we used a TDA to drive a new national coursebook for fifteen- to sixteen-year olds learning English in secondary schools (*On Target*, 1995; Tomlinson, 1995). A team of thirty teachers was divided into ten writing teams. Each team selected a potentially engaging core text from a library of novels, stories, poems, plays, magazines, newspapers, comics, songs and advertisements. They then mapped out a unit for the book using a flexible text-driven framework that had been demonstrated and discussed with them on Day 1 of a six-day workshop in Windhoek. This map was monitored by another team and revised before the actual writing process began. As they wrote drafts of the materials, they added subsidiary texts, making sure that they were using a variety of genres and text types and that their units were coherent in the sense that each activity followed from the previous one and led into the following one. Each night, drafts were taken to the hotel and matched against the new official Ministry of Education syllabus. By the penultimate day, a 93 per cent match had been achieved by the writers with the official syllabus without them being aware of it, a match not only with language items and language skills but also with curriculum objectives such as the fostering of critical and creative thinking, the development of cross-curricular knowledge and skills and the broadening and maturing of the mind. On the last day, some of the missing components from the official syllabus were added as naturally as possible and some were (with the permission of Ministry officials) considered too rarely used or too trivial to worry about. In six days, we had written the draft of a book designed primarily to engage the students affectively and cognitively in texts and activities that were meaningful to them. In doing so we had maximised the likelihood of input progressing to Intake 3 and beyond.

The flexible framework we used consisted of:

1 **Readiness activities**, designed to activate the learners' minds in relation to the location, theme or topic of the core text (thus increasing the likelihood of intake from connections, attention and meaningfulness).
2 **Initial response activities**, designed for the learners to do mentally while experiencing the text, rather than focusing on low-level decoding of its words (thus increasing the likelihood of multidimensional intake from engagement).
3 **Personal-response activities**, designed to elicit learner thoughts, views, attitudes, interpretations, etc. and to facilitate learner deepening and articulation of their understanding of the text (thus increasing the likelihood of intake from multidimensional processing, from connections and from meaningfulness).
4 **Development activity 1**, designed to stimulate the learners to create a related text for themselves by returning to the core text in order to then depart from it by continuing it, preceding it, modifying it, creating it from a different perspective, responding to it etc. (thus increasing the likelihood of intake from repeated encounters, from paying attention, from noticing, from negotiation of meaning (see Chapter 5), from engagement, from multidimensional processing and from auto input (see Chapter 8)).
5 **Input–response activities**, designed to help learners to focus on language items and/or features that are salient and significant in the text and to make discoveries about how they are used, both in that text and in others they find for themselves (thus increasing the likelihood of intake from repeated encounters, from salience, from significance, from paying attention and from noticing).
6 **Development activity 2**, designed to help the learners to improve their text in item 4 or to produce a similar but more effective text by making use of what they have discovered in item 5 (thus increasing the likelihood of intake from repeated encounters, from salience, from significance, from paying attention, from noticing, from meaningfulness, from multidimensional processing and from auto input).

This framework has been used in Botswana, China, Columbia, Ethiopia, Iran, Mauritius, Pakistan, the Philippines, the Seychelles, South Korea, Singapore, Turkey, Venezuela and Vietnam to develop syllabuses and then units for courses of materials. For more details and examples of this framework, see Tomlinson (2013d) and Tomlinson and Masuhara (2018b). The key point is that it is an effective and efficient way of developing a syllabus organically while simultaneously developing materials that have the potential for learner engagement because they are driven by texts selected with that objective in mind. This is in contrast to materials following a language syllabus, which tend to be driven by teaching points, topics or themes illustrated by texts selected or developed for their relevance to a pedagogic syllabus and to the pedagogic objectives of the unit. Of course, in highlighting the text-driven syllabus we are not insisting that this is the only one that can facilitate intake. In our view, task-based syllabuses, project-based syllabuses and CLIL/CBI syllabuses can also be useful in facilitating language intake.

An interesting recent development in language teaching has been a concern with curriculum authenticity. According to Bouziri (2017, p. 28), this can be achieved by ensuring "relevance, scope, coherence, proximity, and feasibility". In relation to learners achieving Intake 3 relevance and proximity are of particular value. Proximity "has been defined as closeness to learners' cognitive maturity as well as to contexts of use" (Bouziri, 2017, p. 38) and has been likened to Pienemann's (1985) concept of learnability of items in a syllabus. A lack of proximity is certainly likely to inhibit intake, as much of the input will probably be too complex and demanding for successful processing and the absence of opportunities for re-encountering and making use of any initial intake is unlikely to create a sufficiently strong record in the brain. For discussion of curriculum authenticity see also Macalister and Nation (2011), Nation and Macalister (2010), Tatsuki (2006) and Trabelsi (2010).

> **Readers' Task**
>
> You are a senior official in the Ministry of Education in Betu, a country with a population of about 500,000, consisting of many small islands in the South Pacific. The main sources of income are fishing, copra and palm oil, with most people being employed by international companies as fishermen or plantation workers. Well-educated Betu tend to go to Australia or New Zealand for their tertiary education, and many stay on there afterwards to start a career.
>
> You have been asked by the Minister of Education to propose changes to current LPP in relation to the learning of English and to use the following template to make notes for a future meeting with the Minister.
>
> Make the notes in Table 3.1 on page 122 which you will use in your meeting.

Application to L2 Methodology

There is no doubt that, although the aptitude, attitude and application of instructed learners are major determiners of intake, the methodology of their instruction is a major determiner too. For example, Morgan-Short and Ullman (2012, pp. 293–294)

Table 3.1 The learning of English in Betu: A proposal for future policy and planning

Feature	Current Situation	Proposal	Reason(s)
1 Medium of Instruction			
Primary	Betu		
Secondary	Betu		
Tertiary	English		
2 The Teaching of English			
Primary	No English lessons		
Secondary	Three hours a week		
Tertiary	Three hours a week		
3 Resources			
Primary	None		
Secondary	1 A national forms-focused coursebook written for the Ministry of Education by a University in Australia. 2 Language laboratories donated by the USA.		
Tertiary	1 A library of books relevant to the subjects studied.		
4 Curriculum			
Primary	None		
Secondary	A forms-focused curriculum listing the grammatical forms to be taught in each grade, together with the four skills of reading, writing, listening and speaking		
Tertiary	None. Each subject department specifies what should be taught and how it should be taught (usually the explicit teaching of language items considered necessary for the study of the subject).		
5 Assessment			
Primary	None.		
Secondary	Weekly tests of the language items taught, using the same test types as the Ministry of Education end of year examination (i.e. multiple choice, true/false, matching, gap filling and sentence completion). There are no speaking tests or examinations.		
Tertiary	No examination of English, only of the subjects studied.		
6 Teacher Training			
Primary	No training of English teachers.		
Secondary	A two-year initial teacher-training course focusing on the teaching of grammar and of the four skills.		
Tertiary	No training of tertiary lecturers.		
7 Proposals for Other Changes and Developments			

report studies that show that both learners who have been trained implicitly and learners who have been immersed in the L2 exhibit the ability to process syntactic structures using both automatic and controlled processes, whereas those trained in "more explicit contexts such as traditional grammar-focused classroom settings . . . evidenced controlled but not automatic processing".

Mishan (2013a, p. 269) provides a very useful survey of "currently influential language pedagogies, outlining their basis in second language acquisition (SLA) theory". She describes the communicative approach, task-based language learning, problem-based learning, consciousness-raising, data-driven learning, the lexical approach and humanistic approaches. She does not, however, describe CLIL, project-based approaches or TDA. Interestingly, she does not mention the PPP paradigm, which in our experience has in fact been the prevailing methodology in classrooms and coursebooks for over forty years, presumably because she, like many other researchers, does not consider it to have a basis in SLA theory. See, though, Criado (2016) for a justification of the PPP paradigm in relation to skill acquisition theory (Lyster & Sato, 2013; DeKeyser, 2015), which claims that PPP can be used to move learners from "declarative knowledge to procedural to automatized knowledge" (p. 122).

The Communicative Approach

The term "communicative approach" refers in fact to the many approaches that share the common goal of helping learners to communicate effectively in their L2. Originally, it referred to experiential approaches that focused on the provision of comprehensible input (Krashen, 1981), on opportunities for interaction (Long, 1996) and on facilitating comprehensible output (Swain, 1985). The emphasis was on language functions, on language skills and on vocabulary, rather than on grammar. Unfortunately in our view, this theory-based approach was rarely implemented in many institutions or materials and, when it was, the texts and tasks were often boringly trivial (e.g. buying a coffee, arranging a meeting, inviting to dinner). Nowadays, syllabuses and coursebooks call themselves communicative whilst openly focusing on the teaching of grammar through a PPP approach (see Tomlinson & Masuhara, 2013 for a critique). The original concept of the communicative approach had the potential to facilitate Intake 3 through significance, meaningfulness, engagement, motivation and negotiation of meaning, but often its actual implementation ignores those determiners of intake and relies on the teaching of language items deemed to be important for communication. The original experiential approach described above is often referred to as the strong communicative approach, and the subsequent teaching approach is often referred to as the weak communicative approach. See Richards and Rodgers (2014) for a detailed discussion of the communicative approach.

Task-Based Language Teaching (TBLT)

As we said in Chapter 1, task-based language learning in its strong form encourages learners to make use of their existing linguistic resources in order to complete a communicative task with a clearly defined outcome (e.g. designing a persuasive advertisement for a new car). Whilst engaged on the task (preferably with other learners) a learner will seek language that they need from peers and from the teacher, and after task completion the learner will gain feedback from their teacher (and possibly their peers) on the effectiveness of their use of the L2. This is very much a form-focused in meaning-focused approach, in other words, the learners' main concern is on successful completion of the task, but in trying to achieve this they will also focus on form when they need to. This approach has great potential for achieving Intake 3 through psychological readiness, salience, significance, engagement, motivation, noticing, negotiation of meaning and meaningfulness. Unfortunately, in many classrooms and in many task-based materials, the approach has been weakened into a forms-focused approach, in which tasks are selected to practise particular language items or features that are pre-taught before the task is introduced. Such an approach, in our view, risks ignoring such determiners as psychological readiness, salience, significance, engagement, motivation, noticing, negotiation of meaning and meaningfulness, because everything is predetermined by a syllabus, coursebook or teacher rather than by learner needs and wants. For information about the theory and application of TBLT see Long (2016), Mackey, Ziegler and Bryfonski (2016), Masuhara and Tomlinson (2008), Tomlinson (2015) and especially Van den Branden (2006) and Van den Branden, Bygate and Norris (2009). For accounts of how TBLT approaches are being used in different contexts around the world, see Lambert and Oliver (2020), and for accounts of how they have been weakened (sometimes into task-supported approaches) in order to achieve face validity and to prepare students for examinations, see Masuhara (2015), Thomas and Reinders (2015) and Tomlinson (2015). For a concise overview of the literature on TBLT see Moore (2018), and for accounts of recent research on the effectiveness of TBLT, see Samuda, Van den Branden and Bygate (2018).

One problem with TBLT is that one of its main advocates, Michael Long, seems to be opposed to the use of texts when he says, "Use task not text, as the unit of analysis" (Long, 2015, p. 305) and that "[t]exts are frozen records, often unrealistic records, of task accomplishment by others, i.e. a by-product of tasks". As a result of this, and possibly of the tasks exemplified by researchers in their publications, the tasks used in the classroom are often of rather trivial speech events such as, "asking for directions, ordering a meal, spotting the difference between two pictures, telling the story of a picture" (Tomlinson, 2018c, p. 4). These tasks might be "ideal for research because they make it easy to control and to assess task performance but they are far from ideal for classroom use as their lack of stimulating content and of cognitive challenge can make them very unappealing to intelligent learners" (Tomlinson, 2018c, p. 4). Using such trivial tasks without texts or contexts can also mean that there are many fewer opportunities for facilitating intake, as there is much less input, less likelihood of affective and cognitive engagement and less likelihood of the task being meaningful to the learners. Our preference would be for a text-driven task-based approach, as in the following example adapted from Tomlinson (2018c) and targeted at overseas nurses and doctors in a UK hospital who are obliged to take language improvement classes.

BOX 3.1 Time to Listen

1. Please get into groups of three.
2. One of you is a doctor, one is a patient and one is an observer.
3. If you are the patient, you are going to tell the doctor what is wrong with you.
4. *The teacher tells the doctor and the patient to face the back of the room and then shows this instruction to the observer, "Time how long it takes before the doctor interrupts the patient."*
5. *The learners act out the doctor/patient scenario and the observer notes the time of the first doctor interruption. The teacher then asks observers to report their times.*
6. Listen to what happened when a doctor decided not to interrupt a patient. *The teacher summarises what is reported in A time to listen (Barr, 2004), which focuses on the problems caused by doctors prematurely interrupting patients (and especially on the case of the old lady whose cancer was only revealed because the doctor let her talk for twenty-two minutes) and concludes by reading aloud a quote from the old lady: "Oh, don't worry about all that. I've had a good life. But I just wanted you to know – this is the best doctor visit I've ever had. You're the only one who ever listened to me.").*
7. Read the text "Time to Listen" and, as you read it, try think of a way of allowing patients enough time to talk about their problem without creating long queues of patients waiting to see the doctor.
8. Write a letter to your hospital authority telling them about your idea. You can do this individually, in pairs or in a small group.
9. Show your letter to another individual, pair or group and ask them for suggestions for improvement.
10. Compare your letter with the one your teacher has written.
11. Revise your letter making use of the suggestions from 8 and what you've learned from the letter you looked at in 9.

This unit of material follows the following flexible procedure for developing text-driven tasks for the classroom, a procedure with many similarities to the one outlined in the section on curriculum development above:

1. A **readiness activity** to activate the learners' minds in relation to the topic of doctor listening time.
2. An **experience** of a potentially engaging text that focuses the students' minds on the meaning of the text rather than on the language it uses to express the meaning. In this example, the text is first summarised orally in order to focus on its potential for affective and cognitive engagement.
3. A **personal response** to the experience of the text, which helps the students to deepen and articulate their interpretation and reaction to the text.
4. A **task** driven by the text.
5. **Peer monitoring** of the task performance by individuals or groups of students with a view to offering advice both on the content and the expression of the task performance.
6. **Comparison** with a proficient user of the L2's performance of the task – preferably focusing on a particularly salient lexical, structural or pragmatic feature of the text.
7. **Task revision**.

N.B. The teacher is encouraged to teach responsively in stage 4 by providing help and advice when invited.

It is our view that such a text-driven task provides rich and meaningful input and enhances the likelihood of Intake 3 through experiences with the potential for salience, significance, meaningfulness, psychological readiness, spaced recycling, affective engagement, cognitive engagement, multidimensional processing, challenge and motivation. Another text-rich, task-based approach, in which short stories drive tasks is described in Baleghizadeh (2017).

For a detailed account of the theoretical underpinning of TBLT, see Mackey, Abbuhl and Gass (2012) and for an application of interactionist theory to TBLT materials development see Mackey, Ziegler and Bryfonski (2016).

Problem-Based Teaching (PBT)

Another type of task-based approach is PBT, in which the task consists of resolving a contextualised problem. According to Mishan (2013b, pp. 273–274), this is a constructivist approach that is "student-led, enquiry-fuelled and self-reflective" (p. 273), and that involves groups of students working together to solve a problem and then reflect on the learning process. When we have used this approach, we have found that it has a great potential for facilitating intake providing that the task is significant, relevant to the learners, challenging, stimulated by a text, conducted in the L2, has an outcome other than just a solution and is facilitated by a teacher who is available to help with language problems. For example, a group of engineering students in a Japanese university were highly motivated by a problem-based task that involved reading a text about water shortages, inventing a cheap device for saving water, presenting their device to an international company and then designing newspaper and television adverts for their device. This turned out to be cognitively engaging and challenging, affectively engaging (they had great fun, for example, performing their adverts) and meaningful (as engineering students they were often presented with such problems on their course). The tasks also promoted visualisation and provided multiple opportunities for paying attention to and noticing form in meaning-focused activities.

See Ansarian and Teoh (2018) for a survey of the literature on problem-based approaches and for suggestions for classroom implementation.

Text-Driven Approaches

A TDA is a learner-centred, experiential approach in which a core authentic text, selected for its potential to engage, drives the activities in the classroom rather than a syllabus or a predetermined language or skills teaching point. A principled, flexible framework for a TDA is described, justified and exemplified in Tomlinson (2013d) and in Tomlinson and Masuhara (2018). In this framework, a readiness activity (e.g. the learners visualising and talking to themselves about their experience of travelling by train) precedes the core text and activates the learners' minds in relation to it. The learners are then given a mental task to perform (e.g. visualising the train journey being described) whilst reading, listening to or viewing the text. After experiencing the text, the learners answer personal-response questions designed to facilitate the development and articulation of their representation and/or interpretation of the text (e.g. drawing a scene from the journey described in the text; giving their explanation for the way the passengers behaved). Then the learners write a continuation of the text individually or in groups. Before this text is handed in, the learners go back to the original text and make discoveries about how a particular language feature is used (e.g. the passive voice) and then make any revisions they want to their text.

In this approach, the learners are provided with input by the core text, by themselves in the readiness activity, by peers during various interactions and by the teacher when responding to requests for assistance. If the core text and the activities succeed in engaging the learners affectively and cognitively, then there is considerable potential in this approach for achieving Intake 3.

Consciousness-Raising (C-R) and Discovery Approaches

C-R is an approach advocated by many SLA researchers (e.g. R. Ellis, 2003; Loewen, 2015). It is based on the claim quoted in Mishan (2013a) from Schmidt (1990, abstract) that "noticing is the necessary and sufficient claim for converting input to intake" and involves learners being provided with language data that they make use of to make discoveries about how a particular language feature is used in the L2. The data could come from corpora accessible on the web, from student-created corpora, from teacher- or coursebook-created examples or from authentic texts. Unfortunately, our experience in classrooms and when evaluating coursebooks is that often when C-R is used in practice the samples provided and the accompanying tasks are strictly controlled, so as to push learners towards predetermined answers. Our preference is for a discovery-based language-awareness approach, in which learners experience and then respond personally to an authentic and potentially engaging text before returning to it to make discoveries about how a particular language feature is used (for examples, see Tomlinson, 1994c, 2007c, 2010a, 2018a and Tomlinson & Masuhara, 2018b). We have also found it useful to get learners to construct their own corpora from which to make further discoveries (e.g. half the class find authentic examples of the use of "some" and half find examples of "any" before forming groups to develop a some/any corpus to make discoveries from). The main differences between discovery-based language-awareness activities and consciousness-raising activities are that the former are text-driven and contextualised whereas the latter are typically not, and the former encourage open-ended learner discovery and autonomy whereas the latter often do not.

Data-Driven Learning (DDL)

DDL is a discovery-based approach in which the learners are provided with (or find for themselves) concordance lines in which a focused lexical item or linguistic feature is exemplified in cotextual use, as in the following example:

> "I haven't actually started that book yet."
> "I'm sorry. He's already gone home."
> "Let's go to Valencia. We've been to Seville before."
> "Many novelists have been influenced by James Joyce over the years."

The learners look at and discuss the use in the samples of the focused item or feature and then make and share discoveries about it. Mishan (2013a) is a proponent of this approach and usefully refers her readers to Johns (1997) for more information about it and to O'Keefe, McCarthy and Carter (2007) for ways of using it in the classroom. Our experience is that it can facilitate Intake 3, provided that the examples are comprehensible, contextualised and meaningful to the learner. One problem, though, is that the learners can only discover how to use the item not when to use or not use the item. Maybe a pedagogical approach should be taken to the assembly of the corpus, so that only authentic instances of the item are used that are informative about when, when not, and how to use the item, as in the following example:

"He didn't really make it at Inter Milan ... or rather should I say, he hasn't really made it at Inter Milan." (*Sky Sports News* – 16/02/2020).

Even with this example, though, the learner needs to know something about the context to work out the difference in use between the simple past and the present perfect. "He" refers to a footballer who was bought by Inter Milan, did not feature for the first team and was then loaned out to another club. The reporter corrects himself because the simple past would imply the player no longer had a contract with Inter Milan, whereas the present perfect correctly implies that he does still have a contract with Inter Milan.

The Lexical Approach

The lexical approach is an approach developed by Willis (1990) and by Lewis (1993) to facilitate the acquisition of a store of ready-made lexical units. The emphasis is very much on experiencing and noticing lexical chunks in use (e.g. "stable government"; "at rest"; "has had to have an operation") and the approach usually follows a "notice, discover and use approach", or as Lewis (2000, p. 177) phrases it, "Observe, hypothesise, experiment". Again, we feel that this approach could facilitate Intake 3 providing the input is contextualised and meaningful, and we think one way of achieving this is to follow a text-driven lexical approach (see Tomlinson, 2016b for an example of a poem used to drive discovery activities focusing on the lexical chunk "Not now ___.")

Content and Language Integrated Learning Approaches (CLIL)

CLIL approaches focus learners on "learning content knowledge and skills (e.g. geography, learning a sport, cultivating crops) whilst gaining experience of using" their L2 (Tomlinson & Masuhara, 2018b, p. 36). The pedagogic approach could be either: 1) to pre-teach the language and skills the learners will need in texts and activities that focus on the subject content; 2) to help the learners to focus on language and skills that have been significant and/or problematic in texts and activities already experienced; or 3) to simply immerse the learners in the L2 when studying the subject content. The first risks becoming PPP with an emphasis on explicit teaching, but the second has great potential for facilitating Intake 3 provided the learners find the subject content meaningful and they are helped to make discoveries for themselves. The third can be very effective in helping the learners develop communicative competence, but can also cause fossilisation of grammatical errors because of the lack of encouragement to notice form (as happened on the Canadian Immersion Project before they introduced language-awareness classes – see Swain, 1985, 2005). See Coyle, Hood and Marsh (2010) and Lasagabaster and Ruiz de Zarobe (2010) for more information about CLIL, an approach with great potential for facilitating Intake 3, providing that the learners are helped to notice significant language forms and features as well as experiencing them in use, and see Sylven (2019) for a research study of the effects of CLIL as used in secondary schools in Sweden. See also Brinton (2003) and Snow and Brinton (2017) for information about a very similar approach CBI that preceded CLIL and was developed in the United States and Canada.

Humanistic Approaches

Mishan (2013a, p. 279) defines humanistic approaches as "those taking a holistic view of the learner and the learning process and implicating 'whole-brain' activities". Tomlinson (2013e, p. 140) defines a humanistic coursebook as "one which respects its users as human beings and helps them to exploit their capacity for learning through meaningful experience". He also advocates humanising coursebooks by "adding activities which help to make the language learning process a more affective experience and finding ways of helping the learners to connect what is in the book to what is in their minds". Mishan exemplifies humanistic approaches with references to Gardner's concept of multiple intelligence (1993), to neurolinguistic programming (Revell & Norman, 1997), to Suggestopedia (Lozanov, 1978) and to books by Rinvolucri (2002) and Puchta and Rinvolucri (2007). She also characterises humanistic approaches as multidimensional approaches. Tomlinson (2013e, p. 148) also focuses on the importance of multidimensional language learning "based on the principle that using affect, mental imagery and inner speech is what we do during effective language use and what we do during effective and durable learning too". Tomlinson (2013e) provides many examples of multidimensional, humanistic activities and recommends in particular using TDA, using literature, using text-free generalisable activities that learners use with texts of their own choice, and using localised materials. He also recommends awareness activities, saying that "once learners have engaged with a text, achieved a multidimensional representation of it and developed and articulated their personal responses to it, I've found it very useful to help them to make discoveries for themselves" (Tomlinson, 2013e, p. 152). Humanistic approaches for young learners receive a rich coverage in Bland (2015, 2018), with much emphasis being given to multimodal approaches and to the use of challenging literature to stimulate engagement, thought and creativity. Advocates of a mythic language approach (for example, King, 1990; Stewart, 1996) also emphasise the importance of providing a rich stimulating experience for language learners and of stimulating creativity and personal expression. This is an approach that makes use of myths, folk tales, fairy stories, fantasies and dreams to help students to access their inner lives and to generate and share images and feelings. We found King (1990) especially persuasive when she argues that using myths to stimulate images and stories enables learners to discover more about who they are and to continue to develop themselves.

Humanistic approaches have great potential for facilitating Intake 3, as they can achieve many of the determiners outlined in this chapter (e.g. significance, meaningfulness, multidimensional representation, affective engagement, psychological readiness, noticing). For a detailed list of the characteristics of humanistic teaching see Grundy (2013).

Drama-Based Approaches

We have found that drama-based approaches can provide multiple opportunities for facilitating intake through meaningful and engaged exposure, as well as interaction, creativity and recycling. This is especially true if learners are asked in groups to act out poems, songs, jokes, short stories, advertisements, cartoons or scenes from plays or films, or to improvise dramas from a given situation or scenario, or even to act out a text from the coursebook. We never force groups to act in front of the class and favour an approach in which groups prepare, rehearse and then act out to another group. We have found that the sillier or more sensational the drama is, the more impactful and memorable it is too.

One approach that has become very popular is process drama, an approach in which the whole class and the teacher together improvise a dramatic version of a situation initially described by the teacher or textbook. There is no script and no audience. One of our ex-PhD students, Hae-ok Park, has recently been given permission by the Ministry of Education to replace the curriculum and the coursebook with a process-drama approach in a school in South Korea. We will be very interested to find out what effect this has on the learners' acquisition of English.

For discussion of the use of drama in L2 learning see Maley and Duff (2005) and Wilson (2008), for a review of the literature on process drama and a report of a process-drama experiment see Park (2010) and for suggestions for the use of drama and of scenarios with young learners see Tomlinson and Masuhara (2018b).

Project-Based Approaches

Project-based approaches, in which learners work in groups to prepare for, carry out and report on a project, have great potential for facilitating intake. They are meaning-focused, form-focused approaches, in which the learners' main objective is to make and communicate meaning but also in which, at various preparation and monitoring stages, they attend to form, and possibly seek help from peers and from the teacher, which can result in meaningful explicit learning. For example, they might be researching the views of the college staff on a proposal to build high-rise flats on an area of nearby parkland. Whilst carrying out their project, they will need to read about the proposal, interview members of staff, record the views of the staff and report the findings of their research. In doing so, they will gain many opportunities for implicit learning through motivated and engaged exposure, through interaction and through production and they will also gain opportunities for explicit learning when trying to understand the proposal document, when devising their interview questions and when writing their report.

For discussion of the value of project-based approaches and for ideas for implementation, see Wicks (2000) and Stoller (2002, 2006).

The Action-Orientated Approach (AoA)

The AoA shares many of the principles and procedures of TBLT, of TDA, of project approaches and of process-drama approaches, in that it is an experiential approach (see Kolb & Kolb, 2001) focusing on learning through doing. It also shares principles and procedures with the scenario approach (DiPietro, 1982, 1987), an approach featuring strategic interaction, in which one group is given a role to prepare for and then enact in a specified situation in order to achieve a specified outcome, and another group is given a different role to prepare for and then to enact in order to achieve a different outcome in the same situation. Neither group knows what the other group is aiming to achieve, nor what they will say and do. After the preparation time, each group chooses a representative to play their role and the situation is enacted (with the group able to call a time out to coach or substitute their representative). After the scenario has been enacted, the teacher leads a post-mortem on the effectiveness of the representative's attempts to achieve their intended outcome.

The AoA aims to help learners to develop sociolinguistic, pragmatic and strategic competence. It is, to a large extent, influenced by the Common European Framework of Reference (Council of Europe, 2001) and its Companion Volume (2018), documentation that, in proposing competencies for learners of languages to aim to attain, "emphasises meaningful action in the target language in the classroom" and sets "goals in relation to 'can do' descriptors" (e.g. "Can explain why something is a problem", B1 Informal Discussion (With Friends), Piccardo & North, 2019, p. 149). The foundation for AoA is very much the "centrality in the CEFR model of the co-construction of discourse in collaborative, interactive, real-life tasks, and a new, positive, interpretation of communication strategies by a language user fulfilling a mission in a realistic context" (Piccardo & North, 2019, p. 149). In AoA the learner is viewed not as a passive learner of a language but as a "user", "an agent in a social context", "a social agent" (Piccardo & North, 2019, p. 245). Learning "is constructed around action" and involves "strategic activation of competences in order to achieve a particular outcome" (Piccardo & North, 2019, p. 248).

See Piccardo and North (2019) for a very thorough description of the principles and procedures of AoA, and for examples of AoA scenarios such as "launching a new blog to help promote a language throughout the school and beyond" (p. 265).

Like many of the other approaches we have advocated so far, AoA could be considered a usage-based approach, in that the emphasis is on extracting language from usage events (i.e. when language is actually used to achieve purposeful communication). For discussion of usage-based approaches, see Lowie, Michel, Rousée-Malpat, Keijzer and Sterinkrauss (2020).

Multidimensional Approaches

"A multi-dimensional approach is one that enables the learners to make full use of the resources of their minds ... and which to do so follows the principles of personalization, affective engagement, cognitive engagement, mental imagery, use of the inner voice and raising of esteem" (Tomlinson & Masuhara, 2018b, p. 263). Such an approach is ideal for facilitating Intake 3, as it has the potential to combine linguistic and nonlinguistic information in a powerful series of connections, for example by learners visualising and using their inner voice to articulate their emotional responses whilst reading a short story. For more information about this approach, see Masuhara (2005) and Tomlinson (2000b) and for an example of multidimensional materials created in Columbia to replace a coursebook considered by learners to be boring see Bonilla and Vargas (2015).

Extensive Reading/Listening/Viewing

Extensive reading, extensive listening and viewing of audio-visual materials can (but does not always) provide input with great potential for facilitating intake because it is rich in quantity, quality and variety of input, because it stimulates affective and cognitive engagement, because it connects with the learners' lives and because items and features are recycled many times. Providing learners with a choice of what to read, listen to and view is essential to achieve meaningfulness and connections. Encouraging them to experience texts that aim to engage rather than teach is important too, as is exposing them to the L2 in authentic use so as to ensure that their intake includes information about pragmatic use as well as semantic meaning and linguistic form (see Maley & Tomlinson, 2017). Extensive reading, listening and viewing is particularly powerful if connected to a language-awareness course in which learners are helped to make discoveries about meaning, function and form for themselves. Having noticed and made discoveries about items and features in awareness activities will help them to notice them again in use in their experience of extensive reading, listening and viewing.

For persuasive research-based arguments for the power of extensive reading see Elley and Mangubhai (1981), Davies (1995), Day and Bamford (1998), Krashen (2004), Maley (2008), Fenton-Smith (2010) and the Extensive Reading Foundation web site (www.erfoundation.org).

Looking Out for the L2

No classroom-based course can really provide enough input to facilitate sufficient intake (Barker, 2010a, 2010b) so it is vital that learners are encouraged to look out for their target language in use outside the classroom. This could involve such activities as surfing the web, gaining access to newspapers and journals, befriending native speakers, joining clubs, watching television programmes in the target language, watching films in the target language and forming clubs in which the members only speak to each other in the target language when they meet (Barker, 2010a, 2010b). Such activities are likely to facilitate intake because they are probably meaningful and engaging to the learners who have chosen to do them.

For discussion and demonstration of ways of getting learners to look out for their L2, see Cooker (2008, 2010), Tomlinson (2010c, 2011b, 2014a), Benson and Reinders (2011), Nunan and Richards (2015) and Pinnard (2016).

We have focused on the approaches above because we feel from our research, our reading and our experience that they are the most likely to facilitate the achievement of Intake 3 – Integration. We feel, though, that we need to say a little more about PPP (Mishan, 2013a; Tomlinson & Masuhara, 2013), which is probably still the most widely used methodology in L2 classrooms, as well as the most widely taught methodology on initial teacher-training programmes, despite the fact that it gets very little mention these days in books on methodology (this is true, for example, in McDonough, Shaw & Masuhara, 2013).

PPP

PPP follows a procedure in which a linguistic item or feature is selected for learning and is then taught through explicit presentation (e.g. of examples, rules, descriptions), followed by learner practice (usually controlled and then guided) and then learner production (usually with suggestions for what language expressions to use). PPP seems to have prevailed for the last fifty years, despite many applied linguists pointing out that there is little support for it in SLA research and theory (e.g. Willis & Willis, 1996; Skehan, 1998; Tomlinson, 2011a; Burns & Hill, 2013; Masuhara, 2016). Recently though, there have been a number of attempts to provide theoretical justification for PPP.

Hadley (2014) follows a PPP approach in using a coursebook in a Japanese university because, "[b]ased on what was then ten years of experience with teaching Japanese university first year students, I knew that most craved a presentation-practice-production (PPP) approach" (p. 221). He claims that he has provided empirical support that global textbooks "can play an important part in helping ... second language learning based upon six years empirical testing with nearly 700 learners" (p. 230). Unfortunately, his empirical evidence is derived from pre- and post-testing of students using the placement tests for the coursebook that he taught (a test which "lasts for 50 minutes and consists of 70 multiple choice items divided into three sections that assess listening (20 items), reading (20 items) and grammatical knowledge (30 items)" (p. 222). Hadley's finding, that in general there was some improvement in the learners' scores between the pre-test and the post-test of a textbook placement test, reveals little about the communicative competence of the students and is hardly empirical support for the textbook or the methodology of its use.

Criado (2016) makes a strong claim for the value of PPP by relating it to skill acquisition theory (SAT) (DeKeyser, 2015), which claims that declarative knowledge of the language can be proceduralised and made automatic by practice. She provides a lot of theoretical support for SAT from the literature devoted to it, but no actual research evidence of its effectiveness.

Anderson (2017) is a very strong advocate of PPP. He claims that there is methodological support in Arnold, Dornyei and Pugliese (2015) and empirical support in Spada and Tomita (2010). However, Arnold et al. (2015) only actually mention PPP once in their book. On p. 9, when referring to their principled approach to communicative language teaching, they say "interestingly, the sequence of declarative input – controlled practice – open-ended practice is reminiscent of the well-known methodological progression of presentation – practice – production (PPP)." But they also propose other principles, such as the language-exposure principle and the focused-interaction principle, which do not typically feature in PPP methodology. Spada and Tomita, (2010, p. 263) do provide evidence from their meta-analysis of studies that "the results indicate larger effect sizes for explicit over implicit instruction for simple and complex features". The findings also suggest that explicit instruction positively contributes to learners' controlled knowledge and spontaneous use of complex and simple forms. However, such evidence is not empirical support for PPP as such. There are many different approaches to explicit instruction and the survey does not attribute the effects reported to PPP. As Schmidt (2017) says in summarising Spada and Tomita (2010):

> Explicit instruction can come up quite organically in any class, from PPP, to TBLT, to Dogme. It can and should be embedded in meaningful communication. According to Dr. Spada in a personal email, "…explicit attention to language form does not exclude attention to meaning/communication/content other than language. Furthermore, most of the research investigating the effects of instruction on L2 learning indicates that a combination of language-based and meaning-based instructions works better than an exclusive focus on either one".

And, of course, explicit instruction can play an important role in consciousness-raising, discovery, CLIL, problem based and project-based approaches; it can be mediated by a teacher, by a textbook or by a learner and it can be in the form of teacher and student recasting or of responsive teaching when learners need help and of feedback on communicative performance. Also, Spada and Tomita (2010) only compared the effects of explicit grammar instruction with the effects of implicit grammar instruction (i.e. with no explicit instruction at all).

Loewen (2015, p. 84) summarises both sides of the argument about PPP. He points out that it "may not be closely based on the psychological constraints of L2 development", he mentions in particular that "it will not help learners skip steps in the natural order of acquisition", and he considers as contentious the assumption of PPP that "what is taught explicitly can be used to develop the ability to use the language for spontaneous production". However, he does also outline "the skill acquisition theory perspective" that "practice is precisely what is needed to turn declarative knowledge into procedural knowledge".

After considering the evidence, as well as our experience, our view is that PPP can help learners to notice language items and features (and therefore to achieve Intake 1– Perception and Intake 2 – Transfer). However, its typical lack of full contextualisation, of spaced recycling, of meaningfulness and of affective and cognitive engagement make it unlikely that it will consistently achieve Intake 3 – Integration, unless:

> the learners have already encountered the language feature in an engaging text and/or task, have found it problematic and/or interesting and have asked the teacher for information ... providing that the presentation, practice and production relate to the text and/or task and to what the learners found problematic and/or interesting. (Masuhara, 2016, p. 29)

Even then, Intake 3 could only take place if there was spaced recycling of the item or feature and if the learners have opportunities to use it for communication and not just to practise it.

Applications of Neuroscience Research

There is very little literature on the application of what we know from neuroscience to ways of teaching second and foreign languages, but Lethaby and Harries (2017) provide useful advice in making use of research findings in neuroscience to stress the importance of pre-tasks to activate old information in the brain so that it can connect with relevant new information, and when they recommend supporting text with visuals to reduce cognitive load, spreading out practice (i.e. distribution) and encouraging retrieval (all of which are likely to facilitate intake). They also recommend teachers to read Roediger and Pyc (2012) for applications of cognitive psychology to educational practice and Van Kestern et al. (2014) for ways of building on prior knowledge. In addition, we would recommend Masuhara (2016) for suggestions on the application of brain studies to materials development for language learning and Tomlinson (2013a) for discussion of readiness activities designed to activate the learners' minds in relation to relevant previous experience prior to reading or listening to a text.

> **Readers' Task**
>
> 1 Which two of the pedagogic approaches described in this section would you like to use? For each approach, say why you would like to use it, what problems you might have in using it, and how you would try to overcome these problems.
> 2 Choose one of the approaches you have selected in 1 and develop a lesson plan for using it with a particular type of class in an institution you are familiar with.

Application to L2 Materials Development

An analysis of almost any two coursebooks at an equivalent level, whether they be global coursebooks from a major commercial publisher, local or Ministry of Education coursebooks, or institutional coursebooks, will reveal that they follow a PPP approach, that most of the texts and activities are determined by preselection of lexical items and/or structural features and that they follow the same format in every unit (Masuhara & Tomlinson, 2008; Tomlinson & Masuhara, 2013; McGrath, 2016; Tomlinson & Masuhara, 2018b). It will also probably reveal that the two coursebooks are very similar in approach, and maybe in content too.

We have just analysed Unit 2 of *Intermediate Outcomes* (Dellar & Walkley, 2010) and Unit 6 of *Speakout Intermediate* (Clare & Wilson, 2012). Unit 2 in *Intermediate Outcomes* is on Feelings and Unit 6 in *Speakout Intermediate* is on Emotion.

It is noticeable that very few of the determiners of intake outlined in Chapter 2 are catered for in the two units we analysed. Both do include personal questions about the learners' feelings and emotions that could create meaningfulness but, despite the titles of the units, neither attempts to stimulate affective engagement through the texts and activities, and neither caters for psychological readiness, salience, significance, noticing, contextualisation or multidimensional processing. The focus in both books is very much on presentation of lexical items and structural features, practising those items and features, producing them in guided activities and practising listening, speaking, reading and writing. There is very little exposure to English in actual use, and very little opportunity to use English for communication. Most of the activities are practice exercises or tests. For example, there are twelve sentence-completion activities, ten matching activities, five listen-and-repeat activities, two translation activities, two sentence-reordering activities, two choose-the-correct-word activities and two true/false activities. These are all standard coursebook activities, for which there is little research or theoretical support and which achieve a very weak match with the determiners of intake outlined in Chapter 2. There are some questions eliciting personal responses but they are mainly decontextualised and without communicative purpose (e.g. "Complete the sentences so that they are true for you. Compare your ideas with your partner. When I get older ..." (Speakout Intermediate, p. 69); "... write your story ... Use ... the key phrases to help" (Speakout Intermediate, p. 77); "Has your government tried to stop something popular? Why? Was it successful?"; (Intermediate Outcomes, p. 37)). There are also some activities that focus attention on input exemplifying a specific feature but the samples are decontextualized and the activity is without any apparent significance or value to the learner (e.g. "Underline the correct alternative to complete the rules." [Speakout Intermediate, p. 69]). See Tomlinson (2008b, 2013b) for analyses of coursebook activities in relation to SLA research and theory, and Freeman (2014) for an analysis of question types in recent coursebooks.

There are some exceptions to what we have described about coursebooks. We know, for example, of published coursebooks in Ethiopia (Tomlinson, 2004), Japan (Tomlinson & Masuhara, 1994), Namibia (*On Target*, 1995), Norway (Fenner & Nordal Pedersen, 1999, 2006) and Singapore (Tomlinson, Hill & Masuhara, 2000) that provide many opportunities for intake by following a TDA. This is true also of a current project in which the coursebooks for secondary schools in Shanghai are being revised by SCRELE, a research centre for English-language education in the Shanghai International Studies University. Unfortunately, most of these books are constrained by having to match the map of the book to an official syllabus, leading in some cases to a selection of texts that feature prescribed language items and features rather than prioritising their potential for learner engagement. We know also of post-graduate students developing text-driven courses of materials, for example, for China, Columbia, Pakistan, Turkey, United States and Vietnam. Most of these courses follow a strong TDA in which a potentially engaging core text drives each unit rather than teaching points. There are also some courses that follow a CLIL approach (see Coyle, Hood & Marsh, 2010) and some that follow a task-based approach (see Van den Branden, 2006) in which the units of materials are driven by a core task rather than by teaching points. Unfortunately, many courses weaken their task-based approach by pre-teaching language items and features prescribed by an official syllabus and/or examination. See Thomas and Reinders (2015) and especially Tomlinson (2015) for an analysis of such weakened approaches in Asia.

Recently, at the MATSDA/Fontys University of Applied Sciences Conference on Meaning-Focused Language Learning Materials, there were presentations from twenty-five countries describing and demonstrating materials that were meaning-focused. Most of them were informed by many of the determiners of intake that have been outlined, and many of them were text-driven and/or task-based. For example, there was a report from Austria of the PALM Project (Promoting Authentic

Language Acquisition in Multilingual Contexts), a web-based resource for young learners in which videos are made by learners as texts to engage other learners and then drive meaning-focused activities; there was a demonstration of a video course from India (the CLIx English course) in which animated videos telling locally based stories were used to engage learners affectively before involving them in meaning-focused activities; and there was a demonstration of a course from Iran that combined a text-driven and a corpus-based approach in order to maximise intake from input.

Our recommendation is that language-learning materials are most likely to facilitate intake if they:

- accept that not all the input in the materials will become intake;
- accept that predetermined teaching points in the input are unlikely to become intake unless the texts and activities match many of the determiners of intake we have outlined above (especially salience, meaningfulness, spaced repetition, noticing and psychological readiness);
- focus on providing rich and varied inputs in written, spoken and audio-visual texts that have the potential to engage the target learners affectively and cognitively;
- provide activities that offer achievable challenges, stimulate personal responses, offer choice, encourage interaction and give scope for creativity;
- focus on discovery of form from meaningful and contextualised input and from communicative use rather than from instruction and practice;
- encourage responsive teaching to help individuals and groups during task preparation.

From our experience in institutions around the world and with publishers, we know that we do need to acknowledge the reality of the need of Ministries of Education to standardise, to provide equal opportunities and to achieve face validity in the eyes of politicians, administrators, parents, employers, teachers and students. We also need to acknowledge the need of institutions to cover syllabuses, to prepare learners for examinations and to be accountable for learner success and learner failure. So, it would be unrealistic to expect the situation to change overnight. And if it did, this would also be threatening to experienced teachers, teacher trainers, inspectors and principals whose careers have been built up on the strength of their knowledge of and expertise in the current norms (see Kennedy & Tomlinson, 2013 for examples of the above and also of innovative language policies that have been weakened at the implementation stage by materials developers and teachers). It would also be unrealistic to expect publishers to risk developing dramatically innovative materials when their lack of face validity could result in financial loss. We know, for example, of a text-driven textbook published in Japan that was popular with our students but sold very few copies (Tomlinson & Masuhara, 1994), of a text-driven language-through-literature textbook published by a major UK publisher that was popular with our students and received critical acclaim (Tomlinson, 1994) but was not a commercial success, and of a coursebook that was a resource book facilitating teacher and learner choice of entry point, route and activity, which did not sell as well as expected. One thing we also know though is that learners are less resistant to change than is generally thought, especially if the change promises something more interesting and potentially useful than what they are accustomed to (see Tomlinson, 2005a; Darici & Tomlinson, 2016).

See R. Ellis (2010a, 2016a), Ellis and Shintani (2013), Harwood (2010), McGrath (2016), Tomlinson (2008a, 2010, 2011b, 2013b, 2013c, 2016a, 2016b) and Tomlinson and Masuhara (2018b) for recommendations for the application of principles developed from SLA research to the development of L2 learning materials. Tomlinson (2011b) lists sixteen principles derived from SLA research and suggests how each can be applied to materials development. For example, he recommends lots of white space between activities so as to prevent clutter, anxiety and cognitive overload, he advocates creating readiness to acquire through motivating activities which require the use of features not yet taught, and he favours activities that support rather than test learners, particularly those in which the materials developers' voices are relaxed, personal and supportive and "chat to the learners casually in the same way that good teachers do" (p. 9) (see Beck, McKeowan & Worthy, 1995 for research evidence of the value of the use of a personal voice in textbook instruction).

Just in case you get the impression that we are the only researchers who are critical of the disconnect between current SLA theory and typical ELT materials, here is a quote from Steve Brown:

> [T]here is much about popular ELT materials and their provenance that is problematic. The mismatch between their design and widely accepted principles of SLA, the lack of inclusion of topics that encourage learners to engage critically with issues of injustice or inequality, the seemingly uncritical presentation of dominant global, neoliberal values such as materialism and competitiveness, and the excessive reliance on standardisation as a means of quality assurance, all raise questions about the validity of these materials as effective teaching aids. (Brown, 2020)

Application to L2 Teaching

For the reasons discussed in Chapter 2, teacher input cannot all become learner intake. Each learner will achieve a different intake and it will always be a lot less than the input they are provided with. However, in addition to using methodologies and materials with a potential for facilitating Intake 3 – Integration, teachers can also help their learners to achieve intake through:

Task-Free Activities

A task-free activity involves the teacher "performing" a potentially engaging authentic poem, story, joke, article, song, extract from a novel, play, film or newspaper or a personal anecdote at the beginning of each lesson. No tasks follow the "performance", but learners who have been engaged by the text can take a printed copy of it at the end of the lesson, put it in a file of texts that have engaged them and read it whenever they want to. The teacher does not interrogate the learners about the texts, but the learners often ask the teacher questions about them days or even weeks later.

Experience in our classrooms, and of many of our workshop participants, has shown that learners tend to enjoy and appreciate this stress-free activity (for example, learners of German at the then Leeds Metropolitan University found it to be both the most interesting and the most useful part of their course). For many learners, it massively increases their engaged exposure to the language in use, it encourages tolerance of ambiguity and multidimensional processing, and the subsequent reading of the text can encourage noticing of the use of language items and features.

Chatting with the Learners

Many learners have no opportunities to experience the L2 in use outside their classroom and are therefore dependent on the teacher for input and interaction. Instead of teacher talk being discouraged, as it is on many teacher-training courses, we believe that it should be encouraged, providing that it involves the teacher chatting with the learners about topics that interest them and not lecturing them about topics they are not interested in. When such chat occurs, it can enrich learner input and learner opportunities for interaction and offer opportunities for Intake 3 – Integration as a result of salience and noticing from repetition and clarification, of affective and cognitive engagement and of meaningfulness.

See Tomlinson (2014b) for more discussion of the value of teacher talk.

Responsive Teaching

We believe that learners learn best what they need and want to learn. They have their own agendas, which rarely coincide with the teaching syllabus used in coursebooks and in PPP teaching in the classroom. These needs and wants are often not evident, but can be made overt (and even created) during classroom activities, especially those involving the learners using the target language in TBLT, CLIL, AoA, problem-based, text-driven, creative writing and project-based approaches. It is during such production tasks that explicit teaching is most useful, as the teacher's input is likely to be much more significant, meaningful and comprehensible than during the presentation stages of forms-focused approaches.

Provision of Supplementary Input

It is generally agreed that coursebooks and teachers are not able to provide sufficient input during class time and that therefore the provision of supplementary input is essential. Teachers can do this by establishing class self-access centres, or at least class libraries, if funds are available, or by getting their learners to develop their own class self-access centres or libraries. In many ways, getting learners to do it for themselves is more likely to lead to Intake 3 – Integration, as not only are they likely to find reading, listening and viewing materials that are meaningful and engaging for their fellow learners but they can gain valuable experience of the language whilst looking for such texts. This is what happened when, for example, a teacher in Jakarta encouraged her learners to bring an interesting text in English each week to put in the class library (a huge cardboard box) and when a teacher in Japan encouraged her learners to record something interesting in English each week to add to the class listening library. The learners in Jakarta actually looked up English-sounding names in the telephone directory and then went knocking on doors asking people if they had anything interesting to read in English; they also went to embassies, hotels, travel agents etc. and had some interesting conversations in English when doing so. The learners in Japan listened to a lot of songs, films and discussions in English whilst making their selections.

Of course, nowadays the Internet is a rich source of supplementary input and many written, spoken and audio-visual texts are freely available from, for example:

- world-wide news in English (www.thebigproject.co.uk/news/);
- poems from such websites as www.poemhunter.com/, which makes thousands of poems available;
- fiction on the web (for example from www.fictionontheweb.co.uk/);
- free sources of TV adverts on the web such as www.tellyads.com/, which makes 21,000 adverts available to download;
- sources of videos such as https://plus.google.com/+YouTube, https://www.youtube.com/?gl=GB and https://www.ted.com/talks

These web links are taken from Tomlinson and Masuhara (2018b). For many more recommendations go to pp. 391–398 in Tomlinson and Masuhara (2018b) and, for suggestions for rich supplementation for young learners, see Bland (2015, 2018).

Provision of Supplementary Interaction

Teachers can help their learners to gain from extra opportunities for purposeful interaction in the target language by:

- organising clubs in which voluntary members agree to always talk to each other in the target language when they meet inside or outside their institution (Barker, 2010a, 2010b);

- inviting proficient speakers of the target language to meet their learners at social events in the school;
- arranging for Skype exchanges with learners in other schools;
- arranging for chats and/or email exchanges with learners in other schools;
- making films and/or putting on plays in the target language;
- chatting with a small group of learners whilst the others are engaged in a focused activity.

Recently, there has been increased interest in the value of out-of-class provision of opportunities for supplementary input and interaction, with an AILA 2020 Symposium being conducted at the AILA World Congress in Groninghen on "Learning through leisure: Informal second language learning in the 21st century". The focus of this symposium is on the research conducted so far on online, informal learning of languages, referred to in the literature as Informal Digital Learning or Online Informal Learning. Much of this research has been on the attitudes and inclinations of learners and their willingness to communicate in in-class, out-of-class and digital contexts (see, for example, Jurkovič, 2018; Lee, 2019; Lee & Hseih, 2019) as well as on the value of informal online engagement with a target language (see, for example, Sockett, 2014; Lech & Harris, 2019). The findings suggest that:

- confidence is the major factor in willingness to communicate regardless of the context;
- "contemporary EFL students may feel more comfortable with digital methods of communicating than conventional offline approaches, whether they use L1 or L2)" (Lee & Hseih, 2019, abstract);
- "digital environments may provide social support and additional psychological benefits, which potentially contribute to creating a less L2 anxiety-provoking environment for EFL students" (Lee & Hseih, 2019, abstract)
- unintentioned learning can result from informal engagement with online use of native or non-native use of English for purposes of gaining entertainment or information (Sockett, 2014);
- "the use of online informal learning of language activities with students learning English as an L2 results in higher fluency, lower error rates, and greater engagement" (Lech & Harris, 2019, p. 39).

Establishment of a Positive Learning Environment

The more positive the learning environment is, the more likely it is that language features and items in the input will become intake. The teacher can maximise positivity by:

- establishing rapport with the learners
- encouraging the learners to make their learning environment attractive (bringing pictures, flowers, ornaments, etc. to the class)

- being pleasant and cheerful
- having a sense of humour
- being interesting
- being supportive
- being understanding
- being patient
- getting to know the learners
- not being judgemental
- not being sarcastic
- minimising tests

Permitting Silence

Teachers do not seem to be comfortable with silence. Often when they ask questions, they demand immediate answers and deny their learners the silent time they need to process the input and prepare their output. Often teachers set a reading task and then interrupt their learners by giving advice, making comments, setting activities, etc. and thus deny their learners the silence they need to process the input. Very often teachers do not allow students to hide in discussions and deny them their right to be silent whilst thinking about what other people are saying.

For research and discussion of the value of silence in the language-learning classroom see Bao (2014), which reports research in Vietnam, for example, that reveals that learners are often talking to themselves in or about the L2 when they are silent, and that learners who do not contribute orally to group or class discussions often gain a lot through attentive listening to interaction. See also Bao (2020) for discussion of East-Asian students use of silence during task response in an Australian university and King and Seiko (2020) for other research reports of East-Asian perspectives on silence in English language education.

Application to L2 Assessment

Many tests are administered in classrooms immediately after attention has been paid to input, either from instruction or from revision for a test. The same is true even for high-stake examinations when the syllabus for an examination is prescribed and students pay a lot of attention to linguistic items on the syllabus immediately prior to taking the examination (e.g. in China, and many other countries where the lexical items to be taught and tested are prescribed by the Ministry of Education). In such cases, the learners are being assessed on their ability to intake from input (an important enabling ability) rather than on their acquisition of language and their ability to use it (the main objective of most language-learning courses). We all know of learners who get good marks on language tests (and even examinations) but never acquire the ability to actually communicate in their target language. Brian, for example, passed "O" Level and

"A" Level French at school (mainly as a result of assiduous revision) but cannot communicate in French.

In order to ensure that learners are assessed on their acquisition of language and their ability to use it, it is important that they are not just assessed on their ability to intake language items from input. This ability is a prerequisite for acquisition, but it is an unreliable indicator of eventual acquisition as many of the items taken in never get passed on to long-term memory and never receive the further processing they need for acquisition. In order to ensure authentic assessment, it is important that:

- there is a considerable gap between teaching and testing;
- if learners are going to be tested on language items, the learners (and ideally their teachers) do not know which items they will be tested on;
- learners are examined on their ability to use the target language rather than their ability to recall what is stored in their short-term memory.

Another important point is that in many school and coursebook tests, learners are deemed to be unsuccessful if they fail to demonstrate intake of prescribed items and features from the input. The lack of intake might have nothing to do with aptitude or application. It might instead be a result of the lack of salience and/or significance of these items or features in the input, of the inability of teachers and/or materials to engage the learners affectively and cognitively, of lack of encouragement to process input multidimensionally, of lack of relevance or meaningfulness of the input, of lack of opportunities for spaced encounters, of lack of developmental or psychological readiness or of an excessive learning load imposed by a syllabus or coursebook. If we are to persist in setting such tests, it would be useful if we analysed the results to find out which items and features in the input did not progress to Intake 3, to try to find out why they did not become part of the learners' intake and to work out ways of facilitating intake of the items and features still considered to be potentially significant for the learners. It would also be useful if the tests were devised in ways that facilitated Intake 3 prior to, during and following the tests. For discussion of ways of testing to learn see Tomlinson (2005b) and see Hattie (2011), *Getting started with assessment* (2018) and Hattie and Clark (2018) for discussion of currently popular Assessment for Learning (AFL) approaches in which the teacher creates opportunities for feedback to learners that could help them to improve the communicative performance in the L2. See also Hughes (2002) for discussion of connections between teaching and testing, Mueller (2018) for a powerful indictment of current ways of assessment and Davies et al. (2018) for a book that focuses on ways of assessment and evaluation that are useful for both teachers and learners, and unusually contains a chapter on the use of assessment to help identify neurolinguistic correlates of proficiency.

Implications for L2 Teacher Development

Awareness of all the applications of SLA theory and practice outlined above should be an important goal of development courses for language teachers (especially the applications for methodology and for materials development). It will not be achieved by trainee or in-service teachers taking theoretical courses in applied linguistics in general and in SLA in particular. But it can be achieved by facing teachers with current realities and problems in their teaching contexts and by guiding them towards the SLA research that could help them to come up with solutions. In relation to this particular chapter, it could be very useful if teachers in training were given information about intake and then set the task of developing ways of helping learners to achieve it. Awareness could also be achieved by encouraging teacher exploration in the sense that they observe and evaluate the effects of syllabuses, of methodologies, of materials and of assessment practices on their learners, and that they conduct action research projects to see if they can influence positive change. For example, they could use observations, questionnaires, interviews and focus groups to find out the views and opinions of learners as well as conducting research featuring pre-testing and post-testing to discover the actual effects of methods, materials and instruments of assessment. From 2020, MATSDA intends to run learner conferences, in which language learners will give presentations on their experiences of materials in action. We are hoping this will prove useful for learners, for teachers, for teacher developers, for researchers and for materials developers.

Readers' Tasks

1 Take any coursebook.

Analyse a unit from the coursebook to discover how many of the determiners of intake outlined in this chapter and in Chapter 2 are catered for by it.

Suggest ways of catering for more of these determiners in an adaptation of the unit designed to maximise its potential for intake.

2 Evaluate each of the following approaches in relation to its ability to maximise intake from the input it provides:
- PPP
- Task-based Teaching (TBT)
- CLIL
- The TDA

For descriptions of these approaches, see Application to L2 Methodology in this chapter, Richards and Rodgers (2014) and Chapter 8 of Tomlinson and Masuhara (2018b).

3 Now you have read the whole of Chapter 3, go back to the table you used in the first Readers' Task in this chapter and make any modifications or additions you would now like to make.

FURTHER READING

Ellis, R. (2010). Second language acquisition, teacher education, and language pedagogy. *Language Teaching. 43*(2), 182–201.

Ellis, R. & Shintani, N. (2013). *Exploring language pedagogy through second language acquisition research*. New York: Routledge.

Loewen, S. (2015). The acquisition of grammar. In *Introduction to instructed second language acquisition* (pp. 76–94). New York: Routledge.

Tomlinson, B. (2013). Language acquisition research and materials development. In B. Tomlinson (Ed.), *Applied linguistics and materials development* (pp. 11–30). London: Continuum.

(2016). Achieving a match between SLA research and materials development. In B. Tomlinson (Ed.), *SLA research and materials development for language learning* (pp. 3–22). New York: Routledge.

Tomlinson, B. & Masuhara, H. (2018). Developing materials for the acquisition of language. In B. Tomlinson & H. Masuhara, *The complete guide to the theory and practice of materials development for language learning* (pp. 189–219). Hoboken, NJ: Wiley-Blackwell.

4 Further Processing, Acquisition and Development

Part One: Theory

Introduction

So far, in Chapter 1 we have defined input as *multimodal data that the receiver is exposed to during communication*. We have identified the kinds and nature of input, and have discussed contemporary and interdisciplinary issues that have tended to be overlooked in past studies.

In Chapter 2 we have explored intake (i.e. *language and the accompanying nonlinguistic and extra-linguistic features from the learner's input that have been taken into the brain for comprehension and for potential processing*). We have considered what the existing literature says about the process and product of L1/L2 learners' intake, and we have proposed six possible types of determiners that interact with each other and influence intake (i.e. linguistic, psycholinguistic, sociolinguistic, environmental, experiential, pedagogic).

In this chapter, we will investigate further processing, acquisition and development. The questions that we aim to find indicative answers to include:

- What happens after a learner extracts elements of input as intake?
- When and how does language acquisition happen?
- Once language acquisition has occurred, what happens to the acquired language?
- Will the acquired language change? If so, in what way?

The developmental language-learning process is complex, dynamic and individualistic. However, we will leave individual differences for discussion in Chapter 9: Some Salient Issues in SLA Research.

Let us begin by providing definitions of the three terms in the title of this chapter. By "further processing" we refer to the mental processes in which features of the existing intake are recycled, reactivated, revised and strengthened in different contexts before acquisition can be said to have taken place.

By "acquisition", we mean an emergent stage in which learners display some consistency in their ability to achieve communicative effect as a result of new elements that are being integrated into existing neural systems (e.g. a baby starts to use "mama" to mean mother in an intelligible and consistent manner; an adult manages to differentiate in her L2 between using the simple present and using the present continuous when answering a doctor's questions).

We are using "development" to mean further refinement, complexity and sophistication in our acquired networks, which may be manifested as competent language use in numerous socioculturally appropriate and effective ways.

Our distinction follows on from that made by Tomlinson (2007a, p. 1):

> between "acquisition" as the initial stage of gaining basic communicative competence in a language and "development" as the subsequent stage of gaining the ability to use the language successfully in a wide range of media and genre for a wide variety of purposes. Acquisition in this distinction is viewed as gaining mastery of an efficient restricted code which makes use of a limited repertoire to achieve effective communication, whilst development is seen as a process of gaining mastery of an elaborated code capable of achieving effective communication in a wide variety of situations.

This distinction between acquisition and development seems to us to be a useful one when learners are being taught to acquire language items listed in a syllabus; but it is not always useful, if ever, when they are given further opportunities to develop their use of the acquired linguistic items to the level at which they can consistently achieve real-life outcomes through effective communication in the target language – something that not all native speakers of a language manage to achieve.

Historical Approaches to Exploring Invisible Mental Processes

The phenomena of "Further Processing, Acquisition and Development" are mental "constructs" i.e. invisible inner mechanisms in our mind that are not easily amenable to direct observation, analysis or measurement. Various attempts have been made though, with available investigation methods, in order to probe into mental processes by researchers in such different fields as linguistics, applied linguistics, first-language acquisition, SLA, psychology and neuroscience.

Recently, increasing interdisciplinary efforts have been made in order to capture the complex nature and procedures of language processing, acquisition and development. The advancement of technology has contributed to more sophisticated computer simulations, to the construction of language interactional corpora and to the more direct exploration of biological architectures and chemical and physiological activities in the human brain in both non-invasive and invasive ways. N. Ellis (2019) provides a useful and up-to-date review of various strands of thought in psychology as well as in sociocultural and computational psycholinguistic fields. The Douglas Fir Group (2016) reappraises SLA studies from a contemporary multilingual perspective, focuses on language-learning environments (as well as learners and language-learning processes) and identifies future directions.

In order to understand the current situation, we need some understanding of the historical linguistic and psychological theories that have influenced the development of language acquisition and pedagogy. Saville-Troike and Barto (2017) provides introductory accounts and Gass and Mackey (2012) offers collections of representative authors in the major relevant disciplines.

We will first review some of the influential strands of theories and arguments in various fields that have emerged in relation to L1 acquisition since the field of L2 acquisition developed around the 1970s and 1980s. Then we will further discuss what has been studied in relation to L2 acquisition and development that we have found to offer potential for application to many actual contexts of learning. The literature we are reviewing is relevant to the focus of this chapter but does not directly address our distinctions between further processing, acquisition and development. So, following our review we will propose possible accounts of what might be involved in L2 "further processing, acquisition and development", supported by reference to our experience as learners, teachers and researchers and to what relevant research the literature does report. Then we will discuss implications for practice.

Snapshots from L1 Acquisition

When we explore the sea of theories, we find it useful to have a compass that points to the final destination – i.e. the most plausible theoretical accounts of the phenomena in question. Our ultimate question is: what kinds of processes are involved in our language learning, acquisition and development?

Peccei (2002, p. 1) provides us with an example of acquisition and development in English as an L1:

Christian, one month old, not keen on having a bath:
Waaaaaaa!
Christian, two years old, not keen on hearing a scary story:
No talk!
Christian, 4 1/2 years old, not keen on leaving for his first day at school:
Mum, I don't think I want to go through with this!

Christian in this example entered a world surrounded by more competent users of L1. At first, all the physical and verbal interactions with adults around him must have meant very little. Within a few years, he has become able to use more and more words in different combinations to achieve his communicative purposes. Increasing cognitive maturity then allows him to apply what he has acquired, not only to the "here-and-now" but also to different times (past, future) and to virtual worlds, as in stories and in his imagination. Language enables him to be part of the community, which in turn helps him to enhance his repertoire of language use. In the same way, a young, teenage or adult L2 learner, surrounded by more proficient users of the language, can go through the same stages of bewilderment, accommodation, comprehension and eventual competence, a process it has been assumed can be accelerated by putting learners together at the same level of accomplishment and supporting them with a teacher. What have theorists proposed to account for this progression?

Exploring Invisible Constructs of Learning: Reappraisal of Past Attempts and Implications for Further Processing, Language Acquisition and Development

Throughout the twentieth century, especially since the 1950s, various hypotheses of the process of language acquisition have been proposed. Some of the insights have created the foundations of contemporary views of further processing, acquisition and development. We will sample many of the influential strands and consider their tenets, their investigatory tools and the approaches used for their theory building, before we attempt to extract a generalised account in a later section in this chapter.

Universal Grammar and the Language Acquisition Device – Linguists' Theoretical Proposition

Linguists in the transformational generative grammar (TG) tradition, originally led by Chomsky (1957, 1965, 1995) and other TG theorists, such as Lightfoot (2006), proclaim an innate view of L1 language acquisition. They envisage that all languages share basic mechanisms and they theorise the existence of a universal grammar (UG), which consists of a finite set of principles and parameters that are genetically encoded in the brain. They argue that human children are endowed with a mental faculty, what Chomsky calls the language acquisition device (LAD), which recognises cues in the often ill-formed input in their environment and autonomously manages to develop a sophisticated system of language in their minds. When Krashen describes how SLA takes place (1981, 1985), he assumes the existence of the LAD (see Chapter 1 Input for more details) in both L1 and L2 acquisition.

How might the UG/LAD theory explain Christian's language development phenomena introduced in the section "L1 Acquisition – Snapshots from L1 Acquisitions"? If we follow the logic of the UG/LAD theory, Christian was exposed to a variety of inputs in his environment during pre-birth and post-birth. His innate LAD recognised appropriate language elements in the light of the UG in his brain. He filtered out extraneous data and retained the possible varieties of UG as intake. The further processing by Christian's LAD might have involved matching, accumulating and autonomously developing more complicated and refined grammar systems that would enable Christian to produce grammatically well-formed output, even though some real-life constraints (e.g. memory lapse, physical conditions) might affect his actual performance. A very similar process could be experienced by an adult immigrant immersed in an English-speaking environment and who makes use of exposure to gradually progress from gestures and "grunts" to interlanguage utterances, to recognisable English use and eventually to the achievement of intended outcomes in near native-like English.

Do note here that the concepts of UG and LAD were theory driven and did not derive from empirical studies of L1 acquisition studies. The main focus of the TG theorists has been to identify components and the mechanism of sentence generation and transformation, from deep to surface structures, and the influence of UG and LAD has been pervasive "in theories of language evolution, language acquisition, neurocognition, parsing and speech recognition, and just about every branch of the cognitive sciences" (Evans & Levinson, 2009, p. 429).

As we will see though, the fundamental assumptions that support UG/LAD concepts have been challenged in the light of newer research instruments and an emphasis on empiricism (i.e. data-based studies):

Arguments against the Existence of Universal Grammar Cross-linguistic studies seem to show more diversity than uniformity between languages. Based on their survey of decades of cross-linguistic studies by typologists and descriptive linguists, Evans and Levinson (2009) and Levinson and Evans (2010) question the existence of UG across languages, as in:

> A widespread assumption among cognitive scientists, growing out of the generative tradition in linguistics, is that all languages are English-like but with different sound systems and vocabularies. The true picture is very different: languages differ so fundamentally from one another at every level of description (sound, grammar, lexicon, meaning) that it is very hard to find any single structural property they share. The claims of Universal Grammar, we argue here, are either empirically false, unfalsifiable, or misleading in that they refer to tendencies rather than strict universals. Structural differences should instead be accepted for what they are and integrated into a new approach to language and cognition that places diversity at centre stage. (Evans & Levinson, 2009, p. 429)

Arbib (2015), from the perspective of the evolution of the neural development of language use, supports the views of Evans and Levinson, arguing that the recurrence of some features across languages may be explained by different factors such as human's physical–cognitive constraints and/or historical–cultural factors influencing across languages rather than the so-called UG.

Arguments against the Premise of the UG/LAD The poverty of the stimulus contained in natural input was one of the main reasons for the argument of the existence of LAD. The corpus studies of child-directed speech (e.g. Motherese; Caretakers' speech), however, reveal systematicity and richness of input, displaying abundant and systematic phonological, morphological, lexical and/or syntactic examples of communicative language in use (e.g. Ambridge & Lieven, 2011, 2015; Clark, 2015, 2017).

Clark (2015), for example, explains the importance of establishing personal, local and communal commonality through communication, which results in children's overall development. Such communication includes much needed abundant repetitions and emphasis on the kind of forms that children need in order to understand what others intend, to convey their own intentions and to be understood. Child-directed speech is also known to change as children grow, in terms of kinds of language features and levels of complexity, resonating with the sociocultural theory by Vygotsky (Vygotsky, 1978, 1962/1986/2012) in relation to the concepts of zone of proximal development and more-knowledgeable others, which facilitate children's cognitive and language development. The same could be said of an L2 learners' experience of learning an L2, except that often their input in classrooms is impoverished and their restricted exposure to communicative language in use might be responsible for many of them not achieving sufficient intake from their input, not further processing what they do intake, acquiring very little and never achieving development.

Implications of UG/LAD for our Discussion of "Further Processing, Language Acquisition and Development"

Going back to the phenomena of Christian's L1 development in the earlier section "L1 Acquisition – Snapshots from L1 Acquisition", it is vital that we are grounded in the reality of language use in communal surroundings when we consider that:

> children's language acquisition is ... a by-product of ... their use of language as a social tool. Children are not "trying" to learn syntax; they are not conducting formal analyses of linguistic structure, combining content-free algebraic symbols, setting parameters, or building abstract linguistic categories for their own sake; they are using language, to cajole, to control and to communicate. (Ambridge & Lieven, 2015, p. 478)

Ambridge and Lieven describe what children are not trying to do during their successful natural acquisition of language. Interestingly, these are all things that instructed learners of an L2 try to do (e.g. trying deliberately to learn syntax). It could be that such explicit efforts to learn inhibit successful acquisition. Or it could be that, as most L2 teachers might argue, instructed L2 learners need these extra activities to compensate for the poverty of input, the brevity of instructed time and the lack of immediate need for successful acquisition. The likelihood is that there is truth in both positions, but we are inclined to favour providing as many opportunities for natural acquisition as possible in and out of L2 classrooms while also providing explicit support.

Psychological Studies

Various psychological theories have influenced the fields of L1 and L2 acquisition, applied linguistics and our own views of learning (i.e. what is called in this book "further processing, acquisition and development"). We will consider the following influential strands in psychology:

1. Classical conditioning, behaviourism, operant conditioning and the audio-lingual method
2. Cognitive science, information processing (IP) and parallel distributed processing (PDP)
3. Neuroscience and neurocognition

Classical Conditioning Pavlov's experiments involving dogs responding to a "bell" (see Todes, 2014) are widely known. Pavlov's theory (Pavlov, 1927/1960/2003; 1928) is often called "classical conditioning" and inspired behaviourist psychologists such as J. B. Watson and B. F. Skinner. As behaviourist psychology was behind the influential audio-lingual method, we will trace how these psychological theories have influenced language-teaching practice in the past (and, in our experience around the world, even now in a surprisingly persistent and pervasive manner).

Pavlov was not a psychologist but a Nobel prize (1904) winning physiologist who investigated the anatomy, cells and biological compound secretions of digestive systems and their mechanisms. When he was furthering his studies in later life through strict objective "scientific research methods", Pavlov came across a puzzling phenomenon, which led to the discovery of how the mammalian brain learns a new conditioned behaviour by adapting existing unconditioned behaviour (Pavlov, 1927/1960/2003; 1928).

The theory can be summarised as follows:

- The stimuli of food in the mouth triggers salivation due to an inbuilt reflex that requires no training or learning (i.e. unconditioned stimulus – unconditioned response). Though the experiment was performed with dogs, Pavlov explained in an interview with journalists that humans share the same unconditioned reflexes (Todes, 2014).
- Neutral stimuli, such as the ticking of a metronome or a research assistant's white robes, do not cause a dog's salivation. However, when Pavlov's dogs repeatedly noticed the assistant approaching to give food, or heard the metronome prior to eating food, they started to salivate. The neutral stimuli began to spark off salivation even when the actual food was not given. Pavlov realised that the dogs had been conditioned to respond to neutral stimuli through associative learning (i.e. a modified neural circuitry in the cerebral cortex occurred through association and adaptation of existing inbuilt unconditioned circuitry).

- Pavlov's repeated studies revealed that such conditioned behaviours can be lost (extinction) without the continued association, or in some cases revived (spontaneous recovery) when the conditioned connection was activated again.

Note here that, though Pavlov strongly argued for a strict, objective, data-based approach to scientific investigation, his ultimate aim was to eventually uncover the physiological explanation of human psychological phenomena such as consciousness, as can be seen in his Nobel lecture (Pavlov, 1904):

> Essentially only one thing in life interests us: our psychical constitution, the mechanism of which was and is wrapped in darkness. All human resources, art, religion, literature, philosophy and historical sciences, all of them join in bringing light in this darkness. But man has still another powerful resource: natural science with its strictly objective methods. This science, as we all know, is making huge progress every day. (www.nobelprize.org/prizes/medicine/1904/pavlov/lecture/)

Natural sciences, such as physiology, use a reductionist approach (i.e. studying a simple system in order to explore a more complex system). According to detailed biographical records by Todes (2014), Pavlov was open to logical generalisations and speculations. For example, as the basics of the neural components and mechanisms throughout mammals are identical, he was confident that the adaptive/associative learning principles of conditioning apply to human beings. He was also aware of the possible involvement of subcortical parts of the brain (considered in Pavlov's era in Russia to be the source of "instinct") in conditioned learning, which are widely considered nowadays to be the fundamental areas of whole brain learning that contribute to the human's mind, affect, behaviour and language acquisition.

Implications of Pavlovian Classical Conditioning for our discussion of "further processing, acquisition and development" Let us go back to the case of Christian in the section "Snapshots from L1 Acquisition". Christian had accumulated an auditory memory of his mum during the latter part of pregnancy and spent his first year being exposed to multisensory and linguistic input in an embodied manner through his sensory–motor bodily interactions with himself, his family and his communal surroundings.

Christian, as a new-born baby, repeatedly experienced such pleasant tactile sensations as being cuddled, his mother's gentle voice and the smell and taste of milk during the breast-feeding period. Eventually, Christian realises that the same auditory signal "mum" or "mummy" is being repeated when the same or similar pleasant and life-sustaining events happen.

The linguistic symbol "mum" in itself is a neutral stimulus. It could be a metronome, buzzer or dummy, or even a car, provided that the symbol is simple and easy for the infant to learn and utter.

What matters is that the word "mum" for an infant is associated with feeding and pleasant sensations. Put in physiological terms, some basic unconditioned stimulus and unconditioned response reflex is cultivated as a life-sustaining mechanism across species as a result of evolutional development. When Christian utters the sound "mum" one-and-a-half years after his birth, he realises the likely effects are enthusiastic responses and more nourishing experience of cuddles and pleasant sensations. He learns to call out "mum" when he is hungry, thirsty or in need of care. When mum is not around, he may start to cry out for "mum". The neutral word "mum" has been acquired by adaptation of and association with various life-sustaining, nonverbal, unconditioned reflexes such as sucking a nipple and feeling close when cuddled.

In sum, language acquisition could be seen as an extension of classical conditioning, in the sense that humans, as a species of mammals, become conditioned to comprehend and eventually use the neutral stimuli of linguistic symbols (a word or combination of words) and expressions (words with syntax) by adaptive and associative learning through existing unconditioned networks (Arbib, 2015).

Classical conditioning happens to human adults as well as children. When you think of the word "lemon", you may experience saliva in the mouth. Acidic food in our mouth triggers salivation as our body tries to counteract the acid by releasing saliva, which is slightly alkaloid, prior to digestion. This is an unconditioned reflex to protect our digestive systems. The word "lemon" is a linguistic symbol that is a neutral stimulus. As we consume lemons and experience the unconditioned response in our mouth, the co-occurring neutral stimulus of the linguistic symbol "lemon" can trigger our unconditioned response of salivation, even without an actual lemon. This is another example of classical conditioning.

This classical conditioning can be observed in a more abstract, cognitive and affective manner in the lives of individuals. Remarkable developments in neuroscience have allowed us to discuss classical conditioning from contemporary perspectives with what we understand about neural learning. For example, a smell can trigger vivid memories and reactions. Olfactory areas of the brain are specialised (but not exclusively) to process smell. They are physically close to, and have robust connections with, the limbic systems, which are associated with crucial functions for survival and well-being. The limbic systems consist of various anatomical areas in the brain: e.g. the hypothalamus and thalamus – the control centres for fundamental life sustenance; the amygdalas – areas that add positive or negative emotional colouring; the hippocampi – central areas for memory formation. It makes evolutionary sense that such strong links exist between the sensation of smells and the limbic system in any organism so as to immediately ignite "fight or flight" reactions.

The limbic systems lie deep between the outer layer called the "neocortex" and the core areas of the brain (i.e. the brain stem and cerebellum – the so-called little brain). The neocortex is associated with cognition, sensory and motor processing and memory storage. Core areas of the brain control breathing, perspiration, balance, movement and other functions that are fundamental for survival. The limbic systems connect the primitive core with a more newly developed outer-layer neocortex, while adding emotional colouring and forming memory. Thus, all parts of the brain work together to create a whole brain experience in order to ensure survival, be it biological or social/communal in the case of some animals, including humans.

Going back to the example of smell, in classical-conditioning terms, specific smells, such as coffee or perfume, are neutral stimuli. However, the smell of coffee or perfume may come to be associated with life-enriching experiences. Then these smells could become conditioned stimuli and link with unconditioned responses. Strong association, in fact, could lead to strong emotional and cognitive reactions and behaviours. The best-known example of the power of smell evoking memories and emotions is known in psychology as the "Proust effect", based on the section of the novel "*Remembrance of Time Past*" by French writer Marcel Proust, in which the experience of having tea and a cake led to a sudden and strong evocation of the long forgotten memory of childhood (for a neuroscientific explanation, see Shepherd & Shepherd-Barr, 2009). We have similar experiences with tastes, with for example the taste of gravy evoking clear images for Brian of childhood lunches at his grandma's house.

Behaviourism The theory of behaviourism originated in the United States. Pavlov (1928) conducted some invited lectures there and his works were influential in the United States around that time. J. B. Watson was familiar with Pavlov's works, as can be seen in his PhD thesis on psychology.

Watson is one of the prominent pioneers in the behaviourist movement because of his contribution in defining the scope and methods for psychology. In an effort to establish psychology as a respectable field of science, Watson publicised the behaviourist principles, for example, in a journal article, "Psychology as the behaviorist views it" (1913, p. 158), which is sometimes described as the "behaviorist manifesto":

> Psychology as the behaviorist views it is a purely objective experimental branch of natural science. Its theoretical goal is the prediction and control of behavior. Introspection forms no essential part of its methods, nor is the scientific value of its data dependent upon the readiness with which they lend themselves to interpretation in terms of consciousness. The behaviorist, in his efforts to get a unitary scheme of animal response, recognizes no dividing line between man and brute. The behavior of man, with all of its refinement and complexity, forms only a part of the behaviorist's total scheme of investigation.

The behaviourists' principles can be characterised as follows. Behaviourism:

- aims to predict and control behaviour of both humans and animals rather than rely on such unusable concepts as consciousness or cognition.
- uses scientific methods of enquiry that are replicable and reliable i.e. use of objective experimental research methods of analysing external behaviour.

- denounces unscientific psychological approaches, such as introspection or interpretation of elusive inner thoughts, as being subjective and unscientific.
- searches for simple mechanisms that constitute complex behaviours (e.g. stimulus–response, classical conditioning).

Note here that Watson (1913) dismissed introspective and interpretative approaches as unscientific and excluded any non-observable inner workings such as mind, memory, beliefs, consciousness or genetic heredity as unworthy of psychological studies. He assumed all behaviours can be explained by "stimulus–response" mechanisms that manifest as observable external behaviours. He did not consider investigating possible cortical or subcortical substances that underlie the behaviours. These views differ from the ones the physiologist Pavlov emphasised: i.e. the ultimate goal of discovering the mechanism of "psychical constitution" through strictly objective methods in natural science (Pavlov, 1904; Todes, 2014). Watson's methods may be "strictly objective" but his decisions, it seems to us, may not be so.

Implications of Watson's Methodological Behaviorism for "further processing, language acquisition and development" The "nature vs nurture" metaphor is sometimes used to describe different views regarding language acquisition. Universal Grammar/LAD proponents would occupy a position close to the primacy of "nature" i.e. learning comes from innate biologically endowed ability. Watson's view, on the other hand, points to the opposite end of "nurture" i.e. learning derives from upbringing.

Watson viewed a child as a blank slate, which requires environment and training. He applied classical-conditioning approaches to his own children and publicised his views widely, as in his comment about child rearing written for the general public in Watson (1924):

> Give me a dozen healthy infants, well-formed, and my own specified world to bring them up in and I'll guarantee to take any one at random and train him to become any type of specialist I might select - doctor, lawyer, artist, merchant-chief and, yes, even beggar-man and thief, regardless of his talents, penchants, tendencies, abilities, vocations and the race of his ancestors. I am going beyond my facts and I admit it, but so have the advocates of the contrary and they have been doing it for many thousands of years. (Watson, 1924/1998/2017, p. 104)

In order to prove that human learning takes place through classical conditioning, Watson and Rayner (1920, 2000) report the results of an experiment on nine-month-old Little Albert B. (pseudonym) and argued that emotional reactions such as phobia can be conditioned. Watson was so confident that he had the experiment filmed (available on YouTube). As he predicted, Little Albert did acquire a phobia against a white rat and other furry objects, plus a mask of a Santa Claus with a white beard. The study of Watson and Rayner (1920/2000) is controversial in many ways (Harris, 1979), not to speak of its ethical violations when considered against current accepted standards.

Contemporary psychology, psychiatric therapies and L1 acquisition studies have been influenced by concepts from classical conditioning and behaviourism. For example, we hear about "development of conditioned behaviour", "extinction" (i.e. acquired conditioned responses disappear after a while unless stimulated), desensitisation (i.e. conditioned learning can be replaced with a more positive association e.g. a barking dog can be trained not to do so by shifting its attention to something positive other than the object that stimulates barking), generalisation (i.e. expansion of the association to similar objects e.g. a child calls any furry animals "doggie") and discrimination (i.e. further refinement of selective conditioned responses e.g. a child eventually learns to differentiate between a cat, dog, rabbit, etc.).

Operant Conditioning and Radical Behaviourism Burrhus Frederic Skinner (more commonly called B. F. Skinner) is known for his concept of operant conditioning and the notion of reinforcement in animal and human learning (Skinner, 1938, 1953). According to the theory of operant conditioning, the repeated effects of a behaviour lead to learning. This concept of consequence-induced learning had been proposed earlier by Edward Thorndike in his theory of effect (Thorndike, 1898/1956) by using mainly cats and his puzzle box (a kind of a cage). A cat is placed in the puzzle box and it is encouraged to reach for the food outside the cage. The cat tries to obtain a fish through the puzzle box. The puzzle box has a lever that can result in the door of the cage opening. The cat, by accident, touches the lever, comes out of the puzzle box and manages to get the food. After repeated trials, the cat starts to use the lever more quickly. The process and time taken are carefully recorded.

Skinner designed an "operant conditioning chamber" (more commonly referred to as "Skinner's box"), which enabled him to measure and record the effect of consequences on the behaviours of rats and pigeons in a repeatable and reliable manner. He conducted a systematic exploration of how novel behaviour can be predictably trained by positive/negative reinforcement and punishment. He showed how complex behaviours can be gradually built up by accumulating simpler learned behaviour.

Skinner's operant conditioning differs from Pavlovian classical conditioning. Operant conditioning occurs when there is no correlated stimulus–response mechanism, to begin with, when an animal's spontaneous behaviour results in positive consequences and the behaviour is positively reinforced. For example, a hungry rat moves around in Skinner's "operant conditioning chamber" and touches a lever. As a consequence of the rat's behaviour, a food pellet appears in a tray. The repetition of positive results strengthens the rat's behaviour of pressing the lever. Negative reinforcement results in weakening of the conditioned behaviour (e.g. the rat presses the lever but no food appears therefore it stops pressing the lever). Pavlovian classical conditioning, on the other hand, is a resultant conditioning to external stimuli (the co-occurrence of an unconditioned stimulus and a neutral stimulus achieves associative/modified learning).

Skinner did not negate the possibility of neurological explanations of the behavioural data. As relevant neurological studies were not available, he chose to take a behavioural approach to record the varieties of reinforcement and temporal changes in the strengths of condition for possible future neurological explanation.

Implications of Skinner's Operant Conditioning to "Further Processing, Language Acquisition and Development" The notion of positive operant conditioning is widely used in education, animal training, marketing and business, even today. Note here that Skinner's theories and the applications concern external management and control of behaviours.

Going back to Christian's case, we saw that, if Christian behaves well, the parents are likely to give positive reinforcement such as praise, encouragement and affirmation. On the other hand, if he behaves badly (e.g. a tantrum), the parents can show negative reinforcement by not giving him the kind of attention he is seeking. Skinner (1953) warns of the danger of punishment and explains how it could possibly result in unproductive behaviours such as avoidance and resentment.

Similar positive reinforcement can be introduced in school education. When students make an effort, the teacher can give the positive reinforcement of approval and affirmation. A variable ratio of praise can be provided to raise the performance level. For example, at first a teacher may praise students for volunteering to answer questions regardless of correctness. If many students start to volunteer, then the teacher can praise only the correct answers. The teacher may further raise the challenge level when the students are becoming stronger by only praising exceptional responses. The use of a token (e.g. stamp, medal, prize) is also a kind of positive reinforcement, which is used widely in schools and society.

Skinner considered language acquisition as a complex combination of simpler conditioning like any other behaviours (Skinner, 1957). He devised a teaching machine (Skinner, 1958) that provides programmed learning for skills (e.g. music) or language learning, which can be used from preschool learners to adults with varying levels of challenges and rewards. The basic idea influenced the field of computer-assisted language learning and is still used in the design of contemporary language-learning applications.

In our view, conditioning can play a role in language learning (through, for example, positive reinforcement of certain linguistic and pragmatic behaviours, but it certainly cannot in itself be responsible for intake, for further processing, for acquisition or for development.

> **Readers' Tasks**
>
> 1 Of these theories and approaches, which ones, if any, do you think influenced the way you were taught a foreign language? What influence do you think they had?
> 2 Have any of these theories and approaches influenced the way you teach? If they have, what influence have they had.
> 3 What do you think are the pros and cons of each of the approaches?

The Audio-Lingual Method In the United States toward the end of the 1950s after World War II, the growing awareness of international competition led to increased attention and funding for the reappraisal of foreign-language policy and the implementation of a new approach to language teaching. Linguists, psychologists and language-teaching specialists were called upon to develop a language-teaching method (for a detailed account, see Richards & Rogers, 2014, pp. 58–79):

> Language-teaching specialists set about developing a method that was applicable to conditions in US. They drew on the army programs which used the Aural-Oral Approach or Structural Approach developed by Fries and his colleagues, adding insights taken from behaviorist psychology. This combination of structural linguistic theory, contrastive analysis, aural-oral procedures, and behaviorist psychology led to the Audiolingual Method. (Richards & Rogers, 2014, p. 61)

The principles of the audio-lingual method included:

- The primacy of aural-oral dialogue (Fries, 1945, 1952) as a model
- Emphasis on native-speaker-like pronunciation and sentence formation (based on written language, not spoken)
- Habit formation through teaching techniques such as mimic and memorise, substitution, repetition and drills. (Lado and Fries, 1943/1953/1957/1958; Skinner, 1957, 1958)
- Error correction at the earliest possible point as negative reinforcement to avoid developing wrong pronunciation or grammar.

The audio-lingual method and materials such as the Lado series in English (1977) were considered to change language teaching from an art to a science and were widely employed in the United States, Canada and around the world for English as a Foreign Language (EFL) and for major European languages. Note here the rise in the need for adult L2 acquisition.

> **Readers' Task**
>
> 1 Do you agree with each of the principles of the audio-lingual method referred to here?
> 2 Why? Why not?

The audio-lingual method and the behaviourist theories behind it were challenged in the late 1960s. The habit-formation approach to the production of linguistic sentences or dialogues did not transfer to spontaneous, unpredictable and creative communication outside classrooms. Learners found the materials and the audio-lingual procedures of learning a language too mechanical, boring and demotivating. The development of brain sciences and the field of artificial intelligence fuelled the rise of cognitive science, which explores more elusive constructs such as memory, mind, intelligence, consciousness and feelings through speculative reflective qualitative methods (see Estes et al., 1983 for arguments supporting cognitive science and Skinner, 1985 for a retort). The legacy of the audio-lingual method is still widely seen though in language education all over the world. We will explore this further in the later section in which we discuss the application of theory to learning.

Cognitive Science, Information Processing (IP) and Parallel Distributed Processing (PDP)

The battle between cognitive scientists and behaviourist psychologists was based on the fundamental differences in their philosophical views. Skinner (1985) explains:

> Cognitive science takes the traditional position: behavior starts within an organism. We think and then act; we have ideas and then put them down into words; we experience feelings and then express them; we intend, decide, and choose to act before acting. Behaviorists, on the other hand, look at the antecedent events in the environment and environmental histories of both the species and the individual. ... The environment *selects* behavior. (Skinner, 1985, p. 297)

The humanities and some psychological branches tend to take what Skinner calls a "traditional approach", which focuses on the possible cause of behaviour (e.g. thoughts and feelings) investigated by introspection, psychoanalysis and insight supported by knowledge. This philosophical stance is sometimes called "mentalism" and can be traced back to Greek philosophers such as Plato, and later Descartes (Descartes, 1983; Sorrell, 1987), who discussed the theory of mind. Chomsky's theory of syntax and his hypothesis of a LAD is a typical example of a mentalist approach.

Medicine, physics and computer science, on the other hand, take a positivist approach, in which behaviour or physical substance itself is investigated through objective means such as experiments and repeatable and verifiable analysis.

Watson and Skinner were critical of the mentalist tradition and considered that its methods elicit unverifiable accounts that are beyond objective analysis. In Skinner's (1985, p. 300) words, "a theory in which feelings and states of mind observed through introspection are taken as the causes of behaviour rather than as the collateral effects of the causes".

Cognitive scientists in Estes et al. (1983) argued that brain sciences and computer simulations will enable the scientific investigation of the inner workings of human minds. They wrote in their report: "Cognitive science and artificial intelligence stand together in taking information processing as the central activity involved in intelligent behavior . . ." (ibid., p. 21).

Information Processing (IP) in the 1970s commonly shared a basic procedural model (Broadbent, 1958; Estes, 1983; Skehan, 1989) of Input → Central Processing → Output. During the Input stage, perception takes place. Central Processing is where the knowledge is stored, retrieved and the information taken in gets processed in a rule-governed way, then represented and restructured before production follows as Output. The process is bottom-up, and one process has to be completed before the next process resumes.

Cognitive scientists in the 1970s realised that analysis of linguistic components in a text was not sufficient to lead to computer comprehension (i.e. an output consisting of a summary of the text). The computer needed world knowledge to interpret the text. This is a finding that obviously applies to human reading too. If you are unfamiliar with the content of a text, it is going to be difficult to read in the L1, and even more difficult in the L2.

The development of an awareness of the neural architecture of the brain inspired "connectionist approaches", especially PDP in the 1980s – see Rumelhart, McClelland and the PDP Research Group (Eds., 1986) for historical developments. By then, the neuroscience of the brain was developing rapidly and the understanding of the neural architecture did not support the idea of a central control system. The most significant contributions of PDP to the computer simulation of the mind include:

- Information Processing (IP) is parallel, not serial.
- Knowledge is stored in a distributed way, not in central memory storage.
- Knowledge is stored according to the "connection strengths", not stored in memory as patterns.

Questioning the Generalisability of IP and PDP Findings When we return yet again to Christian in the section "Snapshots from L1 Acquisition", we find the fundamental analogy of the human mind and the computer, and the narrow focus on purely cognitive linguistic processing, to be as unconvincing as Watson's (1913) exclusion of internal constituents that are unobservable. It is as if the target of enquiry has been lost during the vigorous pursuit of the so-called scientific methods of computer simulations and verifiable data. In the 1950s to 1970s, input meant text, and processing equalled linguistic analysis. In the 1980s, parallel processing did take into account the brain's parallel-processing mechanism and distributed storage of knowledge (i.e. linguistic and schematic world knowledge). There was no consideration, however, of social–cultural learning or of the biological learning that organisms are designed to seek for survival and development from a Darwinian evolution perspective.

"Artificial intelligence" just means an inanimate entity that is programmed by cognitive/computer scientists and engineers. The computer's statistical calculation and linguistic analysis of an input and consequent parallel processing of nodes supported by encyclopaedic data storage may result in the output of simulating certain aspects of human behaviour. Smart computers, such as Chat Box with different disguises supported by statistical analytics of human responses, or by humanoids that are capable of facial recognition and of making their own facial expressions, may be able to learn and modify their actions according to human actions and make calculated choices of preprogrammed reactions. But for a computer there is no "meaningfulness" to its processing that distinguishes between living organisms and machines. For living creatures, survival and development is crucial for posterity and the meaningfulness of processing derives from it. In relation to this point, Skinner discusses the "little man" (1985, pp. 292–293):

> A molecular biologist, Stent (1975), traces the processing of visual data, beginning with the roughly 1,000 million receptor cells in the retina and the roughly one million ganglion cells which, according to Stent, process the information coming from them by signaling light-dark contrasts and edge effects. The fibres of the ganglion cells connect the eye with the brain, where the "signals converge on a set of cortical nerve cells" (1975, p. 1056) ... As Stent notes, "[The] visual system of the frog abstracts its input data in such a way as to produce only two meaningful structures, 'my prey' and 'my predator', which in turn evoke either of two alternative motor output, attack or flight" (p. 1057) ... Stent concludes in a traditional way: "No matter how deeply we probe into the visual pathway, in the end we need to posit an 'inner man' who transforms the visual image into a percept". (Stent, 1975, p. 1057)

Science fiction may present different pictures, but it would be illogical to expect a little man/woman inside a computer.

Implications of Cognitive Science, IP and PDP for "Further Processing, Language Acquisition and Development" Christian, in the section "Snapshots from L1 Acquisition" in this chapter is a living organism. Some aspects of what Christian does may allow computer simulations, and they may help deepen our understanding of the inner mechanisms in Christian's brain and human biological constitution that results in his behaviours. However, the ultimate answers might best be obtained through cellular and molecular studies of the brain, and interdisciplinary efforts by researchers in different fields.

McCauley, Monaghan and Christiansen (2015) provide an update on how language acquisition and development are being studied from a computational perspective.

> In recent years, the computational limitations of connectionist techniques have led to a shift away from artificial neural networks, towards higher-level models capable of scaling up to deal with input in the form of entire corpora of child-directed speech. A number of such models have made contact with emergentist principles, demonstrating that learning structure from input through general cognitive mechanisms can account for specific developmental patterns in syntactic production . . . , the acquisition of construction and construction-like units . . . , and semantic role learning . . . , in addition to capturing the emerging complexity of children's grammatical knowledge more generally . . . . (McCauley, Monaghan & Christiansen, 2015, pp. 415–416)

They introduce two recent computational models of language development. "The first model captures children's discovery of linguistic units in the speech stream, while the second simulates learning to use such units and their distributional properties to comprehend and produce speech" (ibid., p. 416).

L1 researchers such as Ambridge and Lieven (2015, p. 501) predict the future directions of interdisciplinary studies in which L1 acquisition behavioural data studies will be compared with those of computer-simulation studies in order to explore the complex process of how child-directed speech as input leads to output and of what happens in between (Ambridge & Lieven, 2011; Daelmans, Zabrel, Van der Sloot & Van den Bosch, 2010).

Neuroscience, Cognitive Neuroscience and Neurocognition of SLA

We will leave detailed historical accounts to Gazzaniga, Ivry and Mangun (2019) and just say that the study of the brain was a branch of biology that focused on nervous systems (e.g. the anatomy, biochemistry and physiology of neurons and neural circuits) when Pavlov was inferring how the central nervous system learns. The recognition of the significance of the discipline was shared around the 1950s onwards in the United States and resulted in the establishment of neuroscience centres and in diversification of specialities in relation to medicine, psychology, applied sciences and philosophy. The launch of the BRAIN Initiative (Brain Research through Advancing Innovative Neuro-Technologies) in the United States in 2013 and of the International Brain Initiative in 2017 provide evidence of the level and scale of recognition of the significance of neuroscience.

Gazzaniga et al. (2019) provide a comprehensive introduction to the fundamental elements of neuroscience (e.g. architecture, memory mechanisms, consciousness, neural learning, investigation methods). The availability these days of brain maps and of anatomical, cellular and molecular explanations of brain functions facilitates our understanding of language processing and acquisition from biological, chemical, physiological, developmental and evolutionary perspectives. These developments are helping us understand the substrates and processing of short-term, long-term and working memory, hemispheric differences, implicit and explicit learning and L1 and L2 differences. We will be referring to some of these known insights later in the chapter.

Cognitive neuroscience is a field that investigates the neural constitutions and processes of cognition. The subfield of the neurocognition of second language uses various behavioural tests, temporal event-related potentials (ERP) and functional Magnetic Resonance Imaging techniques (fMRI) to explore empirical evidence for language processing. Computer simulations are also used to test hypotheses and explore detailed mechanisms through comparisons of human and machine processing.

Morgan-Short and Ullman (2012) explain how neurocognitive research takes place as well as its typical investigation tools and procedures. Morgan-Short and Ullman (2012), for example, involved L1 and late-learning L2 learners, trained them to understand an artificial language, and measured their performance on language tasks together with the electrophysiological activity in their brains with ERP. The results reveal that:

> [L]earning under an implicit input condition designed to approximate immersion led to the full spectrum of native-like brain patterns for aspects of language processing (...), whereas learning under an explicit input condition designed to approximate traditional classroom settings did not (...). Thus, the study suggests that, at least in certain cases, the attainment of L1 neurocognitive mechanisms in second language acquisition appears to depend not only on the level of proficiency but also on the conditions under which the L2 was learned. (Morgan-Short & Ullman, 2012, p. 945)

Morgan-Short and Ullman (2012) provide, with caution, some implications of various neurocognitive studies for some of the controversial issues in the field of L2 acquisition:

Controversial issue 1: Are late-starting L2 learners capable of achieving L1-like neuroprocessing?

Morgan-Short and Ullman (2012) point to research results that late-starting L2 users can show very similar patterns as L1 users, especially for lexical processing and some syntactical processing.

Controversial issue 2: Can types of training and instruction (e.g. explicit vs implicit) influence the achievement of L1-like neurocognition mechanisms?

Morgan-Short et al. (2012) confirm that types of instruction do influence processing capability. Their view is based on their comparison between those who learned an artificial language under more implicit contexts such as immersion with those who learned it through more explicit contexts such as traditional grammar-focused classroom settings. The results of the behavioural tests did not reveal statistically significant differences. The ERP results, however, showed marked differences. Implicitly trained learners through immersion displayed both automatic and controlled processes, whereas explicitly trained learners showed controlled but not automatic processes.

Implications of Neuroscience, Cognitive Neuroscience and Neurocognition of Second Language for "Further Processing, Language Acquisition and Development" We welcome the prospect of being able to analyse intact brain activities in relation to language tasks. As researchers themselves rightly note, however, we need to be careful in the interpretation and generalisation of the available results, as everyday communication with natural language in social contexts involves complex factors that are often carefully controlled to create experimental conditions (e.g. the selection of the participants, the kinds of language training, behavioural tests, use of contrived language as opposed to natural language). It is promising that more and more interdisciplinary efforts are being made to ensure the validity as well as reliability of neurocognitive studies of how language is processed and acquired.

Readers' Tasks

1 Brian was taught French at school with a grammar translation plus behaviourist-drills approach, in which he learned by heart the definitions of French words, read aloud and translated texts with no relevance to his life, learned grammatical rules and recited declensions and conjugations. He hardly ever communicated in French in class, and never out of class. He passed A Level French but today cannot communicate with anybody in French.

   Hitomi was taught English with a grammar translation plus behaviourist-drills approach. She excelled in her exams, went to the United States on a fellowship and initially had great problems communicating with her host family and new American friends. However, her very high intrinsic motivation to learn English, her love of Beatles songs, her daily interactions with peers and her determined efforts to improve her pronunciation and fluency in a self-access centre helped her to eventually become the bilingual speaker of Japanese and English that she is today.

   Hitomi was taught Spanish at university using a mixture of dialogue repetition, grammar translation and teacher-controlled speaking practice. Her lack of motivation and opportunities to use Spanish for communication resulted not only in average examination scores but an inability to communicate at all when she visits Spanish-speaking countries.

> Of all the theories and approaches outlined in Part One above which one(s) do you think informed the way you were taught an L2. What were the results of this teaching?
> 2 Is there anything you would do to make the way you were taught an L2 more effective?
> 3 If you have acquired English as an L2, you have obviously developed your ability to use it to a high level. What do you think you have done to achieve this level?
> If you are an L1 user of English, have you tried to acquire an L2? If so, have you succeeded? What do you think has contributed to your success (or lack of it)?
> 4 What do you learn from your answers to 1–3 above about language acquisition and development?

SLA Studies – Past and Present

Past

"SLA's early research efforts drew on scholarly developments from the fields of linguistics and psychology as well as on practical concerns for language pedagogy in the post–World War II era" (The Douglas Fir Group, 2016, p. 19) We have discussed such developments in this chapter in relation to the Audio-Lingual Method that stemmed from structural linguistics and from behaviourism in psychology. We have also reflected upon how mentalist traditions, including Chomsky's UG/LAD theory (1960s onwards) and cognitive psychology, have influenced our views of how language learning may take place. What lies behind the historical sways of approaches and arguments are philosophical beliefs as to how such an invisible and unobservable phenomenon as language learning can be studied, and what we think is happening in our minds. Rather than finding indicative answers, what we have been able to present so far has been how language processing and acquisition have been studied and what researchers have said about the phenomena, rather than a synthesised account of what may be involved in further processing, acquisition and development.

What then has been happening in the field of SLA? Have the global demands for English language teaching in the 1970s and the consequent world-wide spread of the communicative approach helped develop the field of SLA?

As was extensively discussed in Chapter 1, Krashen's (1981, 1982, 1985) language acquisition theories stimulated the development of SLA studies. Krashen made links with and applied insights from L1 natural acquisition studies to L2 acquisition. Krashen argued for the vital importance of input (the input hypothesis), which has inspired further L1 and L2 acquisition studies. Krashen, following the Chomskyan LAD hypothesis, believed in learners' innate language acquisition capabilities, thus regarding the role of instruction to be peripheral (the monitor hypothesis).

Long (1981, 1983a, 1983b) investigated how comprehensible input might be made available during classroom learning, and realised that negotiations of meaning during interactions could be rich sources of language acquisition. Long's proposal of the interactionist view of language acquisition (Long, 1996; Mackey, Abbuhl & Gass, 2012) is still widely held to be applicable. Swain (1985; Swain & Lapkin, 1995), based on experience of immersion programmes in Canada, realised that comprehensible input in its own may not help learners become accurate and appropriate users of language. Swain also argued how output plays important roles in language acquisition and proposed "the comprehensible output hypothesis" (see Chapters 7 and 8 in this book). Schmidt (1990, 2012; Schmidt & Frota, 1986), through his own experience of learning Portuguese and of case studies of a Japanese immigrant, Wes, argued for the necessity of paying conscious attention to language form during implicit language acquisition.

Note here that, as we pointed out in Chapter 1, SLA studies from the 1980s onwards have focused mainly on the linguistic development of an additional language. Concepts and terms such as "interlanguage", "native speakers" and "L2 learners" are based on the assumptions that the ultimate goal of L2 language learning is to achieve an idealised "native-speaker competence", deriving from Chomsky's theoretical notion. The success or failure of L2 learners has been measured against the assumed performance models of monolingual "native-speaker" educated elites (detailed discussion in V. Cook, 1999; Ortega, 2019). Typically, SLA research compares L2 learners' performance against the idealised "native-norm" using methods such as grammaticality judgements, noting the occurrence of the use of formulaic expressions and of lexical chunks and error analysis. L2 learners are in fact bilinguals or multilinguals with their own cultural heritages and repertoires of experience and abilities. For example, the timing of their additional language learning could start from their own family and community-based surroundings at an early age and ESOL in the UK is for a minority community, political refugees and immigrants with or without mother-tongue literacy.

Learning contexts in SLA studies have also been mainly limited to classroom ESL (English as Second Language) or EFL. Even in the so-called communicative approach era, accuracy of linguistic knowledge according to written grammar has been taught, tested, researched and often prioritised. English for academic purposes has meant, and still largely means, training L2 learners to be able to cope with Western discourse styles employed in the universities in English-speaking countries such as Australia, the United States, and the UK. As was noted in Chapter 1, global

English users do not feature in the well-known past SLA studies, even though there are "well over a billion speakers for whom English is an additional language compared to fewer than 400 million native speakers today" (Kirkpatrick, 2016, reported in Garton, Copland & Mann, 2016, p. 241; see also Kirkpatrick, 2010; Pennycook, 2010; Saraceni, 2015; Jenkins, 2015; Jenkins et al., 2018; Jenkins & Leung, 2019). These global English users, when they use English as a lingua franca successfully, may not conform to "native English norms", which the past SLA literature tends to be based on. Instead, these multilingual L2 users, with their different cultural identities, may prefer to use "Translingua franca English" (Pennycook, 2010) i.e. as users of English as a tool of communication in multilingual settings, in which participants use whatever resources are available to them from their repertoires of Englishes.

In privileged situations, access to technology and digital tools provides individual choices of learning contexts and methodology. Blended-learning, individuals choosing the means of learning from purely autonomous online learning and formal institutional learning plus individual informal learning are some of the choices being made by today's learners (e.g. see Castaño Muñoz et al., 2013 for an explanation of the Open Education Plan in the membership countries of the European Union).

Present

An innovative transdisciplinary framework for restructuring the field of SLA has been proposed by The Douglas Fir Group (DFG; 2016), which consists of fifteen scholars who form a team with specialisms not only in the field of SLA but also in other related disciplines, such as sociology, cognitive psychology and education.

The DFG argue that:

> A new SLA must be imagined, one that can investigate the learning and teaching of additional languages across private and public, material and digital social contexts in a multilingual world. We propose that it begin with the social-local worlds of L2 learners and then pose the full range of relevant questions – from the neurobiological and cognitive micro levels to the macro levels of the sociocultural, educational, ideological, and socioemotional. (The Douglas Fir Group, 2016, p. 20)

In order to achieve such expanded foci, they propose a "transdisciplinary" approach in which scholars from different disciplinary perspectives and approaches collaborate with one another in order to address real-world issues involving stake holders (e.g. learners, teachers, administrators, institutional and governmental agents). These transdisciplinary researchers from different traditions would seek to "integrate the many layers of existing knowledge about the processes and outcomes of additional language learning by deriving coherent patterns and configurations of findings across domains and 'over many different levels of granularity and timescale'" (N. Ellis, 2014, p. 399; The Douglas Fir Group, 2016, p. 20).

Implications of SLA Studies for "Further Processing, Language Acquisition and Development" We welcome the suggestion by the DFG that:

- L2 learners are in fact bilingual or multilingual learners who may be preschool or school-aged children, adolescents, or adults at any point in life with various experience and sociocultural backgrounds;
- Learning and teaching should be approached as a whole from perspectives of the real world as well as from researchers' laboratory experiments and from classroom discourse studies of formal language teaching;
- Feelings, emotion and affect are important aspects of language acquisition;
- Collaboration is vital between researchers from relevant disciplines in a transdisciplinary manner;
- Research should involve and benefit various stake holders (e.g. learners, teachers, teacher developers, materials producers, institutions, communities, governments);
- Multimodal semiotic processing is one of the vital aspects of communication that has been overlooked in SLA;
- Anytime, anywhere learning and teaching is an important development for the near future, and technological development is taking place to support it (e.g. learning analytics such as chat boxes, humanoid computers and gesture-based computing).

> **Readers' Task**
>
> Is there anything you have learned from the above section that would inform your teaching of an L2? If so, what would it lead you to do?

Most of the findings and recommendations we have referred to above relate to the location, media and "delivery" of learning opportunities, or to the focus of second-language research. But what of the insights into what happens in the learners' brains after intake has been achieved, which we promised at the beginning of this chapter? We have to admit that so far, our literature search has not been very enlightening in relation to further processing, acquisition and development, mainly because most researchers have not made these distinctions and have positioned their findings and conclusions under the general term "acquisition". However, we still think it is worthwhile making these distinctions, and in the following sections we will focus specifically on what we could find in the broader literature and what we have experienced and think ourselves in regard to further, processing, acquisition and development.

What Is Involved in Further Processing, Language Acquisition and Development?

At the beginning of the chapter, we asked some questions:

- What happens after a learner extracts elements of input as intake?
- When and how does language acquisition happen?
- Once language acquisition happens, what happens to the acquired language?
- Will the acquired language change? If so, in what way?

We will now attempt to provide our interpretations of what may be happening during the further-processing period, after a learner extracts elements of input as intake.

Researchers in evolution, cognitive science and L1 and L2 acquisition studies seem to be supporting the likelihood of the following observations:

- Humans are born with a brain that affords the acquisition of languages as an extension of sensory- and motor-processing capabilities;
- Evidence seems to suggest that humans are capable of acquiring and developing language throughout life from pre-birth till death, with various factors affecting achievement levels;
- L1 monolingual and bi-/multilingual learners share convergent language processing with some differences;
- Continuing richness of input is vital, not only from a linguistic point of view but also because of the multimodal, emotional and social associations that come with it;
- Intake involves short-term and working memory. Further processing works towards achieving retention in long-term memory, but is itself fed by further intake;
- Language acquisition involves the formation, retention and strengthening in long-term memory of associative networks, any part of which could spark off associative memories in flexible and varied ways. Rich, engaging, recycled, multimodal, multisensory, embodied input is a prerequisite for the successful achievement of this process;

- Acquired potential neural networks (language acquisition at different strengths) may be reinforced, become dormant or disappear; Reinforcement of useful networks is vital in the progress towards acquisition and eventual development;
- When acquired potential neural networks are reactivated, reinforced, expanded and made use of as a result of further rich experience, these networks facilitate the learner's development towards becoming a highly proficient user;
- The close community of family, friends and neighbours and the larger community (such as schools) affect acquisition and development through the provision of resources, opportunities, encouragement and support;
- Motivation has evolutionary and neuroscientific underpinnings and is activated by such goals as survival, satisfaction and success;
- Feelings, emotion and affect exert a vital influence on successful acquisition and development.

Going back to Christian in the section "Snapshots from L1 Acquisition", L1 acquisition studies seem to suggest that:

- Child-directed speech involves a considerable amount of here-and-now multimodal input;
- The level of input approximates the levels of the child's perception and comprehension capacity;
- Children's curiosity-driven actions influence the object and manner of child-directed speech;
- Children pick up short and easy whole chunks (such as "Don't do that") in the surrounding speech stream (see Grimm, Cassani, Gillis & Daelmans, 2019);
- Multiple exemplars facilitate word learning (Twomey, Ranson & Horst, 2014).

The observations above are based on linguistic studies of child–carer corpora (e.g. https://childes.talkbank.org/) but all could apply at early stages of L2 young-learner, teenager or adult acquisition. These learners would benefit from here-and-now multimodal input from teachers, peers and materials that approximates to (or offer a slight challenge to) their current cognitive, experiential and linguistic levels. They would also benefit from participation in activities that stimulate curiosity, offer engagement, pose a challenge and promise success whilst immersing the learners in input that exposes them to meaningful chunks and multiple exemplars used in authentic communication. Gradually increasing the level and the challenge whilst still stimulating positive affect, involving learners in more and more communicative interaction and production, and providing more and more constructive feedback on communicative use can help the progress towards acquisition and possibly the eventual development of communicative competence.

> **Readers' Tasks**
>
> 1 We mentioned above that "L1 monolingual and bi-/multi-lingual learners share convergent language processing with some differences". What do you think the differences might be between the mental processing of an L1 learner and that of an L2 learner?
> 2 We have stressed the importance of rich input. How do you think L2 learners could gain rich input in a learning context that you are familiar with?

When and How Does Further Processing Take Place in L2 Learning?

Put very simply, further processing takes place when equivalent intake is achieved (i.e. previous input is recycled either identically or in a similar form and this is taken in as a result of such determiners as salience, significance, meaningfulness, utility, engagement and noticing). This "new" intake is "compared" to the equivalent previous intake, new neural connections are created, old neural connections are strengthened and, if even further equivalent intake is achieved, patterns are consciously noticed and hypotheses are generated and used. If still further equivalent intake is achieved as a result of reception or production, then hypotheses are tested and possibly revised and made use of. So, for example, a learner who initially intakes many instances of the regular simple past (e.g. "He lived ...", "She worked"; "I jumped ...") might generate a hypothesis that when you refer to somebody or something doing something in the past you add -ed to the verb. This overgeneralisation could lead to the production of such utterances as "I buyed a new shirt" and "It costed eighty dollars." However, noticing of apparently negative feedback plus frequent exposure to irregular simple past tense forms could eventually lead to revision of the hypothesis and to a distinction being made between regular and irregular verbs and to such utterances as "I bought a new shirt" and "It cost eighty dollars" being produced. Overgeneralisation and/or undergeneralisation appear to be the initial norm in further processing and often result in non-native-like uses that can be viewed positively as manifestations of progress (often referred to as developmental errors), which require more time and input rather than correction. For example, lexical items are often initially overgeneralised to represent their category (e.g. apple = any fruit, car = any vehicle, water = any drink, chair = anything to sit on, brush = anything for tidying the hair) or they are undergeneralised to represent a particular sub-type of a category (e.g. cinema = a drive in, ship = a cruise liner, ball = a football).

Notice that crucial to progress, from intake through further processing towards acquisition, is rich and recycled input, which continues to be salient and significant and is encountered in contextualised and potentially engaging texts or interactions. Equally important are opportunities to use the language feature in order to achieve intended effects in activities in which support is available from peers and the teacher and feedback is provided both situationally and linguistically. Learner noticing (either consciously or subconsciously) can also play an important part in the process, both of the effects of the learner's reception or production and of the gap between the learner's accuracy, appropriacy and effectiveness of production and that of a proficient user on an equivalent task. If these conditions are not achieved, weakening, regression and even loss of intake can occur. Often, though, even if the conditions for progression are achieved, the learner stops progressing and their acquisition of a feature is said to fossilise. This can mean that the learner continues to make the same "errors" when using a feature, regardless of the amount of new input or of negative feedback. Many advanced learners, for example, continue to make article errors in English, even in otherwise accurate and effective production. Many learners, however, never reach an advanced stage and their language acquisition fossilises at an intermediate (B2) stage. This is particularly evident with immigrants who have reached a level with which they can live and work in their new environment without undue difficulty, and with students who do not really need the target language and have reached a level with which they can pass their examinations.

Han and Odlin (2006, p. 4) refer to Selinker and Han (2001) when specifying the five properties of fossilisation:

> First, it pertains to IL features that deviate from the TL norms. Second, it can be found in every linguistic domain (e.g. phonology, syntax, morphology). Third, it exhibits persistence and resistance. Fourth, it can occur with both adult and child learners. Fifth, it often takes the form of backsliding.

The reasons for fossilisation could be that the learner:

- is able to operate sufficiently well in the language in order to achieve their language-learning objectives;
- is demotivated by the apparent lack of progress and "switches off";
- moves away from an environment in which the language is used for communication;
- finishes their course and makes no effort to maintain contact with the language outside the classroom;
- has a very negative experience with a new school, teacher, coursebook or classmate;
- does not want to lose their L1 identity.

See Saville-Troike and Barto (2017) for a view of fossilisation that questions "whether 'progress' should be measured against native-speaker norms" (p. 45) and asks whether we should consider an L2 user who speaks the language fluently with a non-native accent to be exhibiting fossilisation or not.

Of course, hypothesis generation, testing and revision are hidden mental processes, and the learners do not actually articulate the hypotheses, the results of their testing of hypotheses nor their revisions. The process is achieved through the creation and strengthening of neurons, synapses and networks in the brain, See Schütze (2017 – especially pp. 49–66) for a neurolinguistics account of how words are acquired through the creation of synapses, which connect neurons to create networks, which are weakened or strengthened "every time a word is encountered and processed" (p. 62). Schütze (2017) provides a clear account of the role, in language acquisition, of neurons ("nerve cells that can transmit information" (p. 49) and of synapses ("A synapse is a point of contact between two neurons", p. 49). In doing so he stresses that, "What we know about a word, the form and meaning – and how we use it – can change. When a synapse adds or deletes information it becomes modified" (p. 50). See also Myan (2010) who says, "Words representing similar concepts tend to excite the same neurons thus creating a similar internal representation for words or phrases with similar meanings." Likewise, learners do not typically make conscious decisions that result in fossilisation. The phenomenon is subconscious, but sometimes learners are aware of it and make conscious efforts (which are not always successful) to remedy the situation. For a detailed investigation of fossilisation see Han and Odlin (2006), a book of chapters that consider the definition, causes and consequences of fossilisation, with some researchers questioning the value of using the term at all because of its lack of precision and the way it has been interpreted in many different ways (e.g. with global reference to a learner's general proficiency and local reference to the learner's persistent specific "errors"). What the researchers do agree on is that the phenomenon of ceasing to progress (or even backsliding) is a problem for very many learners of an L2 (whether it be with regard to general proficiency or to specific language features).

N. Ellis (2012) provides a clear account of processing and SLA. N. Ellis asserts that "[l]anguage learners have to acquire the constructions of their language from usage [in our term 'use']. Learning is dynamic, it takes place during processing ..." (p. 202). He provides evidence to support this assertion and stresses the importance of frequency, recency and context in the language acquisition process when he says:

> Learning, memory and perception are all affected by frequency of usage: the more times we experience something, the stronger our memory of it, and the more fluently it is accessed. The more recently we have experienced something, the stronger our memory of it, and the

more fluently it is accessed. The more times we experience conjunction of features, the more they become associated in our minds and the more these subsequently affect perception and categorisation; so a stimulus becomes associated to a context and we become more likely to perceive it in that context. (N. Ellis, 2012, p. 195)

We completely agree with Ellis, but we would add that intake is only strengthened if the input satisfies such other conditions as comprehensibility, meaningfulness and engagement as well as frequency, recency and context.

Van Patten (2012) defines processing as, "Processing refers to making a connection between form and meaning/function." (p. 269). He then goes on to establish and elaborate on the following principles:

Primacy of Content Words: Learners process content words in the input before anything else.

Lexical Preference Principle: If grammatical forms express a meaning that can also be encoded lexically (e.g. the grammatical marker is redundant), then learners will not initially process those grammatical forms until they have lexical forms to which they can match them.

The First Noun Principle: Learners tend to process the first noun or pronoun they encounter in the sentence as the subject.

The Lexical Semantics Principle: Learners may rely on lexical semantics, where possible, to interpret sentences instead of the First Noun Principle.

The Event Probabilities Principle: Learners may rely on event probabilities, where possible, to interpret sentences instead of the First Noun Principle.

Van Patten and Cadierno (1993) made use of these principles to develop a pedagogic intervention, which they called input processing. In this approach, they attempt to "alter particular processing strategies" in order to achieve "better grammatical intake for acquisition" (Van Patten, 2012, p. 273). We would accept Van Patten's principles, but would prefer to apply them by developing a meaning-focused approach to teaching beginners (see the Application section of this chapter).

Pienemann is also interested in developmental sequences and has made a distinction (for example, in Pienemann, 1985 between developmental readiness, which determines whether a learner is ready to acquire a structure that can only be acquired after other structures (e.g. the present continuous after the simple present) and psychological readiness, which determines whether a learner is ready to acquire a structure that is not constrained by a fixed sequence of acquisition. There is some disagreement among researchers about how rigid the universal stages of development are, what the actual sequence is and whether or not it makes sense to follow Pienemann's Teachability Hypothesis (Pienemann, 1998), which advocates teaching structures in the order they are naturally acquired. We are particularly interested in psychological readiness as we believe that learners only learn when they are ready and need or want to learn, and that readiness can be influenced by pedagogic tasks (such as those in text-driven and task-based approaches), which require understanding or use of a not-yet-acquired structure for successful completion.

When and How Is Acquisition Achieved?

Acquisition can either be of a particular language feature (e.g. a structure, a lexical item, a chunk, a phoneme, an intonation pattern, the manifestations of a pragmatic function), of the ability to operate in a particular type of discourse (e.g. social interaction) or of a language (e.g. English). We would say that the acquisition of a language feature has been achieved when the learner is able to understand it in frequently encountered situations and genres (e.g. in the classroom, in a shop, in a newspaper, in a film) and to use it with sufficient accuracy, fluency, appropriacy and strategic competence in order to achieve communicative purposes in those situations and genres (e.g. to buy new clothes, to ask for directions, to write an e-mail of complaint). We would say that the acquisition of competence in a specific type of discourse or the acquisition of a language has been achieved when the user consistently achieves sufficient understanding and sufficient accuracy, fluency, appropriateness and effect to operate comfortably and with a degree of success in that type of discourse or when using the language normally. It is obviously impossible to locate an exact moment of achieved acquisition, or to quantify it precisely in an evaluation, but we would say that consistently achieving sufficient effectiveness would be an indicator of acquisition. Notice that we differ from most SLA researchers by not relating acquisition to native-speaker competence and performance. Most learners are aiming at becoming effective communicators rather than native-speaker clones and, after all, most native speakers have acquired their language but not all of them consistently achieve sufficient effectiveness in different situations and genres.

In order for the acquisition of a language feature to be achieved, learners need:

- frequent and spaced exposure to that feature in significant use;
- whenever exposed to the feature, to be influenced by many of the factors which can determine intake (as specified in Chapter 2);
- whenever exposed to the feature, to trigger further processing in the brain of the language feature taken in and of associated extra-linguistic and nonlinguistic features;
- to subconsciously detect patterns and make generalisations about the use of the feature;

- to subconsciously test the hypotheses generated;
- to subconsciously revise and/or strengthen the hypotheses;
- to continue to experience and use the structure.

The process above is an as-yet invisible and unobservable process, revealed both by analysis of data generated by learner use and by neurolinguistic investigations of the brain in action. There is evidence that explicit noticing of the feature in use (whilst not in itself sufficient to trigger acquisition) can contribute positively to the achievement of acquisition, and especially to the comprehension of problematic text and the production of language in situations that afford sufficient time to achieve the recall of explicitly learned declarative knowledge. However, acquisition cannot be achieved without implicit learning from exposure to language in contextualised use, nor without the intake derived from it.

You could say that our specification of what learners need in order to eventually achieve acquisition constitutes a series of stages in the progress towards acquisition. We are reluctant, though, to label them as stages as they are not distinctively sequential. Achieving further intake could, for example, occur whilst or after making generalisations, at the same time as testing a hypothesis or after hypothesis revision.

Some researchers have attempted to list stages of acquisition. Hill and Bjork (2008), for example, list the five stages of acquisition proposed by Krashen and Terrell (1983): preproduction, early production, speech emergence, intermediate fluency, and advanced fluency. Like many such stages, the specification is of what learners can do rather than of the mental processes that promote the achievement. Like many methodologists at the time, Hill and Bjork recommend frequent teacher questioning throughout lessons so that learners can practise their new language and they specify types of teacher questioning (rather than of learner interaction) to facilitate progress through the stages (e.g. Yes/No questions for early production and "What would happen if ..." questions for intermediate fluency). In our view, this provides an impoverished experience for the learners. It might help them to become competent answerers of questions and to perform well in interviews and interrogations, but it is unlikely to help them to become competent at initiating, participating equally in, or closing interactions.

When and How Is Development Achieved?

Development is achieved when L2 users become highly effective in understanding, interacting in, and producing the L2 in multiple contexts, situations and genres. Very few users of a language can ever be said to have achieved development, whether they be using the language as an L1 or as an L2. However, L2 users can progress towards this goal if they are immersed in rich experience of the language in use, not just in everyday life or the classroom but in many different contexts, situations and genres. They need to be motivated and determined to progress, to seek out and exploit opportunities for language use, to notice how features of their input are used to achieve effect and, ideally, to have access to socially cohesive interaction and to teachers who challenge and encourage them. Hitomi, for example, when working as an English teacher in Japan, sought out opportunities for further exposure to English in use and for opportunities to use it but also continued her explicit studies of the language independently. So did one of our MA students from China at the University of Liverpool. She talked to her host family whenever possible, transcribed the conversations and studied them in order to make discoveries. She also kept a diary of her use of English, and found out that doing so considerably aided lexical acquisition. It also revealed hesitation and weak performance when interacting with English speakers she did not know, and this made her determined to rectify this situation.

In order to achieve development, users of an L2 probably also need to have achieved high levels of cognition, creativity and criticality, attributes that can facilitate acquisition but are not absolutely essential for its achievement. Fortunately, though, we have found that determined use of English at high levels of performance can help to develop higher levels of cognition, creativity and criticality, and this in turn contributes to further development.

You do not need to acquire a language before you start developing communicative competence in it. Acquisition and development can progress in parallel, and even those learners who are never going to achieve total acquisition can be helped to develop. They need to be treated with respect as intelligent individuals and to be engaged in activities that involve them affectively and cognitively. They need achievable challenges not easy practice.

Part Two: The Application of Theory to Learning

Application to Language Planning and to Curriculum Development

Language planners and curriculum developers would do well to consider the following intentions of The Douglas Fir Group and to invite like-minded researchers and a group of local stakeholders to work with them in developing a curriculum designed to maximise opportunities for language acquisition and development.

> A main target of its research efforts would be to understand the varying conditions that enable and constrain opportunities for and outcomes of language learning across private, public, material, and digital contexts of social action and interaction. Another main goal would be to

communicate with and serve learners themselves and other stakeholders, including teachers; administrators; appointed and elected officials; parents; community members; business leaders; and educational, business, and health organizations. In sum, the new, rethought SLA would contribute to the development of innovative and sustainable lifeworld solutions that support language learners in a multilingual world. (Douglas Fir Group, 2016, p. 22)

Language planners and curriculum developers could also benefit from considering the following:

New mobile technologies that increasingly integrate in complex ways diverse data sources and networks have reached even seemingly remote corners of the globe and are changing L2 users' worlds. We have come to understand that they are neither neutral nor innocent but, in oftentimes subtle ways, reproduce social, economic, and cultural inequalities (e.g. Van Deursen & Van Dijk, 2014). At the same time, they have also transformed the ways in which language learners interpret and make meaning, and thus the ways in which they need and want to use language. For example, although meaning and communication were always multimodal, using the many technologies of the body (Mauss, 1973), with new technologies multimodality has reached a qualitatively new level. (The Douglas Fir Group, 2016, p. 23)

We would recommend the development of plans and curricula that are locally relevant but that also prepare learners for communication, both actual and virtual, with users of the language located elsewhere. Ideally, the curriculum needs to make provision for rich, varied and multimodal experience of language in use both in the classroom and outside it, and to focus not on the teaching of discrete forms but on providing opportunities to acquire communicative competence through purposeful, supported communication.

Application to Methodology and Materials Development

The most obvious application of what we know about further processing, acquisition and development is that language features need to be experienced many times in order for further processing, acquisition and development to take place. This continuing experience needs to provide multiple opportunities for responding to the feature in contextualised, communicative use when encountered during listening, reading, viewing and interactive activities, as well as opportunities to use the feature in order to achieve communicative intents in speaking, writing and interaction. In our opinion, learners need classroom activities and materials that are experiential rather than studial, meaning-focused rather than forms-focused, form-focused rather than forms-focused, challenging rather than insultingly easy, affectively and cognitively engaging, and that encourage the learners to make use of their existing linguistic and nonlinguistic resources as well as to respond to, and to try to use, new resources. Such experience can be provided by the teacher chatting with learners, by learners interacting with each other and, above all, by learners looking out for opportunities to use the target language outside the classroom. It can also be provided if the teacher makes use in their classroom activities and materials of such experiential approaches as task-based language teaching, text-driven approaches, problem-based approaches, project-based approaches, discovery approaches, drama-based approaches, CLIL, and extensive reading/listening/viewing approaches. All these approaches focus on learning by doing, on implicit learning and on the acquisition of procedural knowledge, but all of them can (and should in our view) also sometimes make use of follow-up activities in which there is an explicit focus on problematic or significant language or in which discourse features are encountered or used during the experiential activities. For information about these approaches. see Mishan (2013a), Tomlinson (2013d) and Richards and Rodgers (2014). See also the Application to Methodology and the Application to Materials Development sections of Chapter 3 in this book for information about how approaches can not only facilitate intake (the focus of that chapter) but also facilitate further processing, acquisition and development.

As we have said, most coursebooks do not make use of the experiential approaches listed above but are dominated by discrete-item, syllabus-driven, declarative-knowledge focused, practice-driven approaches such as PPP (see Chapter 2 in this book). Such approaches can stimulate further processing and facilitate acquisition and development if they are supplemented by engaging texts and activities, if they encourage learner creativity, criticality and exploration, if the learners are highly motivated, if the learners have a rich experience of the target language in use outside the classroom and if they are used by a brilliant teacher. Unfortunately, not many of the current coursebooks that use such approaches are likely to stimulate much further processing or to facilitate acquisition (rather than learning) of the language or the development of communicative competence. Because of the perceived need for the explicit teaching of all the important structures, vocabulary and skills, their syllabuses are massive and there is only time for one unit to focus on each teaching point. Because of the perceived need to provide activities that can be used as easily and reliably marked tests and to prepare learners for examinations, most of the activities are closed exercises, such as filling in blanks, matching and Yes/No questions. This leads to a lack of opportunities for self-expression and communicative interaction (Freeman, 2014; Tomlinson, 2018b). The insufficiency of recycling, of contextualised exposure and use, of exposure to and experience of authentic use and often of cognitive and affective engagement means that it is unlikely that learners who are dependent on the coursebook will achieve acquisition and development (Tomlinson, 2020b).

What we said about the application of SLA theories of intake to methodology and to materials development in Chapter 3 is directly relevant to the application of theories about further processing and acquisition. Rather than repeat it, we would like to outline a course design that would maximise the likelihood of the occurrence of further processing, the achievement of acquisition and the eventual development of a high-level communicative competence. First though, we would just like to make a few comments about methodologies and materials that would be likely to facilitate the development of communicative competence.

The methodologies and materials should:

- focus on contextualised communication in which the goal is to achieve intended outcomes;
- set tasks that initially require learners to make use of their existing linguistic, extra-linguistic and nonlinguistic resources;
- include peer collaboration in which peers pool their resources and provide support and feedback to each other;
- make use of the teacher as a resource during activities and a provider of feedback after activities;
- encourage the teacher to focus feedback on the degree of success of outcomes prior to considering with the learners how modifications of outputs could have increased outcome effectiveness;
- encourage learners to be autonomous and to make discoveries about language use;
- above all, involve learners in out-of-class comprehension, interaction and production activities as well as in activities involving researching how the language is actually used.

A Proposal for a Language Acquisition and Development Course

The following course has been designed to help learners to achieve intake, to activate further processing, to eventually achieve acquisition and to ultimately develop a high and versatile level of communicative competence.

Stage One (equivalent to but not necessarily the same as Beginner or A1)

Approach:

An experiential, meaning-focused, comprehension-based stage.

Components:

1 TPR Plus, 2 Dramatic Reading, 3 Teacher Drama.

Activities:

1 The teacher tells stories while the students act them out physically, the teacher gives instructions for games and the students play them, the teacher gives instructions on how to make a meal and the students eat it (Tomlinson, 1995; Bui, 2018).
2 The teacher reads a dramatic story aided by visuals, props, sound effects, etc. The students respond by drawing their representation and/or answering "why" questions in the L1.
3 A scene from a play, film or novel is acted out, either by a teacher playing all the parts or by two or more teachers.

Materials:

Stories, instructions, scripts.

Comments:

The emphasis is on using a comprehension approach involving listening, seeing, visualising, connecting, feeling and thinking to achieve understanding plus affective, cognitive, kinaesthetic and social engagement. The learners use drawings, their L1 and their bodies to express their understanding and to respond. The teacher ensures that recycling is achieved from one activity to another. The learners are not asked to use the L2 yet.

Activities 1, 2 and 3 are performed in parallel throughput Stage One, with the teacher playing the roles of performer, supporter, supplier of comprehensible input and available informant.

Stage Two (equivalent to, but not necessarily the same as, Elementary or A2)

Approach:
A comprehension, meaning-focused approach plus initial attempts at production and some learner noticing of form.

Components:

1 TPR Plus + Production.
2 TPR Plus from Reading.
3 Extensive Reading.
4 Shared Reading.
5 Discovery Activities.

Activities:

1 As for Stage One, for example, the teacher tells stories while the students act them out physically. But then the students retell the story in a plenary

session prompted by the teacher (e.g. "The people on the beach ...") before working in groups to develop and tell their own extension of the story (Tomlinson 1994b).
2. At first, the students are given written versions of TPR Plus activities they have already done to read and then act out or follow. Later on, they are given new written texts to act out or follow. In both stages, they retell the text in a plenary session after performing it, and then extend the text in group writing activities.
3. The students read short stories located locally in which approximately 50 per cent of the content words are "good friends" (e.g. tv, mobile, taxi).
4. The students read illustrated stories from a screen and discuss (in a mix of L1 and L2) the meaning and form of each screenshot with each other and the teacher before moving on.
5. The students focus on a language feature that is salient in a text they have experienced in 1 or 2, and try to make discoveries about how it is used and to articulate them in a mix of L1 and L2 (Tomlinson, 2018a).

Materials:
Stories, instructions, illustrated readers, discovery activities.

Comments

This a very much a meaning-focused approach, with the emphasis on understanding the target language in engaging use, on providing and recycling rich and comprehensible input, and on stimulating attempts to use the language for communication.

Stage Three (equivalent but not necessarily the same as Lower Intermediate to Upper Intermediate or B1 to C1)

Approach:
An essentially interactional and experiential approach with learner attention also paid to form and its contribution to meaning and to the achievement of communicative intent.

Components:

1. Text-Driven Approaches (TDA)
2. Task-Based Approaches (TBLT)
3. Content and Language Integrated Approaches (CLIL)
4. Problem-Solving Activities
5. Extensive Reading/Listening/Viewing
6. Discovery Activities
7. Out-of-Class Activities

Activities:

1. The learners do readiness, response, development and discovery activities driven by a potentially engaging written, spoken or multimedia text (Tomlinson, 2013d; Tomlinson & Masuhara, 2018b).
2. The learners make use of and pool their existing linguistic resources to perform tasks with intended nonlinguistic outcomes (e.g. designing a persuasive advert to sell a product). The teacher is available as a language resource during the task and as a provider of feedback after the task (Van den Branden, 2006; Samuda, Van den Branden & Bygate, 2018).
3. The learners learn something new through the medium of the target language about a content subject (e.g. geography), an interest (e.g. Sumo wrestling) or a skill (e.g. pottery) (Marsh, Coyle & Hood, 2010; Mahan, Brevik & Odergaard, 2018).
4. The learners in groups use the target language to work out and present solutions to problems (e.g. how to stop motorists from speeding) (Mishan, 2016).
5. The learners select extensive texts from a library and experience them in their own time. No activities are set but learners sign their names when they complete a text and maybe form a discussion group with other learners who have experienced that text (Maley, 2008; Krashen, 2011).
6. The learners focus on language or pragmatic features of texts they have experienced in 1, 3 or 5 and try to make discoveries about how those feature are used in those texts, in their own texts and in any other authentic texts they can find (Tomlinson, 2018a).
7. The learners are encouraged and guided to make use of their local environment and of the Internet to find and make use of opportunities to experience the target language in use (Tomlinson, 2014a; Pinnard, 2016).

Materials:

A library of spoken, written and multimedia texts selected for their potential to achieve affective and cognitive engagement, a library of informative texts on academic subjects, human interests and skills, a library of extensive texts, a menu of discovery activities, a list of suggestions for out-of-class activities.

Comment:

All the texts in this Stage are authentic, in the sense that they are not written or spoken for teaching purposes but for such communicative purposes as to inform, entertain, arrange, provoke, persuade. All the activities either involve contextualised communication aiming at intended outcomes or exploration of the ways in which intended outcomes are achieved in such communication.

Ideally, learners are given a choice of texts and of activities and they work most of the time with peers who have made similar choices.

The teachers' roles are as providers of resources, organisers, stimulators, supporters, suppliers of comprehensible input, available informants and suppliers of constructive feedback.

The activities should be challenging but achievable, should contain intelligent content, and should help learners to connect the familiar with the new and the local with the global.

The texts for many of the activities can be brought to class by the learners.

Stage Four (equivalent but not necessarily the same as C2)

Approach:

A primarily experiential approach but also with emphasis on exploring and researching how the target language is used to achieve communicative effect.

Components:

As for Stage Three but with the addition of:

1 Research Approaches
2 Presentation Approaches
3 Project Approaches
4 Data-Driven Approaches
5 Publication Approaches

Activities:

As for Stage Three but with the addition of activities that require the learners/users:

1 to research how particular structures, lexical items and chunks, registers and pragmatic strategies are used in the language (Tomlinson, 2007c, 2010a, 2018a);
2 to make presentations to the class and to other audiences on subjects and/or issues of their choosing;
3 to participate with other learners in projects that require investigation and interaction outside the classroom as well as written and oral presentation of reports, conclusions, recommendations etc. (Wicks, 2000; Stoller, 2002, 2006);
4 to analyse corpus data in order to come to conclusions about how particular language features are typically used (O'Keeffe, McCarthy & Carter, 2007);
5 to publish, in the institution and ideally outside it too, a creative artefact (e.g. a poem, story, play, journalistic report, song, vlog, video).

Materials:

As for Stage Three but with the addition of access to corpora of the L2 in use and to a menu of project tasks, as well as a widening of the library to include texts from more specialised fields (including applied linguistics).

Comment:

At this stage the learners should be challenged both linguistically and cognitively and should be expected to understand and use the target language accurately, fluently and effectively with a wide variety of topics, genres and objectives.

The learners should be given as many opportunities as possible to interact with peers and to express their personalities, opinions, views and ideas.

Stage Five (all levels)

Approach: The teacher encourages learners who are about to leave a course to continue acquiring and using the target language outside the classroom. The teacher gets the learners to think about how they can continue to experience the language after the course and to design an autonomous learning course for themselves. The learners get feedback on their course from the teacher and then share their revised course with other learners. They make further revisions and then establish peer groups who will communicate with each other in the target language after the course.

Application to Assessment

The most obvious application to assessment is the need to reduce the risk of negative washback on classroom activity as a result of over-emphasis on such closed activities as filling in the blanks, answering Yes/No questions and matching words to pictures, sentences, definitions etc. In order to progress, learners need the opportunities for rich exposure and contextualised use that more open-ended activities can provide. So, examinations and tests need to find ways of still achieving reliability and speed of marking whilst using open-ended assessment tasks that encourage positive washback in the classroom. For a fuller discussion of ways of doing this, see Chapter 3.

Application to Teacher Development

In our experience, teacher-development courses tend to focus on helping teachers to acquire techniques designed to facilitate language learning at the lower levels or, at the first encounter stage at higher levels. The emphasis is very much on introducing "new" language features through presentation and exemplification, and then on providing practice activities that help learners to familiarise themselves with the feature and to gain some mastery over it. We would very much welcome teacher-development courses that also help teachers to provide learners with the incentives, resources, input, tasks and support they need to achieve further processing and acquisition and to start progressing towards development.

CONCLUSION

It is obvious from the infrequent reference to further processing, achievement of acquisition and development of communicative competence in the literature that more research actually does need to be done. We would really like to know more about:

- what promotes, what does not promote and what inhibits further processing;
- what learners need in order to acquire (rather than just learn about) a language feature;
- what learners need in order to acquire (rather than just learn about) a language;
- why many classroom learners of an L2 do not acquire the language;
- why many classroom learners neither acquire the target language nor develop communicative competence;
- why some classroom learners acquire the target language but do not develop communicative competence.

We would like to conclude this chapter by providing our brief answers to the questions that we asked at the beginning.

What happens after a learner extracts elements of input as intake?

The intake becomes available for further processing and eventual acquisition. For this to actually happen, though, further rich exposure to equivalent instances of use are needed, as well as opportunities for relevant use (see Chapter 6). If the conditions are right (e.g. the input is salient, meaningful, engaging, contextualised and embodied) further intake will be achieved and networks will be strengthened. However, if there is no further intake, then networks will be weakened and records could disappear.

When and how does language acquisition happen?

As a process, acquisition of a language feature is a dynamic, longitudinal continuum. It happens as a result of instances of equivalent intake being experienced at spaced intervals and made use of to achieve comprehension and/or effective use. The acquired feature is strengthened or weakened according to the amount and quality of its use.

As a product the acquisition of a feature or a language can be said to have been achieved when sufficient comprehension of its use by others is consistently achieved and when the learner consistently uses it with sufficient accuracy, fluency, appropriateness and effect. Features of a language are acquired in a sequence that is dependent on developmental readiness (i.e. some structures can only be acquired after the acquisition of other structures) and psychological readiness (i.e. after mental and environmental conditions have been satisfied).

Once language acquisition happens, what happens to the acquired language?

The acquired language becomes available for use by selecting elements of it from options activated in the brain and by combining them with other elements to achieve comprehension or communicative use. There is normally a progression in effectiveness of use but there can also be fossilisation and regression if the conditions for progress are not met (e.g. frequent motivated, meaningful, engaging exposure and/or the need to use with accuracy and effect).

Will the acquired language change? If so, in what way?

The acquired language can change both in form and in communicative use. What might have been acquired as an over- or under-generalisation might be revised. What might have been acquired with, for example, an L1 pronunciation, spelling or word order, might move closer to an L2 form as a result of further exposure and feedback.

The most obvious point we are making is that further processing, acquisition and development cannot be achieved by focusing on a language feature intensively in one unit of a coursebook and then having very little experience of it afterwards. What is needed above all is continuing rich exposure, opportunities for noticing and opportunities to use the feature naturally for purposeful, contextualised communication.

Readers' Tasks

1 Is there anything in this chapter that has made you reflect on your approach to language teaching and consider making changes? If so what changes, if any, do you think you might make?
2 Is there anything we have said in this chapter that you disagree with? Say why you disagree with it?

FURTHER READING

Gass, S. & Mackey, A. (Eds.). (2012). *The Routledge handbook of second language acquisition*. New York: Routledge (especially Part III, "Psycholinguistic and neurolinguistic perspective").

Schütze, U. (2017). *Language learning and the brain*. Cambridge: Cambridge University Press.

Tomlinson, B. (2013). Humanising the coursebook. In B. Tomlinson (Ed.), *Developing materials for language teaching* (pp. 140–155). London: Bloomsbury.

5 Recognition, Recall, Rehearsal and Retrieval

Part One: Theory

Introduction

Recognition, recall, rehearsal and retrieval are important processes in both the acquisition and the use of a language. We will discuss these four processes separately, but they often operate in combination and not always in the sequence we have used. We are using the term "recognition" to refer to an awareness of familiarity when encountering a word, phrase, chunk, sound or structure, either mentally through use of the inner voice, visually when reading or auditorily when listening. By "recall", we mean consciously accessing records in long-term memory. By "rehearsal", we mean mental repetition of recalled or retrieved items. And by "retrieval", we are referring to the subconscious process of bringing back information spontaneously from long-term memory in order to make use of it in acquisition, comprehension or production.

All four of these processes are activated through the use of the inner voice (Tomlinson, 2000b, 2020a; Tomlinson & Avila, 2007a). Although these processes are commonly discussed in studies of memory, we had problems in finding much reference to them in the mainstream literature on SLA, and we discovered that the terms recall and retrieval are often used interchangeably.

Recognition

As indicated above, recognition involves awareness of familiarity. This can be conscious or subconscious, and can be of a combination of letters or sounds, of actual words or phrases or of forms or structures. However, recognition does not necessarily imply comprehension. For example, the word "stattness" could be recognised as an English noun without any awareness of what it means. Recognition is a prerequisite for intake, but the word "astute" is unlikely to become part of a learner's intake if it is encountered in isolation. However, if it were met in the cotext "She was very astute", the learner might work out that "astute" is an adjective that refers to some sort of human characteristic and it might achieve Intake 1 – Perception If "astute" were met a number of times over an extended period in contexts indicating somebody is being praised for their discernment and, in particular, their ability to assess people or situations, then it might achieve Intake 2 – Transfer and Intake 3 – Integration. If the encounters with "astute" were accompanied by affective and/or cognitive engagement and were meaningful to the learner (e.g. they were described as astute by somebody they respect), then the word might be processed further and eventually acquired.

Roles of Recognition in Acquisition

As we have said in Chapter 2, perception is an important prerequisite for achieving intake from input. However, perception of an utterance is unlikely to aid intake if the constituents of the utterance are not recognisable as elements of the target language. This would be the case if we can hear an utterance in the L2 but cannot segment it into recognisable phonemes, syllables or words (see Weber and Broersma, 2012 for discussion of the problems of segmenting L2 utterances). We both, for example, have problems in segmenting spoken utterances in German and in Chinese and in recognising L2 words that we have previously encountered if they are written in a script we are unfamiliar with. And all language learners have problems in recognising language they have previously encountered when they hear it being used by speakers with strong regional accents. For example, Hitomi initially had problems recognising the English spoken around her when she went to live in Wisconsin in the United States, and our overseas MA students at the University of Liverpool have big problems in recognising the English spoken by local people with a Scouse accent. And, of course, all learners initially have problems recognising words they have heard but not seen written down, and vice versa. For example, a learner recognises and understands "rough" when hearing it in a film set at sea, but does not recognise it when reading a story (but might possibly work it out if the story was also set at sea). Another example would be Brian recognising and understanding the Japanese verb form "*desu*" (meaning "is") but not initially recognising it in speech because of the almost silent "*u*". In our view this is one of many good reasons for multimodal experience of texts (e.g. the teacher reading aloud a story while the learners read it from the page; the learners watching a film in which the dialogue is repeated for each scene in subtitles). This is especially true for learners of English, a language notorious for its lack of correspondence between sound and spelling (for example, a learner seeing "*ghoti*" might pronounce it as "fish" because of the pronunciation of "*gh*" in rough, "*o*" in women and "*ti*" in motion).

If learners cannot recognise the language they hear or see, that language cannot become intake because they will not be able to hold it in short-term memory and will not be able to rehearse it with the inner voice. If the unrecognisable language is new to the learner, it will have no impact on acquisition, except perhaps to contribute to its inhibition as a result of frustration and negativity. If the language is actually recycled language they have previously encountered and recognised, then it loses its potential for maintaining or strengthening records in the long-term memory if it is unrecognisable. However, if new language is recognised it becomes a candidate for intake, and if recycled language is recognised it becomes a candidate for strengthening and maintaining as intake. The more learners are exposed to the target language in use whilst motivated and engaged, the more likely they are to recognise items and features characteristic of that language. However, if learners are exposed to language use that is not meaningful to them and in which hardly anything is recognisable, then they are likely to become demotivated and inattentive and to not recognise items and features they have actually encountered before. On the other hand, if they are exposed to language use that is meaningful and engaging but contains many items and features that are not recognisable, they might recognise the few items and features they have encountered before, and intake of some of them might be achieved. A catchy and moving song with lots of repetition would be a good example of such language use, as would a very dramatic scene from a film or a bizarre advert that is repeated many times.

Recognition in an L2 is more difficult than in the L1. The input might not be perceived accurately, it might not be recognised as L2 input, it might not be recognised as equivalent to previously encountered and recognised input or it might lack the linguistic, contextual and extra-linguistic redundancy typical of most instances of L1 use. In addition, language learners tend to lack tolerance of ambiguity and to give up if they do not immediately recognise a word they hear. On the other hand, native speakers often achieve retrospective recognition when subsequent cotext or context gives clues as to what the missed word might have been. For example, "The xxxxx eventually took off thirty minutes late but we still landed in Rome on time." There's a strong argument for making learners aware of their ability to achieve retrospective recognition in their L1 and to help them to transfer it to their use of the L2.

Readers' Tasks

1 Here is an extract from a book written in Bislama, one of the official languages of Vanuatu. Which language items and features are recognisable to you? Do you think that they could help to make other items and features recognisable if you continued reading the book? It helps if you read it to yourself using your inner voice.

   Republik blong Vanuatu fastem oli kolem Anklo-Franis Kondominium blong Niu Hebridis. Tudei yumi hapi tumas mo yumi praod long niu nem blong

> *kaontri – Vanuatu, we iminim se Kondominium system we istap 70 yia ipas naoia ifinis mo yumi get Kafman blong yumi nomo.* (*Vanuatu*, University of the South Pacific and South Pacific Social Sciences Association, 1980, p. 10)

2 Here is an extract from a book written in English. How much of it is recognisable to you? How much of it is comprehensible?

> The N.S.R. had some fine superheated 4-4-2 tanks, similar in appearance to the Brighton "I3" class and, although the load was less in those days than it became later, these tanks, and their 0-6-4 successors, did some magnificent work on the first stage, to Stoke ... (Allen, 1953, p. 100)

Roles of Recognition in Comprehension

In many spoken and written utterances, recognition is a prerequisite for comprehension. For example, if you cannot recognise the words "benzied" and "distappers", you will not be able to comprehend the utterance "we benzied our distappers today". However, if the input is rich in linguistic, extra-linguistic, sensory and contextual redundancy, an unrecognised expression could become comprehensible. For example, if you hear somebody shout threateningly, "Put that bongle down. If you hit her with it, I'll kill you", you will probably see a mental image of some sort of weapon being held in a hand. Such achieved recognition could facilitate a partial intake of the word "bongle", which, plus the dramatic impact of its initial encounter, could aid its recognition in any future contextualised encounter and this could elaborate and strengthen the record of "bongle" in the intake.

McQueen (2007) and Weber and Broersma (2012) discuss the difficulties that L2 learners have in word recognition in trying to comprehend spoken utterances in the L2. Weber and Broersma (2012) refer to the two processes that are activated when listening to words in spoken discourse, multiple word activation and competition. Hearing a word calls up similar and associated words from long-term memory, which then compete to be recognised as the word heard. For L2 learners, this process is more problematic than for L1 listeners, as both L1 and L2 lexical items are activated and compete for selection. Weber and Broersma (2012) give the examples of Dutch listeners activating the Dutch word *lief*, meaning "sweet", when they hear the English word leaf and the Dutch word *deksel*, meaning "lid", when they hear the English word "desk". A problem of recognition can also occur when hearing one member of a minimal pair, for example "ship" and "sheep" for learners whose L1 does not use one of the vowel sounds and "rice" and "lice" for Japanese learners, whose L1 does not have exact equivalents of the initial consonants. Obviously, context can help clarification (for example, if the rice is being served in a restaurant with a curry) but anxious L2 learners do not always make use of the contextual information available to them.

L2 learners can also have problems recognising L2 words they already know when reading. This is true if a word is in a different form than in previous encounters (e.g. "mistaken" rather than "mistake"), if it is used with a different meaning than previously encountered (e.g. "Ramos was not even booked"), if it is spelled differently (e.g. "practice" vs "practise") or if it occurs in the midst of a flood of unrecognisable items (e.g. "His wood knocked the jack into the gutter").

Known structures can also be unrecognised in L2 utterances, especially in colloquial speech when short forms are used (e.g. "He'll 've gone to the pub with his dad."), when utterances are elided ("When shall we go? Tomorrow?") or when an utterance is spoken so quickly or quietly that some unstressed syllables are not perceived by the L2 listener (e.g. "He lived in Kobe for three years" is heard instead of "He's lived in Kobe for three years").

Recognition is normally a prerequisite for comprehension but it does not ensure comprehension. For example, we both recognise "hirsute" in the utterance "He's hirsute and handsome". But we are not sure what it means. Recognition is also a prerequisite for acquisition but it is not a reliable indicator of it. For example, we would both get a mark for recognising "hirsute" on a word-recognition test and for choosing it to fill the blank in the sentence, "His ———— appearance always disturbs me" from the options "harmonious", "hirsute", "happy" and "heuristic". But neither of us has acquired the word and we certainly never use it.

Recognition can sometimes help in working out apparently incomprehensible utterances, especially if they are used in context and there are nonlinguistic clues available to connect what is not recognised to what is recognised. For example, if you hear, "Broad comes to the crease on a pair ... Broad is off the pair", what do you recognise? If you recognise Broad as a surname, "comes" as a verb of motion in the present simple, "crease" as some sort of line, "pair" as indicating two of something and "off" as indicating something has changed, it still does not help you to understand the utterance. However, if you hear the utterance while listening to commentary on a televised cricket match, see Broad walking to the middle of the stadium for his second innings, putting his bat on a white line, facing a ball from the bowler and then scoring a run, what you have recognised in the utterance might help you to work out some of the meaning of the utterance. Then, if you encounter a similar utterance in a similar context in future you will confirm or disconfirm your hypotheses and understand more. Eventually, after a number of such encounters, you might acquire "crease" with the meaning of the space where the batsman stands in a cricket match and "pair" as scoring zero in both innings of a cricket match, providing you have sufficient motivation to continue to pay attention to such utterances and to connect recognised language to contextual clues in order to work out its meaning.

Roles of Recognition in Production

As we will see later in this chapter, whenever we attempt to communicate in an L2, we can do so in planned discourse by recalling and selecting from learned language in our long-term memory (e.g. when preparing in our minds a question to ask during a lecture or when writing without the pressure of time constraints), but in unplanned discourse we need to retrieve and select from acquired language in our long-term memory (e.g. when answering a question in a lecture, when engaged in spontaneous conversation and when writing with time constraints). In order to achieve recall and retrieval, we need to be able to recognise language items when we access our long-term memory. The stronger the record of an item, the more likely we are to recognise it accurately, and the weaker the record, the more likely we are to not notice it, to be unsure of it or to recognise it erroneously. Factors that strengthen the record and facilitate our recognition include the number of meaningful encounters with it, the number of encounters in contexts similar to the context of our attempted communication, the number and richness of our sensory and linguistic associations with it, the ease with which we can express it with our inner voice and whether it was acquired primarily through implicit or explicit learning.

CONCLUSION

It could be argued that explicit learning, which sometimes involves paying attention to and practising the spelling and pronunciation of words as well as repeating structures in drills, is more likely to facilitate recognition than implicit learning in which form might not be paid much attention to. However, in our view, an exclusive focus on explicit learning could inhibit progress to Intake 3 – Integration because the intake would be impoverished and would lack meaningfulness, engagement and contextualisation, and it would thus be highly unlikely to contribute positively to acquisition. What is needed is a focus on implicit learning to facilitate the acquisition of communicative competence, plus enough explicit learning to facilitate recognition, noticing, monitoring and recall.

Readers' Tasks

1 Do you think language learners should be made familiar with the roles of recognition in comprehension and production?

Do you think language learners should be trained to make use of recognition in comprehension and production?
    Give reasons for your answers to the questions above.

2 Develop a classroom activity that could help learners to make use of recognition in comprehension and/or production.
3 Develop a research activity that could help us find out more about the roles of recognition in acquisition, comprehension and production.

Recall

In our definition, recall involves the deliberate and explicit calling back of records from long-term memory. We do this when we are consciously trying to learn "new" language, when we are practising what we have just learned, when we are revising what we have previously learned and when we are answering discrete-item examination questions. We also do it when we are translating, when we are writing in the L2 and have time to construct what we are writing with reference to our store of explicit knowledge about the language, and also when we are constructing with our inner voice what we intend to say with our outer voice. Recall is obviously important in the learning and use of an L2, but by itself is insufficient as a facilitator of acquisition as it does little to aid spontaneous communication in unplanned discourse and can only bring back what has been learned explicitly from instruction and study and not what has been acquired implicitly. See Krashen (1981, 1982, 1994) and Rebuschat (2015) for detailed discussions of the distinction between explicit learning and implicit acquisition, and N. Ellis (2015) for reasons why implicit acquisition is vital for facilitating communicative competence.

Roles of Recall in Acquisition

If we are defining acquisition as the gaining of the ability to communicate receptively, productively and interactionally with effect, then recall has limited roles to play in the development of this skill. It is indisputably helpful in promoting the explicit learning of an L2 and thus in aiding successful performance in classroom practice, in planned discourse, in examinations, in translation and when we have time for mental construction of what we intend to say. We have, for example, just managed to construct, rather slowly and painfully, a rough translation into Spanish of "Two beers and a still water please. And Gallician octopus, prawns and anchovies". We think in Spanish it is something like, "*Dos cervezas y una agua sin gas, por favor. Y pulpo Gallegos, gambas y boquerones*". We have probably made structural and syntactical errors, and we certainly could not have produced this utterance spontaneously. We also wanted to order pigs' ears but we could not recall the Spanish equivalent. We also have to add, rather embarrassingly, that we could not recall the Spanish word for "and" and had to google it.

It seems that recall can be facilitated by nonlinguistic contributors to the learning and recall experience. Brian, for example, recalls using a visual image of an edam cheese and of a Mamet drama on stage to help him consciously recall the Japanese word "*edamame*", which he needed to order green soya beans in their pods in a bar in Japan. And Murteira, Sowman and Nickels (2018) showed in two experiments that naming an action picture with a verb was helped by seeing a meaningful gesture, and that such priming effects were affected by gesture transparency. Recall can also be triggered by the bizarreness of the original input. As we said in Chapter 2 it seems that the more bizarre comprehensible input is the more memorable, and presumably recallable, it is too. For example, a learner of English who first encountered the lexical item "sock" in a story about a man who always wears a blue sock on his right foot and a red sock on his left foot is more likely to be able to recall the item than a learner who has only encountered it in sentences like, "I bought a pair of blue socks". For research on the bizarreness effect in recall see, for example, Richman (1994), McDaniel and Geraci (2006), Geraci, McDaniel, Miller and Hughes (2013).

Some researchers (e.g. Anderson, 1981, 1993; DeKeyser, 2007b, 2015; Criado, 2016) claim that explicit learning can become implicit acquisition through the automatisation of learned language and skills (a claim usually referred to as skill acquisition theory). If this was the case, recall would play a vital role in eventually promoting acquisition, as it is a prerequisite for the successful explicit learning that would need to precede implicit acquisition. However, most researchers (including N. Ellis, 2015, R. Ellis, 2015 and ourselves) dispute skill acquisition theory and claim that explicit declarative knowledge and implicit procedural knowledge are stored separately in the brain and that there is no automatic progression from declarative to procedural knowledge. We would argue, however, that recall does have the following limited roles to play in promoting acquisition. It can, if successful:

1 aid recognition as a result of frequent recollection of the graphic and phonetic forms of language items;
2 increase learner confidence and self-esteem;
3 encourage learners to read, listen and interact more;
4 aid learner self-monitoring during and after language use (see Chapter 7);
5 become auto-input which could reinforce acquired procedural knowledge (see Chapter 8).

Roles of Recall in Comprehension

So far, we have only considered recall as the bringing out of forms from long-term memory. The term "recall" can also refer to the bringing out of associated meanings and functions from long-term memory. When we encounter a word, expression or structure in an L2 that we recognise but cannot understand, we sometimes try to recall stored meanings or functions associated with this problematic input. This is very difficult if the input is decontextualised and the record created by previous encounters is weak. This is especially true when listening or interacting because of time constraints, but sometimes when we are reading, repeating the problematic input with the inner voice can help us recall associated meanings. For example, when encountering (and recognising) the Japanese word "*migi*" in isolation, Brian remembered using it to give instructions to taxi drivers in Japan but could not remember whether it meant "left" or "right". Then he remembered telling a story of how, when he lived in Kobe, he could direct taxi drivers to his apartment in Sumiyoshidai from Sumiyoshi by saying "*migi*" at every junction. When he said that all the turnings were to the left and therefore he did not know the Japanese for right, Hitomi corrected him and said it was the other way round. Remembering this correction of his story helped Brian to recall the meaning "right" for "*migi*". However, when revising this chapter six months later, he was again unsure whether "*migi*" meant left or right.

A similar procedure could be enacted for a structure. For example, if a learner of English reads "whenever the train was very late, we would have to catch a bus from the station" and recalls having to do this herself many times on her way to school, she might be able to work out the force of the expression "would have to".

Recall is much easier when reading or listening to contextualised texts than when encountering bits of language in isolation, as there are many more cues to aid recall. This is an advantage enjoyed by learners who are immersed in the L2 compared to those whose exposure is restricted to that experienced when learning the L2 explicitly in a classroom.

Because recall in our definition is a conscious, deliberate procedure there is a danger that, when encountering a problematic but recognised word or structure, we recall what was salient and noticed explicitly without being aware of its potential for contextual incongruity. For example, we might recall learning that the imperative is used in commands, directions and instructions and misunderstand the utterance, "Give Joe the money, I don't care" and think the speaker wants the interactant to give Joe the money, when in fact it might be the opposite.

Roles of Recall in Production

When participating in planned discourse, recall can play an important role, provided the writer has the time and skill to pause, recall, select and combine, as well as the ability to write some of the text spontaneously through retrieval from the acquired stores in long-term memory. Brian has just tried doing this to write about football in French (a language he has very little fluency or accuracy in) and composed the following:

"*Mon equipe favorite est Liverpool. J'adore la chemise rouge et le (way) l'equipe jouent*" (My favourite team is Liverpool. I love the red shirt and the way the team play).

That one sentence took a painful five minutes to compose, and is almost certainly full of errors. It was composed almost entirely from attempts to recollect bits of language learned from explicit instruction at school, and only the function words were retrieved spontaneously (the result presumably of very little experience of French in use in the classroom at school). Interestingly, some of the words were used because they could be recalled rather than because they actually represented what Brian wanted to say.

In spontaneous speech, and especially in interaction, recall can only play a very limited and occasional role, as constantly spending time trying to recall words learned explicitly would inevitably lead to halting monologues lacking fluency, coherence and impact and would result in frequently having to yield turns in interaction. This is what seems to happen with many language learners whose learning has been almost exclusively explicit. They lose potential turns in a conversation because by the time they have composed an utterance from recalled declarative knowledge someone else has claimed the turn. This is also what can happen in classrooms when a teacher asks a question and gets annoyed when no answer is immediately offered, as recorded by Bao (2002, 2013, 2014) in his reports of a research project in Vietnam investigating reticence in the classroom. The teachers attributed students' reticence to answer questions to their fear of losing face, their lack of confidence and even their laziness, whereas the students said they wanted to answer but the teacher did not give them enough time to compose an answer in their heads in order to respond. However, recall can be useful in spontaneous discourse when speakers pause momentarily in search of the right word for themselves or their interlocutor(s).

If a learner is in a situation in which she has the opportunity to compose an utterance before offering it (e.g. in a lecture or meeting) then recall of learned declarative knowledge can be combined with retrieval of acquired procedural knowledge to precompose, monitor and revise an utterance in the inner voice prior to asking a question or making a comment.

Readers' Tasks

1 Develop a classroom activity to help learners make effective use of recall.
2 Develop a classroom activity to help learners to lessen their dependence on recall during unplanned discourse.

Rehearsal

Rehearsal involves instant repetition of encountered input, either subconsciously with the inner voice, consciously with the inner voice or consciously with the outer voice. This repetition is often instant but could occur at a later stage when a learner is reinforcing classroom learning or revising for an exam.

Roles of Rehearsal in Acquisition

Rehearsal plays a very important role in acquisition, as when we are listening or reading all the words we encounter are automatically rehearsed in the phonological loop in Broca's area of the brain. In order for this to occur, when reading a word the graphic representation of the word we see is converted into a phonological representation through the use of the inner voice. This rehearsal of words helps us to refresh the initial representations of words in Intake – 1 Perception, to maintain records of words already encountered and taken in and to create records of words not previously encountered. Without this rehearsal, new records will not be created. However, their creation depends also on processing new information about "phonemes and lexemes, in connection with other sensory–emotional data" (Schütze, 2017, p. 14). The strength of a new record created in the hippocampus and stored, it is thought, in the neocortices adjacent to the hippocampus (Tranel & Damasio, 2002), as well as the strength of the eventual maintenance of this record, will depend on the richness of the extra-linguistic and nonlinguistic information associated with the word in its intake, as well as on the spaced recycling of the word in the input. For discussion of the role of rehearsal and the phonological loop, see Gazzaniga, Ivry and Mangun (2019).

Deliberate rehearsal of a word many times on initially encountering it in order to memorise it might aid progress to Intake 2 – Transfer but instant rehearsal without sensory–emotional associations and spaced recycling is unlikely to facilitate progress to Intake 3 – Integration and to further processing. In addition, any records achieved are likely to quickly weaken and decay. Or, as Schütze (2017, pp. 153–154) says, "when acquiring a new word, there is no point in repeating it several times in a row. In that scenario, the phonemes and lexemes would not stop being processed. In order for repetition to be effective, the process has to start anew every time a word is repeated".

Schütze (2017) describes how rehearsal plays a vital role in the initial recording of a lexical item. He gives the example of how the item "*der Kaffee*" comes to mind when drinking a "very strong and very hot and very small coffee" (p. 32) in an airport in Germany. He describes how in order to be able to "recall that word at any time in the future" (p. 32) the words "*der Kaffe*" need to get your attention so that the executive control function in the frontal lobe can direct attention to the words and the words can be rehearsed in the phonological loop. The phonemes are rehearsed in Broca's area until they are identified and can be stored temporarily in the left side of the parietal lobe, so that they can be compared to phonemes already in the repertoire which are stored in Wernicke's area.

> In order to match the German phonemes to the ones you know, the loop will work together with Wernicke's area to rehearse English phonemes ... as well as German phonemes ... Once identified, the phonemes are matched to a lexeme ... in Wernicke's area ... Wernicke's area contacts the non-mesial region, where the index of records of words that are already known are stored, to see if the new word matches a lexeme that is already known, in this case the lexeme of "coffee". (Schütze, 2017, p. 33)

In addition, information from the senses, for example the smell and texture of the "*Kaffe*" and the "image of the café and music that was playing in the background" (p. 33) is fed from the cortices to the hippocampus, where a record of the word is created and then moved to the non-mesial region for storage.

Roles of Rehearsal in Comprehension

As we have noted, when we are listening or reading all the words we encounter are automatically rehearsed in the phonological loop. This ensures we hold the words long enough in Intake 1 – Perception for us to retrieve associated images and meanings in order to select those that match the context in the input, and to pass this information on to Wernicke's area of the brain for meaning-processing to take place. Sometimes we pause in our reading or listening because of retrieval failure, and we consciously rehearse a word in order to recall an appropriate meaning. The more experience we have of extensive listening and reading of meaningful and comprehensible input, the more likely we are to develop facility in automatic retrieval.

Roles of Rehearsal in Production

Production involves recalling or retrieving learned or acquired elements and then combining them to produce an utterance. During this process, elements are rehearsed to ascertain their degree of fit. For example, in unplanned discourse the identity and form of a word to be used is determined after matching phonemes to lexemes, taking into account other words in the utterance and then adding appropriate morphemes. Before actual production, "a morpheme feeds information back to the lexeme which has been matched to its phonemes, because if it does not fit, either another morpheme is tried or another lexeme with its phonemes is rehearsed" (Schütze, 2017, p. 10). In spontaneous speech this is a subconscious process, which is performed in the brain in "hundreds of milliseconds" (Schütze, 2017, p. 10). However, facility in such spontaneous rehearsal requires rich, massive, motivated and engaged exposure to meaningful and comprehensible language in contextualised use. If learners are pushed into premature production without experience of such exposure, they are forced into using recall in order to compose utterances and are likely to be prone to excessive hesitation, lack of fluency and lack of accuracy. This is one of many reasons why many researchers advocate a comprehension approach for beginners, in which learners are provided with a rich experience of reading and listening to the L2 being used before they are encouraged to produce the L2 themselves (Barnard, 2007; Richards & Rodgers, 2014; Marczak, 2018).

> **Readers' Tasks**
>
> 1 Take any L2 coursebook and open it at any page at random.
>
> Analyse each of the activities on the page and decide whether it is more likely to facilitate recall or rehearsal.
>
> 2 Focus on an activity in 1 that you found to be likely to only facilitate recall. Adapt the activity so that it becomes more likely to facilitate rehearsal.

Retrieval

Brian has been in workshops a number of times when Hitomi has demonstrated a TPR Plus (Total Physical Response Plus) lesson in which she sings a Japanese song and the participants perform the actions. Brian has just been able to retrieve without effort snatches of the song by visualising images of people performing it. The images were not in their original sequence but, he thinks, in order of the impact they made on him. He remembered, "*Te o utte*" (Clap your hands), "*Te o musunde*" (Clench your hands), "*Te o agate*" (Raise your hands), "*Te o sagate*" (Lower your hands), "*motto*" (more). This instant and effortless recollection of chunks of language is one type of retrieval, and is particularly useful when needing to use formulaic language. It is often stimulated by associated sensory and/or affective images, and is a reminder of how useful it is to learn an L2 through experience of it in meaningful and contextualised use. Another example of such retrieval is a TPR Plus (Tomlinson, 1994b) activity in which Brian told a dramatic story about strange creatures kidnapping a man and a woman from a beach (Tomlinson, 2001) whilst all the students acted it out and then retold the story collectively from retrieval. Students in a number of countries, and at a number of levels (including beginners), have managed to act it out and then to retell it spontaneously and successfully.

Other types of retrieval involve retrieving hypothesised generalisations and components of language items from stores in the brain, in order to select from them in the creation of an utterance. In unplanned discourse, this is normally an instantaneous and subconscious procedure. For example, in response to someone on the phone asking, "Can I speak to Bernard, please?" you might see images of Bernard putting his coat on to leave the office, hear him say "Just going to the Red Lion. Be back at two", retrieve the pronoun "he", retrieve the verb "to go", retrieve generalisations about the simple past and the present perfect, retrieve the preposition "to" and retrieve the expressions "Red Lion", "the pub", "out" and "lunch" and say, "He's gone to lunch". If you had to recall all these components consciously, Bernard would be back from lunch before you responded to the request.

Of the four procedures described in this chapter, retrieval has received the most attention in the literature, and this reflects its perceived importance in the acquisition process. There are sections on the role of retrieval in SLA in a number of books and articles. Some of these publications, though, use "retrieval" to refer to both the subconscious, spontaneous process of bringing back from acquired procedural knowledge and the conscious, deliberate process of bringing back from learned declarative knowledge (what we are referring to as "recall") (e.g. Lalonde & Mack, 1994; Barcroft, 2007; Karpicke & Roediger, 2008; Martin, Wiggs & Nakata, 2017). Some of the publications use "recall" to refer to both processes (e.g., Schütze, 2017; Gazzaniga, Ivry & Mangun, 2019) and some use the term "access" to refer to both processes, especially with reference to lexical retrieval during oral production (e.g. Levelt, 2001; Costa & Santesteban, 2004; Bialystok, Craik & Luk, 2008). Many of these publications also use the terms "retrieval" and "recall" interchangeably (e.g. Pyc & Rawson, 2009) and some deservedly respected books on SLA make no reference to either term in their Contents or Index (e.g. Ortega, 2009; Gass & Mackey, 2012; R. Ellis, 2015; Loewen, 2015; Long, 2015; Saville-Troike & Barto, 2017). This is a reflection of how large and complex a field SLA research is, and how researchers tend to focus on those aspects of it that they have researched and/or that they consider to be the most important. It also reflects the split in the field, whereby some SLA researchers include research from brain studies in their considerations and some do not. We believe that brain studies, though rarely providing conclusive proof, are yielding valuable indications of the role of the brain in language acquisition, and we also believe that both the terms "recall" and "retrieval" should be used, and used distinctively and consistently, as they do distinguish between two distinct and important processes.

Roles of Retrieval in Acquisition

Whenever language is retrieved from the brain, the effort and process of doing so strengthens its record and assists in the process of maintenance. This occurs when "new" language is being stored in association with other language retrieved from the brain (e.g. similar sounding words, words with similar meaning), when meanings and associations are being retrieved during comprehension of input and when intended meanings are being mapped onto linguistic options prior to language production. The more frequent and useful retrieval of a language feature occurs, the more likely it is to be maintained and eventually acquired. One reason for this is that retrieval is likely to stimulate subconscious noticing, especially if a feature has been retrieved as a candidate for selection in use. Another reason is that retrieval triggers sensory and emotive associations that strengthen the record of the language feature.

Schütze (2017) gives a detailed account of the roles of retrieval (which he refers to as "recall") in acquisition on pp. 34–39. He says that in order to retrieve a word you need, the executive control calls up a number of related words (e.g. if the need is to order a coffee in German, the words "*Kaffe*", "*Espresso*" and "*Tee*" might be called forward, as well as associated lexemes such as "*Zucker*" and "*Milch*" and phonemes with similar sounds). If the desired word is not immediately retrieved, then the hippocampus can review the associated sensual information as well as the other nonlinguistic information stored when the record of the word was created. This can then trigger the memory (especially if emotions are stimulated) and the word can be retrieved. This in turn strengthens the record of the word and contributes to maintenance and acquisition. This process also reminds us how important rich and meaningful exposure to contextualised use is in the processes of intake and retrieval.

Believers in skill acquisition theory seem to ignore the evidence of brain studies and claim that explicit declarative knowledge can be proceduralised through constant practice and can eventually lead to automatic production. DeKeyser (2007b, p. 95), for example, claims that "proceduralised knowledge ... no longer requires the individual to retrieve bits and pieces of information from memory and assemble them into a 'program' for a specific behavior; instead, that 'program' is now available as a ready-made chunk ... to be called up in its entirety each time the conditions for that behaviour are met". This might have some relevance in relation to such skills as swimming and cycling, but we cannot believe that skill acquisition theory is relevant (as DeKeyser claims) to language acquisition, as so much of the credible research evidence on SLA acquisition (and especially that from brain studies) contradicts it.

Roles of Retrieval in Comprehension

When we are listening or reading, we make use of retrieval to assist our understanding of the language we are experiencing. Sometimes we retrieve associated words (e.g. "bed" when we hear "pillow", and "chair" when we hear "cushion") but often our retrieval is of the sensory and emotive associations that we stored when first experiencing the language feature (e.g. seeing Miles Davis playing and hearing a slow ballad when we hear the word "trumpet"; seeing a huge sign by a busy road in Indonesia with "AWAS" printed in red letters and feeling a sense of danger when reading the Bahasa Indonesian word "*awas*"; seeing a picture of a mother cat warning her kittens about a dangerous dog when the Japanese word "*abunai*" was also immediately retrieved on retrieval of the meaning of "*awas*"). Such retrievals are instantaneous and automatic, and are dependent on rich processing of linguistic information and extra-linguistic and nonlinguistic associations during the intake and further processing stages of acquisition. Retrieval failure in the L1 usually tells us to tolerate ambiguity and wait for eventual clarification. However, many L2 learners lack the confidence to tolerate ambiguity and resort to attempted recall. This, of course, takes time, and if resorted to frequently, delays comprehension when reading and prevents it whilst listening. It can also lead to slow and painful micro-processing of the text, failure to respond to the text holistically and frustration. Rich experience of listening to and reading the L2 in meaningful, contextualised and, ideally, multimodal use can aid retrieval. Topic familiarity (see Rydland, Aukrust & Fulland, 2012) can also be a facilitator of retrieval as it can encourage visualisation and positive confidence. Impoverished experience of only hearing and reading the L2 in decontextualised and mono-modal practice can lead to the excessive use of recall during comprehension.

Roles of Retrieval in Production

In spontaneous speech, retrieval plays a vital role, as fluency, accuracy, appropriateness and effectiveness are dependent on automatic retrieval, monitoring and selection from acquired options stored in the brain. L2 learners who are unable to achieve this automatic retrieval resort to attempted recall, speak with excessive pauses and nervous hesitation, and are unlikely to achieve effective communication.

When writing in an L2, automatic retrieval facilitates speed, fluency and confidence. The ideal is to write automatically from inner speech prompts, and then to make use of recall when monitoring what we have written for accuracy, appropriateness and effectiveness. This reliance on retrieval is quite normal when writing in the L1, but often when writing in the L2 we need to pause and think consciously in order to recall a word or expression or to check the accuracy of a structure or spelling.

Visualisation, emotive association and topic familiarity are powerful facilitators of retrieval for production. For example, if you are talking or writing about a topic you know well, can easily visualise and with which you have emotive associations, then doing so in the L2 should facilitate retrieval much more than if talking or writing about a topic that we do not know much about, have problems visualising and have no emotive associations with (see Schütze, 2017, pp. 4–39). The retrieval achieved when talking or writing can facilitate effective communication, which then becomes rich auto-input (i.e. input produced by the self) and a powerful resource of maintenance and acquisition (see Chapter 8 in this volume).

For detailed discussion of the development and roles of automatic retrieval, see O'Malley and Chamot (1990) (who review literature that views development from controlled retrieval to automatic retrieval as a process seen primarily as accompanying progress from lack of proficiency to proficiency), Galian-Lopez (2018) and Chapter 6 in this volume. Schütze (2017) makes many references to the roles of "recall" in comprehension, production and acquisition, but in many cases he is using the term "recall" to cover what we mean by "retrieval".

SUMMARY

In this chapter we have focused on recognition, recall, rehearsal and retrieval.

Recognition is the process of noticing that a language item or feature in the input conforms to something you are familiar with. It could be that a word is recognised as Italian, that an utterance is recognised as informal, that a structure is recognised as referring to the past, that the pronunciation of a word conforms to the expected norms of the target language, that a word is recognised as a noun, that an intonation pattern is recognised as questioning, that a voice is recognised as angry or that a word is recognised as familiar. The process of recognition can be conscious or subconscious, and is a prerequisite for Intake 1 (i.e. Perception). If nothing can be recognised from a stream of language, then nothing in that stream can be acquired.

Recall involves a deliberate and conscious attempt to bring back stored explicit intake so as to contribute a language item or feature to planned discourse, to understand recognised, but not immediately comprehended, input, and sometimes to pause momentarily to search for a word or phrase to contribute to unplanned discourse that has been mainly constructed automatically.

Rehearsal involves the deliberate or automatic repetition of immediate or previous input either overtly through speech (or occasionally writing) or covertly through the use of the inner voice. It plays an important role in acquisition in the conversion of graphic images into sound to facilitate comprehension, and in the strengthening of input for conversion into Intake 1 (Perception). It also plays a role in comprehension, for example, when the learner rehearses an utterance to aid recall and in production, for example, when a learner rehearses options in the mind before making a selection and then combining selections to make an utterance and rehearsing the utterance before producing it.

Retrieval is the process of automatic selection from the store of implicit knowledge that facilitates and expedites fluent unplanned discourse as well as fluent reading and listening. It is a mental process that the user is unaware of, and that not only facilitates language use but language acquisition too. This it achieves by strengthening intake as a result of successful use, or revising it as a result of unsuccessful use. It also creates original auto-input (see Chapter 8) as a result of combining retrieved elements into novel utterances.

As we have seen, recognition, recall, rehearsal and retrieval play very important roles in language acquisition and use. What we need to ask now is how we can apply what we know and what we surmise about them in the practice of language learning.

Readers' Tasks

1a Think of a topic that you are very familiar with, can visualise easily and have emotive associations with. Try to write a paragraph about this topic for a children's encyclopaedia in an L2 you have acquired.

1b Write a paragraph for the same encyclopaedia as in 1 above on a topic you are much less familiar with, have problems visualising and have no emotive associations with.

1c Compare your paragraphs in 1 and 2 above by considering how long each one took to write, how much resort to recall was necessary and how effective you think the paragraphs are.

1d What implications, if any, do you think your comparisons have for the acquisition of an L2?

2 Devise a classroom activity that could help learners to improve their use of retrieval during unplanned discourse.

Part Two: The Application of Theory to Learning

Application to L2 Language Planning

One obvious application to language planning is for administrators to ensure the provision of resources to enable the massive and rich exposure to the target language in use that can help learners to develop a repertoire of stored items capable of achieving automatic recognition as well as the capacities for automatic rehearsal and retrieval which they need in order to acquire and use the language. Ideally, these resources would be housed in a self-study centre, such as the one at Kanda University in Japan:

> The Self-Access Learning Self-Access Learning Center (SALC) at Kanda University of International Studies is a learning community designed to help KUIS students to develop

lifelong language learner autonomy. The SALC provides a social space to help motivate learners and to facilitate the development of fluency and confidence. The SALC is filled with resources in order to provide learning opportunities to suit all students. There are also different areas and rooms within the SALC where students can carry out language study or use. The SALC is designed to enable students to learn in their own time, in their own ways, and to develop language skills for the real world. Learning advisors and other staff are on hand to help users and the SALC offers modules and courses designed to promote learner autonomy. www.kandagaigo.ac.jp/kuis/salc/

This facility features collections of books, journals, magazines, comics, audio CDs, videos, films, television programmes and advertisements that can provide learners with extensive, multimodal and contextualised experience of the target language in use. Obviously, not every institution can afford such a facility. We have, however, seen many examples where the provision of extensive experience of the target language has been provided in schools by a small library of written, spoken and audio-visual texts with donations of resources from local businesses and aid organisations, and even in classes where the teacher has got her learners to build libraries of potentially engaging texts in cardboard boxes by using their initiative in soliciting resources from local donors they have succeeded in persuading to help. All that was needed initially was impetus and examples from the planners.

Another application to language planning is the recognition of the value of extensive exposure to the target language in use and the provision of time on timetables for such experience. This experience could include simply reading a book, listening to a recording or watching a film. The problem is usually that so little time is available that it is typically allocated exclusively to the explicit teaching of language items and features. Many projects have demonstrated that planning for a classroom period in which the students simply experience the target language in use without any interventions by the teacher is a valuable investment of time. See, for example, Elley and Mangubhai (1981), Krashen (2004) and Maley (2008) for examples of how such allocation of classroom time has resulted in dramatically improved learner performance in reading, listening, speaking and writing. We would argue that one of the reasons for this is the gradually improving facilities of automatic rehearsal and retrieval that can develop as a result of such experience over time.

Application to L2 Curriculum Development

We know of no curriculum or syllabus that makes any reference to recognition, recall, rehearsal and retrieval as capabilities to aim to develop. We would like to see explicit specification of these capabilities as targets to help learners to develop, with suggestions to teachers as to how to facilitate such development.

Recognition

As we have discussed, recognition is necessary but not sufficient in order for encountered language to be acquired. Recognition can be identification as being in the target language, as having a function in the utterance, as having been encountered before and as having specific meanings. Ideally, the syllabus should facilitate recognition by making provision for learner experience of likely phoneme combinations, of likely spelling combinations, of sound/spelling correspondences, of the functional use of intonation, stress, volume and pause, of likely syntactical combinations, of words that typically prime the use of other words (Hoey, 2005), of words that typically collocate with other words (Evert, 2007), of common prefixes and suffixes, of recycled structure and lexis (Nation & Macalister, 2010) and of semantically significant hand and facial gestures (Gullberg & McCafferty, 2008).

We believe that a curriculum or syllabus can also help teachers to facilitate learner recognition by specifying, or at least recommending, that teachers should:

- perform stories, scenes from novels and scenes from plays for the learners, having first planned and rehearsed their intonation, stress, pauses and gestures;
- read texts aloud to learners before asking them to read them silently (especially at lower levels);
- expose learners to all the likely phonemic, spelling and syntactical combinations of the target language without necessarily drawing attention to them;
- provide rich multimodal exposure to the language in use through the use of films, videos, television programmes, advertisements, cartoons, comics, illustrated magazines, etc.;
- provide exposure to different varieties, dialects and accents of the target language through films, videos and television programmes and through inviting speakers of the target language to talk to their learners;
- devise activities in which the learners are asked to recognise target-language utterances, permissible target-language combinations, target-language collocations and typical target-language extra-linguistic indicators of meaning.

Recall

We would like to see curricula specify time to be spent on revisiting what has already been explicitly learned, with a view to facilitating its recall. These would not be revision sessions in the conventional sense of reteaching and then testing the same points that have already been taught, but a new and explicit focus on these teaching points in different contexts and with some additional information. These sessions would also include activities in which the learners are prompted to recall what they have already learned, by encouraging them to use visualisation to recall images previously stimulated by the language being focused on, to use their inner voice to repeat language items internally, to talk to themselves about what they are trying to recall, to make again discoveries they have previously made, and to share their recall with other learners so as to stimulate further recall. Obviously, these recall strategies would work best if the original explicit learning was achieved with the aid of visualisation, the use of the inner voice, discovery activities and the sharing of declarative knowledge.

The revisiting sessions would also feature activities in which the learners make use of recall during intensive reading of texts that they need a detailed understanding of and during planned discourse tasks, such as preparing a speech or writing instructions for a game, when they have the need and the time to make sure they get it right. These activities should not be treated as revision tests, and the learners should also be taught and encouraged to make use of paper and online reference materials to aid recall.

Retrieval

We would also like to see curricula specify time to be spent on revisiting what might have been implicitly acquired. These activities would be meaning-focused, and targeted at achieving communicative intent. They would include purposeful reading and/or listening to extensive texts previously encountered, as well as reading and/or listening to elaborated, extended or changed versions of texts already encountered, to texts on topics already focused on, and to texts belonging to text types (e.g. persuasion) and genres (e.g. newspaper editorials) already encountered. The activities would also include unplanned discourse production activities similar to those already experienced receptively (e.g. being interviewed on a topic the learners have already watched other people being interviewed on), interactions similar to those they have experienced before either receptively or productively and impromptu presentations on topics they have researched but have not prepared presentations on. They could also include such novel and challenging activities as providing a spontaneous commentary to a muted video of a sporting event they have previously watched with the sound on, making up the continuation of a story in a circle of peers, with each learner contributing the next sentence spontaneously in turn round and round the circle, and teaching a group of peers about a topic they have recently been taught about.

Application to L2 Methodology

Obviously, a lot of our suggestions above for syllabus specifications to teachers to help their learners to develop recognition skills are relevant to methodology as well. In addition, we would like to make the following suggestions to teachers:

1 Make use of methodologies that feature massive and meaningful exposure to the target language in use. Such methodologies include:

- Content-based language teaching (CBLT), in which learners focus on learning a topic or an academic subject through the use of the L2 (Coyle, Hood & Marsh, 2010; Lopriore, 2018);
- Extensive reading, in which learners read an L2 book, magazine, newspaper or comic for pleasure, without being monitored or assessed (Elley & Mangubhai, 1981; Krashen, 2004; Maley, 2008);
- Language through literature, in which learners are engaged in experiencing accessible and meaningful poems, stories, novels, plays and films (Paran & Robinson, 2015; Saito & Wales, 2015; Bland, 2018; Jones, 2019; Tomlinson, 2019a);
- Text-driven approaches, in which learners' experience of a potentially engaging spoken, written or multimodal L2 text drives response, analysis and production activities (Tomlinson, 2013d; Tomlinson & Masuhara, 2018b);
- TPR Plus approaches, in which learners respond physically to the teacher telling a story, giving instructions to play a game, advising on the painting of a mural, instructing the creation of body sculptures, stimulating the creation of a meal from specified ingredients, etc. (Tomlinson, 1995);
- Task-based language teaching (TBLT), in which learners make use of their existing linguistic resources to perform a meaning-focused task with intended communicative outcomes (for example, designing an advertisement) (Van den Branden, 2006; Long, 2015; Ellis, Skehan, Li, Shintani & Lambert, 2019).
- Project driven approaches, in which learners do research in order to make a written and/or spoken presentation on a particular issue or topic (Haines, 1989; Wicks, 2000).
- Action-oriented approaches, in which learners are active agents of their own learning in real life scenarios in which they collaborate with others in order to achieve intended situational outcomes (Piccardo & North, 2019).

All these methodologies provide opportunities for recognition of language items and features, recall of meanings and functions, rehearsal of previously and newly encountered items and retrieval of images, associations and meanings. We have found, for example, that CBLT has facilitated easy retrieval through repeated focus on the same topic, that Language Through Literature has stimulated retrieval of elements of texts that have achieved engagement and stimulated imaging, and that TPR Plus activities, in which the learners have mimed dramatic stories narrated by the teacher, have enabled learners to retell the story both instantly and at a distance, as well as to make use of their retrieval in order to continue the story for themselves.

2 Train and encourage learners to visualise and to use their inner voice when responding to spoken, written and multimodal texts. Visualisation and inner voice use are vital facilitators of recall, rehearsal and retrieval, yet research shows (De Guerrero, 2005, 2017; Tomlinson & Avila, 2007a; Tomlinson, 2011d, 2020a) that

L2 learners who habitually make use of visualisation and their inner voice in their L1 typically do not do so at the early stages of acquiring an L2. See Tomlinson and Avila (2007b) for suggestions for activities that train learners to visualise and to use their inner voice (e.g. turning a story into a film whilst reading it; creating visual connections to previous experience whilst listening to a talk; providing an inner voice L2 commentary to what can be seen from the window whilst travelling; composing questions with the inner voice before asking them).

3. Provide repeated encounters with "new" language a number of times at spaced intervals as the rehearsal involved creates a new and probably stronger record each time and thus facilitates recall and retrieval. For long-term acquisition, Schütze (2017, p. 152) recommends repeating exposure to a word at uniform intervals and says, "a general guideline is to repeat a word four times using a 'one plus four' (initial encounter plus four repetitions) design for a total of four practice sessions" over a period of two weeks. He also recommends elaborative processing, which involves the learners not only recognising the words but using them too, and he stresses that nonlinguistic information (provided, for example, by pictures, emotional connotations and sensory involvement) can strengthen records and fast-track words "into long-term memory".

Another approach to providing repeated encounters with the same language involves the learners reading the same text a number of times. For example, Serrano and Huang (2018) report studies demonstrating the beneficial vocabulary-gain effects of repeated assisted readings of the same text or of similar texts with the same target lexical items, and they investigate the optimum time gap between readings. In their own study, they found that an intensive distribution approach, in which learners read and listened to the same text once a day for five days, led to the learning of more items than a spaced distribution approach, in which the learners read the same text every week for five weeks. However, the learners in the spaced distribution group retained the items they had learned far better than those in the intensive distribution group. Tomlinson's (2013d) text-driven approach (TDA) also involves returning to the same text many times, with the difference being that the text has been selected for its potential for affective and cognitive engagement and the text is returned to during the same unit for different purposes.

Task repetition is another way of providing learners with repeated experience of language in use and is supported by research evidence in, for example, Shintani (2016), Vrikki (2017) and Bygate (2018).

4. Provide learners with opportunities for planned discourse, during which they are encouraged to use strategies for recall, as well as plentiful opportunities for unplanned discourse and face-to-face interaction during which there is no time for recall and effective retrieval is essential.

5 Ensure that retrieval for comprehension and for production is required in situations with the potential for achieving affective and cognitive engagement. This can involve the hippocampus in facilitating retrieval of the nonlinguistic information that has been recorded with the L2 features being reviewed for receptive or productive use. For a detailed discussion of the role of affect in the language acquisition process, see Mates and Joaquin (2013).
6 Encourage learners to make contact with their target language outside the classroom for gaining entertainment, information and social interaction as this can lead to informal acquisition. See, for example, Sockett (2014) and Lech and Harris (2019) for evidence of the positive role in acquisition which can be played by informal online learning.
7 Above all, make sure that when learners are asked to read or listen to the L2 and when they are asked to use it, they do so in situations rich in the sensory, contextual and other nonlinguistic information that has been shown to facilitate storage, recall and retrieval.

Application to L2 Materials Development

Very few of the suggestions for activities we make above in relation to curriculum development and to methodology are currently applied in commercially published coursebooks.

We have just taken from our shelves *The Big Picture Intermediate* (Goldstein, 2012), a popular coursebook with many good qualities. We have analysed the first four pages of Unit 8 to see if we can find any application of what is known about recognition, recall, rehearsal and retrieval and found:

1 An activity asking learners to look at two images and say whether they have positive or negative associations (I on p. 82) and an activity encouraging affective association and therefore possibly facilitating subsequent recall and/or retrieval.
2 Activities asking learners to relate the topic to their own lives and to respond to the opinions expressed in the texts (6 on p. 83), activities encouraging personalisation and cognitive engagement and therefore possibly facilitating recall and/or retrieval.
3 Questions inviting learners to reveal the complete story of their country, good and bad, and to say how they would like people to see their culture (4 on p. 84), activities that can encourage personalisation and cognitive engagement and therefore possibly facilitate recall and/or retrieval.
4 An activity asking learners to think of "five positive non-stereotypical images of your country" and then to present one of these images to the class and explain

what it shows about their country (Speaking 1 and 2 on p. 85). Also, activities encouraging personalisation, cognitive engagement and affective engagement and therefore likely to facilitate recall and/or retrieval.

We welcome these activities, but we have to say that most of the other activities on these four pages are unlikely to facilitate the use or development of recognition, recall, rehearsal or retrieval, or even contribute at all to the likely acquisition of language or the development of the ability to use it effectively. They include such activities as answering surface questions about short texts, filling in blanks, matching words to synonyms, true/false questions and turning direct speech into reported speech, explicit learning and practice activities that also dominate the units in other currently used coursebooks we have looked at (Tomlinson & Masuhara, 2013, 2018b).

When flicking through *The Big Picture Intermediate* (Goldstein, 2012) we were pleased to notice that many of the illustrations not only were interesting and aesthetically engaging but were used to stimulate personal connections or cognitive engagement (e.g. a photo which juxtaposes a barren brown desert with an adjoining green golf course on pp. 38–39). We were also pleased to see that there is at least an attempt at recycling, with the provision of a one-page review at the end of every three units. Although these review pages tend to be dominated by tests of language items taught in the preceding units, they do provide some further experience of encountering and using language met in those units.

We would like to see far fewer of the stereotypical coursebook activities which provide decontextualised language and depersonalised language-focused practice. Instead, we would like to see far more activities that involve experience of the extra-linguistic and nonlinguistic features of contextualised use of language. They are much more likely to stimulate personal, affective and cognitive engagement, which enriches and facilitates intake and retrieval. We would also like to see far more recycling of language than is currently attempted in coursebooks, as the typical lack of recycling weakens records in the intake and makes retrieval problematic (see Tschichold, 2012 for an analysis of a textbook that fails to recycle the vocabulary it introduces).

Readers' Tasks

Look at the first four pages of a unit in any coursebook and:

1 Try to find any activities likely to facilitate or contribute to the development of recognition, recall, rehearsal or retrieval.
2 Find an activity in the unit that does not contribute to the development of recognition, recall, rehearsal or retrieval, and think of ways in which the activity could be adapted so that it does contribute to the development of effective use of one or more of these procedures.

Application to L2 Assessment

Recognising, recalling, rehearsing and retrieving are procedures that can facilitate the acquisition of a target language and the development of communicative competence in that language. They are not competences whose mastery should be assessed and evaluated.

Recognition of lexis and structure is sometimes tested in L2 classes and often assessed in SLA research. Such tests are temptingly easy to set and mark, and can achieve a high degree of reliability. Here are some examples of such tests:

1 Which of the following words are English?

substance; entrada; mazui; enlightenment; distraction; secola; sensation; samma; electrician.

2 Which of the following words do you know?

street; sandle; avenue; belt; kild; shield; sunshine; bicker; effective; sensational; bully; prite.

3 Which of the following refer to the past?

He works there. He's worked there. He'll work there. He was working there. He would have been working there. He was going to work there. He had been working there. He's going to work there. He's working there.

These tests might be easy to set and mark, but how valid and valuable are they? A mistake in 1 could indicate no previous experience of the word, students who say they know "shield" in 2 might not be able to understand or use it in context, and getting 100 per cent in 3 does not equate with ability to understand or use the functions of the structures in communication. However, provided the limitations of such tests are recognised they can be of some value as preliminary exercises in phases of explicit teaching, for example of English noun-indicating suffixes in 1.

Recall is often tested in revision exercises requiring learners to explicitly recall lexis, structural items or structural rules in order to do fill in the blank exercises, matching exercises, true/false exercises and sentence completion exercises. Recall could more usefully be assessed and encouraged in activities in which the learners make use of recall in activities requiring comprehension and/or production of language in communication. Here are some examples of such assessment activities.

1 You are going to listen to instructions on how to make a paper aeroplane. Write down words and expressions that you associate with paper and with aeroplanes, as well as instructions you expect to hear.

Look at each of your words or expressions and try to see pictures in your mind of what it represents.

Listen to the instructions and make a paper aeroplane with the piece of paper you have been given. You can look at your list of words and expressions and you can ask your teacher questions about the instructions.

2 Think of a game that is popular in your country. You are going to write instructions so that people who do not know the game will be able to play it.

Write down in English all the words you think you will need to use in your instructions. If you cannot think of a word you need, see pictures in your mind of yourself playing the game to try to stimulate your memory.

Write your instructions and then give them to a partner and ask them to underline anything they do not understand. Then use the underlinings to help you to revise your instructions.

3 Think of an interesting conversation that you have taken part in or listened to. You are going to use that conversation as part of a short story that is intended to amuse, puzzle or excite the other members of your group. Think of a way to use the conversation in your story.

Before you develop your story write down everything you can remember about:

1 Direct speech
2 Reported speech.

Develop your story in your mind by first of all thinking of expressions. Then tell your story to yourself in your head.

Write your story and use your notes about direct and reported speech to help you whilst and after writing the story.

Retrieval, being automatic and subconscious, cannot be assessed directly. It can be assessed indirectly though by setting tasks that involve the learners in communication in unplanned discourse and face-to-face interaction. Noticeable hesitation and non-communicative pausing would be indicative of retrieval problems, and would be of diagnostic value in determining what further experience learners need in order to facilitate future retrieval.

Application to Teacher Development

Recognition, recall, rehearsal and retrieval could be explicitly discussed during teacher-development sessions and the participants could be tasked with developing activities which apply theory to practice. These activities could be shared, evaluated and revised before being tried out in peer teaching and classroom planning sessions.

They could then be used as the basis of action research projects when teachers go (back) to schools.

Readers' Tasks

1 Develop the following activities:
- An activity in which the learners have to recognise the meaning of target-language prefixes and suffixes by working out the meaning of non-existent words such as "reget", "post-summer", "truesome" and "painish".
- An activity that gets learners to recall the lexical items they "know" in relation to the semantic area of a popular sport before writing a newspaper report in their L2 of that sport in action.
- An activity which pushes the learners to use retrieval for production by asking them to provide a spontaneous commentary of an event from the news, a sporting event or a documentary.

2 To what extent (if at all) do you agree with each of the following statements? Give reasons for your answers.
- Most students only have a few hours a week to learn their L2. What they need is clear, focused instruction plus lots of controlled and guided practice. They don't have time for extensive reading or watching films.
- If you give learners activities that push them to rely on retrieval, they will make lots of mistakes and become demotivated. It is important that they have time to use recall in production activities.
- In order to help learners make effective use of recognition, recall, rehearsal and retrieval, it is vital that they gain as much and as rich an exposure to language in use as possible, that they respond personally to this exposure, that they pay attention to salient features of this input and that they have many opportunities to use the L2 for communication in both planned and unplanned discourse.

FURTHER READING

Schütze, U. (2017). Chapter 9 – Learning and teaching. *Language learning and the brain: Lexical processing in second language acquisition* (pp. 152–163). Cambridge: Cambridge University Press.

Tomlinson, B. & Masuhara, H. (2018). Chapter 8 – Developing materials for the acquisition of language. In B. Tomlinson & H. Masuhara, *The complete guide to the theory and practice of materials development for language learning* (pp. 189–219). Hoboken NJ: Wiley.

6 Comprehension of the L2

Part One: Theory

Introduction

The term "comprehension" often features in language learning, teaching and assessment e.g. comprehension check, comprehension questions. What does comprehension mean? What is involved in the mental process of comprehension? How does comprehension contribute to language acquisition?

In this chapter, we will review the literature on theories relating to comprehension and on application of the research, and we will offer our own suggestions for application based on our experience in teaching, teacher training, curriculum development, materials development and assessment.

What Does Comprehension Mean?

According to dictionary definitions of "comprehension", "ability to understand" seems to be the convergent element across established dictionaries. As for "level" of the ability to understand, however, definitions vary from "the ability to understand *something*" [italics added by the authors] (the first definition in the Collins English Dictionary) to "the ability to understand *completely* and be familiar with a situation, facts, etc." (the first definition in the Cambridge English Dictionary).

We are surprised to see the word "complete(ly)" in a few dictionaries being included as one of the main definitions of "comprehension". It seems counter-intuitive when we consider the fact that comprehension involves multiple factors that could influence meaning: e.g. who is saying what, to whom, for what purposes, when and in what contexts. All these factors influence the meaning of what we hear and read. It seems to us that the word "interpretation" seems to represent more closely the reality of "comprehension", be it in L1 or L2. Interestingly, "interpretation" was not the main synonym of comprehension in the dictionaries and thesauruses we consulted.

Imagine a scene with an English husband and wife in a living room in a suburban house with a garden after breakfast on a sunny summer morning.

The wife is looking out at their garden and starts a conversation with her husband, who is reading a paper on a sofa. What would readers "comprehend" from the following conversation? If you were a husband and were looking forward to watching a football match later that afternoon, how would you respond to your wife?

Wife: Darling, have you noticed the grass is getting long?
Husband: Yeah?
Wife: We're having guests for dinner tonight ...

> **Readers' Tasks**
>
> Please pause for a moment, reflect upon what you have just experienced during your effort to "comprehend" this conversation. Make notes on your reflections. Your notes will be useful in the next section, when we discuss "The Mental Process of Comprehension".

Comprehending the wife's utterance will require not only linguistic processing but also interpreting the implied pragmatic force of the utterance within the context.

If L2 learners focus only on the lexis and grammar of the wife's first utterance: "The grass is getting long", it would just mean that the wife is describing the length and growth of the grass in their garden. Most L2 learners are unlikely to understand her intention or the projected effect that she is trying to achieve on her husband. Being able to guess the tone of her voice, her stress and her pauses would make a difference in understanding the shades of meaning. Imagining her facial and bodily expressions, gaze and distance from the husband may add to fuller understanding of the communicative meaning of her utterance.

"Language use" involves reasons and target outcomes of speakers and listeners. Why did the wife talk about the length of the grass, and what is she trying to achieve by telling her husband about it? Why did the husband choose to respond in a vague, evasive and non-committal way?

L2 learners might also benefit from some contextual background knowledge of English "suburban houses", "with a garden", "guests", "dinner" and the concept of "sharing the house chores", as well as the assumed roles of husband and wife. The choice of words and indirect expressions, as well as the contexts, all reveal their upbringing and social status.

If a speaker/writer/producer does not share sociocultural backgrounds with the listener/reader/viewer, then comprehension may become even more complex. Hitomi witnessed such an event in a pharmacy in England between an English elderly lady and a young L2 user.

Imagine a scene in a store in which an elderly lady crouched down to pick up an item on the lowest shelf. The L2 user happened to be browsing next to her. The lady realised that she could not stand up on her own because of her ageing knees. She said to the L2 user with an embarrassed chuckle, "I don't seem to be able to stand up". The L2 user hesitated for a moment. Another bystander lifted her up. Why do you think this L2 user hesitated?

> **Readers' Tasks**
>
> Please pause for a moment, reflect upon what you have just experienced during your effort to "comprehend" this conversation and take notes. Your notes will be useful in the next section, when we discuss "The Mental Process of Comprehension".

In order to achieve "understanding", this L2 user needs to connect what he is experiencing in a multimodal manner (i.e. what he sees as well as what he hears), process linguistic information and recognise emotional and affective implications (see Chapter 2 Intake in this book). In the case of this L2 user, he hesitated. It could be that he did not understand what the lady said or her pragmatic force of implied request for his help. It could be that he understood what the lady said and meant, but his faith did not allow him to touch the lady and he was embarrassed about the situation. He might have been torn between sympathy toward her and his inability to help her. This led to a pause before he could utter a word or resort to action.

Some of our observations so far on the factors that influence comprehension are being investigated in various fields of language processing (R. Ellis, 2008; Grabe, 2009; Saville-Troike & Barto, 2017; Schütze, 2017). Researchers seem to agree that comprehension is likely to involve all or any combinations of the following:

- linguistic processing (e.g. phonology, lexis, syntax, semantics, discourse)
- pragmatic and sociocultural processing (i.e. relationship, intent and purpose of the speaker/writer/producer and also of the listener/reader/viewer)
- real life and world knowledge
- contexts (e.g. who, to whom, where, what, when, why) of the event
- emotional and attitudinal reactions which could influence interpretation.

Each area above was traditionally studied separately in different disciplines in the past: e.g. a predominant emphasis on language descriptions in linguistics, processing of syntax in psycholinguistics and computer simulation in cognitive psychology.

Since then we have seen various welcome developments: e.g. more awareness of the importance of processing lexical and larger units (e.g. discourse) in linguistics; situated studies of overall contexts and participants, real-life/world communication from the perspective of the sociocultural environment in sociolinguistics. For a long time, direct investigation of the inner workings of mental processes was considered impossible. The availability of detailed brain maps and the technological advancement of various brain scanning and imaging tools of healthy brains, however, have enabled us to have a glimpse of mental activities in process. In addition, artificial intelligence has been used to gradually verify our insights in a transdisciplinary manner (e.g.; Foucart & Frenck-Mestre, 2013; Morgan-Short, 2014; The Douglas Fir Group, 2016; N. Ellis, 2019).

In this light, we define "comprehension" as a "process and product of interpreting incoming information of various kinds and figuring out the likely meaning and intention of the speaker/writer/producer from the perspective of the listener/reader/viewer".

> **Readers' Tasks**
>
> According to the *Longman Dictionary of Language Teaching and Applied Linguistics* (Richards & Schmidt, 2010, p. 108), the definition of "comprehension" is:
>
> > the identification of intended meaning of written or spoken communication. Contemporary theories of comprehension emphasize that it is an active process drawing both on information contained in the message (BOTTOM UP PROCESSING) as well as background knowledge, information from the context and from the listener's and speaker's purposes or intentions (TOP DOWN PROCESSING).
>
> 1 What do you think are the similarities and differences of the definitions between Richards and Schmidt's and ours that comprehension is a "process and product of interpreting incoming information of various kinds and figuring out the likely meaning and intention of the speaker/writer/producer from the perspective of the listener/reader/viewer"?
> 2 How would you define "comprehension"?
> 3 Do you think tests and exams are typically designed to assess capability to "interpret incoming information of various kinds and figure out the likely meaning and intention of the speaker/writer/producer from the perspective of the listener/reader/viewer"?

The Mental Process of Comprehension

Mental Representation during Comprehension

In the previous section, two anecdotes were introduced: i.e. interactions between a husband and wife and between an elderly lady and an L2 user. The readers' task was to reflect upon the mental processes during comprehension of the two cases.

When you were reading the interactions, did you see images of the wife, husband, elderly lady and L2 user? Did you hear their voices? Were these images like a movie with actions? Or were they a series of slides, flickering by? Did these mental activities help you to achieve comprehension?

McTigue (2010) reports how L1 primary school second graders (approximately seven- to eight-years old) describe what happened when they listened to a story:

> One student tried, "There is no monkey at all ... except in your head. You have to make the picture in your head." Another explained, "When you make a picture in your head, you just think about the word monkey and a picture comes. If you thought about an elephant, an elephant's picture would come." Another student explained, "I see a movie in my head; my monkey is swinging." Multiple students concurred with the movie analogy. (McTigue, 2010, pp. 54–56)

Mental imagery and its role in comprehension (and also in production) has been studied in various fields, such as cognitive psychology, philosophy, literary studies and reading research (Kosslyn, 1980; Sadoski, 1985; Paivio, 1986; Sadoski & Paivio, 1994). Tomlinson (2011d) conducted a series of studies involving L1- and L2-proficient adult users of English. He describes consistent results across his own studies, as well as related past studies on imaging. In all, over a hundred proficient L1 users were asked to read an extract from a descriptive or narrative text and to introspect their mental experience. "Ninety-six percent reported that they visually imaged the content of the texts as they read them ..." (ibid, p. 358). He also describes differing degrees of vividness, frequency and effect of visual imaging and identifies some of the influential factors, such as motivation, topic familiarity, interest and relevance to previous experience. However, when he did similar experiments with L2 learners, he found that very few of them reported visualising. "For example, in one experiment only 7 out of 41 students reported any visualization when they were asked to describe what they had done in order to try to understand the poem *River Station Plaza*" (ibid, p. 363). Interestingly, Tomlinson (2011d, p. 363) found: "In all my experiments the few students who reported using visual imaging tended to achieve greater comprehension and recall than those who did not" – a finding replicating that of Padron and Waxman (1988).

Mental Representation in the Brain during Comprehension

Masuhara (1998, 2000, 2005, 2016) explores the substrates of mental representation, arguing that what we call "comprehension/interpretation" is a result of neural activities in the brain involving cortical areas (language-related areas; sensory- and motor-related areas) and subcortical areas associated with memory formation (e.g. limbic areas including the hippocampus, which is known to be where short-term memory is created and reactivated, and the amygdala, which is associated with emotional colouring of memory) and with core areas of the brain that ensure vital survival (e.g. the thalamus, hypothalamus and all the core areas of the brain that are involved in breathing, perspiration, balance, etc.) (see Kandel, 2006; Gazzaniga, Ivry & Mangun, 2019).

Our visual imaging during listening/reading may be more noticeable but, depending on the incoming stimuli, our mental representation is also likely to involve other sensory experiences (e.g. hearing, smell, taste, touch), motor reactions (e.g. sensation of movement), cognition (e.g. concepts, evaluation of values) and affect (e.g. feeling, emotion, attitude).

From a neuroscientific point of view, Llinás explains: "The world we see is reality manufactured in the brain ... and integration of all the internal and external information gathered through sensory processing" (1990, preface). The involvement of individuality in our mental representation seems to explain, for example, why one person remembers a photo or story as "scary" and another one does not. It depends on the perceiver's past experiences and personal reactions.

Linguistic and Nonlinguistic Processing in Creating Mental Representation

Language is an extension of the mammal's ability to create multidimensional mental representations (Roth & Dicke, 2005; Arbib, 2015). Language supports and strengthens the retention of otherwise ephemeral mental representations. By attaching a linguistic code to a phenomenon, for example, "acute pains in the head" as "headache", one can wrap the whole series of associated phenomena into a compact chunk. Through physical experience within social contexts accompanied by language use, we develop neural associative connections between "headache" and various associative networks in the brain. These associative connections then remain in our awareness longer than the word that sparked their recall or retrieval.

Masuhara (1998, 2000, 2005) explains how reading comprehension relies on the connections between the language codes and non-verbal mental representations stored in the brain, and how the extensiveness and robustness of the neural connections determine the depths and kinds of individual comprehension. Listening involves modal-specific processes, but meaning construction (i.e. comprehension/interpretation) requires the fundamental mechanisms of parallel processing and associative connection, resulting in our mental representation (Buchweitz, Mason, Tomitch & Just, 2009).

We believe that mental representation is the equivalent of intake as we defined it in Chapter 2, i.e. *language and the accompanying nonlinguistic and extra-linguistic features from the learner's input that have been taken into the brain for comprehension and for potential further processing.* That representation sparks connections with the various components of previous representations stimulated by equivalent input and the resulting combination contributes to comprehension.

Mental Representation in L2

Based on the data from various think-aloud and introspection studies, Auerbach and Paxton (1997, p. 238) describe the convergent phenomena of L2 reading:

> [L]earners ... feel they have to know all the words in a text in order to understand it, rely heavily on the dictionary, are unable to transfer productive L1 reading strategies or positive feelings about reading, spend long hours laboring over sentence-by-sentence translation, and attribute their difficulties to a lack of English proficiency.

The L2 learners in these studies were from Vietnam, China, Haiti, Ethiopia, Thailand, and several Latin American countries, and were enrolled in university preparatory courses. Masuhara (2013) and Tomlinson (2011d) conducted literature surveys of studies (including their own) using think-aloud, questionnaires and interviews and they confirm very similar text-bound reading behaviours among L2 learners, which often result in poor comprehension and low self-esteem, regardless of age, nationality, gender or, in some cases, scores of language-proficiency tests. What is remarkable is that, in most of these cases, the L2 readers are proficient and avid readers in their L1 (e.g. Stevick, 1982; Kim & Krashen, 1997; Masuhara, 1998; Masuhara, 2000; Tomlinson, 2011d). In L2, they read in a bottom-up linguistic manner with very fragmented mental images based on individual words, even though their L2 proficiency is well above the linguistic threshold. Yet, when they read in their L1, they report seeing coherent movie-like imagery and enjoying personal associations with the content. The transfer of L1 reading skills is not taking place for these L2 learners.

Readers' Task

What do you think the reasons may be for the differences in mental representation when reading in the L1 and when reading in the L2? Language proficiency? Lack of vocabulary? Age? Instructions? Lack of confidence? Apprehension caused by fear of being tested by comprehension questions?

In listening/reading, the main stimuli come in the form of linguistic codes. It is left to the listener/reader to process the linguistic codes in the input and to activate the associative networks in sensory, motor, affective and cognitive systems of the brain.

In L1 listening/reading, the connections between the linguistic networks and multidimensional non-verbal networks tend to be extensive and robust. For instance, hearing/reading a familiar word instantly sparks off simulated experiences of images, tastes, aroma, affect and other associations in our brain.

In L2, on the other hand, if the necessary neural connections are less extensive and robust, then comprehension/interpretation may require a longer decoding process, which results in vague and fragmented mental representation.

In response to studies indicating learners' L2 processing difficulties, SLA studies, L2 teaching methodology and L2 materials have emphasised the importance of automaticity of word recognition (Hill & Laufer, 2003; Schmitt, 2008; Nation, 2013; Schmitt & Schmitt, 2014) and of learner strategy training (Carrell, Pharis & Liberto, 1989; Oxford, 2011).

Thus, L2 training books often include linguistic training (e.g. pre-teaching of vocabulary, vocabulary-building exercises). The assumptions behind such teaching methods and materials seem to include:

- meaning construction relies on quantity of vocabulary knowledge and syntactical processing;
- extensive listening and reading requires a certain vocabulary size;
- acquisition of a large vocabulary requires a huge amount of implicit learning; therefore learners need explicit vocabulary teaching (e.g. textual flooding, enhancement such as highlighting, pre-/post-reading focus on vocabulary);
- explicit teaching of vocabulary knowledge will somehow turn into implicit knowledge;
- helping L2 listeners and readers requires provision of lexically controlled readers or audio materials selected based on statistical calculation of frequency and ranking of words and chunks;
- explicit strategy training will somehow turn into implicit comprehension skill through habit formation.

The list above seems to us to show a worrying prioritising of linguistic processing and an explicit cognitive approach to L2 teaching. However, our recent experience of observing classes all over the world and working with teachers, methods and materials (for example, our reviews of adult courses in Tomlinson & Masuhara, 2013) reveals that L2 learners still seem to be struggling to create vivid mental representation when they are reading and listening (see also the literature on L2 teaching found in Garton & Graves, 2014; Masuhara, Mishan & Tomlinson, 2017; Tomlinson & Masuhara, 2018a). There is a stark contrast in the listening and reading acquisition processes described in L1 acquisition studies and in SLA studies, and we wonder if this is a consequence of explicit teaching interfering with the transfer of skills.

The Roles of Comprehension in Language Acquisition

Tallal (2003) explains how the brain learns in general:

> The brain seems to learn by looking for consistencies, looking for events that repeat themselves frequently. And those events are usually made up of visual input, auditory input, feelings in the mouth for the baby, and feeling on the body the sensory events of the world. And the baby's brain's job is to begin to understand and to code neurally in the brain; to map its own brain through experiences to what's going to matter and what's not going to matter.

In short, the brain seems to be wired to:

- look for consistencies and reinforcement;
- identify events that repeat themselves frequently;
- map its networks according to what is going to matter;
- repeat what gives a sense of wellbeing and pleasure;
- acquire spoken language.

In privileged L1 learning, we can witness how such learning principles operate in acquiring our ability to comprehend. In L2 teaching, however, are we providing the environment and encouragement for L2 brains to be able to function as they are designed to? If not, why not? Be it L1 or L2 acquisition, fundamentally the same brain learns.

We will look at how comprehension facilitates SLA through listening, reading and viewing (multimodal processing) and we will seek convergence and note differences between what happens in the L1 and in the L2 (Buchweitz et al., 2009; Foucart & Frenck-Mestre, 2013). We will do so by considering what we understand about the L1 process and then contrasting this with the typical L2 process.

L1 children normally spend their first five years in aural–oral modes, then reading and writing are gradually introduced in primary school. From the perspectives of neuroscience in her interview for Children of the Code, a Social Education Project, Tallal (2003) explains: "Written language must stand on the shoulder of oral language …". Thousands of years of evolution have genetically programmed the human brain to acquire spoken language. Reading and writing, however, are nurtured skills, just as anyone may be able to appreciate music but when it comes to reading musical notes, we need training to become able to connect the symbols with actual sounds. Even the genetically prepared infant's brain takes five years to acquire a basic repertoire of language and processing skills. It is staggering to consider that L2 learners are expected to cope with L2 sounds, words, spellings, grammar and discourse and to comprehend and acquire all at the same time.

Let us now compare how language acquisition takes place in L1 and L2, in terms of how input is provided. We will mainly compare how L1 language acquisition takes place with what typical formal education tends to provide in L2 language teaching in order to explore how the L2 language-learning environment can be improved through reappraisal of educational policy, curriculum, methodology and materials.

We are not arguing that L1 and L2 learning are the same. L2 learning starts in addition to mother-tongue learning, most probably after L1 neural connections have been more or less established. How the neural wiring takes place in L2 learning may be different, but it would be difficult to argue that the brain changes its fundamental mechanisms for learning. Bilingual/multilingual language acquisition has not been adequately addressed by mainstream SLA literature (see Ortega, 2019 for reference to the increasing call for correcting this bias) but gradually we are seeing an increase in transdisciplinary efforts (e.g. The Douglas Fir Group, 2016).

In L1 acquisition, it is known that the brain first learns to hear the pitch and rhythm of the mother's voice (but not individual words) (Partanen et al., 2013). Then the developing ability to identify phonemes and the ability to manipulate individual sounds eventually lead to speaking and finally to reading, spelling and writing. Soon after birth, babies start to recognise familiar sounds (e.g. /m-i-l-k/) and eventually they link the sounds together with associated sensations detected through various sensory-processing channels. The same recognisable phonetic stimulus recurs frequently and with consistent associations. This gives a sense of wellbeing and pleasure in an embodied and holistic manner, and eventually leads to acquisition (Joaquin & Schumann, 2014). Only after this stage has taken place are children ready to start to learn to read.

Note here that in the L1 example given, linguistic (i.e. phonological and lexical memory) networks regarding the word "milk" are being developed together with associated sensory, motor and emotional networks. Damasio and Carvalho (2013) describe evolutional and neurobiological origins of emotion and Immordino-Yang and Damasio (2007) explain how affective factors have a strong influence on learning.

In L2 learning, there is no separation between language acquisition and reading acquisition. In L2 textbooks, for example, words and grammar tend to be presented as part of a reading text, and in speaking sections native speakers (e.g. Tom and Jane) are often introduced and then converse in dialogues designed to illustrate language points. Unlike L1 babies, L2 learners are not the central participants of communication. Instead, they are the receivers of instruction and language, and are often instructed to learn words with L1 translations, using glossaries in a decontextualised manner. Raising phonemic awareness through listening, for example, is rarely an objective, and often little emotional investment is encouraged or expected.

By twelve to eighteen months, L1 toddlers are reported to use up to twenty simple words, like "cup", "shoe" and "daddy" and to start copying what siblings and adults say. Vocabulary is acquired according to children's needs and wants, and gestures and words are used in pretend play in imitation of adults in their surroundings. In this sense, language acquisition takes place in an embodied and multimodal manner situated in a familiar social environment.

In L2, on the other hand, words in textbooks are often taught without consideration of learner needs or wants or of their experience of life, and are selected possibly on the basis of a frequency database taken from an English-language corpus in UK or the United States. This is often based on spoken and written language in English extracted from newspapers, magazines, books, university lectures, etc. by L1 educated adult monolinguals, and is likely to be far detached from the familiar environment or community of the learners.

By eighteen to twenty-four months, toddlers understand 200–500 words. They enjoy listening to simple stories and ask for their favourite ones to be read to them many times. Child-directed speech during shared reading provides ample evidence of children dictating the amount and frequency of repetition, recycling and feedback in a curiosity-driven way. Research shows eventual effective transition from listening to reading through such shared reading (O'Farrelly, Doyle, Victory & Palamaro-Munsell, 2018; Greenwood, Hutton, Dudley & Horowitz-Kraus, 2019).

Also by eighteen to twenty-four months, syntactical awareness starts to emerge in children's utterances. The toddlers of this age group distinguish clauses by learning the prosody of a language – the rhythm of sounds and pauses, the varying pitch in the voice, the different pattern of loudness and softness (Sachs, Habibi, Damasio & Kaplan, 2018). Recent studies report that toddlers take in short, easy chunks such as "Don't do that" as a whole (Grimm et al., 2019) and repeated multiple exemplars in the input help them to subconsciously work out consistency in syntactical structures (Twomey et al., 2014). They miss out the ending of words (which often carry morphological but not semantic significance – e.g. plural -s; tense -ed) but they are not penalised or corrected, as such phenomena are accepted as manifestations of developmental stages. It is interesting to note the natural and gradual emergence of syntax and the later development of morphology. No explicit teaching of language form takes place apart from interactional feedback in a communication-focused manner.

Prosodic features help the L1 toddler to chunk their input and facilitate lexical and syntactic learning. Multiple examples in frequent and varied contexts (e.g. interactions; listening to nursery rhymes and stories; shared picture book reading) help L1 toddlers to subconsciously work out the grammar of their language.

In L2, on the other hand, grammar tends to be taught in an explicit and deductive way. PPP does allow some repetition, but the context is usually limited and explicit teaching of structures takes away opportunities for the development of learners' own syntactical awareness and of the development of integrated networks in their brain. Materials (including listening and reading materials intended to provide comprehension practice) are usually written to cover a large and predetermined syllabus of vocabulary and grammatical items. Therefore, there is very little recycling of the lexis or grammatical items in different contexts to ensure frequency of encounter or reinforcement of learning.

By four to five years old, L1 preschoolers show some awareness of orthography (i.e. the spelling system). They know about their alphabet and can identify some letters of the alphabet, for example those included in their names. Recent neural studies report how early shared reading and carer's intervention (e.g. drawing attention; asking questions; interacting) can influence successful literacy introduction in later years (Hutton et al., 2017; O'Farrelly et al., 2018; Greenwood et al., 2019). Preschoolers also understand pragmatic meaning and how the context influences the way utterances convey meaning. The same utterance, "It's 10 o'clock", can convey different functions such as "information", "warning" or "threat". Prosodic features mark old and new information. Children learn to differentiate implicit messages from intonation, tone and pitch, with, for example, the intensity of a mother's nagging signalling to them how long they can continue ignoring her order. How many "low level" L2 textbooks include interpretation of prosodic features or of pragmatic use of language in a meaningful context?

Note that all this aural–oral learning for the initial five years of L1 learning is multimodal. When language processing is discussed in SLA or in cognitive psychology, models focus on linguistic processing and rarely, if ever, discuss other modalities involved in communication, possibly because of the lack of other modalities in laboratory experiments.

When formal reading instruction begins, L1 children have 4,000–5,000 aural–oral words (Nation & Waring, 1997). Nation (2013) in one of his chapters lists what it is to know vocabulary. Knowing a word for L1 children involves extensive networks in the brain. Studies of behavioural, neurolinguistic and imaging studies confirm the likelihood of parallel activities in the brain that are associated with mental imaging, semantic processing and subcortical emotional involvement at the same time as linguistic processing (Damasio & Carvalho, 2013; Hutton et al., 2017). Such extensive networks have been built from five years of aural–oral interactions in the home environment with family members.

L1 children are capable of seeing and feeling the language because the associative-memory networks between linguistic and multidimensional neural networks have been established in the initial five years of aural–oral learning in an implicit and embodied manner. Any of the sensory, motor or linguistic stimuli in the children's interactions could spark off associative networks in a varied way each time linguistic input is received. An input may spark off automatic retrieval to working memory from long-term memory (e.g. linguistic, sensory, motor, emotional or episodic). The executive control in the frontal lobe in the brain can then make use of the phonological loop or the visual sketchpad to work out how to use these resources.

In L2 language learning, reading starts when the students have a very small vocabulary, which has often been learned through L1 mediation. Note here that reading is in fact sound-based (Tallal, 2003; Gazzaniga, Ivry & Mangun, 2019). Print is processed as visuals in the brain and transformed into sound to be processed in Wernicke's area in which sound-meaning connections are known to take place. If reading lacks sound-meaning connections with established networks, it remains simply an impoverished exercise in linguistic decoding – a typical L2 behaviour reported in much of the L2 reading literature (for example in Auerbach & Paxton, 1997; Kim & Krashen, 1997; Masuhara, 2007; Tomlinson, 2011d).

When the literature discusses "automatic word recognition" or "strategy training" in L2 language processing, we need to question how extensive the necessary neural networks are in the L2 learners' brains in the first place. L2 learners receive teaching of phonology, morphology, lexis, syntax, listening, speaking, writing and reading all at the same time and we would argue that reading is often taught to L2 beginners prematurely. In the PKG Project referred to earlier in the book (Tomlinson, 1990) beginners focused first of all on listening, then on speaking and only then on reading and writing. And when they did start reading, they read elaborated versions of stories they had already dramatised in TPR activities, as well as potentially engaging stories in which 50 per cent of the content words were good friends (i.e. words similar in meaning and in pronunciation or spelling to words in Bahasa Indonesia).

In our view, weak or fragmented mental representation in L2 is a sign of the lack of associative neural networks involving linguistic, sensory, motor, cognitive and affective areas of the brain. The development of such networks takes place mainly implicitly through experience. The depth and width of vocabulary depends on the richness of frequent encounters with meaningful language in an embodied, situated and engaged manner. It is not something we can fix by giving the learners wordlists with L1 translations to memorise, or by teaching L2 learners how and when to use strategies. Explicit learning involving conscious attention paid to vocabulary will help only as a support in addition to the foundation of linguistic and multidimensional networks in the brain.

There are some issues related to comprehension in terms of unique elements of L2 language processing. For example, future discussion needs to pay attention to the processes involved in adult bilingual and multilingual language acquisition (e.g. Whitney et al., 2009; Foucart & Frenck-Mestre, 2013; Grey, Sanz, Morgan-Short & Ullman, 2018) and to the processes involved in multimodal learning (e.g. Brown, Waring & Donkaewbua, 2008; Van Leeuwen, 2015; Schüler, 2019).

CONCLUSION

In this chapter, we have considered the characteristics of comprehension, mental representation (i.e. the psychological term for comprehension/interpretation), neural substrates of mental representation and how listening, reading and multimodal comprehension may facilitate acquisition. In addition, we have compared what may be involved in L1 and L2 acquisition through listening, reading and multimodal comprehension. In our view, the best solution for L2 listening- and reading-comprehension problems would be to reappraise language planning, curriculum development, methodology and materials to support L2 brains to learn effectively in ways in which they are designed to do (i.e. in ways that are rich, rewarding, engaging, comprehensible, recycled, purposeful, multimodal and embodied). Only then will learners develop the networks in the brain that they need to facilitate L2 comprehension, which in turn can facilitate the enrichment of new intake, the strengthening of existing intake and the furthering of acquisition. In our view, the richer the comprehension, the greater the potential for acquisition and development.

Readers' Tasks

Use the following framework to help you to write a brief summary of Part One of this chapter.

Definitions of Comprehension	Our Definition of Comprehension	Ways of Facilitating Comprehension	Salient Points of Part One
1	1	1	1
2		2	2
3		3	3
4		4	4
			5

1. How do you think ways in which L1 learners acquire language through reading and listening can be applied to L2 learning contexts?
2. Develop a classroom activity that could help learners to develop mental representations of what they hear and read.

Part Two: Application of Theory to Practice

Application to L2 Language Planning

One obvious application to language planning is for administrators to recognise the vital importance of comprehension in acquisition. This could lead to creating conditions in which L2 learners can willingly receive abundant repeated, recycled and meaningful exposure to interactional target language in an engaging manner. This might include provision of multimedia centres for teachers and learners to make use of. In such a space, collections of books, films, DVDs, computers with internet access and audio materials can be made available (see Chapter 5 for an example in Kanda University in Japan). In addition, in such centres time can be scheduled for teachers and students to meet and hold informal discussions on what the students have listened to and read, as well as on topics of learner choice (Cooker, 2008; Cooker, 2010).

Provision is one thing, utilisation is another. Ideally, integration in the whole ecology of the educational system needs to be established, involving curriculum development, teacher development, materials and student guidance. Loh and Renandya (2015) report such an attempt in Singapore. They describe STELLAR (Strategies for English Language Learning and Reading), a Singaporean national literacy reform programme for all six levels in primary education. The approaches include shared reading, the text-driven approach, the language–experience approach, sustained silent reading and a writing process cycle. It is noticeable how comprehension-based approaches are central to this approach to facilitating language acquisition.

The STELLAR programme is accompanied by an in-service professional-development scheme and by countrywide mentoring and grouping support systems, which are informally interactive rather than top-down, rigid or evaluative. The ongoing evaluation of the six-year implementation of the new programme so far seems to indicate positive changes taking place with innovative adaptations that enhance the STELLAR principles.

Considering the nature of comprehension and ways of nurturing comprehension capabilities, we feel that language policy may benefit from considering two fundamental issues: one is the chosen variety of the target language, and the other is assessment. Any reforms that do not consider these two issues have very little possibility of success.

The first point involves re-evaluation of non-native teachers and the target variety of the foreign language of choice. In the case of English, from the 1970s until recently the aspiration of L2 language learning has been towards the "native-speaker norm", deriving from the Chomskyan notion of "native competence". As a result, native speakers and native-speaker teachers tended to be treated consciously or subconsciously as "superior", regardless of educational and professional achievements, their actual ability, suitability and personality. Such a phenomenon is sometimes called "Native speakerism" as in "racism" and "ageism". Holliday (2006) defines "Native speakerism" as:

> a pervasive ideology within ELT, characterized by the belief that "native-speaker" teachers represent a "Western culture" from which spring the ideals both of the English language and of English language teaching methodology (Holliday, 2006, p. 385)

The Chomskyan notion of monolingual elite native speakers' "competence" has been counter-argued on many grounds (see Chapters 2 and 4 in this book). When global Englishes are prominent on the Internet and in communication in commerce, scientific endeavours and technology, the traditional target of "speaking like a native speaker" is becoming irrelevant (Pennycook, 2010). Readily available digital means (e.g. YouTube, social media, translation, interpretation apps) allow global communication, and native-like accuracy is certainly not the main concern in such situations.

What would be the target accuracy and fluency for bi-/multi-lingual users who do not require native-like English for their future career? What will examinations of International English look like and what will the marking criteria be (Tomlinson, 2020)? The biggest and most crucial issue is the fact that English is taught all around the world by millions of EFL teachers who are multilingual English users (Kirkpatrick, 2010; Copland, Garton & Mann, 2016; Kirkpatrick & Liddicoat, 2017; Ortega, 2019). Traditionally, fearing that their accented English might lead to inferior varieties of the target language, teachers have relied heavily on language CDs and native-speaker materials whose content may not be socioculturally appropriate or relevant to the learners. L2 learners themselves may not have welcomed peer or group interactions in the target language, thinking that they do not want to pick up their friends' accents or wrong use of words. However, teachers and peers are the best providers of comprehensible input (slightly above the learners' level), which is considered in SLA theories as vital in acquisition. Just as mothers provide nourishing child-directed speech that facilitates language acquisition, multilingual English teachers are in a position to provide the necessary environment for successful additional language acquisition, provided that they get the resources and support. Users of International English, including native speakers, need to develop tolerance of ambiguity and the skills of accommodation, negotiation of meaning, and collaborative communication. Peer interaction can provide opportunities for the development of such communication skills and more provision for this is needed in lesson planning. Also, the materials and topics of L2 lessons need to be what the learners and teachers find relevant and interesting rather than talking about "Tom and Jane" in London or New York. Language policy needs to clarify the kind of target language and level, and give due credit and a rightful place to "non-native" bi-/multi-lingual language teachers.

The second issue is "Assessment". Assessment backwash determines the quality of teaching and learning. Even in the STELLAR programme in Singapore, Loh and Renandya (2015) report that the teachers in an elite school continue their own exam-orientated syllabus and traditional exam preparation, thus clashing with the language-learning philosophy of the STELLAR programme, which is in line with current thinking in SLA and learning theories. Ultimately, exams need to be designed so that they genuinely measure the capabilities of the learners in L2. The assessment design must consider backwash effects and ensure positive impact on teaching and learning. See Tomlinson (2010d, 2020c) for suggestions for ways of evaluating the capabilities of users of English as an International Language (EIL), which could have a positive backwash effect on L2 teaching and learning, and see Tomlinson (1981) for a library of communicative tasks to be used either as classroom tasks or as examination tasks (an approach that Brian also took with his classes at Kobe University and with primary classes in Vanuatu (Tomlinson, 1981).

Application to L2 Curriculum Development

We know of no curriculum or syllabus that explains what comprehension is, how rich and deep comprehension can be achieved and how comprehension capabilities can be nurtured.

Instead, traditional syllabuses tend to specify target achievements in general terms, provide an inventory of language and skills and specify learning sequences for different levels. During implementation, materials writers tend to focus on coverage and on the sequence of teaching items in the syllabus. The teachers, parents and learners are all aware of exams and tests, therefore teaching becomes ticking off the syllabus items and practising them in preparation for assessment.

Often, there seems to be confusion between linguistic items (i.e. declarative knowledge – knowledge about language) and procedural knowledge (i.e. ability to make use of language to achieve communication). A term such as declarative "knowledge" in psychology may give an impression that it can be itemised and directly and explicitly taught. As was described in this chapter in relation to "mental representation", comprehension means developing associative networks in the brain, linking linguistic, sensory, motor, cognitive and affective activation. Acquisition involves frequent activation and reactivation with strong internal reinforcement of our short-term memory (i.e. intake) and eventual long-term memory (i.e. acquisition). Such brain networks can only be developed through experience of hearing, speaking, touching, feeling and understanding in individual ways, connecting with learners' own lives. Such experience needs to be abundant and genuinely enjoyable so that learners will want to repeat, revisit and go on learning without worrying or thinking about learning (i.e. implicit learning).

We would like to see in the curriculum explicit specification of the capabilities of comprehension/interpretation as targets to help learners to develop, with suggestions to teachers as to how to facilitate such development.

The main application of our discussion on listening, reading and multimodal comprehension is to consider ways of providing an environment in which communication in the target language can take place in an embodied, situated and engaging manner. What becomes clear in L1 acquisition is how much L1 children are immersed in a positive language-learning environment in an aural–oral manner to begin with. We could create a similarly positive environment for L2 learners. After gaining some vocabulary with all the associative nonlinguistic and contextual learning, and some ability to listen and speak, reading and writing could be introduced. Rather than being tested and being corrected for making mistakes, it would be more educational and motivating to be encouraged to experience creative thinking, hypothesis testing and experimenting with use of the language.

It is vital that teachers and peers interact and work together. When they are not able to perform, learners can help each other. Such collaboration creates opportunities for genuine interaction (see Chapter 2 for research that provides evidence of beneficial effects of peer interaction in SLA; see also Chapter 9 about the constructive use of L1 to enhance L2 learning).

In this sense, curriculum developers may like to consider different kinds of syllabuses that are different from conventional language or skill-based syllabuses. For example, a shared-reading programme at early stages has been demonstrated to be useful (Ghosn, 2013; Mourão, 2015; Bland, 2015, 2018). For more mature learners, a task-based syllabus, a text-driven syllabus, a project-based syllabus or a content-and-language integrated-learning syllabus might be more productive, and a performance-based syllabus (Park, 2010) using drama may suit some learners in some contexts. Such syllabuses share such characteristics as being meaning-focused, potentially engaging, potentially multimodal and using comprehension and production as means to achieve purposeful communication rather than as means to learn declarative knowledge.

The curriculum would be genuinely educational if it recognised the value of extensive exposure to the target language in use, and the provision on timetables for such experience (e.g. reading a book, listening to a recording or watching a film). Spending much of the classroom time on explicit teaching of discrete items gets very little support from learning theories, and could be replaced with more experience of purposeful comprehension and production supported by teacher help and feedback when needed.

Application to L2 Methodology

In this chapter, we explained that a good foundation of listening can lead to the development of speaking, reading and writing competence. Starting with listening/viewing followed by speaking and then by reading seems to match the natural sequence (Tallal, 2003).

Methodologies that make use of and facilitate the development of comprehension capabilities are similar to the ones suggested in Chapter 5 – Recognition, Recall, Rehearsal and Retrieval. They include CBLT, extensive reading, language through literature, text-driven approaches, TPR Plus, task-based approaches and problem-solving approaches.

We would also like to recommend extensive listening (Renandya & Farrell, 2011), extensive viewing (Keddie, Lessonstream; Keddie, 2009; Keddie, 2014), comprehension approaches (Barnard, 2007) and process drama (Park, 2010). Interestingly, the authors of the literature referred to in this paragraph are all teachers as well as researchers, and the approaches they recommend have been tried and tested in actual classrooms in, for example, China, Singapore, Korea, as well as many other places. What they have in common is the fact that the stories, videos, and images are aesthetic, striking, thought-provoking and engaging, as they are taken from real life for the purpose of entertainment, enjoyment and stimulus of the listeners and viewers. The activities involve collaborative acting, drawing, miming, shooting videos, creative writing, projects and tasks. Lessonstream by Keddie, for example, is freely downloadable (http://lessonstream.org/lessons/) as this project was crowd-funded. He provides lesson plans, but we found it very easy to use a text-driven sequence with the "texts" and to create different lessons for our own learners.

Note that in reading pedagogy, there is a confusion between "teaching reading" and "teaching language through reading". If the objective of teachers is to help learners to enjoy reading and gain language and confidence from doing so, for example, then extensive reading is likely to serve this purpose more than exemplifying language teaching points in reading texts (Krashen, 2004; Maley, 2008; Krashen, 2011; Uden, 2013).

Application to L2 Materials Development

Very few of the suggestions for activities we make above in relation to curriculum development and to methodology are currently applied in commercially published coursebooks. Comprehension in coursebooks seems to be heavily influenced by testing techniques (e.g. gap filling, multiple choice, true or false, comprehension questions). If a mother read a bedtime story to her child and asked comprehension questions or set true or false questions afterwards, how would the child react? Would they be asking for a bedtime story ever again?

We have had opportunities to look at textbooks in various countries, and what we almost invariably find is that a linguistic syllabus dictates the texts and activities regardless of what the blurb of the books say. Texts tend to be simplified or enhanced for the purpose of teaching vocabulary or grammar, thus offering very little of communicative value, and not providing engaging listening or reading experiences. Even if the content of a text happens to be potentially engaging, often the activities take away the opportunity for learners' exploration of meaning as the exercises are there to check learner comprehension or to draw learner attention to language points contained in the text (see the example later in this section).

Some readers, especially those who have very little time or freedom to adapt or develop materials in their work, may feel that our suggestions and/or recommended approaches seem to require effort and time. There is a simple selection and adaptation procedure we can recommend: instead of focusing on language points when developing or adapting materials, look for "potentially engaging texts" and let them drive your activities. When selecting a coursebook or unit, look for texts that may stimulate curiosity and interest within yourself and your learners.

Once you have found potentially engaging texts, you may be surprised how easy it is to come up with ideas for activities and sequences. For a more systematic approach to exploiting potentially engaging texts though, see The Text Driven Framework described in Tomlinson (2013d) and in Chapter 3 of this book.

We would like to "practise what we preach" and use an extract from a published global coursebook and demonstrate how we would adapt it in order to realise what we have recommended about comprehension in this chapter. We will provide our observations of the original coursebook extract and offer examples of adaptation to demonstrate how our discussion in this chapter can be applied to materials and to classroom teaching.

We have selected Unit 2 Lives and Legends in *Global Intermediate* (Clandfield & Robb Benne, 2011). We have chosen this section because it uses a Grimm brothers' story, Hansel and Gretel, and we have found Grimm brothers' stories to be potentially engaging. We thought we knew this story of a brother and sister, but when we actually revisited the story we were surprised to notice some dark undertones.

The story goes like this. Hansel and Gretel were abandoned deep in the forest by their father (a wood-cutter) and their stepmother because the family were extremely poor and had no food. Left on their own Hansel and Gretel walked all night and day to get back home, but without success. They came across a cottage made of bread and cakes. They were so hungry they started to eat a small part of it. The witch who lived there kindly invited them in and fed the hungry Hansel and Gretel. But soon they realised that the old woman was in fact a child-eating witch. Hansel was kept in a small room, and Gretel was ordered to feed him so he would be good for the witch to eat. The story includes many scenes that stimulate vivid images and emotional responses (e.g. Hansel and Gretel eating pieces of the house made of bread and cakes; the wicked witch with weak eyesight trying to check if Hansel is fat enough to eat) but the frightening elements are somewhat counterbalanced by how Hansel and Gretel think creatively to manage to solve problems. In the end, they manage to escape and return home.

The coursebook section starts with a Speaking and Listening section.

Activity 1:
The learners are instructed to look at the picture from the fairy tale of Hansel and Gretel and are asked if they know the story.

Our observations:
We think this is a good multimodal and personalised start, preparing the learners to activate their background knowledge (some people use the term "schema"). The only reservation we have is the teacher's question: "Do you know this story?" The learners may just answer "yes" or "no" and this may not lead to extensive imaging or recall from long-term memory.

Our adaptation:
We might ask "Have you heard of the story of Hansel and Gretel?" "What do you know about the story?" "Share what you know in groups". In this way we think that the learners will need to visualise and recall whatever they know from their long-term memory into their working memory. Then the group work would encourage articulation and sharing of images with the use of language. There is a real-life information gap and sharing of ideas as in real-life communication. It would be a good readiness activity before listening to the story.

Activity 2:
Then the learners are instructed to work in pairs and describe the picture:

- Who can you see?
- Where are they?
- What is happening?

Immediately below this Activity 2, there is a "Useful phrases" section with a list of possible expressions to use:

- There's a forest/cottage/witch.
- The picture shows ...
- In the foreground/background ...
- It/He/She looks ...

Our observations:

We wonder about the value of describing the picture in pairs when both of them can see it. What would be the communicative reason for doing so? We suspect this pair work is just trying to elicit vocabulary and expressions.

From the point of providing opportunities to establish associative networks we think that this "Useful expressions" section turns the potential "exploration and discovery activity using a picture from a story" into a comprehension test and language practice. We can easily imagine the pairs discussing how to complete the sentences, rather than focusing on the content of the story.

If this was shared bedtime reading in L1, the mother may show the picture and let her child guess what is happening. The child may come up with his/her own stories and the mother may go along with it or ask further questions, which may or may not link with what is coming next in the story. The main point of doing so is for the children to play with their imagination and with language, sharing outrageous and funny ideas, laughing together and feeling close. Similar ludic experiences can facilitate L2 language acquisition, not only for children but for teenagers and adults too (Cook, 2000).

Our adaptation:

Our instruction would be: "I will read you the story in a minute. Look at the picture first. Guess what is going to happen in the story." There will be no questioning and we will then experience the first part of the story.

Activity 3:
Read the questions. Do you know the correct answers?

1 Why were the children alone in the forest?
   a Their parents took them into the forest and left them there.
   b They went for a walk and got lost.
2 What happened at the witch's cottage?
   a The witch killed Hansel but Gretel escaped
   b Gretel killed the witch

Activity 4:
Listen to the story of Hansel and Gretel and check your answer to Exercise 3.

Our observations:

In Global Intermediate (Clandfield & Robb Benne, 2011), this Activity 3 is a pre-listening activity. Possible objectives may include inviting the learners to predict what is going to happen in the story and providing scaffolding for the story structure. It seems to us that the instruction: "Do you know the correct answers?" creates a closed activity with only one answer. As we predicted, Activity 4 is for the learners to listen to the story and check if their answers are correct or not. So, listening becomes an exercise in confirming correct answers rather than enjoying the story itself and exploring its personal significance.

In L1 bedtime story reading, would a mother ask her child to guess what the story is about and let them listen to the whole story to find out whether their guesses were correct or not? Would the child remember what he/she had guessed? In the case of L2 learners, is it not the case that having to find correct answers would stop them from living in their mental representations that change from moment to moment, being scared by the witch, feeling the heat of the oven and being burnt to death?

Our adaptation: We would not use the recording of the story on the CD which is provided. Instead, we would read section by section while noticing the learners' reactions. If "non-native" teachers feel worried about their pronunciation, they can listen to the CD and practice in advance. We would strongly argue that live interactive reading by the teacher provides a far superior authentic listening experience, in which natural pause, repetition and repair occur and the language is embodied. We may stop and ask prediction questions. We may ask the learners to mime to the story. Depending on the story, we may give roles or tell the learners to act as all the characters and even inanimate objects such as trees. Afterwards, we might ask them to remember their favourite moment and create a group tableau (a motionless human picture) to perform in class. All these activities would involve the teacher's repeated reading and learners thinking about and responding to the scenes in linguistic, sensory, motor, cognitive and affective ways, linking linguistic codes with corresponding mental representation.

After listening, we may set a collaborative task of creating a picture book and then give out the story for reading. We may set a writing task of rewriting the story in their own local context with their names. The class can exchange their stories and recommend a few for the teacher to read out.

None of the suggestions we have made require much preparation or equipment. They all involve creating mental representations: e.g. visualisation, prediction, creative reproduction (e.g. tableaux, picture books) and using multimodal expression (miming, picture books), thus providing opportunities to connect linguistic networks with sensory, motor, cognitive and affective networks. While they work on their linguistic output, there might be an explicit focus on accurate form in a meaningful context and then collaborative production.

Automatic word recognition, frequency-based selection of vocabulary and lexical chunks are all important. L1 children, however, are not given corpus-based frequency vocabulary or enhanced texts. Motivated exposure and interactions about what matter to them provide opportunities for repetition, recycling and noticing in the context of form-meaning-function associations and similar experiences would benefit L2 learners more than being explicitly taught language items whilst trying to comprehend an engaging text.

> **Readers' Tasks**
>
> Look at the first four pages of a unit in any coursebook:
>
> 1 Try to find any activities likely to facilitate or contribute to the development of comprehension that are similar to what L1 children do when reading or listening to a text.
> 2 Find a "comprehension" activity in the unit that is actually unlikely to contribute to the development of comprehension and think of ways in which the activity could be adapted so that it does contribute to linking linguistic networks with sensory, motor, cognitive and affective networks in the learners' brains.

Application to L2 Assessment

For listening and reading, established high-stake examinations often use certain testing techniques that test products of comprehension rather than proficiency in its process (Khalifa & Weir, 2009; Coombe et al., 2012; Flowerdew & Miller, 2012). High-stakes tests are developed and administered on a worldwide scale, and statistical measures need to be produced to justify their reliability. Marking needs to be standardised and inter-rater reliability must be assured. Various measures of validity need to be satisfied. These tests assume a large number of testees and therefore the logistics of test administration need careful consideration. As a result of all these requirements, the tests often resort to objective (and therefore easily, quickly and reliably marked) test types such as yes/no comprehension questions, gap fill, multiple choice, true or false, etc. Each of these test types ensures that there is only one correct answer in order to achieve marking consistency and, in doing so, focuses on surface linguistic understanding of discrete sections of a text rather than holistic representation and interpretation. If this is the case in high-stakes tests, you can rely on it being the case in classroom tests and in classroom teaching too.

These testing techniques may test products of comprehension, but they are not designed to measure proficiency in its process. The mental processes that learners' brains might have gone through are invisible and therefore not typically explored in testing. As we have discussed in this chapter, listening and reading comprehension ideally involve developing mental representations through activation of associated networks and, as this skill is not normally tested, it is not normally developed in classrooms either.

Activating multidimensional associative networks may help learners to produce some correct answers in listening and reading tests, but testing only the knowledge of linguistic items or the level of mastery of strategies is not likely to measure comprehension (i.e. multidimensional associations in the brain) nor to encourage its development or to promote effective and durable acquisition.

Typical high-stakes testing techniques not only influence exams and quizzes at the levels of institutions or classroom assessment but also materials and teaching. As was shown above in our analysis of activities for Hansel and Gretel taken from *Global Intermediate* (Clandfield & Benne, 2011), correctness of understanding and knowledge of vocabulary and expressions are often emphasised at the expense of creating mental representations of texts that can lead to personal enrichment and language acquisition through listening and reading. Such blind applications of traditional testing techniques could end up in preventing the development of the ability to create mental representations, a damaging example of negative backwash (Menken, 2008; Bailey & Masuhara, 2013).

How then can comprehension be assessed? The concept of direct testing is relevant here, that is testing what learners can actually do. We would argue that if we want to see if learners are creating multidimensional mental representations, then we need activities that require them to do so. For example, we could ask learners to:

- follow instructions to do something e.g. *The tester requests the learner to "put Hansel in a small room and lock the door", either by drawing this, manipulating a model or miming.*
- draw their representation e.g. *The learners are asked to listen to or read the relevant section and then draw how Gretel avoided having to go into the oven.*
- mime their representation e.g. *The tester reads a text and the testee demonstrates what is happening in it.*
- describe what they see in their mind e.g. *The testees are asked to listen to or read a passage and to recall their mental experience.*
- solve a problem e.g. *The testees need to listen to or read a problem and provide a solution to it.*

In other words, classroom activities have the potential to be used as assessment activities. Testing experts may question the reliability of marking such activities. However, when we have used TPR Plus activities as assessment activities (listen and draw; listen and mime; listen and cook; listen and create a tool) we have supplied marking criteria and inter-rater reliability has been acceptably high. This was probably because when we established criteria, we specified what to take into account and what not to include when marking. For example, when recreating the sequence of an event was the objective of assessment, the spelling of words was not marked as long as the intended meaning was clear. Such classroom tests encouraged teachers and learners to focus on comprehension (i.e. creating mental representations) during classroom activities, thus resulting in positive backwash (Menken, 2008; Bailey & Masuhara, 2013).

Testers are reliant on the theory of mental constructs, components and processes. When mental processing is still very much debated, high-stakes tests continue to use techniques that may or may not actually measure the construct. Meanwhile, it seems to us to be sensible to make educational decisions that prioritise the benefit of learners (Tomlinson, 2005b; Menken, 2008; Brown & Priyanvada, 2010).

Application to Teacher Development

As we have discussed in this chapter, comprehension is a term widely used without being clearly defined or its substrates and processing being agreed upon.

The main points we have highlighted include:

- Comprehension involves pragmatic, sociocultural and contextual understanding as well as linguistic processing.
- Learners need a lot of rewarding and implicit listening, reading and viewing experience to achieve comprehension.
- The vital importance in listening of phonological segmentation and prosody in meaning construction must be recognised.
- Comprehension activities often confuse teaching, learning and testing.
- Teaching discrete linguistic items does not lead to comprehension.
- Automatic word recognition depends on connecting linguistic codes to multidimensional networks in the brain.
- Strategy training is useful as a support when there are problems in automatic meaning construction.

In relation to teacher development, we would advise teacher developers to reflect on their own listening and reading experience, and to read about how the brain understands and acquires language in order to conduct a critical evaluation of the received dogma about reading and listening comprehension, which tends to remain unchallenged. One example of a belief that we think needs to be challenged by teacher developers is that teaching and testing declarative knowledge of grammar and vocabulary will somehow generate the procedural knowledge needed for successful holistic comprehension. Another very different example is the rejection of shared reading by many teacher developers as being too teacher-centred. The value of shared reading, in which the teacher reads aloud and discusses with the learners a text in a very large format, is widely recognised in L1 and L2 young-learner reading acquisition research (e.g. Bland, 2015, 2018). However, we have encountered cases in which EFL teachers who have just completed training programmes in the UK were advising against teachers reading stories in a shared book manner because of the length of teacher talking time. The teacher reading aloud stories in a dramatic, embodied and interactive manner whilst learners read the text can help EFL learners to create mental representations and to strengthen neural networks while activating linguistic, sensory, motor, cognitive and affective areas of their brains. We feel that it is very important that teacher developers do not blindly adhere to what could be considered unprincipled and unresearched dogma without challenging it and thinking carefully about how to advise teachers on their courses. Of course, it would help if some examiners on teacher-training courses would reconsider what candidate behaviour they will reward and what they will "punish", by for example focusing on whether in a given context the teacher talking seems to be potentially facilitating or hindering learner acquisition rather than predetermining that teacher talking time is bad (Tomlinson, 2014b). It would also help if assessment on such courses focused on the effectiveness of what teachers do to support learners, rather than on the teacher's demonstration of approved techniques.

Readers' Tasks

To what extent (if at all) do you agree with each of the following statements? Give reasons for your answers.

1 Most students only have a few hours a week to learn their L2. They need to prepare for exams. They don't have time for extensive reading or watching films.
2 Unless the learners are pretaught new language, they will not be able to understand what they hear or read.
3 Rich and ample exposure to language in use is a prerequisite for acquisition, but learner motivation also needs to be considered when choosing materials and approaches for comprehension lessons.
4 Teachers need to encourage their learners to tolerate ambiguity when reading and listening rather than worrying about the meaning of every word they encounter.

FURTHER READING

Tomlinson, B. & Masuhara, H. (2018). Chapter 9 – Developing materials for the development of skills. In B. Tomlinson & H. Masuhara (2018), *The complete guide to the theory and practice of materials development for language learning* (pp. 220–245). Hoboken NJ: Wiley.

7 Production and Monitoring of the L2

Part One: Theory

Introduction

In the nineteen seventies, Steven Krashen put forward what has become both a controversial and an influential model, which he referred to as the Monitor Model (Krashen, 1979, 1982, 1994). He actually put forward five hypotheses, which are sometimes given the name of the Input Hypothesis (his fourth hypothesis) and sometimes the Monitor Model (his third hypothesis). His basic thesis was that adults can learn a language consciously from explicit transmission of declarative knowledge, but that this learned knowledge does not help them to communicate spontaneously. In order to achieve this, they need to acquire the language from exposure to comprehensible input (see Chapter 1 in this volume). In Krashen's view, the only role for learned declarative knowledge was to help learners monitor their utterances prior to and subsequent to production of language. While acknowledging that this could be a useful (but limited) role, he pointed out that excessive monitoring could slow down a speaker and make their hesitant speech very difficult to listen to. He also categorised learners into three types: over-monitors, who nearly always monitor their production and suffer the communicative consequences of hesitation and reticence; under-monitors, who rarely monitor their production and thus make many errors; and optimal monitors, who monitor when it is appropriate and significant (e.g. in formal writing or in speech situations where accuracy is important). Whilst not disagreeing that the main role of explicitly learned knowledge is monitoring, we would go further than Krashen and say that such monitoring takes place before, during and after production, that monitoring is not just of accuracy but of fluency, appropriateness and effect, that implicitly acquired procedural knowledge can play a crucial role in spontaneous monitoring, that effective monitoring facilitates effective production and that effective monitoring can make a valuable contribution to language acquisition. Amazingly, given its importance in the process of producing language, monitoring has received very little attention in the research literature on language production, an area which is itself under-researched in our view. In this chapter we will refer to what research literature there is on monitoring and language production, but much of the chapter will be theoretical in the sense that we will be using our experience as researchers in a number of academic fields, our experience as language users and teachers and our informed introspection and intuition to posit a description of the mental processes involved. For some SLA researchers such theorising is taboo and only empirical evidence is acceptable. For us, theorising can help to fill the gaps in the research literature by stimulating thought, provoking controversy, inspiring application and suggesting profitable areas of research. After all, in applied linguistics there is an honourable tradition of philosophical theory with such influential figures as Pit Corder, Strevens, Chomsky, Halliday, Widdowson, Stevick, Faneslow and Maley inspiring thought and exploration with their novel theories rather than with their empirical evidence.

The Process of Language Production

For a language learner there are three types of language production, for communicative use, for language practice and for language display.

Production for communicative use requires contextual awareness and competence in achieving an appropriate level of accuracy, fluency, appropriateness and outcome effect. Each experience of communicative use can make a rich contribution to language acquisition, as it can both add to and strengthen the linguistic, paralinguistic, extra-linguistic, affective and sensory records in the brain.

Production for language practice is typically context-free and is restricted by the focus determined by the practice activity, whether it be controlled or guided. It tends to focus on increasing lexical, structural or phonological accuracy, without regard for fluency, appropriateness or effect. It might achieve some strengthening of linguistic records, but compared to communicative use it usually provides an impoverished experience in relation to language acquisition.

Display tends also to be context-free and to focus on lexical, structural or phonological accuracy without regard for any communicative effect other than impressing the addressee(s) (usually a teacher or examiner). It might achieve some strengthening of linguistic records, but compared to communicative use it provides an impoverished experience in relation to language acquisition. Unfortunately, in our experience many (but not all) L2 assessment tasks and examinations ask learners to display their productive competence rather than to communicate purposefully within a context with the objective of achieving intended effects. And, even more unfortunately, in many language classrooms around the world, learners spend much of their classroom time practising displaying their productive (rather than communicative) competence in preparation for examinations.

Speech

Unplanned Discourse

Participating in unplanned oral discourse is probably the most difficult communicative act in an L2. Not only does it require decisions about appropriate, interesting and effective content, but decisions also about the accurate, appropriate and effective language to use to express this content in order to achieve intended effects. And all this has to be achieved almost instantaneously or else the listener(s) will respond negatively to the speaker's lack of fluency. As Schütze (2017, p. 153) says, in order to use words actively those words "need to be recalled" (we would say retrieved) "from memory, which activates the non-mesial region, the phonological loop, Broca's area, Wernicke's area, and, if needed, the hippocampus", a process that takes "half a second or less per word". Of course, in order for this process to be achieved the required language, as we have seen in previous chapters, needs first to have been acquired through numerous meaningful encounters rich in semantic, sensory and nonlinguistic information, ideally whilst affectively and cognitively engaged. It also needs to have been acquired from exposure to spoken language in authentic use to avoid the development of the habit of speaking in sentences with the lexis and grammar of the formal written variety of the language (see O'Keeffe, McCarthy & Carter, 2007, McCarten & McCarthy, 2010 and Carter, Hughes & McCarthy, 2011 for descriptions and examples of the distinctive features of spontaneous spoken English discourse).

Planned Discourse

When the learner has time to plan what to say (e.g. before asking a question in class or in a lecture or meeting) they can make use of learned declarative knowledge as well as acquired procedural knowledge. They can use both recall and retrieval before using their inner voice to assemble and to try out an utterance (see Chapter 5). When doing so, they need to bear in mind their contextual objectives and their eventual intended outcomes. They need to decide how important accuracy, fluency and appropriateness are in order to achieve their intended effects. In order to achieve effectiveness in planned oral discourse, learners need a lot of experience in attempting to achieve intended effects rather than just practising being accurate. We remember a group of very advanced post-doctoral science students from China who were prepared at a college in the UK to be accurate when speaking to fellow researchers at the University of Cambridge. Unfortunately, most of the interaction with fellow researchers took place in a pub or a coffee bar rather than in a laboratory or lecture room, and the composed, formal sentences of the Chinese researchers, whilst being grammatically and scientifically accurate, were considered to be socially inappropriate and ineffective.

Interaction

Learners of an L2 typically interact with fellow learners, with their teachers both formally and informally and sometimes with native speakers and other proficient users of the L2. Interaction provides potentially rich opportunities to strengthen and develop language acquisition providing it is contextualised and communicative and has objectives other than just language practice or display. When it satisfies these conditions, it can provide valuable and authentic input, opportunities for using embodied language and pragmatic strategies to achieve communicative outcomes, supportive feedback on the effectiveness of the learner's contribution to the interaction and affective, cognitive and social engagement. See Long (1981, 1983a, 1983b) for his research-based interaction hypothesis, which states that communication is achieved in interaction through negotiation of meaning and that such negotiation increases comprehensible input and can facilitate intake and eventual acquisition. Interestingly, both our experience and the research reports in the literature suggest that the most useful type of interaction for facilitating language acquisition is peer interaction. This is especially so if learners are in a small, heterogeneous group in which "expert" learners help "novice" learners with input, suggestions and feedback, if they are engaged in social interaction in collaborative problem solving or task completion, and if the group is socially cohesive (see Sato & Lyster, 2007; Barker, 2010a, 2010b; Choi & Iwashita, 2016; Sato & Ballinger, 2016a, 2016b). Sato and Ballinger (2016b) claim, as we would, that learner–learner interactions can be more useful than learner–native-speaker interactions because learners tend to produce structurally richer input than native speakers (Mayo & Pica, 2000), who often simplify their language and produce foreigner talk, which is reduced in grammaticality and complexity (Sato, 2015). They also claim, as we would again, that learners give each other more, and more useful, feedback (Sato & Lyster, 2007), that learners feel more comfortable when talking to each other, that they are more willing to try out hypotheses (Sato & Lyster, 2007) and that they modify their input more (McDonough, 2004). In summary Sato and Ballinger (2016a, p. 4) say "it seems that during peer interaction learners are able to shift their attention" more "to formal aspects of the target language" and "they engage in quantitatively richer interaction with each other in terms of output".

For us, peer interaction provides probably the richest opportunity of all production activities for furthering language acquisition, and yet in the thousands of language classes we have observed all over the world we have seen so little of it. We see learners practising the language with each other, we see learners answering their teacher's questions, we see learners displaying their ability to produce sentences, but only rarely do we see socially engaged learners actually communicating with each other in the target language.

Writing

Unplanned Discourse

There are times when we have to write spontaneously, without time for prior planning. Examples of such writing would be filling in a form that you have just been given, leaving a message for someone, taking notes for immediate use, responding to questions and comments during a podcast, web or chat, and writing a report of an ongoing event. For most learners of an L2 such writing in the real world would be rare, but experiencing it during learning time would be useful as it requires similar instant access to, selection from and combination from acquired language as unplanned speech does but often does not elicit the same immediate feedback on effect.

Planned Discourse

Planned written discourse is the norm in the L2 classroom and very often learners are asked to display their ability to produce language, either in guided practice activities in which the content and often some of the language is predetermined or in free production activities in which there is no context and no intended outcome other than production of a text (e.g. writing an essay). Such activities not only ignore the realities of real-world writing in which there is a reason and a purpose for writing and in which the context needs to be considered when deciding on content, and when selecting the language and the pragmatic strategies most likely to achieve the intended effects. Replicating such writing in the classroom is not only a useful preparation for real-world use of the L2 but can facilitate language acquisition through the testing and revision of hypotheses and the strengthening of records in the brain. Most importantly of all though, when such writing is dependent on the utilisation of existing linguistic resources (as when completing a written task in a lesson using a strong task-based approach) the learners discover needs that can then be satisfied by collaborating peers, a supportive teacher, a reference resource or self-discovery. Such on-task satisfaction of needs can be a powerful facilitator of language acquisition, as it can create psychological readiness for acquisition (Pienemann, 1985) and match the language acquisition criteria of salience, relevance, utility and impact. Saville-Troike and Barto (2017, p. 173) outline how writing "may contribute to successful L2 learning" and point out that because:

> writers must express ideas without recourse to objects and events in their own immediate physical environment or that of their reader(s), or to gestures or other nonverbal means of communication, and without reliance on immediate feedback or cooperation to fill gaps, writing can push learners closer to their limits of existing knowledge than can speech.

They also claim that this "contributes to SLA by stimulating syntactic development" (p. 173). Whilst agreeing with this, we would warn against over-reliance on writing on a language course, as this could lead to the stilted production of complete and grammatical written sentences in informal oral discourse and could inhibit the development of competence in interpreting and producing embodied language. Saville-Troike and Barto (2017, p. 173) also list other ways in which writing can facilitate SLA. Of these ways, we would agree with:

- Generating input
- Helping learners notice gaps in their own knowledge as they are forced to visibly encode concepts in L2 forms
- Allowing learners to test hypotheses they have formulated as part of their developing linguistic systems, with opportunity for monitoring and revision
- Providing opportunity for others to comment on problems and provide corrective feedback

For a consideration of other ways in which writing can facilitate SLA, see Swain and Lapkin (1995) and for a comprehensive survey of the literature on the acquisition of second language writing, see Polio (2012).

Interaction

Written interaction is becoming increasingly common in the real world, either in real time in the form of computer chats and text messaging or in delayed responses in emails, and sometimes still in letters. Replication of such interactions in the classroom could not only be a useful preparation for real world contextualised and purposeful use of the L2, but could also provide opportunities to strengthen and develop the learners' mental repertoires of language and of pragmatic strategies. As such interaction does typically provide communicative feedback on appropriacy and effect, it can also aid the testing, revision and strengthening of hypotheses.

The Mental Process of Language Production

What we are presenting below is our model of the mental process of language production based on our research, our reading, our experience in the classroom, our reflection and introspection of our own language production and our informed intuition. In unplanned discourse many of the processes described below need to be performed subconsciously and instantly, but in planned discourse some of them are performed deliberately and consciously.

1 Impetus

The starting point for any language production is an impetus to produce. This could be that somebody has asked you a question, that you want to find your way to a station in an unfamiliar city, that you want to tell somebody your good news, that you have been invited to give a presentation at a conference, that you have received an email that requires a response, that you have seen an advertisement for an interesting post and have decided to apply, or that a teacher has asked you to produce a sentence using the past continuous.

2 Appraisal of the context of production

The immediate response to the initial impetus for language use is to ascertain such salient features of the context as who you are producing the language for, what your relationship is to the addressee(s), what previous interactions you have had with the addressee(s), what is expected of you and what the appropriate level of formality would be. However, if the impetus is only for language practice or display then the appraisal will simply be of the level of accuracy required and the experience will be impoverished in relation to its value in the process of language acquisition.

3 Determination of intended effect

Whilst appraising the context of production, the language user is also determining the communicative effect they intend to achieve (e.g. persuading somebody to help them, convincing somebody of the validity of their point of view, getting people to buy a product, amusing people, helping somebody to fill in a form, getting a job). In order to achieve this intended effect, they will need to achieve a competent level of contextual appropriateness, of content awareness, of cultural awareness, of fluency, of accuracy and of strategic skill.

Stages 1, 2 and 3 above are almost instantaneous and overlapping in unplanned discourse, and are probably achieved by a combination of experience, informed instinct, imaging and inner speech.

4 Determination of content

Often in a language class, the focus is on how to say or write something rather than what to say or write. However, in communicative use the main (or at least initial) focus is usually on what to say or write, that is on the content of the intended utterance. Ideally, the content needs to be relevant, focused, informative, interesting and of value to the addressee(s). Without these qualities, an utterance will have little impact on the addressee(s) regardless of its degree of accuracy and fluency.

The determination of content is achieved through a combination of imaging and inner speech. For example, when deciding on the content of the first sentence of "6 Selection of language" below, an image of words in a diagram of the brain came to mind and the words "make choices" were both imaged and uttered silently.

5 Determination of strategies

If we are aiming to achieve a particular effect in a specific context in which we know who the addressees are, then we need to determine not only intent and content but also pragmatic strategy. For example, preliminary praise and future promise are typical strategies when trying to persuade somebody to help, consistent use of the simple present tense to give the impression that facts are being presented is a typical strategy when attempting to win an argument and the use of affirmative adjectives is a common strategy when trying to sell a product. Strategies are determined by intended effect, previous experience and awareness of the addressee(s), they are prompted by visualised images and the inner voice, and they are often revised in speech as a result of monitoring of the initial effect. The determination, monitoring and revision of pragmatic strategies is basically subconscious in unplanned discourse, but can be conscious and deliberate in planned discourse, and especially in careful writing.

Like all the other stages of production, strategy determination is mastered through experience. Unfortunately, many L2 coursebook and classroom production activities do not provide this experience, and it is not uncommon for advanced learners to produce language that is accurate and fluent but lacking in effectiveness. See Taguchi and Kim (2018) and Ostman and Verschueren (2018) for edited volumes that explore how pragmatic effects can be achieved in language production.

Researchers are beginning to pay more attention to what happens in the brain prior to speech production, with an emphasis on the conceptual representations that inform the selection of language to produce. For example, Papafragu and Grigoroglu (2019) agree with Levelt (1993) that spoken production starts with the preverbal, conceptual apprehension of what the speaker intends to talk about. One of their research findings is that conceptualising an event prior to communication depends not only on conceptual and linguistic factors, but also on the pragmatic assessment of what the interlocutor needs and knows.

6 Selection of language

The language needed to express content and achieve intended effects is recalled and/or retrieved from the brain (depending on the amount of time and planning available) as sets of lexical options and the producer makes initial choices. These sets of options can be manifest as visualised and/or silently uttered words, and we are rarely aware of their occurrence, even in planned production.

Rahman and Melinger (2019) investigate the process of lexical selection and conclude that conceptual representation and lexical selection operate in parallel and that there is sometimes a conflict between conceptual priming (i.e. the influence of content, context and intention) and the lexical options available to the speaker.

7 Initial combination of language

The words and phrases selected in stage 6 are combined in a rough mental draft by the addition of structure words and inflexions. This mental draft is manifest as visualised and/or silently uttered expressions (usually in meaningful units), and we are only aware of their occurrence in such planned production events as those requiring careful writing or the mental formulation of intended oral questions or comments in interviews, meetings or lectures.

For an account of where and how stages 6 and 7 occur in the brain, see Schütze (2017).

8 Revised combination of language

The rough mental draft in stage 7 is revised through deletion, addition and modification, and then rehearsed as a complete utterance. The rehearsal is performed with the inner voice, and we might be well aware of it immediately prior to uttering it in planned discourse or to writing it. This rehearsal serves the functions of maintaining the utterance in the mind ready for production, of providing a final opportunity for revision and, as we will see later in Chapter 8, of providing auto-input for potential intake into the brain with the potential for maintaining, strengthening and creating records.

9 Production of language

The revised utterance rehearsed in stage 8 is spoken or written, and possibly further revised during production, as a result of perceptions of inaccuracy, inappropriateness or ineffectiveness. Such perceptions are triggered by a process of monitoring, which also notes when production appears to be successful, a process not only useful for successful communication but for successful language acquisition too.

10 Response to the production of language

In speech the utterance produced in 9 is repeated, summarised, repaired or elaborated if it is considered to have been ineffective in achieving the intended effect determined in stage 3. In writing, the utterance is read with the inner voice and is deleted, repaired or elaborated if it appears to be defective or likely to become ineffective in achieving the intended effect. For L2 learners, apparent effectiveness will reinforce hypotheses in the brain and apparent ineffectiveness can trigger revisions of hypotheses.

All ten stages of the production process above are vital, and the only way of establishing mastery of them is frequent, purposeful use. Many controlled and even guided practice activities often require only the use of stage 9 (and possibly stages 4 and 10) and cannot provide adequate preparation for authentic communication, in which context, intended effects and emotions play significant roles. Nor can they provide rich enough feedback on effectiveness to aid the acquisition process.

One recent publication, which stresses that language acquisition is usage-based, is meaning-focused, is context-dependent and is determined by frequency of experience is Tyler, Ortega, Uno and Park (2018). This book also proposes a pedagogy which, as we do, highlights rich experience of understanding and producing language in contextual use as a prerequisite for the acquisition of language and the development of communicative competence in an L2.

Our listing of stages above gives the false impression that one stage always follows another in a set sequence, when the reality is that language production is dynamic, organic and recursive, with stages overlapping and being repeated. For example, content is determined in stage 4 but it might be further determined during and/or after stages 6, 7 and 8. The listing of ten stages also gives a false impression that it takes a long time to produce language. This might occasionally be true of such carefully planned discourse as an academic book chapter or a legal document, but in spontaneous unplanned discourse the whole process is achieved in a miraculously few seconds. The process is speeded up by the use of set phrases (e.g. "This might be true of such ..."), by words priming other words (e.g. "such" primes "as", "academic" primes "book chapter", "legal" primes "document") and by rough drafting in stage 7 followed by elaboration in stage 8 (e.g. "such planned discourse" in 7 became "such carefully planned discourse" in 8).

A book that covers all the stages of speech production from intention to articulation to monitoring is Levelt (1993). This provides a very detailed description of all the processes involved, and stresses that most of them are automatic and that they can operate in parallel. Although now slightly outdated, it has provided a starting point for most of the subsequent research into what happens prior to, during and subsequent to speech production in communication.

The Literature on Language Production during the Acquisition of an L2

Much of the literature on L2 learner language production focuses on the language required for successful production or on the product rather than the process of language production. For example, it might focus on the language required for effective academic writing (either from prescription, from textual analysis or from reference to corpora), it might focus on the language manifestations needed to achieve pragmatic effect in service interactions, it might focus on the grammar of spoken English, it might focus on the language typically used by students on English for Academic Purposes (EAP) courses or it might focus on typical learner errors. Very rarely does it focus on how learners produce the language that they do, and what effect this has on their acquisition of the L2.

The Literature on the Language Needed for Successful Production

There is a large literature on the language needed for successful production, with success often being defined by the degree of accuracy or of genre appropriacy, or more recently on pragmatic achievement. For example, see Maley and Tomlinson (2017) for chapters on the language needed for authentic production (e.g. Jones, 2017 on authentic conversation), see Burns and Hill (2013), Pickering (2012) and Timmis (2013) for reference to research on what learners need to do when speaking in an L2, see Mukundan and Nimechisalem (2013) and McDonough, Shaw and Masuhara (2013) for research on what learners need to do when writing in an L2, and see Taguchi and Kim (2018) and Ostman and Verschueren (2018) for research on what learners need to do to achieve pragmatic competence.

The Literature on Differences between the Language Used in Speech and the Language Used in Writing

Research in the last thirty years has revealed great differences between the lexis and the grammar typically used in speech and that used in writing, and has had the great value of stressing the need for L2 learners to experience the target language in both typical written and typical spoken use. One example of such a difference would be writing, "Messi is the best player in the world" but saying, "He's the best player in the world, Messi". For information about the differences between the language of speech and of writing see Carter and McCarthy (2006, 2017), McCarten and McCarthy (2010), Carter, Hughes and McCarthy (2011), and McDonough, Shaw and Masuhara (2013).

The Literature on the Language that L2 Learners Use in Production

Now that many corpora have been compiled of learner use of language (for example, ICLE (The International Corpus of Learner English) and the Cambridge Learner Corpus), publications are being written on how L2 learners actually use language in production. See, for example, Gablasova, Brezina, McEnery and Boyd (2015), Granger, Gilquin and Meunier (2015), Tono and Díez-Bedmar (2014), O'Keefe and Mark (2017) and Gablasova, Brezina and McEnery (2017).

The Literature on the Relationship between L2 Language Production and Acquisition

Most of the publications on language production, as we said previously, focus on either the language needed for production or the products of production. However Kormos (2006) does focus on speech production and language acquisition, as do Tarone (2005), Pickering (2012) and Colantoni, Steele and Escudero (2017). Tarone (2005) provides perhaps the widest coverage of aspects of speaking in a second language and reviews the literature on the acquisition of L2 phonology, of transactional competence, of communication strategies and of speaking competence, as well as focusing on ludic discourse and the value of using language for play in language acquisition (a view we fully endorse, as does Cook, 2000 in his detailed overview of language play). Another publication that investigates the relationship between language production and language acquisition and development is Kuiken and Vedder (2012), which looks at the effects of speaking and writing tasks on second language performance and concludes that both the oral and the written modes can be effective in influencing performance but that oral "interaction may … enhance the quality of a written text" because of the "extensive deliberations going on between the participants before they decide to commit something to paper (p. 375). Kuiken and Veddar (2012) focus on the influence of task types on-task performance, but do not point out that immediate performance is not necessarily the same as acquisition and can be a misleading indicator of acquisition.

Perhaps the most significant and influential theory of L2 language production is Swain's output hypothesis (Swain, 1985, 1995, 1996, 2005), which claims that "the act of producing language (speaking or writing) constitutes ... part of the process of language learning" (Swain, 2005, p. 471). According to this hypothesis, output has three functions in second language learning: "1) the noticing/triggering function, 2) the hypothesis-testing function, 3) the metalinguistic (reflective) function" (Swain, 2005, p. 471). Swain argues that learners can gain acquisition by being pushed to achieve comprehensible output through delivering messages that are "conveyed precisely, coherently and appropriately" (Swain, 2005, p. 473). The learners are pushed by noticing problems when they attempt to produce the target language, by testing hypotheses in trial runs "reflecting their hypothesis of how to say (or write) their intent" (Swain, 2005, p. 476), by reflecting on language produced by "others or the self" (Swain, 2005, p. 478) and by teacher feedback. The aim is modification of problematic output and the eventual acquisition of revised hypotheses. Initially, researchers focused on the effect of pushed output on accuracy and appropriacy and found it to be beneficial (see Swain, 2005) but we would claim that it can have beneficial effects on pragmatic competence too if the focus is switched to the effectiveness of the outcome rather than (or in addition to) the accuracy of the output. R. Ellis (2015) provides examples of learner output, which was improved by modifications resulting from being pushed, and he refers to research that reports the benefits to acquisition that such pushed output can provide. R. Ellis (2015) also investigates the research evidence related to learner output tasks and concludes that, "there is in fact substantial evidence that task-based instruction does promote the kinds of performance likely to facilitate acquisition and also a growing body of evidence to show that it can result in acquisition" (R. Ellis, 2015, p. 285).

The prevalence of learner pair and group interaction in many currently popular methodologies (for example, task-based learning, text-driven approaches problem-solving, content-based approaches) has led to increased interest in the value of peer interaction in improving productive communicative competence. One recent book that investigates this in detail is Sato and Ballinger (2016a). This is a collection of reports of studies of the perceived and the actual effects of peer interaction on learner performance and includes a focus on the silent learner, on peer interaction, on metacognitive instruction, on group dynamics, on interactional behaviour, on heterogeneous grouping, on affective and social engagement, on task modality, on meta-analytic talk and on using social discourse for language learning. The consensus seems to be that peer interaction (especially when conducted in heterogeneous but socially cohesive and engaged groups) can help to improve learner communicative competence, even more than learner–native-speaker and learner-teacher interaction.

It seems that "during learner interaction learners are able to shift their attention to formal aspects of the target language more than when they interact with native speaking partners or teachers" and that "they engage in quantitatively richer interaction with each other in terms of output" (Sato & Ballinger, 2016b). Another book that focuses on the beneficial effects of peer interaction is Mackey (2006). Mackey, Abbuhl and Gass (2012) provide an overview of the value of interaction in language acquisition and Mackey, Ziegler and Bryfonski (2016) discuss the value of peer interaction in TBLT.

A recent development in the study of the language used by non-native speakers interacting successfully with each other in English (i.e. using English as a lingua franca) emerges from the findings that ELF (English as a Lingua Franca) users not only make frequent use of lexical chunks but do so in ways that approximate native-speaker use without completely matching target forms. Mauranen (2012, 2017) has been instrumental in focusing on fuzzy processing in ELF, and stresses that it is a feature of successful listening and speaking, which depends on the interlocutors' acceptance of approximations in interaction. See Hynninen (2020, pp. 83–86) for a concise summary of Mauranen's work and that of other contributors to research on cognitive and utterance fluency in ELF.

The consensus in the literature is that producing language to achieve communication can be a powerful facilitator of language acquisition. Whilst agreeing with this view, we would warn against premature production for beginners as we have found that this inevitably leads to the making of multiple errors and a consequent loss of esteem and confidence. We would much prefer approaches to the teaching of beginners that follow a silent-period approach (Asher, 1981; Saville-Troike, 1988; Tomlinson, 1994b) or a comprehension approach (Winitz, 1981; Krashen & Terrell, 1983; Barnard, 2007; R. Ellis, 2015; Marczak, 2018), in which the learners are exposed to the L2 in meaningful and engaging use but respond to it physically or in the L1 until they have achieved sufficient language processing to be ready to start confident production in the L2.

The Literature on What L2 Learners Do Mentally When Producing Language

Literature on this very important topic is scarce. Harley (2008) is a book on language acquisition which does have a substantial chapter on "how we produce language". Harley follows Levelt (1989) in claiming that there are three stages in the process of language production, conceptualisation, formulation and encoding. The "processes of conceptualization involve determining what to say ... The processes of formulation involve translating this conceptual representation into a linguistic form ... the processes of execution involve detailed phonetic and articulatory planning" (Harley, 2008, p. 397). This is similar to our model above but without our specification of the roles of imaging, of the inner voice and of rehearsal in the process. In fact, Harley

(2008) specifically denies that inner speech necessarily plays a role in language production on p. 448 and provides rather unconvincing evidence in substantiation. Harley also refers to Garret (1988) and his model of speech production, which differentiates between the discrete stages of conceptualisation, formulation and articulation and to Hayes and Flower (1986) and their identification of the three stages of writing production, the planning stage, in which "goals are set, ideas are generated and information is retrieved", the translation stage, in which "language is produced from the representation in memory" and the reviewing stage, in which "the writer reads and edits what has been written" (Harley, 2008, p. 447). One difference between our model and those of Garret and of Hayes and Flower is that our model emphasises the interactive, dynamic and recursive nature of the mental stages involved in language production.

As previously mentioned, Schütze (2017) does describe the internal process of selecting, combining and rehearsing lexical items during communicative production and like us he does stress the "fluid and dynamic nature" of the process and that "the components work simultaneously so various parts of the same sentence are at different processing stages at the same time" (Schütze, 2017, p. 21). Schütze asserts that a language producer first locates "the words s/he wants to use from memory", puts "them into a grammatically correct sentence" to form a pre-utterance sentence and then chooses a medium of communication. He also says that fluency is linked to the speed with which we can recall words from memory, whereas speaking accurately refers to being able to recall words correctly as well as to grammatically code them with morphemes' and that complexity "refers to our access to a large variety of words stored in the non-mesial region" (Schütze, 2017, p. 19).

Lintunen, Mutta and Peltonen (2020) refer to cognitive fluency in their summary of definitions. They distinguish it from utterance fluency and perceived fluency, and characterise it as:

> Cognitive fluency includes processing capacity (limitations of the working memory ...) and the automaticity of sub-processes needed for producing basic language skills (reading, listening, speaking, writing). Lexical access (or retrieval), that is, how fast and accurately a language user can access words in their mental lexicon while performing a language task, can also be regarded as a key index of cognitive fluency. (Lintunen, Mutta & Peltonen, 2020, p. 4)

As Lintunen, Mutta and Peltonen (2020) say, most of the research on cognitive fluency has been conducted with reference to its role in promoting oral fluency (e.g. Olkonnen, 2017) but they do refer to Olive (2014), who found "similarities between cognitive levels of processing in speaking and writing" (Lintunen, Mutta & Peltonen, 2020, p. 4). They also refer to much recent research on the process, value and measurement of fluency but not to research on how to promote learner fluency. In our view, it is mainly a combination between exposure to rich input of language in use and opportunities to use the target language for purposeful communication which eventually helps learners to develop the speed of lexical access which promotes fluency in production. We would also agree, though, that helping learners to acquire lexical chunks can facilitate fluency as they increase

> the mean length of runs, they facilitate speed fluency in general (e.g. speed rate) while at the same time reducing features associated with disfluency in terms of breakdown (e.g. long and frequent pauses) and repair frequency (e.g. repetitions). As a whole, formulaic utterances seem to form an important element in enhancing utterance fluency. (Lintunen, Mutta & Peltonen, 2020, p. 6)

With regard to face-to-face communication, we feel that it is important to recognise that gestures can play an important part in maintaining interaction, in achieving conversational fluency and in eliciting comprehensible input. As Peltonen's (2020) multimodal analysis of learner interactions during a problem-solving task reveals, gestures can play both a compensatory and a complementary role in achieving communication. We would certainly encourage the use of gesture in learner interaction and discourage, for example, dialogue practice in which learners are inhibited from gesturing because of holding a book or a card.

Readers' Task

1 Without looking back at the book, write a one-page summary for a friend of what you can remember from your reading of the book about the process of language production.
2 As soon as you have finished writing the summary, reflect on and write notes on what you think you did mentally before, whilst and after writing the summary.
3 What does your reflection tell you about the mental processes of language production?

The Roles of Monitoring

Monitoring is a mental process that is not only important post-production but during and after each of the ten stages listed in our model of the mental process of language production. It is achieved through a combination of imaging, experience-informed instinct, association, analysis and inner speech.

1 Prelinguistic monitoring

In L1 production, the initial decisions with regard to impetus, appraisal of context, determination of intent, determination of content and determination of strategies are monitored during and after each of those stages. For example, a father who has organised a graduation party for his son might decide to urge his son to come down from his room to the party because the guests have all arrived (impetus), to remind himself his son has been rather edgy and moody all day (appraisal of context), to decide to aim to get his son to come down without annoying him (determination of intent), to decide to talk about a friend who is waiting for a ride in the son's new sports car (determination of content and strategy) and to decide to make a subtle appeal to the son's consideration for his parents and their potential embarrassment if he remains in his room (determination of strategies). Notice that for an L2 user, none of these decisions need to involve the use of the L2, the making of such decisions is rarely advised in coursebooks or classrooms (except sometimes the deliberate pre-planning of content in writing activities) and such decisions are often never made at all in L2 learner production. All of these decisions, however, are vitally important in the achievement of effective production and the determination, monitoring and possible revision of these decisions are important communication skills.

2 Monitoring of selected language

Monitoring of selected language refers to stage 6 of the production process (selection of language) and consists of mental appraisal of the lexical options retrieved and/or recalled plus selection from them. In planned, time-friendly discourse, this process might be performed consciously and deliberately through the inner voice, otherwise it is largely a subconscious process.

3 Monitoring of initial combination of language

Monitoring of the initial combination of language refers to stage 7 of the production process and consists of mental appraisal of the initial mental draft of an intended utterance. In planned, time-friendly discourse this process might be performed consciously and deliberately through inner-voice rehearsal and comment, otherwise it is largely a subconscious process.

4 Monitoring of revised combination of language

Monitoring of the revised combination of language refers to stage 8 of the production process and consists of mental appraisal of the revised mental draft of an intended utterance. In planned, time-friendly discourse this process might be performed consciously and deliberately through inner-voice rehearsal and comment, and even in unplanned discourse there might be some conscious deliberation involved.

5 Monitoring of the production of language

Monitoring of the production of language refers to stage 9 of the production process and consists of mental appraisal of an utterance produced. This is the monitoring referred to by Krashen in his Monitor Model (1979, 1982, 1994) and is largely focused on evaluating accuracy with a view to repair or revision. In both planned, time-friendly discourse and unplanned discourse this process might be performed consciously and deliberately through inner-voice comment and this is the process which makes most use of learned declarative knowledge.

6 Monitoring of effect

This is a very important process, which is often missing from L2 instructed learners' experience. Checking to see if we are achieving, are likely to achieve and/or have achieved our intended effect is a natural part of L1 interaction, whether spoken or written. It is achieved by observing and evaluating facial, gestural, intonational and linguistic responses, by imaging likely consequences, by inner-speech self-discussion and by connections to previous experience. However, the emphasis on accuracy in the L2 classroom often means that the context-free, purposeless production required of the learners denies them of vital opportunities to develop expertise in monitoring for effect.

The Importance of Self-Monitoring

A controlled or even guided practice activity often requires monitoring only during and after stage 8 and therefore cannot provide adequate preparation for the monitoring required during authentic communication. What is needed is instruction in how to use recall of learned declarative knowledge to aid pre-, whilst- and post-monitoring of planned discourse, plus frequent and rich experience of such monitoring and even more frequent and rich experience of participation in time-pressed, unplanned discourse for communication. It is very important, though, that explicit monitoring of production is not over-experienced, as this can lead to a reliance that can cause inappropriate explicit monitoring of accuracy in situations calling for instantaneous implicit monitoring. Learners who suffer from such a reliance often lack confidence and fluency, fail to respond during interaction or respond with very short, safe utterances, make very little impact, fail to achieve their intended effect and make their interlocutors feel uncomfortable. Learners need to know when, what and how to monitor.

If learners develop the ability to monitor appropriately and effectively, they can gain extremely valuable implicit and explicit input, which can make an important contribution not only to the learner's repair or revision of their production but also to their eventual acquisition of the L2.

The Literature on Self-Monitoring

There is a considerable literature on self-monitoring and repair (i.e. the production of an improved version of an utterance perceived by the learner to be defective) both during oral interaction and during the writing process. Levelt (1983), for example, stresses that monitoring and repair are essentially mental processes involving continuous parsing of inner or overt speech, and that the detection of trouble requiring monitoring can be followed by the production of the repair, providing the speaker has "access to structural properties of the original utterance" (p. 42). Levelt talks mainly in terms of "correction" and focuses on accuracy. However, interestingly he seems to imply that repair can play a role in acquisition in saying that "[b]y transferring and reusing structural properties of previous speech the speaker may at the same time gain in fluency, and establish discourse coherence to the advantage of the listener" (p. 42). He seems to think though that the speaker has no access to the pre-production processes and to agree with Bock (1982) "that the speaker presumably has no access to intermediate processing results, but only to his communicative intention on the one hand, and to the final products of his formulation process, on the other" (Levelt, 1983, p. 46). We would disagree with that position, and argue that the speaker can have conscious access to some of the pre-production processes (e.g. the revision of initial mental drafts), that their brain (and especially the central control) certainly has subconscious access to and a determining role in all these processes, and that a writer partaking in the luxury of time-friendly planned discourse can have conscious access to all these processes. Another publication that investigates L2 self-monitoring is Broos, Duyck and Hartsuiker (2016). Its research-based conclusion is that both L1 and L2 learners monitor their own speech both externally through perception and internally through internal speech representation, and that doing so plays a role in L2 learning. See also Ellis and Zimmerman (2001) for discussion of how successful learners consciously monitor the effect of their utterances during self-regulated learning of speech, and Schütze (2017) in particular for descriptions of actions and decisions made by the brain during the pre-production stages of speech.

Not many of the researchers referred to consider the value of monitoring and repair in the acquisition process. Instead, they tend to focus on their value in improving the quality of the actual production. However Schmidt (1990, 2001, 2010) puts forward a "noticing" position in which he claims that learners cannot acquire a language item or feature until they have noticed how it is used, and have noticed especially the gap between how they use it and how it is typically used by proficient users of the language. Noticing involves paying attention and gaining awareness, and is often considered to be a deliberate, conscious and explicit process in which declarative knowledge is gained as a result of teacher instruction or teacher-guided learner enquiry. However, we would argue that noticing can also be a learner initiated, subconscious, implicit process in which a gradually increasing procedural awareness is developed as a result of frequent such noticing of the same item or feature in contextual use.

It is noticeable that most of the literature referred to focuses on post-production monitoring and on the achievement of accuracy. We would very much like to see more investigation of pre- and whilst-production monitoring and of the monitoring of appropriateness and effect as well as of accuracy.

Peer Monitoring

Often learners learn more from their peers than from their teachers. This is possibly because peers are less likely to be judgemental, are socially closer, are more likely to be empathetic, are more likely to respond to meaning than to form and are more likely to provide useful feedback than explicit teaching. This seems to be especially so if the learners are working together on pair or group activities in class or are engaged in such long-term cooperative activities as projects, drama productions and unstructured interaction (e.g. talking to each other in the target language whenever they meet out of class (Barker, 2010a, 2010b).

Peer monitoring can consist of help in constructing an utterance prior to production, in help during production and in feedback in response to production. Such monitoring is often interactive and communicative rather than interruptive, as these examples show:

Carla: He answered I don't know! And the guard doesn't ... doesn't
Pancha: permit
Carla: So the wine is good for your ...
Pablo: health

(Sato & Viveros, 2016, p. 102)

Lovella: Okay, so it was "in Liverpool airport" or something like that.
Fabe: Yes.
Lovella: At, or "at Liverpool airport" er ...
Hester: "At" sounds more logical.
Lovella: Yes, "at", okay, but do we say then "at Liverpool airport er the exchange would find place" or something like that?
Fabe: Yeah, "would taken" er ...
Lovella: "Would ha ...
Fabe: "would ..."
Lovella: "Would taken, no, would take place."

(Kuiken & Veddar, 2012, p. 374)

Peer monitoring seems to be a natural instinct, but can also be encouraged and possibly made more useful by:

1 getting the whole class to retell a story they have mimed from the teacher's narrative by shouting out sentences in response to the teacher's prompt (in our experience they often reword other learners' utterances not as correction but as improvement of the collective story);
2 getting learners to make up a story in a circle in which each member takes it in turn to contribute an utterance (often learners seek clarification of the previous utterance before offering their own);
3 getting learners to give suggestions for improvement to first drafts of a written communication (e.g. an application for a particular post) – an activity which can be especially effective if the learners are given a joint mark for both pieces of writing.

If most of the production activities are practice activities, learners have very few opportunities for meaningful peer monitoring as there is little else but accuracy of form for the learners to give feedback on, and in most controlled and guided practice activities satisfactory accuracy is easily achieved.

Choi and Iwashita (2016) concluded their research study of low-level proficiency learners participating in group work by reporting the participants' view that "peer assistance was beneficial in reinforcing previous knowledge that they were unsure about" (p. 128). The researchers claimed that this is explained by the theory of ZPD (the zone of proximal development) which, they agree with Aljaafeh and Lantolf (1994), is best facilitated when the expert provides "no more help than is necessary" (Choi & Iwashita, 2016, p. 128). See Vygotsky (1986) for an explanation of ZPD as the difference between what a learner can do by themselves without help and what they can do with the help of somebody more expert than themselves, and see Donato (1994) and Shooshtaria and Mirb (2014) for discussion of the role ZPD can play in L2 learning through peer interaction. Cho and Iwashita also agree with Lapkin, Swain and Psyllakis (2010) that "assistance should be attuned to the specific needs of the learner and should be provided when learners have internalized the new knowledge within their ZPD" (p. 129). It could certainly be argued that peers who are collaborating are in a better position to provide this sort of assistance than their teacher, providing that teachers "train learners to acquire a positive mindset in terms of peer interaction" and "encourage students to acquire a positive attitude towards other group members as equal contributors" (Choi & Iwashita, 2016, p. 128). This need for effective learner training is emphasised by Young and Tedick (2016), who report a study in which learners in heterogeneous group activities were instructed to provide feedback to each other and in which the more proficient learners then over-corrected and often silenced the less proficient learners. In our experience, if the learners are collaborating on completing a task or writing a joint story for example, they are more likely to provide the amount of feedback needed than if they are competing or having a purposeless discussion. We have also found, like Baralt, Gurzynski-Weiss and Kim (2016), that learners are more likely to be helpful rather than judgemental with their feedback if they are socially engaged and having fun together. For other research on peer monitoring (or peer assistance) see Foster and Ohta (2005), Fujii and Mackey (2009) and Sato and Viveros (2016).

Teacher Monitoring

Many teachers habitually monitor their learners in the pre-, whilst- and post-production stages of writing and in the whilst- and post-production stages of speaking. They check learners' prewriting planning for content and coherence (e.g. their intended paragraphing), they often walk around checking learners as they write to monitor their accuracy and they give feedback on the texts produced by their learners to help them improve their accuracy, their coherence, their cohesion, their appropriacy and sometimes their effectiveness. The literature seems to be agreed that such overt monitoring can have a positive effect on immediate repair, but there is much less agreement on whether or not it makes a positive contribution to eventual acquisition and considerable agreement that overcorrection of written work can have a negative effect on learner esteem and positivity. Teachers also typically monitor learners during speech activities. Some respond with immediate feedback and/or correction and some with delayed and focused feedback addressed to individuals or to the class. Again, many researchers claim that such direct feedback can have a positive effect on uptake and immediate repair, but there is less agreement about its effect on eventual acquisition. This applies also to negotiation of form activities in which the teacher guides the learners into making student-generated repair, with Lyster and Ranta (1997) and Morris (2002), for example, reporting the value of negotiation moves in achieving immediate repair, but Morris (2002) warning that successful repair does not necessarily lead to L2 acquisition. See Loewen (2012) for reference to research on the value of such different types of teacher feedback as recasts, elicitation, repetition, metalinguistic feedback, explicit correction and clarification requests and for an evaluation of the evidence in support of teacher feedback in helping learners to achieve successful uptake, noticing and L2 learning.

For a more detailed discussion of the contribution made by corrective feedback to language acquisition, see Chapter 9 in this volume.

Teacher responses that do seem to have some positive impact on acquisition include recasts and the initiation of remedial discovery tasks. Teacher recasts involve the teacher reformulating a learner utterance to improve it whilst at the same time acknowledging its meaning. This is what parents typically do in the L1 with young children, and what many teachers do either habitually or strategically in the L2 classroom. An example would be a learner saying "I goed to cinema last night" and the teacher responding "I went to the cinema last night too. What did you see?". Many researchers believe that such teacher responses play a useful role in language acquisition, because they juxtapose the original and the improved utterances and provide further salient contextualised input without risking the damage to esteem and attitude that overt correction can cause (e.g. Avila, 2007; Long, 2007b; Tomlinson, 2007b). Other researchers claim that the focus on meaning can prevent the learners from noticing the changes of form and prefer the teacher to initiate negotiation activities as they lead to noticing and student-generated repair (e.g. Lyster, 2004). Our own experience is that teacher (and learner) meaning-focused recasting of form can facilitate both repair and acquisition and that more overt forms of teacher correction can be useful to facilitate repair if they do not interrupt communication, but can be damaging to esteem if they do. See Tomlinson (2007b) for a summary of research on recasting and for a report of an experiment in which Chinese learners of English in the UK wrote comparison accounts in which nobody used the contrastive "but", played a group game comparing two versions of a film without using "but" until the teacher started acknowledging their comparisons and recasting them with "but", and then a few days later wrote a comparison account in which many of them used "but" effectively to highlight contrasts.

Remedial discovery activities involve the teacher drawing learners' attention to their utterances that could be improved and then getting them to make discoveries for themselves that could enable them to improve these utterances. These discoveries ideally involve the formulation and testing of hypotheses and are achieved by analysing teacher (or other proficient L2 user) reformulations of texts in which the learner utterances were produced, by analysing texts provided by the teacher in which similar utterances are used and by finding and analysing texts for themselves in which similar utterances are used. For example, a group of learners might write a story in which they frequently misuse reported speech (e.g. "She said to the giant hello big man"). The teacher might then rewrite the story using reported speech and direct speech effectively and ask the learners to focus on how speech is reported in their story, in her story and in another story she gives them. For homework they might find, read and then analyse another story that uses reported and direct speech and then in the next class write another story of their own that involves the use of reported speech, with the teacher available as a resource to call on for feedback. See Bolitho et al., (2003), Tomlinson (1994c, 2007c, 2018a) for discussions and examples of learner discovery activities.

Part Two

Application of Theory to Practice

Language Planning

The most obvious applications to language planning are that planners should make provision for time and opportunities for the learners to experience purposeful, contextualised communication in the L2, both inside and outside the classroom, with much of this experience consisting of face-to-face, virtual, phone, email and written interaction with fellow learners. In addition to classroom and homework activities, this could include such informal learning opportunities as:

- the use of social media for communicating with speakers of the L2;
- twinning and frequent communication with overseas schools where the learners are L1 users;
- twinning and frequent meetings and communication with local schools where the learners are L2 users;
- provision of experience of visiting (and ideally staying in) areas where the L2 is spoken;
- production of school plays in the L2;
- regional and national L2 speaking, drama and writing competitions;
- school, regional and national learner magazines and blogs;
- visits of L2 speakers to schools for conversation opportunities for the learners;
- classroom assistants who can only communicate with the learners in the L2;
- projects in which learners make presentation videos and vlogs to share with other schools.

See, for example, Sockett (2014) and Lech and Harris (2019) for evidence of the value of using social media for opportunities to communicate to learn.

Curriculum Development

Most curricula these days (other than those for learners aiming to acquire an L2 for specialist purposes) tend to focus on speaking rather than writing. Interestingly though, they tend to list language points to be learned in order to be able to speak accurately (and sometimes effectively) and thus often encourage (either deliberately or otherwise) more allocation of time to the teaching and practice of these points than to the actual experience of purposeful, contextualised oral communication. Some curricula these days, however, do focus on developing the ability to use L2 speech to achieve competencies, such as booking a hotel on the phone, asking for directions or giving an oral presentation. Often though, curriculum writers feel the need to specify manifestations of these competencies (for example, expressions for starting and concluding a service phone call) and this can lead to the teaching, practice and testing of useful expressions being given more priority in coursebooks and classrooms than experience of using the competency for communication. We have just analysed a random unit in a coursebook from our shelf (Unit 7, Clare and Wilson, 2012) and discovered the following activity types related to speaking and writing:

Total number of activities in the unit – 81
Total number of speaking activities – 11
- answering and discussing questions – 5
- discussing and comparing abilities – 2
- giving opinions – 1
- presentation - 2
- contextualised and purposeful communication - 1
- monitoring – 1 (pre-production preparation of content)

Total number of writing activities – 2
- writing notes – 1
- writing a summary – 1
- contextualised and purposeful communication - 0
- monitoring – 0

Total number of activities involving learning or practising grammar, vocabulary or expressions – 39

Clare and Wilson (2012) is a book that impresses us with its use of personalisation and its potentially engaging written, spoken and visual texts. We feel though that like most coursebooks it has been understandably over-influenced by the prevailing curricular focus on the teaching, learning and practice of grammar, vocabulary and expressions. We would like to see a much greater emphasis in curriculum development on getting learners to speak and write for purposeful and contextualised communication and the introduction of specifications of appropriate monitoring abilities to be developed prior to, during and after purposeful, contextualised communication. One problem we have always found with curriculum development is that curriculum developers (including ourselves) feel obliged to specify manifestations of functions and competences and to list teaching points rather than being content to encourage learning by doing, to achieve acquisition through communication.

Methodology

The most obvious application of what we know about the process of producing language is that learners need to be provided with, and to seek out, as much experience as possible in producing language to achieve communicative intentions and in monitoring this production when appropriate. By doing so, they can not only develop their effectiveness as communicators in the L2 but also contribute positively to their further acquisition of the language. If the learners are restricted to production for practice in which the context, content, and language of the production are determined or influenced to the exclusion of choice and the diminishment of affective and cognitive engagement, then the learners might improve their structural and lexical accuracy but are unlikely to improve their communicative competence.

The following methodologies have the potential for affording opportunities for the learners to gain experience in context-dependent production for communicative effect:

- Content based instruction (CBI) - in which learners focus on learning a topic or an academic subject through the use of the L2 and spend a lot of time talking and writing about content they have recently learned (Brinton, 2003; Coyle, Hood & Marsh, 2010). This is an approach in which "**teaching** is organised around the **content** or information that students will acquire, rather than around a linguistic or other type of syllabus" (Richards & Rodgers, 2001, p. 204). This approach is sometimes referred to as CBLT (Content-Based Language Teaching) and sometimes (especially in Europe) as CLIL (Content and Language Integrated Learning). It is an approach that typically provides a rich experience of purposeful communication through immersion in the target language. However, it does seem that immersion approaches often provide lower rates of feedback and uptake than communicative language teaching approaches (Lyster & Ranta, 1997). For an account of what teachers and learners actually do in videoed CLIL lessons see Mahan, Brevik and Odergaard (2018).
- CBLT – an approach that focuses "on the outcomes of learning, as the driving force of teaching and the curriculum" and in which "the competencies needed for successful task performance are ... identified, and used as the basis for course planning. Teaching methods used may vary, but typically are skill-based, since the focus is on developing the ability to use language to carry out real-world activities" (Richards, 2018).
- Extensive Reading – in which learners read an L2 book, magazine, newspaper or comic for pleasure without being monitored or assessed (Elley & Mangubhai, 1981; Krashen, 2004; Maley, 2008). This might seem a strange choice of methodology to promote communicative production skills but there is evidence that massive and enjoyable reading for interest and pleasure provides a rich exposure to language in communicative use, which provides input likely to facilitate the implicit intake required as a resource for communicative production (see, for example, Elley & Mangubhai, 1981).
- Language Through Literature – in which learners are engaged in experiencing accessible and meaningful poems, stories, novels, plays and films and then often

in generating written and spoken creative texts themselves (Paran & Robinson, 2015; Saito & Wales, 2015; Bland, 2018; Jones, 2019; Tomlinson, 2019a);
- Text-Driven Approaches – in which learners' experience of a potentially engaging spoken, written or multimodal L2 text drives response, analysis and contextualised production activities (Tomlinson, 2013d; Tomlinson & Masuhara, 2018b);
- TPR Plus approaches – in which learners respond physically to the teacher telling a story, giving instructions to play a game, advising on the painting of a mural, instructing the creation of body sculptures, stimulating the creation of a meal from specified ingredients, etc. (Tomlinson, 1994b). At more advanced stages, the learners take over the activity and continue the story, instructions, etc. themselves.
- Task-Based Language Teaching (TBLT) – in which learners make use of their existing linguistic resources to perform a meaning-focused production task with intended communicative outcomes (for example, designing an advertisement). Many researchers claim that this approach not only improves task performance but also improves real-world communicative performance too (Van den Branden, 2006; Long, 2015; Samuda, Van Den Branden & Bygate, 2018; Taguchi & Kim, 2018). Some researchers claim that both task and real-world performance can be enhanced as a result of task repetition – i.e. doing the same or a similar task again after feedback on the effectiveness of the first task performance (see Shintani, 2016; Bygate, 2018).
- Usage-Based approaches (Tyler, 2010) – in which the theoretical underpinning is meaning- and communication-focused. The theory has been applied in a number of different ways, for example by Nguyen (2013), who supported the theory that "L2 learning is a non-linear process and develops on the account of frequent exposure to the target language in a communicative, meaningful context" (pp. 32–33) and found that an input approach providing authenticity and frequency of exposure through films facilitated productive proficiency. For other practical applications to language learning, see Tyler, Ortega, Uno and Park (2018).
- Simulation approaches – in which the learners are placed within a simulated real-world situation, given roles to play in the situation and given differentiated objectives to achieve (see Richards & Rodgers, 2014). The learners are usually given time to prepare in advance for their roles and the strategies they will use to try to achieve their objectives. After the simulation, the teacher often conducts a post-mortem with the learners in which their strategies and the language they used to try to achieve their outcomes are analysed and constructive feedback is provided by the teacher, by peers and by the learners to themselves.
- Scenario approaches (DiPietro, 1982, 1987; Tomlinson, 1990) – in which two groups (or halves of a small class) are put into a situation in which two people are in disagreement or are trying to persuade each other (e.g. a boy trying to

persuade his mother to let him stay up to watch a game on TV; a taxi driver trying to persuade a customer to go to a different hotel). One group is given the situation from the perspective of one of the interactants and the other group from the other perspective. As a group, they prepare their strategies and then choose a representative to act out the scenario on their behalf. At any time during the enactment of the scenario they can call a time out and advise or substitute their representative. Afterwards, the teacher leads a post-mortem reflection on the success or otherwise of the interactants in achieving their objectives.

- Project Driven approaches – in which learners do research in order to make a written and/or spoken presentation on a particular issue or topic (Haines, 1989; Wicks, 2000).
- Process Drama approaches – in which the learners and the teacher improvise dialogue within a context and make full use of embodied language, extra-linguistic communication and nonlinguistic communication (Kao & O'Neill, 1998; Bowell & Heap, 2001; Park, 2010).
- Drama performance approaches – in which the learners work towards the performance of a play over an extended period of time, with learners taking on the role of director, actors, stage manager, costume designer, etc.
- Film and other visual media-based approaches – which provide learners with rich experience of responding to and using embodied language, extra-linguistic communication and nonlinguistic communication (Herrero & Yanderschelden, 2019; Tomlinson, 2019b).
- Creative writing approaches – in which the learners, for example, write a novel or write a script for a play.
- Responsive teaching approaches – in which the teacher is available as a resource during learner tasks and interactions to provide guidance and information when it is asked for by learners (thus providing explicit instruction when it is needed, wanted and salient).
- Feedback teaching approaches – in which the teacher's explicit instruction focuses on discovered learner needs. This could be in the form of plenary instruction, individualised instruction or remedial cards designed to provide focused attention on common problems of production and their solutions (see Chapter 9).

Notice that we have not included in our list above the popular PPP (Presentation–Practice–Production) approach – in which a language item, feature or function is taught, then practised and then produced. This is because, typically, the so-called production stage is rarely affectively or cognitively engaging, rarely contextualised, very rarely involves the achievement of intended effects, restricts (and often predetermines) the selection of content, strategies and expression and hardly ever requires the use of embodied language, extra-linguistic communication and nonlinguistic communication. This production stage might reinforce the language just taught and might help it to achieve a weak initial intake, but we very much doubt if it makes a significant contribution to language acquisition, especially if, as often happens in coursebooks, it is not repeated many times at intervals. We do concede, though, that interestingly taught PPP lessons could create an illusion of learning that generates useful learner positivity and that, if the teacher succeeds in focusing engaged attention on a specific teaching point, learner noticing might be stimulated at the time and when encountering the point in subsequent authentic input. This could aid monitoring in contextualised, purposeful, planned discourse. In our view though, the time taken up by a PPP lesson could be more profitably spent on affective and cognitive engagement with an authentic text, followed by communicative production activities, monitoring and discovery activities and then further communicative production.

In these methodologies, learners are often encouraged to write plans of what they are going to write and to check what they have written for errors before handing it in for marking. However, they are rarely encouraged to monitor mentally in pre-production stages, to monitor during production or to monitor for achievement of communicative intent. In order to help learners to improve the effectiveness of their oral and written communication they can be guided to:

1 visualise their intended effect(s) prior to production;
2 use their inner voice to make selections and decisions;
3 rehearse utterances mentally before speaking or writing them prior to planned discourse;
4 monitor for the achievement of intended effects during and after production;
5 revise utterances prior to and during production;
6 clarify or elaborate on utterances immediately after production;
7 reflect on the effectiveness of the communication after completion.

Teachers have to be careful, though, not to over-teach monitoring strategies and to help learners to appreciate when it is appropriate to use them, or else there is a danger of learners becoming over-monitors whose production of language is always hesitant, safe and restricted or of becoming apologetic communicators who are always repairing their utterances even when it is not communicatively necessary.

Recently, a number of publications have put forward ideas for production activities that we think have the potential to contribute towards learners' acquisition of language and development of communicative competence. One of these is Bridges (2018), which proposes activities to help learners to connect the two discourses of social chat and academic speech by combining everyday language with language of the academic register. In these activities the students are at the centre. They generate the communication and the teacher acts as a mediator. The book discusses the research and theories underlying the approach and then focuses on applying these theories to practice. Another such book is Hyland (2018), which explores the metadiscourse that writers use to refer to themselves, to their readers and to their text. Whilst not explicitly focusing on how such metadiscourse can help learners acquire language and develop skills, it suggests to us ways in which writing can be personalised and familiarised in ways more likely to generate such facilitators of acquisition as salience, familiarity, meaningfulness, connectivity and relevance than such decontextualised, impersonal activities as writing essays and formal academic reports. Other publications that advocate production activities to foster acquisition include Ghosn (2007), who advocates the use of children's literature to stimulate young learners to write creatively, McDonough, Crawford and De Vleeschauwer (2016), who value the learning opportunities provided by collaborative writing tasks and Floris, Renandya and Bao (2018), who suggest how social media can be made use of to provide learners with principled opportunities for social interaction in the target language.

See Materials Development below for some examples of production activities that provide learners with experience of authentic communication plus guided monitoring when appropriate.

Readers' Task

1 Think of a context in which you are teaching L2 learners and specify their age(s), level and reasons for learning their target language.
2 From the methodological approaches outlined, choose those you would use with these learners to help them develop communicative competence and decide how you would introduce these methodologies to the learners.

Materials Development

Here are some typical examples of production activities from coursebooks. Do you think they are likely to contribute to the learners' acquisition of language and their development of communicative competence?

Activity 1
D Work in pairs. Look at the pictures. Discuss what is good and what is bad about each way of travelling. Which way do you prefer? Why? (Dellar & Walkly, 2010, p. 92)

Activity 2
Speaking

A Discuss the situations below and decide who is to blame. Use *should have* or third conditionals to explain why.

(Four situations are described in which something goes wrong and nobody takes responsibility)

B Work in pairs. Choose one of the situations. You are going to role-play the situation. Before you start, decide who will take which role and think about how you will try and blame the other person. (Dellar & Walkly, 2010, p. 97)

Activity 3
Writing

Write a report on languages in your country. Use your notes and useful phrases above to help you. Remember to organize your thoughts into paragraphs. (Clandfield & Robb Benne, 2011, p. 16)

Activity 4
Speaking

A Work in pairs. Think of a new project that could improve the quality of life in your area and make notes in the chart.

(There is a chart with the headings "What", "Where", "Why", "Impact".)

Present your plans to the class. Which project would:
- make the biggest impact?
- be the easiest to build?

(Goldstein, 2012, p. 53)

What do you think? In our opinion, the activities above all have some qualities as production activities, but they focus mainly on language practice rather than experience of authentic communication. The writers and/or publishers are reluctant to just provide a rich menu of opportunities to experience communication in the target language, probably because of the perceived need to provide teaching points that can be assessed and an active role for teachers who are unwilling to just let the learners get on with communicating without their explicit help. Interestingly, there seem to be very few writing activities in coursebooks for EFL students. For example, neither Dellar and Walker (2010) nor Goldstein (2012) have any activities at all explicitly labelled Writing.

Activity 1 is personalised and familiar and it gets learners to express and justify their views. However, it lacks context and purpose. Why are the learners saying which means of transport they prefer and in what situation? There is no determination of appropriacy or of intended effect, and no preparation or monitoring.

Activity 2 is personalised and contextualised and it does include a preparation stage with a determination of strategies. However, the content, language and outcome of the interaction are given and the learners are practising rather than communicating.

Activity 3 is personalised and there is a preparation stage. However, it lacks context and purpose and there is no intended effect. Again, the learners are practising rather than communicating.

Activity 4 is also personalised and there is a preparation stage and a stimulus to think. However, it lacks context, purpose and intended effect.

Changes could be made to all the above activities to provide opportunities for producing language to achieve intended communicative outcomes and to provide opportunities for appropriate monitoring:

Activity 1

1 Work in pairs. Look at pictures 1 and 2. Discuss what is good and what is bad about each way of travelling.
2 You are going on a long journey next week with two friends from another pair. Decide which of the ways of travelling in 1 and 2 you want to use for your journey.
3 Decide how you will persuade your friends to use the way of travelling you've decided on. Then practise what you'll say to your friends.
4 Join a pair who've been discussing pictures 3 and 4 and try to persuade them to agree to your way of travelling. Record your conversation.
5 As a group decide on the way of transport you'll use on your journey.
6 When you've finished your conversation, in your pair decide:
   - if you succeeded in achieving your intention
   - why you did or did not succeed
   - what you could have done but didn't.
7 As a group of four listen to the recording of your conversation and then decide for each person:
   - one thing they said successfully
   - one thing they could have improved (suggest an improvement)
8 - As a group say what you liked and disliked about this activity.
   - Suggest one way of making it more interesting and/or useful.

Activity 2
Speaking

A Discuss the situations below and decide who is to blame and why.
B Work in pairs. Think of another situation in which two people blame each other for something going wrong.
   Write a role card for each member of another pair, describing what happened and what that person did which might make them to blame.
C Take a role card each from another pair and read it.
   Think about how you will try and blame the other person for what went wrong.

D Act out the conversation about who was to blame for what went wrong and record your conversation.
E Give your recording to another group and ask them to listen to it and then decide which person was to blame.

Activity 3
Writing

1 You have been asked to write a 500-word article on the languages spoken in your country for a travel magazine aimed at tourists.
2 Decide what you intend to achieve through your article.
3 Decide what style to use in your article. Will it be formal or informal?
4 Decide on the content of each paragraph. Then for each paragraph decide what you intend to achieve and how you are going to try to achieve it.
5 Write a draft of your article. As you write it visualize the content you want to communicate and say to yourself the words you are going to use in your next sentence.
6 Monitor your article for accuracy, organisation and likely effect on the reader. Then revise it.
7 Give your revised article to another learner. Tell them they are reading your article on a plane as they are flying to your country. After they have read it ask them what effect it had on them.
8 Write a final version of your article.

Activity 4
Speaking

A Work in pairs. Think of a new building project that could improve the quality of life in your area.

Visualise what the project would look like, where it would be, and what effect it would have on people's lives. Then make notes on what you intend to say under the headings What, Where, Effect.

You are going to present your project to the local council, who are running a competition to select a project which would be affordable and have a beneficial impact on people's lives. Practise presenting your project and make suggestions to each other as you do so. Then present it to an imaginary audience and record it.
Listen to your presentation and make suggestions to each other on how to improve it.
Present your project to another pair. Then listen to their suggestions for improvement.
Present your project to the class as part of the local council competition.

We would encourage materials writers to include more communication activities in their materials and to ensure that learners are asked to produce purposeful, contextualised language with intended effects and are also asked and guided to monitor the spoken and written texts they produce for accuracy, appropriateness and pragmatic effect. For publications advocating such an approach, see Cohen and Ishihara (2013), Ishihara and Paller (2016) and Bardovi-Harlig and Mossman (2016).

> **Readers' Task**
>
> Go to a coursebook and (as we did) take any speaking activity and any writing activity at random.
>
> 1 Critique the activity as a provider of opportunities for authentic production and monitoring.
> 2 Make changes to each activity to increase their likelihood of contributing to the language acquisition and skills development of the learners who use them.

Assessment

In John Faneslow's new book *Small Changes Big Success* (Faneslow, 2019) he designs an ironic Informed Consent Form for students taking commercial EFL examinations. Here are a few extracts from it:

> Because my teachers are forced to focus on test preparation, they have to teach in ways that stifle my language development and their development as teachers.
>
> I sign this Informed Consent Form knowing that preparing for your exam prevents me from learning English that I can use.
>
> 4. Because fiction, songs, and poetry are rarely, if ever, used in standardized tests, I am forced to read and listen to boring and banal passages and impersonal dialogues, rather than songs, poems, short stories, and other forms of literature.
>
> I object that you are limiting my world view and emotional experiences and stunting my language and personal development by not encouraging me to develop my language abilities in the ways people have learned languages for centuries, by reading and listening to stories, songs, poems, and personal narratives each person selects individually.
>
> The separation of testing from learning and teaching that your commercial tests force us all to experience I do not approve as my signing of this Informed Consent Form indicates.

9. Because gestures and facial expressions, animation, and originality are not evaluated in IELTS I have no confidence in the score I receive and resent the fact that such crucial features of interaction are given no value. (Faneslow, 2019, 262–264)

This sums up very succinctly our objections to the way that high-stakes examinations dictate what happens in the classroom to the detriment of the acquisition of the target language, of the development of the ability to use the language skilfully, flexibly and effectively and of the learners' personal development. For suggestions on how to use "testing to learn" see Tomlinson (2005b), in which similar objections to Faneslow's are made and suggestions are put forward for approaches to testing that can contribute positively to the testees' acquisition of the language. In this article, Tomlinson makes the points that testing should mirror learning rather than the other way round, that learners should actually increase their opportunities for learning from preparing for the test, taking the test and receiving feedback on the test (whether it be formative or summative) and that tests should be prepared not only to achieve reliability and validity but to engage and stimulate the learners too. This is what happened in Vanuatu when a bank of communicative and potentially engaging tasks was prepared to serve both as tasks for the classroom and as instruments of assessment (Tomlinson, 1981). It is also what we both did in our universities in Japan when our classroom tasks and classroom assessments were indistinguishable and the students were not even conscious they were being assessed.

The most obvious implication of what we are saying for the assessment of communicative competence is that the assessment tasks should be actual and potentially engaging tasks in which the learners make use of their available linguistic, nonlinguistic and extra-linguistic resources to achieve contextualised, communicative outcomes rather than decontextualised activities inviting display of their language ability (for example, writing a letter to an international company persuading them to take interest in the water-saving device they have invented rather than writing an essay without an audience or communicative purpose on a topic which is neither relevant nor interesting to them). The former might be more difficult to assess reliably but it can be done through the use of outcome related criteria. And it is well worth the effort.

For discussions of and suggestions for positive ways of testing that can contribute to the learners' language acquisition and development of communicative competence, see in particular Davison (2013) and his description and advocacy of assessment for learning (AfL), an approach to assessment in which "the primary purpose of the information being collected is to improve learning" (p. 263) and in which feedback plays a key role.

Teacher Development

The main implication for teacher development is that trainers need to spend less time on analysis of the products of speaking and writing, less time on encouraging learners to use speaking and writing activities to practise language points previously taught and more time on helping trainees to understand the mental processes of language production in ways that will help them to facilitate their learners' communicative competence and language acquisition.

SUMMARY

In summary, we are saying that the main applications of the SLA research and resultant theories relating to language production and monitoring are:

- Learners need plentiful opportunities to speak and to write in the L2 for communication, regardless of their instrumental needs, because purposeful, contextualised speaking and writing not only aid the development of communication skills but can also contribute positively to language acquisition.
- All writing and speaking activities should have intended outcomes and not just require the production of output. That is, they should require learners to produce language as a means of achieving communicative intentions, such as persuading, informing, clarifying, explaining, justifying, amusing, advising, etc.
- Learners need experience of both unplanned and planned discourse, that is, of communication where conscious, deliberate pre- and whilst-monitoring is not possible and also of communication where such conscious, deliberate monitoring is possible.
- All production activities should be contextualised and should involve the conscious or subconscious determination of intended effect.
- Many of the production activities should involve the use of embodied language, extra-linguistic communication and nonlinguistic communication.
- Learners should be informed about the different types of monitoring and should be helped through instruction, guidance and activities to develop and use, when appropriate, their ability in pre-, whilst- and especially post-production monitoring of accuracy, appropriacy and effect.
- Practice activities might help learners to become more accurate but, if they lack context, intended effects and learner initiation of linguistic and pragmatic strategies, they are unlikely to help learners to become effective communicators.
- Explicit teacher instruction can be of value in increasing learner awareness of the norms of language use, providing that it is in response to discovered learner needs and that it is perceived as salient, engaging, meaningful and useful by the learners.

Readers' Tasks

1 What struck you as the most useful information in this chapter? Why?
2 What struck you as the most useful advice in this chapter? Why?
3 Have you changed your mind at all about the best ways to help learners to achieve communicative competence after reading this chapter? If so, in what ways have you changed your mind?
4 Is there anything you disagree with in this chapter? If so, what do you disagree with and why?
5 Write a page of advice to language teachers about how to develop speaking and writing activities for their learners.

FURTHER READING

Lintunen, P., Mutta, M. & Peltonen, P. (Eds.). *Fluency in L2 learning and use.* Bristol: Multilingual Matters.

Sato, M. & Ballinger, S. (Eds.). (2016). *Peer interaction and second language learning: Pedagogical potential and research agenda.* Amsterdam: John Benjamins.

Schütze, U. (2017). *Language learning and the brain.* Cambridge: Cambridge University Press (especially pp. 18–24).

8 Auto-Input

Part One: Theory

Introduction

We have been using the term auto-input for many years and we consider it to be a very important concept. However, we are aware that it is rarely used in the literature on second language acquisition. We asked a number of applied linguists what they understand by the term auto-input, and these are the answers we received:

> *auto-input* – I am not familiar with this term. I presume it harps back to Krashen's notion of language acquisition as opposed to learning. In this case, it would refer to material that is in the input, not attended to by the learner, but nonetheless finds its way into the learner's receptive and/or productive performance. Andrew Cohen (22/5/2017)

> auto-input is not a term I see much; I think it refers to the phonological loop that is made when a learner listens to him/herself speaking the TL and thus provides him/herself with input. I think this idea goes back to Krashen's initial dismissal of production as important in SLA – it was all about reception for him, and the Silent Period – but here in auto-input we have a kind of acceptable self-seeding production. I dunno, sounds a bit odd, but I wouldn't have thought the term had much traction. Pauline Foster (23/5/2017)

> auto-input – learner's output becomes input that can be processed in the same way as input (e.g. learners may combine two formulaic chunks when speaking and in so doing create input consisting of a larger chunk which is subsequently intaken and stored as a single complex chunk). Rod Ellis (22/5/2017)

On the web we also found the following definitions:

> **Auto-input** refers to language data produced by learners (**output**) that is subsequently analyzed as any other source of **input**. Self-produced **input** is more likely to provide learners with a more accurate picture of their own abilities and limitations in the second language.
> https://coerll.utexas.edu/methods/modules/grammar/02/dictogloss.php
> (accessed 22/1/2019)

Output provides the learner with auto-input – that is, learners can attend to the input provided by their own language production. Rod Ellis – Principles of Instructed Language Acquisition - https://charttesl.wordpress.com/2011/02/10/657/ (accessed 22/1/2019)

We also found out in Ünlü (2015, p. 264) that Sharwood Smith (1981), Gregg (1984) and Schmidt and Frota (1986) have used the term auto-input to refer to "learners' own output ... which learners should make use of to learn a language".

Our own definition of auto-input is that it is *all the linguistic, extra-linguistic and nonlinguistic output generated by a learner that is available to the learner as input, plus all the contextual, sensory and affective associations connected with the output as well as learner awareness of the effectiveness of that output.*

Readers' Task

Do you think auto-input can be valuable in facilitating language acquisition? If so, how and why can it become valuable?

What Is the Value of Auto-Input to the Learner?

Auto-input can be extremely valuable to the learner as it can satisfy most of the conditions for intake. It is likely to be:

- comprehensible, because the learner knows what they are saying;
- meaningful, in that it inevitably relates to the learner and connects with what they want to say (providing it is not part of a meaningless drill or of other types of decontextualised exercise);
- relevant, in that it inevitably relates to what the learner is trying to do;
- salient, if the activity is of apparent value to the learner;
- extensive, if the learner is given opportunities to communicate;
- recycled, because the learner uses their available linguistic resources and inevitably uses the same lexis and structure many times;
- affectively engaging, if the learner is encouraged to express their feelings and views;
- cognitively engaging, if the learner is encouraged to express their opinions, solutions, conclusions, etc.;
- embodied, if the learner takes part in authentic communication and is not holding a book or fixing their eyes on an exercise;
- developmentally appropriate, if the learner is deciding what to say and write and is not being pushed too much to express themselves in language not yet acquired nor being told what expressions to use.

Whether these conditions of intake are satisfied depends on the nature and extent of the learner's output, whether or not the learner pays attention to their output (consciously or subconsciously) and whether or not the learner receives effective situational, self, cooperative or corrective feedback.

Ideally, the learners' output is produced in a context so that there is situational feedback about the effectiveness of the output in achieving the intended effect. For example, if the learner is asking for instructions on how to get to the station and then fails to get to the station, the learner is alerted to the ineffectiveness of either their requesting strategies, their attempts to seek clarification and/or their listening performance.

Ideally, the learner's output is important to the learner and is not something they are being forced to say or write to simply complete an exercise or cover a syllabus. If the learner is actually communicating to achieve an intended effect determined by themselves, then this significance condition is almost inevitably satisfied.

Ideally, the learner's output is produced when engaged and when focused on meaning, and it is therefore processed as intake, together with sensory, emotive and cognitive associations, which maintain and strengthen phonological, lexical, syntactic and pragmatic connections and "records" in the brain. The more this happens, the more likely it is that output becomes input, which becomes further intake, which promotes further processing, and which is eventually acquired. An example of this (and of the value of collaborative communication) would be if a learner is cognitively engaged when contributing to a group solution of a problem and echoes a peer's utterance when using "It could be because …" when suggesting a possible cause. If the group acknowledge this contribution positively, then positive emotive and cognitive associations will be intaken together with the utterance from the auto-input. This could lead to the learner using the expression again in problem-solving situations and in reinforcing and maintaining the intake each time it is acknowledged.

Ideally the learner's output is responded to by interlocutors, by audiences, by readers and, most importantly, by themselves. As we have mentioned elsewhere in this book (see for example Chapters 7 and 9), learners have been shown to acquire language by collaborating in its production with fellow learners and by both providing and gaining corrective and elaborating input (see, for example, Swain & Lapkin, 1995; Swain, 2005). We have also shown how learners have been demonstrated to gain confidence, self-esteem and language input from the opportunities for extensive, elaborated and responded output afforded by peer interaction that is comfortable, collaborative and socially cohesive (see, for example, Choi & Iwashita, 2016; Sato & Ballinger, 2016a, 2016b). If the learners receive situational and positively corrective feedback whilst interacting with peers, their repaired output can become a valuable source of auto-input.

What Types of Auto-Input Are There?

Oral Auto-Input

The most useful type of oral auto-input is gained from interaction, and especially from peer interaction that is comfortable, affectively engaging, cognitively engaging and socially cohesive. If the learner succeeds in completing a communicative turn appropriately and effectively, and this is signalled by peer responses such as nods, smiles and linguistic acknowledgements of comprehension, then the hypotheses and selections that have generated the output receive powerful reinforcement. If a turn is completed less successfully or even interrupted, then the learner might receive repairs, clarifications and elaborations from their peers or be pushed to clarify their expression. Both of these contributions from peers can enhance not only the learner's output but also the auto-input generated both externally and internally by it.

Giving presentations, commentaries, speeches and dramatic performances can also provide opportunities for converting output into input from the self-monitoring of rehearsal, the simultaneous listening to production, the spontaneous clarification, repetition, paraphrasing and repair and from post-production reflection on effect. Though such monologues do not usually permit instant or collaborative feedback, the post-production feedback given by audiences, directors and teachers can stimulate auto-input from learner explanations, clarifications, rephrasings and modified future performance. Also, if speeches and dramatic performances are memorised prior to performance, each instance of memorisation, rehearsal and performance can provide powerful auto-input, providing it is meaningful and engaged.

In both interaction and monologue, learner agency is a significant influencer of rich auto-input. Put simply, learner agency involves learners taking responsibility for their own learning in learner-developed activities, projects and even courses, as well as during teacher-orchestrated activities that encourage learners to express their thoughts, feelings and identity. This takeover of responsibility leads to an intersection between teacher discourse and learner discourse, between the formal and the informal, between the social and the individual, between the academic and the personal. The combination of affective and cognitive engagement that stimulates learner spontaneous expression in activities in which learners invest themselves can create output that can provide impactful input for other learners, as well as auto-input replete with sensory, emotive and cognitive associations. Such input has great potential for generating new intake and for strengthening, maintaining and developing connections and "records" in the brain. For detailed discussions of learner agency, see Kramsch (1993), Gutiérrez (2008), Mick (2011, 2015), Deters, Gao, Miller and Vitanova (2015) and especially Larsen-Freeman (2019), a critical and personal overview of the literature on learner agency in language learning and in particular in relation to complex dynamic systems theory's (CDST) conceptualisation of agency.

Oral auto-input is particularly useful if it is recorded and is available to the learner for playback. Not only does this facilitate meaningful recycling and noticing but it can also be used to raise the learner's awareness of the gap between their performance (in, for example, a task or a presentation) and an equivalent performance by a more proficient speaker, to help them to monitor progress during a course, to promote self-feedback and to raise confidence and self-esteem. On a course at a college in England for businessmen from Lyon, we responded to requests for an experiential course without explicit teaching of grammar by developing a course that featured business simulations, work experience in local companies and shadowing of local businessmen. The participants were enjoying the course, but were also becoming increasingly frustrated at their apparent lack of progress until we got them to record their interactions and to realise that their turns were getting longer, their initiations were more frequent and their lexis was richer and more effective. Listening to their own output not only increased their confidence and self-esteem but provided auto-input that probably reinforced hypotheses and helped to strengthen and maintain language intaken from previous input. It is also likely that some instances of less successful communication were noticed, and the brain was alerted to the need to pay attention to relevant features of future input.

Inner Voice Auto-Input

In our first language, we talk to ourselves more than to anybody else. When learning a foreign or second language, we often talk to our teachers more than anybody else, and it seems we very rarely talk to ourselves in the target language (De Guerrero, 2005, 2017; Tomlinson & Avila, 2007a; Tomlinson, 2020a). This is unfortunate, as inner speech can be a fruitful source of input for the learner. Because inner speech is not monitored or corrected, the speaker can play with language and take risks. Such childlike production of language has been found to facilitate language acquisition for both children and adults (see, for example, Cook, 2000). If encouraged, young children can play with language in private speech (inner speech spoken aloud) and adults can mirror this language by playing with inner-voice monologues and dialogues (Tomlinson & Avila, 2007b). Because inner speech does not have to be understood by anybody else, it can be very personal and meaningful to the speaker. Because inner speech uses a restricted code in which a minimum of linguistic resources is used to achieve a maximum of meaning, there is the frequent meaningful recycling that can be so facilitative for language acquisition. The restricted code normally used by inner speech (for example, simple rather than perfect tenses, the active rather than the passive voice) means that most of the learner's inner-voice utterances are comprehensible and meaningful to the learner. This might not apply to utterances being memorised for external performance by the learner, but the recycling occasioned by internal memorisation and rehearsal can aid eventual comprehension and retention.

The contribution of the inner voice as auto-input can come from inner-speech monologues, inner-speech preparation for speech and writing and inner-speech reflection on outer speech output.

The contribution of the inner voice as auto-input can also come from using the inner voice to accompany apparently silent reading and listening so as to turn input from others into output from the learner. In the L1, we automatically read written texts with our inner voice whilst appearing to be reading silently. We do so in order to personalise the text, to aid retention of the text and to convert graphic images into the acoustic images we need to achieve comprehension, intake and processing (Tomlinson & Avila, 2007a). We also repeat in our own inner voice much of what we hear from other voices, thus providing opportunities for converting output into auto-input.

Written Auto-Input

Writing in the L2 can promote powerful auto-input from:

- the pre- and whilst-writing inner-voice preparation and rehearsal of content and expression (see Chapter 7);
- the recycling achieved by numerous re-readings;
- the modifications occasioned by whilst- and post-writing revisions;
- the retention of expressions accompanied by the visual images and affective associations they have generated.

Such powerful auto-input is only generated, though, if what the learners are writing about is meaningful and relevant to them, and if the writing activity is affectively and cognitively engaging. Auto-input generated by exercises requiring written responses to such decontextualised exercises as isolated sentence completion, matching and filling in the blanks is unlikely to have much impact on hypothesis generation and testing, or on generating, strengthening or maintaining connections and "records" in the brain.

Readers' Tasks

1. a) Talk to yourself about what you have read so far in this chapter.
   b) Reflect on your conversation with yourself. What can you remember about the content and the language of your conversation?
   c) Do you think it would be useful to ask L2 learners to talk to themselves about a text they have just read and then to reflect on their conversation with themselves? Why?
2. Do you think we are right to focus so much on auto-input as a promoter of intake? Why?

Auto-Input Generated by Reflection on Output

Swain (1998) focuses on the value of learners collaborating on the production of output and, in doing so, consciously reflecting on the accuracy and effectiveness of the output they produce. The reflection could take place during the production of oral or written output, or when monitoring a draft that has been produced. Swain (1998) surveys the available literature and reports a study in which most of the learners who had successfully corrected their output during conscious reflection were successful when tested on that language feature a week later, whereas those who were unsuccessful in correcting their output were also unsuccessful on a test a week later.

Learner noticing of gaps between their own production of the L2 and that of proficient speakers of the L2, and between what their output has achieved and what they intended it to achieve, can also generate valuable auto-input. Noticing of output effects (i.e. outcomes) has received much less attention than noticing of language inaccuracy, but it is arguable that it can play a more significant role in the development of communicative competence. Ideally, auto-input does not just consist of linguistic utterances but also of associations and of awareness of the consequences and effects of the language and strategies used by the learner in their attempts to achieve intended communicative effects.

Research into the Processes and Effects of Auto-Input

We know of no research that has specifically focused on why and how auto-input is generated, intaken and processed, or on what the effects of auto-input can be or whether auto-input is potentially more powerful than intake from others. This is understandable, as the existence of auto-input as a phenomenon in language acquisition and use is not generally acknowledged and research into its processes and effects would require much more complex investigations than those needed to find out more, for example, about the value of input from others. We would, however, very much welcome SLA researchers rising to the challenge and increasing our awareness of what we consider to be a potentially very rewarding but much neglected area of study.

We would in particular like to find out more about:

- when learner output becomes auto-intake and when it does not;
- whether auto-input is potentially more facilitative of language acquisition than input from others;
- whether auto-input is needed to recycle and reinforce input from others;
- whether auto-input plays a vital role in strengthening and progressing input from others that is in the process of being acquired by the brain;
- whether auto-input can negate input from others by differing in the way it uses language and strategies already intaken;

- whether auto-inputted pronunciation in particular can corrupt pronunciation input from others (through, for example, learner divergent repetition from a model becoming a more powerful source of input than the original);
- whether the potential value of auto-input as a reinforcer, tester and maintainer of hypotheses is greater than its potential danger as a contradicter and deviator;
- the extent to which auto-input mirrors previous input from others and the extent to which it is original (after all, language use is creative and it is arguable that every utterance is unique).

Readers' Tasks

1 Pick any one of the things we would like to find out more about from our list above and:
  - Turn it into a research question.
  - Hypothesise about what you would expect to find out if you researched your question.
  - Decide how you would go about researching the question.
  - (Ideally apply for a research grant and research the question).
2 What other questions would you like to see researched about the processes, value or effects of auto-input?

Part Two – Application of Theory to Practice

The most obvious implication of a consideration of the theory of auto-input is that learners need as many opportunities as possible to use (rather than just practise) the target language in order to communicate with themselves and with others.

This need can be catered for by curriculum developers focusing on communicative use in their curricula, by materials developers focusing on it in their materials, by teacher trainers focusing on it on their courses and, especially, by assessors focusing on it in high-stakes examinations, which are likely to have a substantial backwash effect on teaching and learning. It can also be catered for by writers of articles, chapters and books likely to be read by teachers, and by presenters at conferences likely to be attended by teachers. If they draw teachers' attention to the existence and potential value of auto-input and to self- and collaborative communication as means of promoting and enriching it, then there is a possibility that they might modify their materials and methodology accordingly. In order to facilitate this process, we would like to focus in our application section on methodologies and tasks with a potential for promoting quality auto-input.

Methodological Approaches

A number of methodologies mentioned earlier in this volume (for example, in Chapter 7) can play an important role in facilitating the production of auto-input with the potential to become powerful intake.

Content-based instruction (CBI), also known as content-based language teaching (CBLT) or content and language integrated instruction (CLIL) is an approach in which learners acquire new content knowledge and/or skills through instruction in the target language (e.g. knowledge about architecture or skill in pottery). It can provide opportunities for purposeful and collaborative communication with the potential for constructive feedback from teachers, peers and the learners themselves. If the content is significant or fascinating for the learner, then there is a good chance that the learner's internal and external output generated in relation to it will become powerful auto-input, as will constructive feedback during collaborative peer interaction and informal interaction with teachers. For information about this approach, see Brinton (2003), Coyle, Hood and Marsh (2010) and Mahan, Brevik and Odergaard (2018).

Text-driven approaches provide learners with experience of potentially engaging spoken, written or multimodal L2 texts, which then drive response, analysis and contextualised production activities (Tomlinson, 2013d; Tomlinson & Masuhara, 2018b). These activities can generate rich auto-input if the learners are engaged whilst reading the texts with their inner voices, when discussing the activities with themselves in inner speech (Tomlinson & Avila, 2007a, 2007b; Tomlinson, 2020a), when discussing the texts and working on the activities with peers and when they are producing texts of their own.

In task-based language teaching (TBLT), learners make use of their existing linguistic resources to perform a meaning-focused production task with intended communicative outcomes (for example, inventing an environmentally friendly vehicle). As we said in Chapter 7 many researchers claim that this approach not only improves classroom task performance but improves real-world communicative performance too (Van den Branden, 2006; Long, 2015; Samuda, Van Den Branden & Bygate, 2018; Taguchi & Kim, 2018). Task performance is often of three types, informal peer interaction during initial discussion, form-focused interaction with teachers by learners with a discovered need, and more formal presentation of conclusions, results, solutions and products. All three types provide opportunities not only for communicative input from peers and teachers but also for auto-input enhanced and enriched by contextual and collaborative feedback. Classroom task performance seems to be enhanced by preparation and rehearsal, and some researchers claim that both task and real-world performance can be enhanced as a result of task repetition (see Shintani, 2016; Bygate, 2018). The recycling and reformulation facilitated by preparation, recycling and repetition is likely to generate salient auto-input with great potential for intake, especially if the learners are affectively and cognitively engaged in the task.

Simulation approaches – in which the learners are placed within a simulated real-world situation, given roles to play in the situation and given differentiated objectives to achieve (see Richards & Rodgers, 2014) can also provide rich opportunities for the generation of valuable auto-input. This is especially true if the context, content and goals of the simulated situation are meaningful, relevant, achievably challenging and engaging for the learners. The learners are more likely to notice their auto-input and to pay attention to features of it if time is given to the learners to prepare in advance for their roles and for the strategies they will use to try to achieve their objectives. They are also more likely to notice their auto-input if, after the simulation, the teacher conducts a post-mortem with the learners, in which their strategies and the language they used to try to achieve their outcomes are analysed and constructive feedback is provided by the teacher, by peers and especially by the learners themselves.

Scenario approaches (DiPietro, 1982, 1987; Tomlinson, 1990) are similar to simulation approaches, but differ in that typically they involve group preparation for one-on-one unscripted, and to some extent unpredictable, interaction. Two groups (or halves of a small class) are put into a situation in which two people are in disagreement or are trying to persuade each other (e.g. a couple disagreeing about where to go on holiday; a salesman trying to sell a car to a reluctant customer). One group is given the situation from the perspective of one of the interactants and the other group from the other perspective. As a group, they prepare their strategies and then choose a representative to act out the scenario on their behalf. At any time during the enactment of the scenario, they can call a time out and advise or substitute their representative. Afterwards, the teacher leads a post-mortem reflection on the success or otherwise of the interactants in achieving their objectives. The preparation activities, the actual interactions and the post-mortems provide opportunities for successful output and reflection on less successful output to become potentially useful auto-input.

TPR Plus approaches (Tomlinson, 1995), although using activities in which learners initially respond to teacher output physically and without speaking, have great potential for generating useful auto-input. At lower language levels, the learners mime stories or play games silently in response to teacher output, but at higher levels the learners repeat, expand on, elaborate and analyse the teacher output, often converting teacher output into learner output into learner auto-input. For example, the teacher might tell an exciting story while the learners act it out without words. Then the teacher might get the learners to retell the story by shouting out completions to her sentence beginnings. The students might then create the beginning of a sequel to the story by taking it in turns in groups to contribute a sentence. One of the group stories could be performed by the group while the teacher copies it onto a whiteboard (or blackboard). The class could then collaborate in suggesting improvements to the story, which the teacher records next to the initial text on the board. Each student could then copy the improved version, add their own ending to the story and then give it to the teacher for feedback. This lesson would create multiple opportunities for valuable auto-input both from successful output and from reflection on and improvement of other output.

In our experience, drama approaches can provide opportunities for generating auto-input, with great potential for intake and processing. This is particularly true of those approaches that involve learner commitment to the performance of a play that really engages them affectively and cognitively, or that require learners to conceive, script and perform short plays, or that (as in process drama) involve the learners and the teacher improvising dialogue within a context whilst making full use of embodied language, extra-linguistic communication and nonlinguistic communication (Kao & O'Neill, 1998; Bowell & Heap, 2001; Park, 2010). We have many memories of learners becoming fully engaged in drama activities, and it is this engagement in creating output aiming at achieving impact both within the drama and with an audience that generates auto-input that satisfies most of the criteria for language acquisition. One such memory is of an activity in which different pairs or groups are given different situations with which to create a drama. They create and assign characters and then perform an initial impromptu drama located in their situation. They discuss their performance and give feedback to each other on their characters. They then repeat this perform-and-reflect routine before performing and recording a third version of their drama. They then use the recording to help them to script their drama. For homework, they learn their parts and then in the next lesson they rehearse their drama before performing it to another pair or group. We do not believe in forcing learners to act in front of a large and potentially critical audience, but those groups who want to can perform their drama in front of the class and possibly even at a school performance of the best dramas from each class (as voted for by the learners). The teacher's role in this type of activity is to energise the learners (maybe by a brief impromptu performance at the beginning of the lesson), to explain the activities, to set up the situations and to be available for learners who request feedback and assistance.

Using project-driven approaches – in which groups of learners do research in order to make a written and/or spoken presentation on a particular issue or topic (Haines, 1989; Wicks, 2000) – is another way of providing opportunities for learners to use the target language for communication, both informally in the peer interaction required during the research and preparation stages and more formally during the written and/or spoken presentation of the group findings. This communicative output is pushed, commented on, repaired and elaborated on by peers and given feedback on by the teacher, and opportunities are thus provided for improved output to become auto-input to become intake rich in both language in use and in sensory, affective and cognitive associations.

Engaged reading activities can provide opportunities for auto-input from both the inner-voice activity that can accompany silent reading and from the inner speech self-interaction that we generate when we are absorbed in reading. Extensive reading - in which learners read an L2 book, magazine, newspaper or comic for pleasure without being monitored or assessed (Elley & Mangubhai, 1981; Krashen, 2004; Maley, 2008) is an approach that can achieve this, as is Language Through Literature - in which learners are engaged in experiencing accessible and meaningful poems, stories, novels, plays and films and then often in generating written and spoken creative texts themselves (Paran & Robinson, 2015; Saito & Wales, 2015; Bland, 2018; Jones, 2019; Tomlinson, 2019a). Film and other visual media-based approaches can also provide learners with rich and engaging experience of responding to and using meaningful language in use, as well as providing authentic experience of embodied language, extra-linguistic communication and nonlinguistic communication (Herrere & Yanderschelden, 2019; Tomlinson, 2019b). The main point is that the aesthetic and engaging experience provided by these approaches can expose the learners to memorable use of language for effect, and that this is strengthened as input by being focused on, repeated and responded to internally and externally by the learner as auto-input.

A number of recent pedagogical approaches have based themselves on theories of learner agency. An example would be an approach developed by Dirk Lagerwaard and presented in his paper "Through others we become ourselves: Agency in the secondary classroom" at the IATEFL conference in Liverpool on Tuesday 2 April 2019. In his approach, Lagerwaard works with his students to exploit communicative opportunities that exploit scaffolded or even semi-scripted situations in which emotional engagement triggers deeply felt and spontaneous personal expression. An example, which Lagerwaard demonstrated in his presentation, is a Skype interview in which an initially shy student in Barcelona interacts with increasing confidence and independence with Lagerwaard's brother in Denmark, thus producing rich input for her fellow students and powerful auto-input for herself. Lagerwaard (2019a, 2019b) provides details of his methodology, plus examples of learner agency in affective action in the classroom through the implementation of Alexander's (2005) proposal for dialogic teaching, with its five key principles for the classroom of collective, reciprocal, supportive, cumulative and purposeful, and the application of Vygotsky's theory that "it is through others that we become ourselves" (1987). Lagerwaard's methodology relies upon positive collaboration between students and teacher to stimulate, respect and enhance student output, upon stimulating student emotions and upon creating activities that "challenge students to go beyond themselves towards goals that have personal significance to them" (Stetsenko, 2017).

We have enjoyed similar bursts of student self-expression to those reported by Lagerwaard when, for example:

- provoking an excited and articulate argument between male and female students in Oman about who was responsible for Bernard's death in the children's story *Not Now Bernard* (McKee, 1980), in which his mother and father ignore Bernard when he tells them there is a monster in the garden and do not even notice when the monster eats Bernard and then approaches his mother and father, (see Tomlinson (2019a) for the plan of this lesson);
- setting up a student-led filming of a performed version of the poem *The Schoolmaster* by Yevtushenko (1962);
- encouraging a class of domestic-science teachers in a teachers' college in Vanuatu to discard their coursebook and to write a novel set on the island where they lived.

All these approaches value peer interaction (see Chapter 7) and are likely to promote auto-input as a result of highlighting and elaborating engaged utterances in learner output. A recent publication giving valuable advice to teachers on ways of making use of peer interaction is Adams and Oliver (2019). This book provides information about the theoretical justifications for making considerable use of peer interaction, it suggests and exemplifies ways of making effective use of peer interaction in the classroom, and it responds to the typical questions and concerns of teachers about the use of peer interaction.

The teacher can also play an important role in helping learners to generate valuable auto-input by adopting responsive teaching approaches. These are approaches in which the teacher is available as a resource during learner tasks and interactions, in one-to-one tutorials and in self-access centres to provide guidance and information when it is asked for by learners (thus providing feedback to learner output when it is needed, wanted and salient). Any learner repair or uptake during these interactions is potentially useful auto-input, as is any learner output which succeeds in communicating (especially if it elicits signs of teacher approval).

All the pedagogical approaches recommended above are holistic approaches focusing on communication, as well as being humanistic approaches focusing on human interaction. They provide experience of language in use, opportunities to use language internally and externally for meaningful communication and opportunities for salient feedback. They are not discrete approaches focusing on language.

Classroom Activities

Here are some classroom activities that, regardless of the prevailing methodology being used, can promote auto-input with the potential to become valuable intake:

- getting learners to do a presentation on what interests them most in life, with preparation and rehearsal being supported by a teacher if requested, with the presentation being repeated and with learners choosing which of their classmates' presentations to listen to;
- getting learners to listen to a poem or short story and to visualise it as they listen, then to do a different activity for ten minutes and then to use their remembered images to generate the language they need to reproduce the text as faithfully as possible;
- getting learners to recite a favourite poem, song or story and then to answer questions from peers about its language, content and meaning;
- returning learners' written work with feedback on only the learner's use of one salient linguistic or pragmatic feature, getting the learner to read more about this feature (through, for example, a remedial card – see Ellis and Tomlinson, 1980 and Chapter 9 in this volume), and providing the learner with an opportunity to revise the piece of work and to use the feature in a different writing task;
- getting learners at the end of a lesson to think about, write down, draw a picture of and then share with a partner one new word or expression they have learned how to use in the lesson;
- having a pause in the middle of a lesson and getting learners to think about something they have said or written that could be improved, and then to write this down together with an improved version (possibly with the help of a peer or of the teacher).

Out-of-School Activities

As we have argued throughout this volume, the more that learners experience and use the target language outside the classroom the better. Here are some out-of-school activities that, regardless of the prevailing classroom methodology, can promote auto-input with the potential to become valuable intake:

- getting learners to pretend they are making a documentary and to comment with their inner voice on the scenes they are passing on the bus or train or as they are walking home, and then to try to repeat and improve their commentary when they get home;
- getting learners to act out dialogues of couples on the train or bus with their inner voice and then to write down the dialogues as scenes from plays when they get home;

- getting learners to use their inner voice to respond to blogs and vlogs on social media;
- getting learners to take photos of signs and notices in English (either from actual streets or from the web), challenging their peers to work out their meaning and then explaining the meaning to their peers;
- getting learners to find a joke on the web or in a book, to rehearse telling the joke and then to perform the joke to a group, and possibly to the class (or even the school) if willing;
- getting learners to write letters or emails to local speakers of the target language, inviting them to come to the school and take part in an interview, then rehearsing their questions for the interview, conducting and recording a live interview, and then giving self-feedback on their interview performance whilst watching the recording with their peers.

All of these activities, and many similar ones, involve learners in using their inner and outer voices to produce output in meaningful situations, and then paying attention to their output in order to improve or learn from it, thus creating auto-input with great potential to become intake.

Assessment

For many years we have been advocating what we called "testing to learn" (Tomlinson, 2005b), an approach to testing that always makes the main objective of testing the provision of learning opportunities prior to, during and after a test or examination. This proposal was rejected by many assessment experts but, as mentioned earlier in this volume, there is now a growing movement in favour of Assessment for Learning (AfL) (for example, Jones, 2005; Harlen, 2007; Tan, 2011; Lee & Coniam, 2013). "Assessment for Learning takes place during day-to-day classroom practice and while pupils are engaged in learning. It also gives pupils an active role in the assessment process. Pupils work with the teacher to determine what is being learned and to identify the next steps" (Council for the Curriculum, Examinations and Assessment, 2019). If assessors are serious about assessment providing opportunities for learning, then not only will they provide more opportunities for learners to participate in collaborative communication, but they will also find ways of helping learners to create their own feedback (by, for example, comparing their own production with that of proficient speakers performing the same task) and thus to gain valuable intake from the auto-input that this can provide.

Readers' Tasks

1 Without looking back at this chapter, try to complete the following table as a summary of what the chapter says about auto-input and what you think about it yourself.

Question	Answer
1 What is auto-input?	
2 Why can auto-input be extremely valuable for language learners?	
3 Why do you think there has been so little research so far on the determiners and effects of auto-input?	
4 What can language planners do to promote opportunities for auto-input?	
5 What can the teacher do to promote opportunities for auto-input?	
6 What could coursebooks do to promote opportunities for auto-input?	

Read through the chapter again, and then make revisions (if you want to) to your answers in the table above.

2 Design a task-based or text-driven unit of materials that has the potential to create opportunities for both internal and external auto-input.
3 Design an out-of-school task with the potential to create opportunities for both internal and external auto-input.
4 Design an assessment task that not only measures learners' ability to communicate collaboratively but that also subsequently provides them with an opportunity to gain auto-input by monitoring their own performance.

9 Some Salient Issues in SLA Research

Introduction

There have been a number of important issues that have dominated research and debate in SLA for many years without researchers reaching a consensus of resolution. We have touched on these issues throughout the book, but in this final chapter we are going to revisit some of them, review the research, give our opinion and suggest possible applications to practice.

The Use of the L1 in the Acquisition of an L2

Views from the Past

When we were taught foreign languages at school, we were taught an L2 through the medium of our L1. Learning a foreign language was considered to be a useful academic discipline that could help learners to develop analytical skills, to appreciate the value of accurate memorisation and hard work, and to open up their minds to another world. Learner achievement of communicative competence was rarely considered a major objective and was rarely achieved. Not only were we taught an L2 through our L1, but also we used our L1 to talk about and answer questions on the L2 as well as to translate it. It was considered that our goal was to learn about the L2 and that it was much easier to achieve this goal by using our L1 than the L2. Then came the revolution. As air travel opened up the world and more and more people wanted and/or needed to achieve communicative competence in an L2, not only did the objectives of language courses change but, in theory, the medium of instruction changed too. Methodologies became prevalent that recommended the exclusive use of the target L2, both by the teachers and by the learners, the theory being that learners needed experience of understanding and of using the target language in order to acquire it. First audio-lingual approaches and then direct method approaches provided focused practice in understanding and producing the L2 in carefully contrived situations, progressing gradually from the simple to the more complex. Then the communicative approach stressed the need for learners to understand and use the L2 in communication. Approaches such as PPP (Presentation–Practice–Production), TPR, the Natural Approach, Suggestopedia, Project Approaches, Task-Based Language Teaching (TBLT), Text-Driven Approaches (TDA), the Action-Orientated Approach (AoA) and Content and Language Integrated Learning (CLIL) have differed in their underlying theories of language acquisition but they have all stressed (or implied) the importance of the exclusive use in the classroom of the L2. All these approaches have been discussed in previous chapters, but for more information about them see Richards and Rodgers (2014).

For most of the last fifty years, most SLA theorists and most methodologists have advocated the exclusive use of the L2 in the language classroom. Krashen (1985, 1994), for example, in his input hypothesis argued for the availability of comprehensible input in the L2 as an absolute prerequisite for L2 acquisition, Swain (2005) in her output hypothesis argued for the importance of opportunities for using the L2 in order to facilitate its acquisition, and Long (1981, 2015) advocated peer interaction in the L2 as one of the most effective means of gaining L2 communicative competence. All the definitions of input and the considerations of its value in Chapter 1 of this volume (including ours) assume that input should be in the L2 and all the theories as to the value of output in the acquisition process in Chapter 7 assume that output should be in the L2. Although experts have been advocating the use of the L2 in the classroom and methodologists have been insisting on it, our experience has been that this might have actually happened in motivated language school classes taught by native speakers of the target L2 but the reality has been that in many schools and colleges, in countries where the L2 is a foreign language and is taught by non-native speakers of the L2, the L1 has continued to be used by teachers to give instructions and explanations and to ask questions to the learners. The L1 has also continued to be used by learners when asking or answering questions, when involved in pair or group discussion and when involved in collaborative construction of texts. We have observed this reality in English-language classrooms in countries such as China, Indonesia, Japan, Nepal, South Korea, Thailand and Vietnam, where teachers often have little confidence in their own ability to communicate accurately and effectively in English. They continue to use their L1, not out of any theoretical conviction but because they do not think they can provide their learners with a suitable model and they think using their L1 will make it easier for their learners to understand them.

Current Theories

In the last ten years or so, there has been an increasing questioning of the value of the exclusive use of the L2 in the classroom. One of the questioners has been Vivian Cook. In Cook (2003), for example, he questions the validity of insisting on learning an L2 through an L2, and in Cook (2010) he stresses the differences between L1 and

L2 acquisition and questions why, from the direct method to task-based learning, it is assumed that the L1 should play no part in the L2 learning process and why the learner is required to speak only in the L2 when using the L1 might facilitate the acquisition of the L2. Sultana (2018) reviews the literature on learner use of the L1 when learning an L2 and reports, for example:

- Anton and Dicamilla (1999, p. 245), concluding that L1 "enables learners to construct effective collaborative dialogues in the completion of meaning-based tasks";
- Storch and Wigglesworth (2003, p. 768) recommending that "teachers should not prohibit the use of some L1 altogether in group and pair work but acknowledge that the use of the L1 may be a normal psychological process that allows learners to initiate and sustain verbal interaction";
- Swain, Kinnear and Steinmann (2015, p. 43) saying that "if the activity requires complex cognitive processing then the best (or only) way is to discuss it in the first (and strongest) language)".

Much of the research on the effects of the use of L1 in L2 classrooms has been in countries where English is a foreign language and where teachers and learners often seem reluctant to use the L2. For example, Widyalankara (2012) investigates the prevalence and the effects of the use of the L1 (Sinhala) in English classes in Sri Lanka, Wu (2016) focuses on the effects of L1 cognitive resources on L2 reading ability in China and an Indonesian academic, Zulfikar (2018), writes about such benefits of using the L1 in an L2 classroom as clearer expression of ideas by learners and clearer explanations of concepts by teachers.

Most of the recent mainstream SLA publications have sections on the role of the L1 in the acquisition of an L2, but they focus on the connection in the mind between the two languages rather than the actual use of the L1 in the acquisition of an L2. This is true, for example, of Gass and Mackey (2012), Herschensohn and Young-Scholten (2013), R. Ellis (2015) and Saville-Troike and Barto (2017). The focus of most of the studies reported is either related to whether or not the L1 interferes with the L2 to cause errors of comprehension or production, and whether or not the L1 and the L2 are stored separately in the brain or together. Current thinking seems to be that the L1 does not interfere with the L2, but that transference occurs when learning an L2, and this can be positive or negative and can be dependent on the type of knowledge being transferred. As R. Ellis (2015, pp. 120–121) says "transfer may be evident when the L2 is elicited by instruments that tap into explicit knowledge, but may not occur in L2 free production, which is more likely to draw on implicit knowledge". Current thinking is also that the L1 and the L2 are not different language systems stored separately in the brain but are in many aspects interdependent, with researchers differing as to the degree of separation or fusing and most considering that this is variable. For a review of research on the degree of independence of an L2 from an L1 in the brain, see Saville-Troike and Barto (2017, pp. 75-80).

What we find amazing is that there seems to have been very little SLA research into the actual effects of learners and of teachers using the learners' L1 in the L2 classroom. The assumption of most SLA researchers seems to be that the learners and the teachers only use the L2 in the classroom, yet the reality in many classrooms is very different.

Many of the advocates of the use of the L1 in the acquisition of an L2 seem to be basing their assertions on their own experience and views, and there seems to have been very little research conducted on the differing effects of exclusive use of the L2 compared to selective use of the L1.

We would very much welcome experiments which, for example, compare the effects on the development of communicative competence between equivalent classes of learners in which, in one class the teacher and the learners only use the L2, in another class the teacher only uses the L2 but the learners are encouraged to use the L1 when in discussion with each other, and in another class both the teacher and the learners use the L1 when asking and answering questions and when in discussion. Ideally, the classes would follow the same methodology, use the same materials and have the same teacher. They would differ only in the degree of L1 use encouraged in the classroom.

Our Opinion

We believe that whether or not using the L1 can facilitate the acquisition of an L2 depends on who is using it, when they are using it and how they are using it.

Teacher Use of the L1

We would certainly not recommend the use of the L1 by teachers in situations where the L2 is being learned as a foreign language and where there is little or no exposure to the L2 outside the classroom. In such situations, the teacher is often the only source of input available to the learners and the only potential interactant more proficient than themselves. If teachers give instructions and explanations in the L1 in such situations, they might achieve greater clarity but they are denying their learners a valuable source of exposure to the L2 in use and they are denying them opportunities to gain feedback and facility from interaction with a more proficient user of the L2 than themselves. If teachers use the L2 to give instructions and explanations, there is a high probability of intake because such determiners of intake as salience, relevance, meaningfulness, affective engagement, cognitive engagement and achievable challenge are likely to be achieved (see Chapter 2 for discussion of the determiners of intake). We have witnessed the impoverishment of input caused by teacher use of the L1 in English classes in China, Indonesia, Japan and Vietnam and the enrichment of input created by encouragement of teachers on the PKG Project in Indonesia (Tomlinson, 1990) to use English when giving instructions and explanations.

Given our view expressed above, we were very happy to read an article reporting a new initiative by the Ministry of Education in Chile, which "started out by breaking the prevailing paradigm of the day which was teaching English in Spanish". The report stated: "We have been emphatic about the need for English teachers not just to speak English, but to also feel comfortable with that language … to be able to communicate in English" (Pérez, 2018, p. 132). Interestingly though, this focus on the teachers needing to communicate in English was one of the few references to pedagogic principle in a 505-page report on English-language teaching policy in Latin America. In our experience, this is typical of language-teaching policy documents, and one of the recommendations we would make is for language planners to pay more attention to what we know about how languages are best taught and learned rather than making the apparent assumption that any type of language teaching is good and then focusing only on how to resource, fund, deliver and evaluate it.

We would probably make an exception to our stand on the importance of teacher use of the L2 though in the case of teachers giving individual feedback on the progress of beginner- and elementary-level learners as clarity would probably be a more important goal than providing input.

Learner Use of the L1

At lower levels, we would definitely encourage learners to make use of their L1 in order to help them to understand L2 texts they have read, listened to or watched as, without such investigation, all but the simplest and most inauthentic texts could remain incomprehensible and of little value as input. At these levels we would also recommend encouraging learners to use their L1 to develop and to discuss ideas prior to their attempted articulation of their ideas in the L2, to discuss and monitor the expression of their ideas in collaborative L2 writing tasks and to ask the teacher questions they need answering in order to do a task or express an idea. In this way, they will be able to express themselves at the level of their cognitive ability, rather than being restricted to apparent banalities and, in doing so, they will gain valuably modified input (see Chapter 1). An example of this approach is Brian asking students for the first hour of an English-conversation class in Japan to discuss an issue or solve a problem in Japanese and then to spend the second hour expressing and presenting their views or solutions in English.

Code Switching

Switching from L1 to L2 and vice versa is a natural and potentially effective procedure during communication between users who share an L1 and an L2 (regardless of their level of proficiency). It enables efficient and effective communication, and it can increase the likelihood of the L2 components of the communication facilitating intake. This is true for both learner–learner interaction and teacher–learner interaction (see Macaro, 2009 for studies demonstrating the value of teacher use of code switching, and Bhatti, Shamsudin & Said, 2018 for evidence of the benefits of both learner and teacher code switching). Code switching can not only be useful in learner production but also in reading and listening too. There are now many bilingual books that are written using both the L1 and an L2, many of which start mainly in the L1 but gradually use more of the L2 as the book progresses. They often feature repetition, redundancy, contextual signification and illustrations and some are designed to be read aloud by a teacher. See Fowler (2019) for her top ten bilingual books.

Applications to Practice

Here are some examples of L1 included activities we have found to be potentially useful in the L2 classroom:

1 The teacher gives a dramatic reading of an L2 story enriched by sound effects and visuals (e.g. a story about an old man getting out of a taxi, looking at the numbers on doors, knocking on a door, smiling as a woman opens the door and then entering the house, and there is at first laughing from inside the house and then screaming). The teacher asks and then writes on the board an open-ended question in the L2 (e.g. "Why did the old man scream?"). The learners in groups discuss and answer the question in their L1, practise answering it in the L2 and then give their answer to the class in the L2.
2 The teacher gives the learners a written version of the story in 1 that begins entirely in the L1, progresses with a mixture of L1 and L2 and then ends entirely in the L2. The learners in groups continue the story writing their first paragraph in the L1, their second paragraph in a mixture of L1 and L2 and their third paragraph in the L2.
3 The learners are given in the L2 a complicated issue to discuss or a difficult problem to solve. They discuss it in depth in the L1 and then reach a conclusion or find a solution. They then prepare, rehearse and finally perform an L2 presentation of their conclusion or solution.
4 The learners in pairs are given a topic to discuss with one partner using the L1 and the other using the L2. They then change languages before concluding their discussion, with both learners using the L2.
5 The learners perform a TPR Plus story (Tomlinson, 1994) by miming all the parts as the teacher gives a dramatic rendition of the story. The learners retell the story first in the L1 and then in the L2, by shouting out completions of the teacher's prompts. Then the learners make up Part 2 of the story, contributing a sentence each round and round in a circle. They start in the L1 but when the teacher shouts

"Change!" they start to contribute sentences in the L2. Each group then writes their story in the L2, with the teacher acting as a resource when a group gets stuck and needs a word or a translation.

The main benefits of all these activities are that the use of the L1 makes the L2 comprehensible, it helps to develop and articulate concepts, it relaxes the learners and it provides content for the learners to try to articulate in the L2. This can only happen, though, if learners share an L1, that is if the class all speak the same L1, or if the teacher divides the class into groups according to their L1. Of course, as the learners progress, they can be encouraged to use more and more L2 and eventually to do the activities through the exclusive use of the L2.

Readers' Tasks

1 Imagine a specific language-teaching context in which you have been asked to give advice to a young teacher about the use of the L1 in the L2 classroom. Imagine and then write your conversation with the teacher.
2 Devise a case study in which you are trying to find out something about the use of the L1 in an L2 classroom. Specify what it is you are trying to find out and how you intend to gain this information.

FURTHER READING

Cook, V. (2010). The relationship between first and second language learning revisited. In E. Macaro (Ed.), *The Continuum companion to second language acquisition* (pp. 137–157). *London*: Continuum.

Swain, M., Kinnear, P. & Steinmann, L. (2015). *Socio-cultural theory in second language education: an introduction through narratives* (2nd ed.). Bristol: Multilingual Matters.

Feedback and Correction

In our view, there is no doubt that learners need feedback on their effectiveness to communicate in their target language (though some researchers, for example, Krashen, 1985; Long, 2007b) have cast some doubt on the necessity for negative feedback). We feel that without positive and negative feedback learners lack the "information" they need in order to progress. But what form should the "information" take, what should the information be about, who or what should provide it and when and how should it be provided?

Explicit Teacher Correction of Form

We reckon that language teachers can waste years of their lives correcting their learners' so-called errors in speech and in writing. All over the world at this moment teachers are:

- providing a correct alternative and asking a learner to repeat it (e.g. No Toshi. It's not "lice" its "rice". Repeat after me, "We cooked the rice");
- crossing out or underlining an expression, providing a correct alternative and telling the learner to copy it five times (e.g. "I buyed (bought) a new dress". Write out the correct sentence five times).

We gave this up many years ago when we realised what little benefit our efforts were bestowing and how much of our lives we were wasting. Our learners might have repeated the correct utterance or even repaired their "erroneous" utterance themselves but almost inevitably they soon made the same "error" again, and often the learners lost confidence and self-esteem as a result of the constant negation of their efforts to communicate (even when they had requested teacher correction). Brian certainly remembers trying to communicate intelligently and interestingly with his one-to-one teachers when trying to learner Bahasa Indonesia and Japanese, and feeling very frustrated when the usual response was to correct his tenses or pronunciation.

Before we turn to the literature, we would like to list some of the reasons why we think that explicit teacher correction is usually ineffective in contributing positively to enduring acquisition:

1. The "error" might not be an error. It might just be a mistake caused by anxiety, carelessness, rushing, lack of topic familiarity etc. An error is systematic, consistent and predictable, whereas a mistake is untypical and nothing to worry about. Native speakers make mistakes all the time, and especially in spontaneous conversation.
2. If it is an error. it might be just part of a developmental process, which will eventually lead to the learner achieving accurate and effective expression. For example, most learners get the past tense of irregular verbs "wrong" (e.g. buyed, costed) before they eventually get them right. Initially, when they acquire the regular past tense form, they tend to overgeneralise its use to most verbs. A developmental error certainly does not need to be corrected. All that is needed for development to occur is further experience, noticing and time.
3. We know of no neurolinguistic evidence that teacher correction of an error achieves new input that has any positive impact on previous intake. The input provided by explicit error correction is usually restricted to declarative linguistic knowledge and tends to lack affective and cognitive engagement, recycling, extra-linguistic and contextual information and procedural knowledge.

4 Constant error correction can interrupt and inhibit learner attempts at communication and reduce the likelihood of learner production contributing to learner acquisition.
5 If a learner is frequently corrected (especially in front of peers) there is a danger that the learner will feel diminished and negated. If suffered often, this can lead to loss of confidence, esteem and contribution, and thus reduce the likelihood of acquisition.
6 Frequent explicit correction of error communicates a message to the learner that they are failing because they are not achieving native-speaker accuracy, a target that most learners do not need to and never will attain.

We must point out, though, that there has been research that has demonstrated the effectiveness of explicit correction (e.g. Ellis, Loewen & Erlam, 2006; Norris & Ortega, 2000), and R. Ellis (2009) provides a powerful advocacy for explicit correction. It could be that learners have demonstrated the effectiveness of explicit correction with immediately correct repair or uptake and that they have gained the ability to produce correct forms in delayed tests of declarative knowledge, but we have not seen convincing proof of enduring acquisition resulting from explicit correction alone.

For a concise survey of the literature on explicit correction, see Li (2014).

Responsive Teaching

Far more productive in our view than teacher correction is teacher support. We have found this to be especially true if the teacher responds to requests for help when learners are actually engaged in using the L2 for comprehension or production. It could be that learners in a group are trying to decide which is the more effective way of saying something of two alternatives, are disagreeing about the meaning of an utterance in a text or are wanting advice about the most effective strategy to use in a collaborative letter. The teacher eliciting or even providing an effective solution is likely to make a more positive contribution to the learners' acquisition and development than the teacher correcting learners during or after production.

An effective way of responding to learner problems in communication is to set a production task, then provide a text produced by a proficient user in response to the same or a similar task, guide the learner(s) to make discoveries about how specific language features are used to effect in that text and then invite the learner(s) to revise and submit their text. This procedure is commonly used in lessons and materials following a text-driven approach (see Tomlinson, 2013d, Tomlinson & Masuhara, 2018b).

Recasting

If a teacher is going to provide corrective feedback during learner communication, we would recommend recasting. This consists of the teacher reformulating learner utterances as part of the communication, or as Loewen (2012, p. 24) puts it, giving "a type of input-providing feedback that correctly reformulates a learner's erroneous utterance but retains the learner's intended meaning". Loewen (2012, p. 26) provides the following example of a recast from Loewen and Philp (2006, p. 538):

S: to her is good thing (.) to her is good thing.
T: yeah for her it's a good thing.
S: because she got a lot of money there.

Recasting can be implicit or explicit. An example of implicit recasting would be:

T: That's a nice shirt. Where did you buy it?
S: I buyed it in Flannels.
T: You bought it in Flannels? I bought mine in Flannnels too. But I think I prefer yours.

An example of explicit recasting would be:

T: That's a nice shirt. Where did you buy it?
S: I buyed it in Flannels.
T: You mean, "I bought it in Flannels".

The advantages of implicit recasting are that it does not interrupt the communication, it is not judgemental and it makes a positive contribution to the input. The disadvantage is that the learner might be so focused on the communication as to not notice the recasting at all.

The advantage of explicit recasting is that the learner's attention is drawn to the recast. The disadvantage is that it interrupts the communication and can be perceived as judgemental.

An advantage of both types of recasting is that they occur immediately after the error and they provide an opportunity to compare the erroneous form with a form considered to be a model target form.

Recasting is a much researched pedagogic strategy, with most researchers finding it contributes to acquisition (e.g. Ellis & Sheen, 2006; Loewen & Philp, 2006) but with some having reservations about implicit recasting's lack of focus on the error and preferring elicitation, which prompts learner self-correction as a means of providing negative feedback (e.g. Lyster, 2004; Lyster & Mori, 2006). Our thinking is reflected in the statement by R. Ellis (2015, p. 163) that: "Recasts provide learners with positive evidence and thus make it possible for them to acquire *new* features. Prompts ... can help learners consolidate those features they have prior knowledge of, so both are important." We are not so sure that we agree with R. Ellis (2015, p. 162) when he asserts the value of corrective recasts in which the recasts "are made salient to the learners" by first of all repeating the learner's error. He justifies this by reference to Doughty and Varela (1998) and their assertion of the value of "corrective recasts" in which a repetition of the learner's error is used as a prompt and then followed by a recast if the learner fails to self-correct. "Doughty and Varela reported that the recasts resulted in progress through the acquisition sequence of past tense verbs and also in more target like use in an immediate and delayed oral post-test." (R. Ellis, 2015, p. 162).

R. Ellis (2015) provides a useful review of the literature on recasts in his sections on "input-providing vs. output-prompting strategies" and on "implicit v explicit corrective strategies" on pp. 162–163. He asserts that explicit corrective feedback (e.g. metalinguistic comment and explicit correction) is more effective than implicit corrective feedback (e.g. recasts) but does not define what he means by effective. He does, however, refer to research that appears to justify this conclusion, for example, a meta-analysis by Li (2010) of thirty-three studies. It seems to us that the method of testing will inevitably influence findings. If the tests are of declarative knowledge (e.g. recognition tests, matching tests, filling in blanks tests, multiple choice tests) then they will reveal a stronger effect for explicit corrective feedback, whereas if they are of procedural knowledge through evaluation of communicative performance then implicit corrective feedback will achieve a stronger effect. This is a possibility also considered by R. Ellis (2015, pp. 165–166) when reporting the findings of Revesz (2012) that: "As in Ellis, Loewen and Erlam (2006) ... recasts appear to have impacted on learners' implicit knowledge but not on their explicit knowledge".

For a report of a study in which the researcher influenced a class of students to start using the contrastive "but" effectively through implicit recasting (both immediately and after a delay), see Tomlinson (2007b).

Remediation

Remediation attempts to remedy an error rather than just correct an instance of it. It usually involves drawing the learner's attention to instances of the error, providing information about why it is an error and what the correct form should be, providing opportunities to practise the target-language feature and providing opportunities for the learner to go back and correct instances of the error they have made previously. Whilst we are not in favour of using such terms as "correct", "error" and "remedy", with their implication that the learner is at fault for not achieving native-speaker accuracy, and we are uneasy with the concentration on explicit learning, practice and correction, we have found this approach to be of value in helping learners to improve their ability to achieve accuracy and cohesion in planned written discourse. For example, in Zambia in 1970, Brian took part in a project in which teachers from a number of nearby schools first of all brainstormed typical errors in writing, and then wrote a number of remedial cards for each error, with side 1 of the card containing examples and explanations of the error plus examples of correct use, and side 2 containing practice activities. In each of the participating schools, the teacher responded to a student's written work with the number and letter of a remedial card related to a problem conspicuous in the student's work (e.g. 16A). In a timetabled lesson, the students took the recommended card from a box, read side 1, did the exercises on side 2 and then took the corresponding marking card from another box. If they scored 70 per cent or more and there was time left, they corrected their errors in their piece of work and then took another card from the box and worked on it. If they did not score 70 per cent, they took another card focusing on the same problem and worked on that. While the learners were working on their remedial cards, the teacher brought individuals to their desk and gave general feedback and advice on their written work. At that time, there were also boxes of remedial cards available commercially, but we have not seen any in use for a long time. For an example of a remedial card (unfortunately called a correction card) and a description of a taught remedial lesson, see Ellis and Tomlinson (1980). Nowadays, I doubt if we would focus on discrete errors of grammar or spend a whole lesson teaching remedially, but we would use discovery cards to help learners make discoveries about more global problems in their writing (e.g. problems with achieving cohesion or coherence; problems in achieving intended pragmatic effects). We would then get learners to revise a number of pieces of written work they have produced during a course.

Peer Feedback

Recent research (e.g. Sato & Ballinger, 2016a) and our experience reveal that peers are typically less judgemental and more constructive when giving each other feedback. This seems to be especially true during communicative interaction and during collaborative tasks when learners are working together towards a productive goal. Rather than just correcting perceived errors, they tend to give each other opportunities to clarify, to elaborate and to self-repair by asking meaning-focused questions and making meaning-focused statements that seek confirmation, clarification or further information. Or they offer implicit recasts (e.g. "You mean we bring sandwiches to the picnic?"; "I'm surprised you went by bus. I thought I saw you on a tram").

As well as setting many collaborative tasks (e.g. group solving of problems or designing of products), we make use of the rich potential of peer feedback by arranging for each pair or group doing a task in class to have a monitor pair or group to give them feedback whilst any productive work progresses, or for each individual on an online project to have access to peer monitors in a support group. We also use collective peer monitoring of learner's work as in the following example:

1 Learners as a class mime a dramatic story as the teacher narrates it.
2 Learners as a class repeat the story by shouting out completions of teacher prompts (usually in our experience recasting other learners' inaccurate completions without being at all judgemental).

3 Learners in groups make up Part 2 of the story (usually as a circle story with each learner in the group taking it in turns to narrate the next sentence).
4 One group tell their story to the class whilst the teacher copies it verbatim and displays it.
5 Learners as a class offer revisions to the story to improve both content and expression.
6 Individual learners copy the revised story.
7 Individual learners write a completion of the story for homework.
8 Individual learners share their completion with a peer monitor who suggests improvements.
9 Individual learners revise their completion and hand it in for teacher feedback on its impact.

We have found that this procedure offers many opportunities for constructive and communicative feedback that satisfy most of the conditions for facilitating intake (e.g. comprehensibility, relevance, meaningfulness, impact, recycling, engagement, support).

Auto-Feedback
Auto-feedback occurs when learners monitor their own comprehension or production prior to, during or after performance. If they notice potential or actual inaccuracy, inappropriacy or ineffectiveness, then the feedback they provide to themselves can be extremely valuable, especially if they follow up the noticing with attempts to discover or find more accurate, appropriate or effective ways of expressing themselves. The noticing and discovery are usually achieved using inner-voice evaluation of potential or actual effects, and the finding could involve gaining access to relevant input, asking peers or teachers for help, going to a dictionary or corpus or even carrying out mini research studies.

Situational Feedback
In natural language acquisition, the most valuable source of both positive and negative feedback is provided by markers of effect in the situation of the attempted communication. If a learner/user wants orange and gets water, attempts a compliment and receives a scowl, makes a request and receives a curt refusal or orders a shirt online and receives a blouse, then they receive situational feedback on the inadequacy of their attempt, which might contribute to modifications of what has been acquired, especially if they then look out for alternatives that might be more effective. On the other hand, if they make a joke and people laugh, if they give instructions and people follow them, if they book flights successfully, if they persuade somebody to do something, then reinforcement and strengthening of intake can take place.

Unfortunately, most coursebooks and lessons in focusing narrowly on language form fail to provide opportunities for situational feedback, a form of feedback potentially more effective than words alone because of its rich multimodality, contextualisation, meaning focus, effect focus and affective engagement. For example, in Unit Three of *Headway Pre-Intermediate Student's Book* (Soars & Soars, 2012), thirty-nine of the fifty-six activities involve a focus on linguistic form, and none of them provides the learners with a multimodal or contextualised experience of the use of English.

Input Feedback

The more learners experience contextualised language in comprehensible, meaningful and engaging ways, the more likely they are to notice (either consciously or subconsciously) how features of the target language are used to achieve intended effects, and the more likely they are to develop the ability to achieve such effects themselves. This is especially true if they have an opportunity to compare the input with something they have written or said themselves in an equivalent situation for an equivalent purpose. Such experience of rich input is not normally referred to as feedback, but we regard it as such because it not only promotes new intake but also allows the learner (and, more importantly, the learner's brain) to revise, replace or strengthen language features already taken in.

Applications to Practice

In this section we have already applied theory to practice with our exemplification of principled approaches that we would recommend. We would say that for feedback to be of value it needs to be (like most other input):

- supportive
- comprehensible
- constructive
- rich
- relevant
- meaningful
- recycled
- salient

Ideally, it should also be:

- engaging
- memorable
- multimodal

We would also say that from our reading of the literature and from our experience in the classroom the best ways of affording learners valuable feedback are through making use of:

- learner discovery
- peer collaboration
- peer interaction
- situational tasks with intended communicative goals
- teacher response to requests for assistance during task performance
- meaning-focused recasts
- learner noticing as a result of rich input (e.g. through extensive reading, listening and viewing)

> ### Readers' Tasks
>
> 1 From your reading of this section on feedback and your own experience as a learner and a teacher, which means of providing feedback do you think are most effective in promoting language acquisition?
> 2 What would your reply be to learners who say to you: "Please correct all my mistakes. I want to speak correctly"?

FURTHER READING

Loewen, S. (2012). The role of feedback. In S. M. Gass & A. Mackey (Eds.), *The Routledge handbook of second language acquisition* (pp. 24–40). New York: Routledge.

Sheen, Y. & Ellis, R. (2011). Corrective feedback in language teaching. In E. Hinkel (Ed.), *Handbook of research in second language teaching and learning II* (pp. 593–610). New York: Routledge.

Implicit and Explicit Learning

In SLA literature, we frequently see the terms "implicit" and "explicit" in relation to the process of learning (e.g. implicit and explicit learning), to the product of learning (e.g. implicit and explicit knowledge) and to instructional approaches (e.g. implicit and explicit instruction; implicit and explicit feedback). We will first consider the definitions of implicit and explicit learning and of explicit and implicit knowledge. We will then summarise what has been the controversy regarding the two, before discussing our views and suggestions for applications for research and practice.

Implicit Learning and Implicit Knowledge

Often quoted definitions of implicit learning include "acquisition of knowledge about the underlying structure of a complex stimulus environment by a process that takes place naturally, simply and without conscious operations" (N. Ellis, 1994, p. 1)

N. Ellis (2011, p. 35) explains implicit learning by using an example from L1 acquisition: L1 children interact with caretakers in everyday social interactions. L1 children are focused on meaning and communication. Through such child-centred interactions, children gradually, unintentionally and organically achieve intake which, if significant, leads to the acquisition of meaning–form–context associations and of formal elements of the L1 in the brain. A four-to-five-year-old child, when developmentally ready, is able to demonstrate, for example, morphological and syntactical understanding developed in his/her brain i.e. acquired implicit knowledge of language systems that has never been taught to them. When asked about these systems, however, the child is not able to explain. This knowledge of the language system and its use is called implicit knowledge – the product of implicit learning.

What characterises implicit learning is that the process and the use of the product do not involve conscious awareness that learning is taking or has taken place, and they do not involve intentionality to achieve goal-orientated wilful learning. Implicit knowledge is acquired gradually in an incidental, experiential, unplanned and unintentional manner in a natural communicative environment without effort. The learners' focus is on meaning and on the purpose of communication. During such meaning-focused communication, learners are absorbing and abstracting linguistic and associated extra-linguistic features in the brain in a subconscious and automatic manner. The significance and value of the interaction is what matters. Frequent experience of instances and of the meaningfulness of the interactions influences the quality and quantity of intake and acquisition.

Explicit Learning and Explicit Knowledge

N. Ellis (1994, p. 1) defines explicit learning as "a more conscious operation where the individual makes and tests hypotheses in a search for structure". In explicit learning, a learner intentionally pays conscious attention to particular linguistic features in order to learn the target features and their patterns and rule-like tendencies. What is learned through explicit learning is called explicit knowledge.

An example of explicit learning can be found in Schmidt and Frota (1986) in which the first author kept a journal for five months, reflecting upon the processes he went through while trying to learn Portuguese in Brazil. At that time, Krashen's Input Hypothesis (1985) was very influential. Krashen's hypothesis would have predicted that implicit acquisition during the five months of immersion experience should have helped R (Richard Schmidt, the first author) not only to acquire the ability to communicate but also to become able to assimilate the morphological and syntactic features of this new language.

R found, however, that natural and incidental input were not always comprehensible, frequent, salient, intelligible or noticeable. R did attend language classes and learned some key language features in a conventional way (e.g. learning vocabulary and syntax that otherwise may not be available through typical language-teaching exercises). He appreciated the fact that learning Portuguese in language classes compensated and strengthened what implicit learning could not provide outside classrooms. Nonetheless, R also felt that explicit teaching in class did not always result in explicit learning. What R found to be the most significant contributor to learning was his own act of paying conscious attention, what he called noticing, to some language features in the input (i.e. explicit learning).

Consciousness and Attention

It would be wise not to confuse attention and consciousness. For example, our eyes may be following something. Until someone asks, "What are you looking at?" we might not have been conscious that we were doing so. Likewise, we may be paying attention to language features but not be conscious of doing so.

Explicit learning of an L2 involves intentionality and consciousness. Conscious attention is paid to language features. L2 learners' attention may move from one feature to another. But they are conscious that they are paying attention to various different features throughout.

In implicit learning of an L2, which is subconscious and unintentional, attention may be drawn to linguistic features but L2 learners may not be conscious that they are paying attention to them. Imagine a scene in which an L2 learner is curious about a souvenir in a shop in an L2 speaking country. She does not know what the object is called in the L2. So, she talks to the shop owner about purchasing it. Note here that her attention may be drawn to the name of the object but she is not consciously or intentionally trying to learn the word. Her goal and her consciousness are focused on purchasing the souvenir. Once she manages to buy it, she may or may not retain the name. The name of the object could be implicitly learned and become implicit knowledge and remain dormant. When she hears or reads about the object some time later or tries to recall it, she may become conscious of it. More durable learning is likely to take place if she hears it many times in meaningful contexts or she needs or wants to use the name of the object frequently. She may consciously learn the name in an explicit manner by intentionally repeating the name or writing it down for later reviewing (i.e. explicit learning).

Issues in Implicit and Explicit Learning

Research on Comparing the Effect of Implicit and Explicit Learning

Krashen (e.g. 1985) differentiated between acquisition and learning. R. Ellis (2015, p. 16) points out a similarity between the current conceptualisations of implicit and explicit learning to Krashen's conceptualisation of "acquisition (= implicit learning)" and "learning (= explicit learning)".

Krashen (e.g. 1985), belonging to the mentalist tradition and believing in the Chomskyan notion of a "Language Acquisition Device", emphasised the exclusively primary role of acquisition (i.e. implicit learning) and acknowledged only a partial-supportive role of explicit learning through formal teaching of languages in his Monitor Hypothesis. Such a strong assertion provoked numerous studies with research foci such as:

- exploring the kinds and value of L2 instruction
- comparing the effect of implicit vs explicit learning
- evaluating the efficacy of raising learners' metalinguistic awareness of specific L2 forms
- evaluating the efficacy of implicit and explicit feedback
- comparing the effects of comprehension practice and of production practice for learning L2 structures.

A branch of SLA called instructed SLA (ISLA) has gradually developed since the 1980s. ISLA research focuses on investigating the effects of various aspects of instruction on SLA achievement.

Norris and Ortega (2000, p. 417) conducted a systematic meta-analysis of ISLA studies. Their objectives were to standardise and synthesise the findings from experimental and quasi-experimental investigations in forty-nine studies published between 1980 and 1998. They asked two major questions:

1 How effective is L2 instruction (vs simple exposure or meaning-driven communication)?
2 What is the relative effectiveness of different types of L2 instruction?

They also added four further questions:

3 Does type of outcome measure influence observed instruction effectiveness?
4 Does length of instruction influence observed instructional effectiveness?
5 Does instructional effect last beyond immediate post-experimental observations?
6 To what extent has primary research provided answers to these questions?

Their analysis reveals that "focused L2 instruction results in large target-orientated gains, that explicit types of instruction are more effective than implicit types, and that Focus on Form and Focus on Forms interventions result in equivalent and large effects" (Norris & Ortega, 2000, p. 417). They also add that further studies reveal that "the effectiveness of L2 instruction is durable". They note the observed order of effectiveness of instructional types in terms of effect size: i.e. "Explicit Focus on Form > explicit Focus on Forms > implicit Focus on Form > implicit Focus on Forms".

Note here that "Focus on Form" and "Focus on Forms" are the terms that Long (1991) introduced. Focus on Form overtly draws a student's attention to linguistic elements within a meaning-focused environment. Focus on Forms, on the other hand, draws students' attention to often decontextualised and discrete language items, using traditional language teaching/testing techniques such as gap filling, matching lexical items and memorising items. So according to Norris and Ortega's (2000) meta-analysis of carefully selected forty-nine studies, explicit teaching of Focus on Form in a meaningful context seems to be rated the highest. Explicit learning through traditional Focus on Forms comes second. Then implicit Focus on Form comes third. The least effective was coursebook exercises without any interventions.

Goo, Granena, Yilmaz and Novella (2015) conducted a follow up meta-analysis study, looking at eleven studies from Norris and Ortega (2000) and an additional twenty-three studies published between 1999 and 2011. The results confirm the similar larger effect size of explicit learning. Other meta-analysis studies resulted in similar tendencies e.g. Spada and Tomita (2010), investigating the effect of implicit vs explicit learning in relation to grammar and R. Ellis, Loewen and Erlam (2006), on the effect of implicit and explicit feedback on learning grammar items. Schmitt (2008) discusses implicit and explicit learning of vocabulary and emphasises the optimal combination of vocabulary instruction and implicit exposure.

What we are concerned with is how such seemingly overwhelming positive results for explicit learning in a meta-analysis could be misinterpreted as the definitive conclusion to the explicit vs implicit debate. We must remember that all the authors of these meta-analysis studies listed in the previous paragraph add notes of caution. For example, Norris and Ortega (2000) provide an extensive discussion on potential caveats of their studies. They point out that:

- the measurement of the improvement induced by instruction tends to favour more explicit types of performance, thus resulting in supporting explicit interventions;
- the implicit instruction in these studies tends to be a single type of "implicit" exposure, whereas explicit interventions typically involve different types, such as rule presentation, focused practice, negative feedback and rule reviews;
- the durability of learning is only based on the small number of studies that included delayed post-tests;
- the validity and quality of primary research need improving;
- the result of their meta-analysis has limited generalisability, due to problems with sampling, with the comparability of the primary research, and with statistical calculations.

It is the first caveat that worries us most. If the pre- and post-tests feature discrete-item tasks, such as filling in blanks because they are more reliable than open-ended activities, then any treatment that includes performing discrete-item tasks will inevitably be favoured over one that does not. There is also the problem that explicit learning can be achieved fairly quickly and therefore immediate plus delayed tests can give a fairly reliable indication of increased explicit knowledge. Implicit acquisition takes time, plus many meaningful encounters subsequent to the period of treatment. Tests taken immediately after treatment will be misleading and will give no indication of eventual acquisition. Most important, though, is an unasked question about what the tests are intended to measure. If, as surely it is, our main concern is the eventual achievement of communicative competence, then tests of explicit learning of declarative knowledge cannot be used. The pre- and post-tests in any valid comparison of effectiveness must be measurements of the ability to achieve intended effects in a contextualised context of communication.

In addition, we also share concerns expressed in Chaudron (2006) and Simpson (2017) about the misleading term "effect size" and the resulting ranking comparisons.

A meta-analysis tries to summarise a large number of primary studies of interest (e.g. those that have compared the effect of implicit vs explicit treatment on a pre-/post-test improvement measure), using a statistical measurement called the effect size.

Simpson (2017) explains:

> Indeed, it might be argued that "effect size" is badly named. It is not simply a measure of the size of an effect at all and it might have been better named "effect clarity": a large d indicates that, for that particular intervention, between the two groups used and, on the measure, selected, the difference is very clear. But that does not mean the difference is large or important or educationally significant. (Simpson, 2017, p. 463)

In relation to Norris and Ortega (2000, p. 147) saying "explicit types of instruction are more effective than implicit types", according to their ranking of effect size, explicit instruction is ranked highest and implicit Focus on Forms lowest, Simpson (2017) points out how "effect size" could change if the design is scrutinised: e.g. sampling methods; similarity between treatment and tests.

Simpson goes on to advise: "If one wishes to make judgements about more or less effective educational interventions, then studies must use the same comparisons, measures and range of participants." Such studies will show the effectiveness without resorting to standardised "effect size".

If teachers, policy makers, materials developers and researchers mistake "effect size" for what it is not, and prioritise explicit teaching over implicit teaching, then this could have serious consequences for SLA research, and even more serious consequences for its application to practice.

The Neurobiological Explanation of Implicit and Explicit Learning

Converging evidence from human functional MRI scanning of intact brains, from patient research and from computational models seems to indicate that there are separate underlying neurobiological systems associated with implicit and explicit learning and with the storage of the respective memories (Morgan-Short & Ullman, 2012; Gazzaniga, Ivry & Mangun, 2019).

The explicit memory network formation (N.B. more commonly called "declarative memory" in neuroscience) of facts and events, such as episodic memories, is associated with the medial temporal lobe and the diencephalon, including the hippocampus (memory formation) and amygdala (emotional association). Implicit memory, on the other hand, (more commonly called "procedural memory" or "non-declarative memory" in neuroscience) is believed to be processed in various areas of subcortical structures that are not amenable to conscious awareness (e.g. basal ganglia; striatum; cerebellum). For example, we may acquire some kind of habit without intention or awareness. Emotional associations and reflexes are other examples of implicit learning and memory.

The finding, that the processing, storing and acquisition of explicit declarative knowledge seems to involve different areas of the brain from the processing, storing and acquisition of implicit procedural knowledge, seems to invalidate theories that claim that explicit declarative knowledge can be transferred into implicit procedural knowledge through oral practice (e.g. skill acquisition theory – DeKeyser, 2007b). For an overview of the research on skill acquisition theories, see Lyster and Sato (2013).

As we have revealed in our review in the previous section, meta-analysis research has evaluated empirical studies in the last thirty years on the effectiveness of L2 instruction, and found that focused L2 instruction has been reported to result in larger target-orientated gains over implicit types in post-tests and delayed tests. But what do we gain from comparing the efficacy of implicit and explicit instruction?

Neuroscientific insights on declarative and procedural learning and memory testify to how different areas with specific functions in the brain achieve intricate communication and work together as a whole, just as our body parts with different shapes and capabilities function together in a coordinated manner. A mental process such as language learning and processing is no different. Explicit and implicit learning are both involved during the whole process of learning. In this sense, we agree with N. Ellis (2015) when he emphasises and explores how "Implicit *and* explicit learning" facilitate SLA.

Skill Acquisition Theory and Language Acquisition

Skill acquisition theory is based on John R. Anderson's ACT (Adaptive Control of Thought) (Anderson, 2016), which attempted to develop a theory to unify the human cognition system. The ACT theory distinguished declarative knowledge (i.e. the representation of facts), procedural knowledge (i.e. the representation of actions in particular situations) and a gradual automatisation process, in which declarative knowledge becomes procedural knowledge. The ACT theory has since evolved into ACT-R models (Anderson, 2016).

DeKeyser (2007b), one of the proponents of skill acquisition theory for language learning, explains how declarative knowledge develops into automatised procedural knowledge through practice. Language learning starts from conscious, controlled processing (i.e. explicit learning). DeKeyser emphasises the importance of "transfer appropriate processing", which mirrors the situations and conditions required in the target operation. For example, if a learner wants to achieve communication, then the practice needs to involve similar communicative experience. The practice will be domain specific i.e. if a learner wants productive skills then the practice will involve speaking and writing.

Skill acquisition theory is employed to justify the PPP approach (Sánchez, 2016) in which discrete linguistic features are explicitly taught and practised until the learners automatically acquire the skills needed to use the taught features.

Skill acquisition theory assumes direct transformation from explicit to implicit knowledge. Current L1 acquisition studies and SLA studies (N. Ellis, 2015) report numerous studies, showing how chunks and whole formulaic expressions are taken in for later finer neural storage provided there are significant, repeated and abundant encounters, with or without the support of attention and, possibly, consciousness. Such SLA units are meaning-focused and do not always conform to the units we traditionally find in linguistic theories (e.g. phonetics, morphology, grammar), not to speak of prescriptive discrete grammar items isolated from meaningful contexts. Skill acquisition theory does not discuss the substrates of the SLA intake process in terms of neural networks and units of processing. For example, considering that the brain has both explicit and implicit learning routes available for parallel processing, explicit to implicit linear processing arguments seem to be unsustainable. Skill acquisition theory based on the old ACT paradigm in the 1980s seems to us to be unconvincing.

Readers' Tasks

1 Without looking back at the section on explicit and implicit learning, complete the following table with your definitions:

Question	Definition
1 How would you define explicit learning?	
2 How would you define implicit learning?	
3 How would you define explicit knowledge?	
4 How would you define implicit knowledge?	
5 How would you define declarative knowledge?	
6 How would you define procedural knowledge?	

> Now read through the section again and make revisions to your definitions if you want to.
>
> 2 In your view, what is the value of implicit learning, and what is the value of explicit learning?
> 3 From your experience of language learning/teaching, do you think that skill acquisition theory is valid? Can learners acquire the ability to communicate accurately and effectively if they follow the procedure advocated by skill acquisition theory?

Applications to Practice

Despite years of abundant exposure and encounters, non-salient linguistic elements in the input (e.g. morphology, phonologically intricate features) are very difficult for L2 learners to perceive, analyse and acquire, as numerous L2 studies attest (e.g. a case study by Schmidt & Frota, 1986; larger scale studies by Perdue, 1993; N. Ellis, 2015). For example, in everyday conversation, if an L2 learner hears the word "yesterday", a morphological past tense marker such as "walk*ed*" becomes redundant and thus morphological intake or noticing of the past tense signifier might not take place through implicit learning and feedback.

The tendency found in research regarding L2 learners' non-intake of non-salient linguistic features has sparked off SLA research on the role and efficacy of explicit language learning in form-focused instruction (i.e. learners' attention is drawn to linguistic features in a meaningful communication). There are numerous studies demonstrating that L2 learners benefit from opportunities in which their conscious attention is drawn to significant features of language. Such guidance can be explicit (e.g. output-prompting feedback; explicit guidance) or implicit (e.g. recasting).

Note that this does not mean that implicit learning needs to be regarded as less effective. Neurobiological and L1 research clearly testify to the fact that in language acquisition, implicit learning is primary.

How can we incorporate explicit learning in language education planning, syllabus design, methodology, teacher development and materials development?

The first and foremost point we would like to make is the distinction between explicit learning, which SLA researchers discuss, and the explicit teaching that seems to be pervasive in practice and materials.

Explicit learning in the SLA literature focuses on the learner investing motivated attention and conscious effort to the learning of linguistic features that may not be amenable to implicit acquisition. Explicit instruction is likely to involve teachers and materials creating various opportunities in which learners are helped to notice non-salient yet significant elements of language use.

Let us provide a concrete example. A teacher may give a group task that involves learner groups interviewing people in the community, and later presenting their findings in class. The learners are interested, and some of them feel motivated by such a task. The group members need to discuss interview questions and agree before showing the draft to the tutor. The group discussion is likely to involve interactions e.g. asking for clarification, negotiation of meaning. The learners are focused primarily on meaning. When there is a communication breakdown, the members of the group will pay conscious attention to what was said. If particular words or expressions were unclear, learners will pay conscious attention to language and negotiate meaning (e.g. What do you mean by ...?; You mean ...?). When they go on to collaborative articulation of interview questions and noting them down, these learners may pay even more conscious attention to language elements (i.e. explicit learning). Such conscious comprehensible input is believed to contribute to language acquisition. The actual negotiation is explicit (i.e. conscious and attentive) but, at the same time, implicit registering of sound, meaning, contextual association, multimodal accompaniment is likely to be taking place (i.e. implicit acquisition).

During a tutorial, the tutor may give feedback to a group draft of interview questions. The tutor may find a few interview questions to be unclear and therefore ask for clarification. The tutor may recast, prompt self-correction or explicitly suggest alternatives. The group members are consciously paying attention in order to find the best linguistic choices for the communicative effect they intend to achieve. Again, explicit learning is taking place. What is often overlooked is the fact that implicit learning is likely to be taking place at the same time in the background. Eventually, some of the group members will have acquired the expressions and will be using them in a context-appropriate manner in future communication (i.e. a sign of acquisition). It might be the case that some members continue to make mistakes (an example of learner differences).

Then what do we mean by "explicit teaching"? If you reflect upon your own teaching context, does the kind of exchange described in the previous paragraphs take place in textbook exercises? Do curricula and syllabuses specify provision of environment, teaching methods and materials that enable learners and teachers to experience implicit and explicit learning in a meaning-focused, contextualised environment?

Is it the case that the syllabus lists discrete vocabulary and grammar items to be taught in sequence and isolation? Does teaching mean coverage of vocabulary and grammar items in the syllabus by using a coursebook that tests declarative knowledge using techniques such as gap filling, multiple choice, true or false, etc.? Are students asked to do pair work reading aloud of dialogues between, for example, Tom and Jane, with no information about the interactants or their context of communication, with no relevance or meaning to the students' lives, and with no reasons or purposes for doing so other than the practice of a pre-taught sentence pattern? This is how we would characterise the "explicit teaching" we have observed in classrooms around the world. Such teaching is based on theories of what has come to be called "blocking", that is simplifying the learning process by focusing on one feature or skill at a time. Recently, however, psycholinguistic and neurolinguistic research has revealed greater success in learning and retention from activities that follow the theory of "interleaving", in which mixing (or interleaving) practice of two or more new skills or features at the same time and then again at other times is recommended (Pan, 2015):

> [I]nterleaving strengthens memory associations. With blocking, a single strategy, temporarily held in short-term memory, is sufficient. That's not the case with interleaving – the correct solution changes from one practice attempt to the next. As a result, your brain is continually engaged at retrieving different responses and bringing them into short-term memory. Repeating that process can reinforce neural connections between different tasks and correct responses, which enhances learning. (Pan, 2015)

Rohrer (2009) stresses the value of both the mixing and the spacing of skills and concepts in the learning of mathematics. This is an approach that we have been following for many years, but one which only recently has received a lot of positive attention in the literature on learning. It is also an approach that is followed by the holistic methodologies we have been consistently recommending throughout this book (e.g. TDA, task-based teaching (TBLT), CLIL approaches, project-based approaches, problem-based approaches, extensive reading/listening/viewing). It is not an approach that is followed by such discrete-item-focused, forms-focused approaches as PPP.

Note the differences between explicit learning and explicit teaching. In explicit learning, learners are communicating with others while expressing themselves. In order to achieve social bonding and sharing of the same purpose, learners strive for successful communication at the required level of sophistication for a desired effect. This is the kind of explicit learning SLA researchers believe is likely to lead to language acquisition.

What we would advocate, based on our discussion of implicit and explicit learning, is that the curriculum, the syllabus, the specified methodology, and the related teacher development and materials development need to ensure sufficient implicit learning takes place as well as explicit learning. Just teaching declarative knowledge will not provide the environment necessary for language acquisition. No amount of practice will compensate for the lack of nourishing opportunities for explicit and implicit learning that the brain requires. Successful L1 acquisition requires at least five years of implicit learning, with massive meaningful exposure. In L2 acquisition, the developed brain will benefit from conscious attention to non-salient elements in comprehensible input, but the same brain will also require motivated implicit learning at the same time. It seems to us that L2 failure can often be attributed to exclusively explicit teaching, which contradicts what we now know about how the brain learns.

> **Readers' Tasks**
>
> 1 How would you incorporate a focus on implicit learning in your curriculum, syllabus, teaching methods, teacher development and materials?
> 2 How would you incorporate a focus on explicit learning in your curriculum, syllabus, teaching methods, teacher development and materials?
> 3 What proportion of class time would you give to implicit learning? Why?
> 4 What proportion of class time would you give to explicit learning? Why?

FURTHER READING

Ellis, R. (2015). *Understanding second language acquisition* (2nd ed.). Oxford: Oxford University Press.

Rebuschat, P. (Ed.). (2015). *Implicit and explicit learning of languages*. Philadelphia: John Benjamins Publishing Company.

Learner Differences

Introduction

In language schools, it is normal practice to conduct placement tests so that learners can be taught in classes that are approximately homogeneous in level. These tests need to be administered and marked quickly and reliably, and so consist usually of discrete-item tests of declarative knowledge, objective comprehension tasks, a short essay and possibly an interview. They place learners together who display similar levels of linguistic competence on that day (though possibly with very different levels of communicative proficiency), but soon the learners will diverge. More importantly, even on the day of the test, the learners will differ from each other in many significant ways. And they will be different from themselves on other days, too.

In this section, we are going to look at a few of the ways in which L2 learners differ, to consider how these differences affect their learning and to make suggestions for how we can make use of our awareness of learner differences to provide optimal learning experiences for each learner. What we have referred to as learner differences is sometimes labelled individual differences in the SLA literature.

How Do L2 Learners Differ from Each Other and from Themselves?
Language Aptitude

Even in a similarly motivated group of students taking the same course with the same content and teacher, some students seem to learn faster than others. Do these fast learners possess a special talent (i.e. aptitude)? What does aptitude consist of? Can a slow learner be trained to gain stronger aptitude?

A lot of studies on aptitude have been conducted since the 1930s in the field of psychology. Early attempts at aptitude studies centred around developing a test of aptitude that predicted L2 attainment. John Carroll and Sidney Sapon, after many trials, identified four aspects of aptitude measures (i.e. phonetic coding ability; grammatical sensitivity; implicit learning ability; memorisation ability) as the best predictors of the rate of foreign language learning and developed the Modern Language Aptitude Test (MLAT) (Carroll & Sapon, 1959). Through the years, MLAT seems to have demonstrated its robustness against other tests in predicting performance, not only on traditional language tests and formal classroom learning but also in communicative tests and in naturalistic "acquisition rich" environments (R. Ellis, 2015; Skehan, 2015).

Li (2016) conducted a meta-analysis of sixty-six primary studies on aptitude and reports that:

1. aptitude was independent of other cognitive and affective factors: it was distinct from motivation, had a negative correlation with anxiety, and overlapped with, but was distinguishable from, intelligence;
2. executive working memory was more strongly associated with aptitude and aptitude components than phonological short-term memory;
3. aptitude measured using full-length tests was a strong predictor of general L2 proficiency, but it had low predictive validity for vocabulary learning and L2 writing; and
4. different aptitude components demonstrated differential predictive validity for different aspects of learning.

(Li, 2016, p. 801)

Current thinking is that language aptitude comprises various distinct abilities (e.g. phonological sensitivity, working memory, ability to identify patterns of correspondence) that interact dynamically during the learning process (Kormos, 2013; R. Ellis, 2015; Wen, Biedron & Skehan, 2017; Andringa & Dąbrowska, 2019). This means that individual learners may differ in their constituent abilities. Recent research seems to show that aptitude is not a stable, trait-like construct and, in fact, is trainable (Kormos, 2013). Currently, research is investigating how specific abilities contribute to stages in the process of L2 acquisition and how they respond to instructional approaches (Dörnyei & Ryan, 2015; Andringa & Dąbrowska, 2019).

Research is progressing in relation to the role of working memory and the neuroscientific underpinning that may clarify the construct and mechanism of what has been called "aptitude".

There is no doubt that learners who have been placed in the same class at the beginning of a course because they have achieved equivalent scores on a placement test will nevertheless differ in both overall language-learning aptitude and in aptitude related to specific abilities that can contribute to successful language acquisition.

A couple of questions we would like to ask are: how we can explain how a learner can exhibit a weak aptitude at one time and a much stronger aptitude six months later without any deliberate intervention; and how a learner can demonstrate a very strong aptitude when learning one language and a much weaker aptitude when learning another language. Hitomi, for example, displayed a very strong aptitude when successfully learning English, and a very weak aptitude when attempting to learn Spanish and Bahasa Melayu.

The obvious implication for practice of what we know about aptitude is that teachers cannot expect all their learners to learn at the same speed or level, and that apparent failure to learn is not necessarily attributable to teacher inadequacy or learner lack of effort. We would agree to some extent with Loewen (2015) that:

> one of the best methods of ensuring that different types of aptitude are catered for is for teachers to employ a wide range of pedagogical activities, some of which may be more beneficial to some learners than to others. (Loewen, 2015, 176)

We would warn, though, of the danger of unprincipled eclecticism, which can lead to the teacher employing some activities, in order to extend their range, that do not actually benefit any of their learners. We would also suggest that offering choices of principled activities might be more beneficial for the learners. This can be done, for example, by reading the same text to all the learners, then getting them to go round the room reading activity cards, with each one specifying a different type of activity (for example, drawing the text, performing the text, continuing the text, discussing the text, analysing the text, focusing on a language feature in the text). Each learner selects one of the activities, reads the text and then does the activity individually, in a pair or in a group. We need to be careful, though, that learners do not always do the same type of activity that they are good at. One way of ensuring this is to vary the menu of activities, and to design them so that learners have time to do more than one activity in each lesson.

Motivation

Anyone working in education is likely to have witnessed how motivation is one of the major driving forces that spurs learning and, if strong enough, leads to sustained efforts and actions necessary to attain goals. The vital influence that motivation plays in L2 acquisition (be it instrumental motivation related to the achievement of a specific goal, or intrinsic motivation driven by a holistic desire to learn the language) is widely acknowledged by both researchers and practitioners. Without motivation, even a highly intelligent, competent individual may not perform to the level they are capable of. On the other hand, highly charged with currents of motivation (Dörnyei, Henry & Muir, 2015; Henry, Davydenko & Dörnyei, 2015), some learners may surpass any expectations and achieve amazing accomplishments.

Motivation in SLA theory is normally understood as the desire to initiate L2 learning and the effort employed to sustain it, reflecting the historical meaning of the original Latin word, "motivus", which means "to move". Some kind of long-term effort and actions seem to be implied. We would differentiate between motivation and interest by saying that that you are motivated *to do* something but you are interested *in* something. Interest is useful in language acquisition, but it does not always have the potential for action. Motivation is more useful, because it does carry the potential to lead to action.

Dörnyei (2019) makes an interesting comparison of the term "motivation" and of "engagement" as it is used in educational psychology:

> Engagement in educational psychology is understood as active participation and involvement in certain behaviors ... and student engagement – which refers to engagement in school-related activities and academic tasks – has recently been hailed as "the holy grail of learning" and "one of the hottest research topics in the field of educational psychology" ... This behavioral aspect is, in fact, what distinguishes the notions of engagement and motivation from each other most markedly: motivation only indicates a student's potential for actively pursuing learning (rather than how this potential is actually realised). (Dörnyei, 2019, pp. 24–25)

What is fascinating about motivation is that teachers can potentially exert an influence on learner motivation. Each student's motivation levels may vary, and their motivation may ebb or flow in the classroom dynamics. Often students enter the classroom indifferent or unmotivated, but then an appealing activity might motivate them. In some cases, they may be moderately motivated, but then a negative classroom experience could demotivate them. Motivation can be created and strengthened through orchestration of the learning environment through curriculum, assessment, teacher development, methods, materials, technology and teachers' choices of language and activities.

Lamb (2017) provides a very useful overview of studies which are pedagogically relevant, including studies of "motivational strategies" which teachers may consider deploying to encourage learner motivation. He also summarises theories which have direct relevance to learner motivation such as Self-Determination Theory in which Deci and Ryan (1985) discuss intrinsic and extrinsic motivation, Dörnyei's (2009b) L2 Motivational Self System and some more recent theories that are likely to feature in future discussion of motivation. Muir (2020) focuses on directed motivational currents and the implications of research findings on the effects of such currents for the pedagogy of language education. The focus of this approach is on creating intense motivational periods that energise learners into performance beyond their expected level, a goal we have been intuitively trying to achieve for many years through teacher performance of stories, jokes, plays, songs, dances etc. at the beginning of lessons (what we refer to as task-free activities).

Our experience of learners of English in many countries of the world is that, despite all the attention paid to globalisation in the literature, they are not particularly motivated to learn English and they stand to gain very little benefit from doing so. For example, what does a student stand to gain who is living in a remote area of Kalimantan, where all transport is by boat and speakers of English are rare? What we have found, though, is that teachers can motivate such learners to want to read, listen to and view texts, and to participate in tasks that are meaningful, relevant and potentially engaging. And if that happens enough, the learner can gradually not only be motivated to read a text and do a task but eventually to want to make the effort to learn English too. We watched this happen in a school in Turkey, where a class were observed to be unmotivated to participate with a teacher who just went through all the activities in a global coursebook, and were then observed to be eager to participate in lessons in which a different teacher had prepared materials that engaged the learners affectively and cognitively and achieved context and learner authenticity.

We have also observed learners motivating themselves. Hitomi, in fact, is a classic example. As a young teenager, she "fell in love" with John Lennon and wanted to learn English in the hope that one day she might marry him. She learned all the Beatles' songs, and sought out experiences of English in use. She became proficient in English, and this success motivated her to seek even more opportunities for improvement and to become intrinsically motivated. Ironically, at this time Brian was teaching English at Quarry Bank, the school John Lennon went to in Liverpool, and remembers discussing his songs in English lessons, as well as one of his students writing to John Lennon and getting a letter back. Even more ironically, Hitomi is now sometimes mistaken for Yoko Ono.

Brian, incidentally, was not motivated to learn French at school until he was offered a place on a BA course in English Language and Literature at the University of Liverpool, on condition that he passed A-Level French, and his parents paid for a private tutor to help him. The tutor turned out to have recently been crowned Miss Blackpool, and this might have contributed to Brian's instrumental motivation. He managed to pass French, go to the University of Liverpool and fail to develop any communicative competence in French whatsoever.

Our point is that it is possible for teachers to motivate learners, and it is possible for learners to motivate themselves (with varying degrees of success).

> **Readers' Tasks**
>
> 1 Think about a teacher who managed to motivate you to learn. What did they do to achieve this?
> 2 List things you think teachers should do to try to motivate their learners to learn.

Affect

An elephant in the classroom? – As we have stressed many times throughout this book, affect is vital for language learning, yet in our view it has often been overlooked and neglected, both in SLA research and in the classroom.

Arnold and Brown (1999, p. 1), after evaluating various definitions, provide a broad definition of "affect" as "aspects of emotion, feeling, mood or attitude which condition behaviour", and they go on to demonstrate how vital it is in determining the success or otherwise of learners' attempts to acquire an L2.

We also strongly believe that affect (of both teachers and learners) is one of the fundamental factors in successful language learning. Based on our own experience of working as teachers and also of working with teachers around the world, we know that teachers would agree with us regarding the vital importance of learners' motivation, emotion, engagement, moods, attitudes, self-esteem, confidence and aspirations. They would probably also agree with the teachers and researchers writing in Martinez Agudo (2018) about the emotional challenges, requirements and rewards of being an L2 teacher.

We have observed, for example, that teachers all over the world are often conscious that the demands of syllabus coverage and exams exert negative pressure (Roberts, 2020) and often conflict with their desire to provide their learners with motivating and engaging experience of the target language in use. Many of them have told us that they have a hard time trying to persuade not necessarily motivated students to engage with L2 language learning in often underprivileged and demanding conditions.

What makes the situation even more challenging is that the vital importance of affect has not really been fully acknowledged in many SLA theories, in curricula, in assessment, in teacher development, in methodology and especially in materials, as they all still seem to prioritise the cognitive learning of language codes and rules.

"Affective Turn" in SLA theories

SLA researchers themselves are beginning to discuss the predominant bias in the past toward cognitive language processing in the fields of SLA and cognitive psychology. Affective elements have often been "poorly studied, poorly understood, seen as inferior to rational thought" (Swain, 2013) and in fact, "have been almost absent from the applied linguistics agenda" (Martinez Agudo, 2018, p. 4). However, the last decade has seen something of a surge of publications focusing on the affective dimension of language learning (Gabrys & Bielska, 2013; Pavlenko, 2013; Prior, 2019).

There is a growing awareness that the separation of cognition and affect/emotion/feeling distorts what we know about how the brain functions and learns. From a neuroscientific perspective, Damasio and Carvalho (2013, p. 143) define "feeling" as "mental experiences of body states". They explain that the "felt experience" may signify not only physiological need such as hunger, pain, fear, anger and well-being, but also more socially inspired reactions such as "compassion, gratitude or love". The dynamic, individual and complex nature of "motivation" (Dörnyei & Ushioda, 2013) seems to fit well with a visceral biological and cognitive account based on in-built desire for better biological and social survival (Lee, Mikesell, Joaquin, Mates & Schumann, 2009).

Damasio and Carvalho (2013, p. 150) argue that: "Feeling paved the way for the establishment of higher levels of cognition and consciousness, culminating in the modern human mind". In fact, the title of the article by Immordino-Yang and Damasio (2007) "We feel therefore we learn: The relevance of affective and social neuroscience to education" sums up their view of how sentience (i.e. the ability to feel, perceive, or experience subjectively in contrast to reasoning) controls learning, attention, memory, decision making and social functioning. Bolte Taylor (2009, p. 19), a neuroscientist, confirms such a claim based on her own experience of recovering from a stroke, by saying that "Although many of us may think of ourselves as thinking creatures that feel, biologically we are feeling creatures that think".

Immordino-Yang and Damasio (2007, p. 9) warn that "neither learning nor recall happen in a purely rational domain, divorced from emotion, even though some of our knowledge will eventually distil into a moderately rational, unemotional form". They also point out that unmemorable knowledge inherently does not transfer well to the real world situation.

Masuhara (2016) exemplifies how learner behaviours will vary when affect gets involved:

> Imagine an EFL learner who associates reading with painful translation routines. Consciously she may tell herself that she needs to learn to read fluently in L2 as her extrinsic motivation is to pass the exams in order to gain entry to an esteemed university. Right after reading she knows that she will be tested on her comprehension and on the language contained in the text. What would be her internal state and her feeling? What kinds of research data would a researcher get if this girl was a respondent in the questionnaire and interview studies on motivation in relation to classroom language

learning? Would she be able to articulate why she reads in the way she does during reading lessons? The same learner, however, may read with far superior comprehension if she were to receive a love letter in English from the boy of her dreams. What would be her internal states and her feeling then? If there were unfamiliar words, would she be able to work out their meaning and moreover learn them? (Masuhara, 2016, pp. 27–28)

We would like to reiterate that language acquisition is more likely to take place when the learner is affectively engaged by a text or task, when the learner feels positive about the learning experience, and when the learner achieves self-esteem. Such affective experience is unlikely to be provided by simple practice of a grammatical structure in decontextualised sentences. However, it can be provided by immersion in a humorous, dramatic, moving or controversial text, by a task that offers the learner an achievable challenge in relation to a situation that is meaningful to the learner, by a classroom environment that is stimulating and supportive and by achievement in successful communication.

Based on our understanding of how affect drives learning, memory, recall and retrieval, we would strongly argue that teaching approaches should aim ultimately to provide opportunities for the self-fulfilment of learners. The brain is designed to preserve and enhance life by learning. In this sense, relevance, meaningfulness and the engagement value of materials to the individual play crucial roles. Activities should ideally be engaging and contribute so much to the well-being of the learners that they want more and look forward to coming to class or to working in a support group or on their own (Fredrickson & Branigan, 2005). The bias toward factual knowledge and objective analysis in the learning environment needs to be rebalanced with the notion of sentience (i.e. the ability to feel, perceive or experience subjectively) in the mind. The implications here are that the potential for affective engagement should be the prime criterion when writing, selecting or adapting texts and tasks and that learner choice of texts and tasks should be a vital consideration when designing and using materials. Ways of achieving this would include helping learners to select or find a text that they want to use with the tasks specified in their materials or selecting from a menu of tasks those they want to use in response to a potentially engaging text.

We would like to sum up this brief but crucial section on affect by emphasising three things:

1. Learners should be given an engaging and holistic experience of acquiring their target language and not just be restricted to the discrete learning and practice of language items.
2. Teachers should adapt and supplement their coursebook materials with activities which their learners really want to do and which motivate them through enjoyment, fun, laughter and achievable challenge.

3 Good teaching is an emotionally charged event, where teachers connect with each student as they passionately deliver their lesson in a pleasurable environment. Such classrooms reflect an environment where both students and teacher are enthusiastic and excited as they discover learning and risk-taking in a safe environment.

(T. S. C. Farrell, Foreword to Martinez Agudo, 2018, p. vii)

The third point above is obviously a statement of the ideal, and is not always realisable given, for example, the workload of many teachers, the unattractiveness of many classrooms and the demotivated exhaustion of many learners. We believe, though, that it should always be a focal goal of teacher development and an aim for every teacher. We know it can be attained, because we have observed excited classes in Indonesia enjoying TPR Plus lessons with students from other classes crowding the windows to take part too, we have observed efforts by teachers and students in Indonesia to enrich their schools with plants and flowers and murals on the walls, and also in Indonesia we have observed invigorated students going out into their city to look for free copies of books, magazines, comics and even labels to contribute to their nascent class library of extensive readers kept in a cardboard box donated by their ingenious teacher.

Readers' Tasks

1 Think of another learner difference that we have not focused on in 4 and write a paragraph about it.
2 Find references on the web or in your library to the difference you have focused on. Add these references to your paragraph.
3 Think of possible ways of helping learners in relation to the difference you have focused on. Add these to your paragraph.
4 If you are studying with a class or support group, share your paragraph with other members of your class or group.

FURTHER READING

Dörnyei, Z. & Ryan, S. (2015). *The psychology of the language learner revisited.* New York: Routledge.

Ellis, R. (2012). Instruction, individual differences and L2 learning. *Language teaching research and language pedagogy* (pp. 307–335). Chichester: Wiley-Blackwell.

(2015). *Understanding second language acquisition* (2nd ed.). Oxford: Oxford University Press.

Loewen, S. (2015). *Introduction to instructed second language acquisition* (pp. 162–178). New York, NJ: Routledge.

Prior, M. T. (2019). Elephants in the room: An "affective turn," or just feeling our way? *The Modern Language Journal, 103*(2), 516–527.

Swain, M. (2013). The inseparability of cognition and emotion in second language learning. *Language Teaching, 46*(2), 195–207.

Authenticity in Language Acquisition

The notion of authenticity has frequently been discussed and heatedly debated in ELT (for a detailed review, see Mishan, 2005) ever since the advent of the Communicative Approach in the 1970's, which sought "genuineness" and "realism" in teaching and materials development.

Buendgens-Kosten (2014, p. 457) points out, "In the widest sense, 'authenticity' is related to the notion of 'realness' and 'trueness to origin'. What is meant by 'real' and 'true to origin' varies according to the users, contexts and purposes".

In the 1970s, "realness" and "trueness of origin" in relation to the term "authenticity" seem to have been used to mean how English is used in Inner Circle countries (Kachru, 1985) by mainly monolingual "native speakers" (Widdowson, 1979; Quirk, 1991; Ortega, 2019; see also Kachru, 1991 in response to Quirk, 1990).

In recent years, the need for redefining authenticity has been stressed in relation to spoken and written corpora of various kinds of English, the spread of global Englishes and the availability of digital communication (e.g. Internet, social media) at the users' disposal.

We will first establish our definition of authenticity, and then focus our discussion on how authenticity might influence language acquisition and development.

Definition of Authenticity

Often-cited classic definitions of authenticity include those by Widdowson (1979) and by Morrow (1977).

In discussing authenticity, Widdowson (1979) differentiates "genuine text" and "authentic use of them". According to Widdowson (1979, p. 89), genuine text means "an instance of discourse, designed to meet a communicative purpose, directed at people playing their roles in a normal social context".

"Authenticity", on the other hand, "is a characteristic of the relationship between the passage and the reader and it has to do with appropriate response" (ibid., p. 80). He argues that the "desired aim" (Widdowson, 1979, p. 169) is to use a text that will "correspond to [. . .] normal communicative activities" (ibid., p. 80).

It is interesting to note that Widdowson's view seems to be that genuineness resides in the text and authenticity emerges during the interaction between the text and the reader, adding that ideally authenticity reflects the "genuineness" of the original communicative activities.

Morrow (1977, p. 13) defines an "authentic text" as "a stretch of real language, produced by a real speaker or writer for a real audience and designed to convey a real message".

Considering both influential definitions, we wonder what they had in mind when they described "people playing their roles in a normal social context", "normal communicative activities" (Widdowson, 1979) and "a real speaker, writer, audience" (Morrow, 1977).

Buendgens-Kosten (2014, p. 458) notes that the use of the term "'authenticity' for both 'features of a text' and for 'features of its use' ... has remained common practice in ELT discourse, and texts written by a native speaker, or for native speakers, or for non-language-learning purposes, tend to continue to be referred to as 'authentic'".

Such a traditional association with native-speaker use of language does not exactly match the contemporary reality in which English is widely used as a lingua franca around the physical and virtual world, in which varieties of English evolve and proliferate and in which the origins of an output may not always be evident. For example, when Nelson Mandela made the three-hour speech entitled "I Am Prepared to Die" on 20 April 1964 at the Rivonia Trial, Mandela, a non-native user of English, used English as an additional language "to meet a communicative purpose, directed at a people playing their roles in a normal social context ..." (Widdowson, 1979, p. 89). His speech is "a stretch of real language, produced by a real speaker or writer for a real audience and designed to convey a real message" (Morrow, 1977). The authenticity of Mandela's text may be best appreciated in the context of the trial in South Africa, but readers belonging to different generations in different geographical and political contexts may choose to interpret the text in different ways and make use of it within their own contexts.

What is "real" English? Which origin are we talking about? What does authenticity mean in the contemporary context? Which English should we teach and how? At the moment, language policy in many countries, international high-stake examinations and materials are still very much based on the traditional "native-speaker paradigms" and are functioning as gate keepers, while authenticity of texts and tasks in the global and information age is being questioned and debated (Pinnard, 2016; Maley & Tomlinson, 2017; Mishan, 2017).

There is another dimension to the definition of authenticity. Traditionally, authenticity has been discussed in terms of text authenticity and task authenticity, as in Widdowson's (1979) distinction of genuine text and authenticity in its use. Reflecting current developments, Tomlinson (2017) identifies an additional four perspectives of authenticity in addition to text and task authenticity: "context authenticity", "curriculum authenticity", "learner and teacher authenticity" and "theoretical authenticity".

For example, materials developers may have carefully selected a text that is based on a genuine text in the sense that it had been produced for communicative purposes and not for language-teaching purposes (i.e. text authenticity). They may have made use of the authentic text and developed authentic tasks that are meaning-focused, have a communicative purpose and aim to achieve intended effects (i.e. task authenticity). What the producers thought of as authentic in terms of text and tasks for a certain predetermined context (e.g. materials written for the European market), however, may not be received by the users as appropriate and relevant in terms of their learning contexts (e.g. materials users in Africa, Asia, the Middle East). The content of the text or tasks may seem, for instance, to be culturally alien, pedagogically unsuitable and in conflict with the assessment system (i.e. context authenticity). There are cases in which governments request materials developers to produce innovative materials that incorporate methods recommended by experts at the time. Materials developers, however, might find a mismatch between their materials and the existing curriculum (i.e. curriculum authenticity), see, for example, the reports from Asia regarding problems with the implementation of TBLT in Thomas and Reinders (2015). Even when the materials have satisfied authenticity in terms of text, task, context and curriculum, because materials developers have specifically tailor-made their materials according to specifications, there is a possibility that they fail to engage or to satisfy the needs and wants of teachers and/or learners (i.e. learner and teacher authenticity) when they are used in classrooms. Materials, on the other hand, may be well-received by the users but may not achieve consistent adherence to a principled and evidence-supported theory (i.e. theoretical authenticity) and it is questionable whether the materials will actually facilitate language acquisition and development as a result of use. One very obvious way of achieving all the different types of authenticity outlined is through peer interaction focused on an issue of local significance (as in a project approach or a process drama approach). Another obvious approach would be a text-driven approach, in which the learners select the core text from a library of texts with the potential for affective and cognitive engagement, and at each stage select the tasks from a menu. The library would consist of texts chosen both for their potential for engagement and their text authenticity, and the menu of tasks would satisfy the contextual and communicative criteria for task authenticity.

Mishan (2017) adds the dimension of "digital authenticity", in which the text involves multimodality and the co-creation of text by interlocutors through synchronous or asynchronous online interactions. This is an important criterion for teenagers and young adults in areas with easy and reliable connectivity, but this still does not apply to all the parts of the world where learners are trying to acquire an L2. A coursebook, for example, that achieves digital authenticity risks alienating learners by its lack of contextual and learner authenticity if it is used with learners living in areas with low digital awareness or connectivity, for example, remote areas of Sarawak for which no suitable coursebook has been published. At the MATSDA/SISU Conference at the Shanghai International Studies University in 2018, Tamas Kiss and Hazelynn Rimbar, in their presentation on "EFL Materials off the Grid", showed how students in remote secondary schools in Sarawak were bewildered by the modern technical world depicted in the global coursebooks their teachers were obliged to use with them. They also demonstrated though how it was possible to achieve affective and cognitive engagement with these contextually inauthentic materials by linking them to the students' own environment, experience and lives.

As discussed so far, we believe that authenticity is a multifaceted notion and should be defined as such. Therefore, our definition of authenticity refers to communicative production of (or response to) a spoken, written or multimedia text produced for communicative purposes (not for teaching or learning purposes) in order to achieve nonlinguistic real-life outcomes appropriate to the context of production. The interlocutors can be native or non-native speakers, the production can be a monologue or dialogue, the production can be as short as a phrase or as long as a novel, the production can be live (as in group discussion) or recorded, but the response must be meaning-focused rather than pedagogic.

Referring to how authenticity may relate to pedagogy and materials, Tomlinson and Masuhara (2018c) argue:

> [W]hat is considered authentic in design because it is seen as representative of how the target language is typically used might not be perceived as authentic in action or in reflection because the users do not perceive the relevance or value of the materials. The ideal is therefore for the designers to try to ensure that their materials achieve authenticity in design, in use and in reflection. (Tomlinson & Masuhara, 2018c, p. 33)

Readers' Tasks

1 Turn to any two-page spread in a coursebook and evaluate it for:
   - text authenticity
   - task authenticity
   - context authenticity (in relation to a context you would use it in)
   - curriculum authenticity (in relation to the curriculum you would use it with)
   - learner authenticity (in relation to learners you would use it with)
   - teacher authenticity (in relation to your own experience and capabilities)
   - theoretical authenticity (in relation to theoretical principles of language learning that you believe in)
2 Suggest ways in which the two-page spread you have evaluated could be made more authentic.

The Relationship between Authenticity and Language Acquisition and Development

A lot of SLA researchers and experts provide direct or indirect arguments in support of using authentic texts. For example:

- Listening to, viewing and reading authentic texts provides rich and varied input, which is a prerequisite for implicit and incidental language acquisition and development (Mishan, 2005; Gilmore, 2007, 2011; Maley, 2008; Krashen, 2011; Renandya & Farrell, 2011; Tomlinson, 2011b, 2013c, 2016a; Ghosn, 2016).
- Being engaged in interactions between interlocutors (e.g. expressing views, negotiating meaning, requesting for clarification) can provide comprehensible input (Long, 1996, 2015; Mackey, 2006; Loewen, 2015; Sato & Ballinger, 2016) and also push the learner into comprehensible output (Swain, 2005).
- Being asked to clarify or rephrase through feedback helps learners consciously pay attention to language features in a meaning-focused manner (Schmidt, 1990, 2012; Long, 1996, 2015; Mackey, Abbuhl & Gass, 2012).
- Being exposed to genuine texts prepares learners for challenges in real-life communication by sensitising them to the use of English in the real world (Mishan, 2005; Gilmore 2011; Tomlinson, 2016a; Maley & Tomlinson, 2017).

On the other hand, some researchers argue for the simplification or enhancement of authentic texts to reduce the potentially negative effects of using demanding authentic texts. For example, they say that authentic texts may turn out to be too complex and difficult for learners, due to ungraded vocabulary, grammar or cultural associations (Yano, Long & Ross, 1994; Day & Bamford, 1998; Day, 2003). They say that implicit exposure to authentic spoken or written texts may not help learners to notice less salient aspects of language as learners are focused on more meaning-bearing elements, such as nouns and verbs. And they say that authentic texts may not provide the frequency and density of target-language items compared to texts enhanced through flooding (e.g. intentional repeated use of the target vocabulary or expressions), highlighting or elaborating. What is interesting to us is the fact that neither simplification nor enhancement seem to result in significant improvements in comprehension or in acquisition (Leow, 1993; Han, Park & Combs, 2008) whereas engaged reading of authentic texts does (Maley, 2008; Krashen, 2011; Gilmore, 2011; Renandya & Farrell, 2011; Ghosn, 2016).

What we find most significant is that the debate on the values of using authentic texts seems to focus on linguistic processing, and possibly overlooks the role of affective elements such as motivation and the need and want to listen, read or communicate, the role of contextual factors in creating crucial connections in the brain and the roles of affective and cognitive engagement in strengthening networks and records in the brain. Possibly the greatest benefit that authentic input and use of the L2 can provide the learner is experience of situated, embodied, sociocultural, multisensory and multimodal use of the L2. N. Ellis

(2019) stresses the importance of such experience in the acquisition of a language and says, for example:

> Embodied cognition is the recognition that much of cognition is shaped by this body we inhabit – by aspects of the entire body including the motor system, the perceptual system, bodily interactions with the environment (situatedness), and by the assumptions about the world that become built into the structure of the organism as a result of repeated experience. (N. Ellis, 2019, p. 41)

In his article, N. Ellis makes many pertinent points that we would entirely agree with and that offer strong support for an approach to language teaching providing a rich experience of authentic language in use. For example, he says: "Learning and remembering are always situated. Their contexts extend beyond the here and now, streaming backwards in time through our personal and cultural histories" (N. Ellis, 2019, p. 49); he says also "an individual's creative linguistic competence emerges from the collaboration of the memories of all the meaningful interactions in their entire history of language usage" (N. Ellis, 2019, p. 49); and he says: "Language learning involves learning the associations within and between constructions." (N. Ellis, 2019, p. 50). We certainly support the usage-based approaches advocated by N. Ellis and we would hope that he would agree with us that such approaches need to be based on the provision of learner opportunities for experience of authentic language in use.

We are not arguing that every text and every task used in the classroom must be authentic. Contriving texts to facilitate discovery of a language feature can promote language awareness (e.g. Bolitho & Tomlinson, 1995), especially of those features of the language that are not typically salient and might not be amenable to implicit acquisition. Also, pedagogic tasks can facilitate skills development (e.g. getting learners to use the skill of seeking clarification to get information from the only group member who has seen a drawing they have been tasked with reproducing). What we are arguing, though, is that if the learners' classroom experience lacks text authenticity, task authenticity, context authenticity, learner authenticity and theoretical authenticity, the learners are highly unlikely to achieve acquisition and development at a satisfactory level. They are also going to be incapable of operating successfully in their post-course world, as they will have had no prior experience of authentic language use. Of course, on the other hand, gaining experience of authentic communication during their course does not guarantee the achievement of communicative competence, though it does increase the likelihood of doing so. It all depends on the quality of the learner's experience of authenticity. If an authentic text is incomprehensible, or if it lacks meaningfulness or engagement for the learner, it is highly unlikely to stimulate rich intake. If an authentic task is too easy or much too difficult for the learner, if it does not require the understanding or production of authentic use of the L2, or if it lacks relevance or engagement, it is also highly unlikely to stimulate rich intake. What learners need is experience of authentic texts and tasks that is meaningful, relevant, situated, affectively engaging, cognitively engaging, achievably challenging, and ideally embodied and multimodal. They need to exploit the potential of authentic texts and tasks to facilitate the achievement of intake that is rich in "information" about how the L2 is used to achieve communicative effect and that stimulates multiple connections and multisensory associations.

In many ways, what we have just said above about what learners need in relation to authenticity is an apt summary of our position on what we can learn as teachers from what has been found about language acquisition. There is still much to be discovered and many issues unresolved, which space does not allow us to deal with in this volume. For example, what effect on acquisition and development do confidence, attitude, needs, wants, experience, age, cognitive ability and tolerance of ambiguity have, and what explains how the same learner can perform differently on different days, with different people, on different tasks and with different topics? For discussion of some of these issues, see Granena (2013), Granena and Long (2013), R. Ellis (2012, 2015) and Loewen (2015).

To conclude this chapter, we took a coursebook from our shelf and opened it at random on a two-page spread and evaluated the two pages scoring out of five against the following criteria:

- opportunities for implicit learning
- potential for affective engagement
- text authenticity
- task authenticity

The book was Eales and Oakes (2012) and the pages were 92–93. What we found was;

- There were two opportunities for implicit learning from peer-discussion tasks. (3/5)
- There were four texts offering potential for affective engagement because they each focused on a difficult decision. The peer discussions about the decisions also offered potential for affective engagement because they focused on the learners' own views (though the difficulty created by needing to use conditionals could move the focus from meaning to forms). (3/5)
- Three of the texts achieved text authenticity. The fourth was contrived as practice for completion with the correct form of the verbs in brackets. (4/5)
- Six of the eight tasks that followed the reading of the texts were surface-comprehension or practice tasks. Two of them focused on discussion of issues in the texts with the questions phrased so as to elicit use of the target structure (conditionals). The learners did not at any time use the target language with the main purpose of achieving communicative intentions. (2/5)
- If the coursebook was being used in remote areas of Asia or Africa (as it often is) it would be unlikely to achieve learner authenticity, as the topics (the Euro Millions, a

hiker on Mont Blanc, a mother informing on her shop-breaker son, and computer theft in the office) would be unlikely to be meaningful for many learners. (2/5)

This book, like most coursebooks we look at, has great potential to facilitate language acquisition. Unfortunately though, in our view, the priority given to grammar and the typical closed questions the book uses compromise this potential. See Tomlinson and Masuhara (2013) for a detailed evaluation of a number of coursebooks, which came to a similar conclusion.

> ## Readers' Tasks
>
> A
> 1 Do you think you can use authentic texts and authentic tasks with beginners? Why/Why not?
> 2 What do you think are the advantages and disadvantages of using authentic texts?
> 3 How can you overcome the disadvantages of using authentic texts?
>
> B
> 1 Select one of the following: confidence, attitude, needs, wants, experience, age, cognitive ability and tolerance of ambiguity. Write a paragraph on what you think is the role of your selected topic in SLA.
> 2 Find references on the web or in your library to the topic you have focused on. Use these references to revise your paragraph.
> 3 Think of possible ways of helping learners in relation to the topic you have focused on. Add these to your paragraph.
> 4 If you are studying with a class or support group share your paragraph with other members of your class or group.
>
> C
> 1 Select a coursebook you are familiar with.
> 2 Turn to any page at random.
> 3 Evaluate the page in relation to the criteria of:
> - opportunities for implicit learning
> - potential for affective engagement
> - text authenticity
> - task authenticity
> - contextual authenticity (in relation to the context you are working in)
> - learner authenticity (in relation to the context you are working in)
>
> For each criterion, give a score out of five.
>
> 4 Think of ways of adapting the material so as to increase the score for each criterion.

FURTHER READING

Ellis, N. (2019). Essentials of a theory of language cognition. *The Modern Language Journal*, 103, 39–60.

Gilmore, A. (2007). Authentic materials and authenticity in foreign language learning. *Language Teaching* **40**, 97–118.

Maley, A. & Tomlinson, B. (Eds.). (2017). *Authenticity in materials development for language learning.* Newcastle: Cambridge Scholars.

SUMMARY

In this chapter we have focused on five important but seemingly different issues in SLA research and practice. Our five sections, however, are connected by our informed convictions that:

- for input to facilitate intake, it needs to be rich, meaningful and engaging (for example, when learners use their L1 to clarify an L2 text or contribute to an L2 interaction, or when they engage in an authentic experience of the L2 in use);
- learners need to learn their L2 both implicitly and explicitly with the priority being given to implicit learning if the main objective of the course is to facilitate interactional competence (for example, when learners and their teacher cooperate to provide communicative feedback during authentic interaction, but then the teacher follows this up by setting remedial tasks focused on salient linguistic or pragmatic features of the interaction);
- learners need to be agents of their own learning (as, for example, when setting themselves their own out of class tasks, when seeking clarification during interaction, when initiating topics and directions in projects, simulations and tasks and when making discoveries about language use);
- learners need to use the L2 for purposeful communication (rather than just practise its grammar, lexis and pronunciation) so as to strengthen intake, reinforce or revise hypotheses, gain informative implicit and explicit feedback on their achievement of intended effects, gain confidence, elicit rich input and gain experience of the strategies needed to achieve authentic and successful communication;
- learners need to be affectively and cognitively engaged whether they are using their L1 or L2, whether they are learning in their own way or collaborating with others, whether they are gaining implicit or explicit feedback and when they are gaining authentic experience of the language in use.

FURTHER READING

Ellis, R. (2015). *Understanding second language acquisition* (2nd ed.). Oxford: Oxford University Press.

Loewen, S. (2015). *Introduction to instructed second language acquisition* (pp. 162–178). New York: Routledge.

Summary

Introduction

We have decided to finish our book by providing a brief summary of the main points and recommendations we have made. But first we would like to stress the most obvious application of generally accepted theories of SLA. This would be to stop planning for, preparing for and delivering transmission approaches to the teaching of languages, and to start encouraging planners, curriculum and materials developers, teacher trainers, assessors and teachers to work together to promote experiential approaches to language learning in which learners are active agents of their own learning, benefiting from the exposure to language in use, from the opportunities for language use and from the opportunities for discovery they help to create.

Useful Theories of SLA that Could Be Applied to Practice

Here are some of the theories we have discussed, which we feel could and should be applied to practice:

In order to develop communicative competence in an L2, learners need:

- a rich exposure to contextualised, extensive, embodied and purposeful use of the language
- opportunities to use the language for purposeful communication
- to be cognitively engaged
- to be affectively engaged
- to be motivated to make the effort to learn, either intrinsically, extrinsically or by a particular teacher, group of learners, coursebook or even task
- to notice how language items, features and strategies are typically used to achieve communication
- to receive help and feedback from peers and teachers when requested
- to look out for opportunities to experience the language outside their course

- to make discoveries for themselves about how language items, features and strategies are typically used to achieve communication
- to become autonomous learners

In order to help their learners to develop communicative competence in an L2, teachers need to:

- supplement their courses with potentially engaging written, spoken and multimodal texts
- offer extra opportunities for their learners to engage in purposeful communication during and outside the course
- cater for learner difference by offering choices of methodology, texts, activities and commitment
- encourage their learners to take responsibility and initiative
- prioritise the potential for affective and cognitive engagement when selecting and adapting texts and activities
- ensure that texts and activities are meaningful for their learners
- adapt a primarily form-focused in meaning-focused approach
- focus on helping their learners to become appropriate and effective communicators, and not just fluent and/or accurate users of a language
- focus on helping their learners not only to acquire implicit procedural knowledge of the target language but also to help them gain explicit declarative knowledge of it too
- be available as resources to provide help and feedback when requested before, during and after learner activities
- ensure spaced recycling of language items and features in their learners' input.

Ways of Applying Useful Theories to Practice

Here are some of the approaches and activities that we have recommended for applying SLA theories to methodologies and materials. Note that they are all holistic, humanistic approaches providing mixed and spaced experience of skills and concepts, rather than discretely focused linguistic approaches restricting learner attention to one language feature, skill or concept at a time.

Approaches

- Text-Driven (TDA) approaches, in which a potentially engaging written, spoken or multimodal text drives a class or a unit of materials instead of a discrete teaching point
- Task-Based (TBT) approaches, in which learners make use of their existing linguistic resources to try to achieve the specified outcomes of a task

- Action-oriented approaches (AoA), in which learners are agents of their own learning and acquire communicative competence through active participation in real-life tasks
- Content-Based Language Teaching (CBLT) or Content and Language Integrated Learning (CLIL) approaches, in which learners are taught a content subject or skill through the medium of the target language in order to gain both the content subject or skill and proficiency in the language
- Total Physical Response Plus (TPRP) approaches, in which learners respond physically to instructions from the teacher in order to mime a story, make a meal, paint a mural, make a model, make a paper aeroplane, etc.
- Problem Solving approaches, in which learners are presented with a problem and are asked to work out and present solutions
- Simulation (or scenario) approaches, in which learners are given roles to play in a given situation and are asked to interact with or without preparation but without a script
- Drama approaches, in which learners write, direct, improvise and/or act scenes from plays
- Project approaches, in which learners are given a topic or issue to investigate and then make a written or spoken presentation
- Extensive reading, listening and viewing approaches, in which learners experience extended texts of their own choosing without having to answer questions or write summaries of what they have experienced

Activities
- Task-free activities at the beginning of a lesson, in which teachers tell stories, perform poems, songs and scenes from plays and read extracts from news reports in order to provide learners with a rich, relaxed and engaging experience of language in use without any requirement to respond
- Invited guests giving presentations to classes about their job or hobby
- Learner presentations involving learners giving presentations on a skill or topic that they are very enthusiastic about
- Circle stories, in which learners sit in a circle and continue or make up a story by taking it in turns to contribute the next sentence
- Extended creative projects, in which, for example, learners develop and perform dramas, write novels or video a documentary
- Riddles set for learners to solve as a break in the middle of a lesson or at the end (e.g. Where do fish keep their money?)
- Homework activities involving looking for samples of the target language outside the classroom and working out their meaning (e.g. signs, adverts and notices; songs; newspaper reports)

> **Readers' Tasks**
>
> 1 Which three of the approaches recommended would you be most likely to make use of? Why?
> 2 Are there any approaches you would add to the list of recommendations?
> 3 Which three of the activities recommended would you be most likely to make use of? Why?
> 4 Are there any activities you would add to the list of recommendations? Why?

What We Would Not Recommend Without Principled Modification

Throughout our book we have focused on theories, approaches and activities that we feel have been sufficiently tested in practice by academics, by researchers, by teachers and by ourselves, for us to be able to recommend. We have also made reference to theories, approaches and activities that, based on our reading and our experience, we would not recommend without modification, and we have summarised these next.

Theories
1 Behaviourism

Behaviourism, when applied to language learning, claims that language forms can be learned as a result of habit formation and that habits can be formed through stimulus and response approaches in which a correct model is provided by the teacher or the materials and is repeated and practised by the learners until it becomes habitual. Once the correct use of the forms of the language has become habitual, the learners can focus their attention on meaning and communication. This theory was popularised by Skinner (1953, 1976), who claimed that operant conditioning, with behaviour being reinforced by positive outcomes and deterred by negative outcomes, was the key to learning. Although it was challenged by Chomsky as long ago as 1959 (Chomsky, 1959), it has been influential in shaping methodology and materials in classrooms around the world. In our view, although there might be some point in initially drilling basic forms, the basic tenets of behaviourism are contradicted by neurolinguistic research, and the input its application results in is impoverished in being experienced without affective or cognitive engagement and in being devoid of contextual, pragmatic or extra-linguistic support. Also, if the only input the learners receive is correct and the only output they generate is correct but without a context or pragmatic intent, then there is no scope for hypothesis generation and testing in relation to contextual appropriacy and outcome effectiveness. Most researchers seem to share our view, although there are still classrooms and courses influenced by behaviourism and there have recently been reappraisals of its value (e.g. Staddon, 2014; Reimann, 2018).

The only modifications we can think of which would give this theory value would be to relate it to successful outcomes within communicative contexts and to space the repetitions. So, for example, instead of repeating the same context-free form over and over again, the learners would repeat the same context dependent routine, transaction, conversation or task once a week for three weeks (for the value of task repetition, see Shintani, 2016).

2 Universal Grammar

Chomsky (1955, 1957, 1965) claimed that human beings are born with a disposition to learn language and with the basic rules for language intact in the form of a mental universal grammar which is fine-tuned by a language acquisition device (LAD) when exposed to a particular language in use. This belief has been supported by many researchers (e.g. Cook, 1993, 1994, 1997) but is nowadays disregarded by most SLA researchers and neurolinguists who cannot find research evidence to support what was a very elegant concept. Although we accept that there are some language universals (i.e. characteristics shared by all languages), we would not recommend the application of the theory of universal grammar because neurolinguistics has disproved the existence of an LAD, we know of no neurolinguistics evidence to support the theory that humans are hard-wired to learn language, languages do not have rules but norms, and our own experience of the theory being applied in materials development has revealed no positive contribution to language acquisition.

For an interesting account of the arguments for and against universal grammar see Wikipedia (https://en.wikipedia.org/wiki/Universal_grammar).

Although universal grammar has been largely discredited as a theory of language acquisition, many of Chomsky's contributions are still significantly valid. We certainly believe he is right in his criticism of Skinner's behaviourism, in his assertion that language learning is not a process of imitation but of creation and that language users often perform below their competence as a result of such constraints as anxiety, urgency and topic unfamiliarity.

3 Skill Acquisition Theory

We would not recommend basing a teaching approach on skill acquisition theory (SAT). This is a theory that claims that language mastery is a type of skill, like driving, cycling, cooking or playing tennis, and that it is best developed through a process progressing from declaratisation of knowledge (i.e. the receiving of explicit knowledge about language forms) to proceduralisation of knowledge (i.e. the attainment of communicative proficiency) and eventually to automatisation of knowledge (i.e. "full mastery in using language for communicative purposes", Criado, 2016, p. 122). The main means of achieving this remarkable progress is constant rehearsal of the target form, starting from controlled practice and gradually moving through guided practice to elicited production. The main proponents of SAT include Anderson (1982), Johnson (1996) and DeKeyser (1998, 2007a, 2009) and the theory is concisely summarised by Criado (2016). In our view, this theory ignores contemporary research in neurolinguistics demonstrating that intake does not consist primarily of rules and information about language forms but primarily of communicative utterances and their contexts, intentions, effects, associations and supporting extra-linguistic information. It also ignores the evidence of classrooms around the world in which we have witnessed bored and demotivated learners still failing to communicate in the target language after many years of learning it from approaches aiming to give and then proceduralise declarative knowledge.

The only way we can see SAT being made use of to facilitate language acquisition is if the declaratisation stage consisted of the learners first of all experiencing and responding personally to potentially engaging written, spoken and multimodal texts. These texts could then be made use of to draw the learners' attention to a specific language form or feature that is salient in the texts. The learners could be stimulated to make discoveries about the use of this form or feature and then to use it for themselves in a series of contextualised texts, which become gradually longer, more complex and more challenging. This could stimulate both implicit and explicit processing of some of the language encountered in the texts responded to and the texts produced.

Approaches
1 Grammar Translation

This is a very grammar-centred approach, in which the rules of the grammar of the L2 are taught explicitly by the teacher and by the materials (usually in the learners' L1). Vocabulary is taught through word translations, which are memorised, and then the declarative knowledge gained from the grammar and the vocabulary teaching is used to translate words, expressions and sometimes short texts. The emphasis is very much on reading and writing, and the method has had very little success in facilitating the development of oral communicative competence for the fairly obvious reason that its application depends on conscious recall of declarative knowledge.

This method has long been discredited, but it has prevailed for centuries and is still used today in classrooms and coursebooks throughout the world, maybe because the teacher does not have to communicate in the L2 and because of its supposed value as an academic discipline. Brian learned French through this method. He passed all his exams, can just about read simple texts in French, but totally fails to communicate whenever he goes to France.

We can only see this approach contributing to language acquisition if it is taught as an option for studially inclined learners at the higher levels of a course that also offers them a rich experience of language in use.

For a critique of the Grammar Translation approach see Rivers (1981).

2 Direct Method

The Direct Method was developed in the early 1900s as a reaction against grammar translation. It focuses on providing a direct experience of the target language without any use of the L1 by either teacher or learners. There is no explanation of the grammar. Instead, the grammar is taught inductively through experience and practice of examples of it. Realia, visuals and demonstration are used to reinforce the meaning of the example sentences presented, and the emphasis is on listening and speaking and, especially, on questioning and answering.

Although there is little research or theoretical evidence to support the Direct Method, it has been popular in classrooms for over one hundred years. Versions of the direct method are used in international language schools such as Berlitz and Inlingua and many of the language departments of the Foreign Service Institute of the US State Department adopted it in 2012. It provides an illusion of acquisition, as learners typically develop an ability to repeat the examples and to "use" them in guided practice. In our experience, though, its impoverished input of constructed examples fails to facilitate communicative competence unless the learners have ample opportunities to experience and use the target language outside the classroom. We can only see the direct method making a positive contribution to language acquisition if it is used as an occasional approach on an otherwise input-rich experiential course and it succeeds in drawing learners' attention to salient features, which they might then notice in subsequent contextualised input.

For a fairly positive view of the Direct Method see the blog by STEVIE D at www.fluentu.com/blog/educator/direct-method-of-language-teaching/ and for discussion of the Direct Method plus a view of eclecticism in language methods and in the language classroom, see Thornbury (2011).

3 Audio-Lingualism

This is an approach based on the theory of behaviourism in which the teacher and/or the materials present a correct spoken model, which the learners first of all repeat and then manipulate by putting different words into the same pattern (e.g. "He's sitting on the chair", "He's sitting on the table", "He's sitting on the floor"). If the learners get it right, the teacher rewards them with praise, if they get it wrong the teacher corrects them and then they repeat the correction. This is a very teacher-centred, forms-focused, restrictive approach, which matches none of the criteria for acquisition that we have been detailing throughout our book. However, it is still a popular approach in many classrooms, possibly because it is easy for the teacher to prepare, the teacher can easily maintain control of the lesson and the transfer of the teacher's output to the learners' short-term memory provides an illusion of learning. We believe that this illusion can only be converted into actual acquisition if the approach is supplemented by considerable experience of contextualised language in use.

For more information and discussion on audio-lingualism see Harmer (2001) and Larsen Freeman (2000).

4 Presentation–Practice–Production (PPP)

PPP is an approach in which a discrete language point is taught by the teacher and/or the materials, is practised by the learners and is then produced by the learners in tasks designed to require use of the item taught. It is based on an assumption that declarative knowledge explicitly learned can be proceduralised through practice. This is an assumption we have challenged a number of times in this volume because it does not recognise the inevitably delayed and accumulative nature of acquisition nor the need for rich, contextualised input and opportunities to use the language for communicative effect. We have found that this approach only makes a positive contribution to acquisition if you subvert it into a PPPP approach in which contextualised, communicative production is followed by presentation of what was demonstrated by learners in the production stage to be problematic, followed by practice of that feature, followed by contextualised production activities that might or might not elicit use of the problematic feature.

5 Other Discrete Item Teaching Approaches

We personally do not really see much point in any forms-focused approach which teaches in isolation a discrete item (such as the present perfect tense) because it is in the syllabus rather than because it has been significant in a text experienced by the learners, it is needed by learners in a communicative task that is proving problematic or it has been noticed or asked about by the learners. Without learner need, affective and cognitive engagement and contextual and pragmatic association, the chances of intake being strong enough to promote eventual acquisition are remote.

> **Readers' Tasks**
>
> 1 Do you disagree with anything we have said about what we would not recommend? If so, provide a rationale for your disagreement based on your experience and/or the literature.
> 2 Is there any approach we have not mentioned that you would definitely not recommend? If so, say what it is and why you would not recommend it.

Activities

1 Memorisation

Memorising translations, definitions and rules is still a common practice in language classrooms throughout the world. For example, Brian's son is currently learning Japanese in a school in Kyoto and has to learn fifty new words every night. While this might be useful when trying to achieve recall during planned discourse and reading, it seems to be of little value during unplanned discourse and listening when there is no time for conscious access to declarative knowledge. There might be some point though in memorising routine chunks of language that aid fluency (e.g. "for example", "not now", "my main point is ...", "but what about ...?").

2 Literal Translation

Translation is still a popular activity with teachers in language classrooms around the world, even though at all but the highest levels it often involves little more than conscious processing of learned declarative knowledge and, as a classroom activity, it is often more of a test than a provision of learning opportunities. We would certainly not recommend literal word-for-word, decontextualised translation, as both the input and the output are likely to be impoverished. However, we have found that getting learners to read an engaging text, to visualise the content of the text whilst and after reading it, to produce a version of the text in the other language and then to compare the version with the original is a potentially useful activity. The engagement, visualisation, contextual awareness, pragmatic awareness and creativity involved are likely to result in rich intake and the comparison of learner output and original output are likely to facilitate auto-input.

Other uses of translation we would recommend include the use of L1 subtitles for L2 videos and films (Caimi, 2006; Frumeselu, 2019), learners translating a text from L2 to L1 and then back again into L2 before comparing this text with the original, learners comparing their translation with that of a proficient user of the translated language, learners producing L1 versions of L2 poems or songs, and learners working with a teacher to translate a scene from an L1 play into L2 and then performing it. These activities involve creativity, awareness of context and noticing. This can be true, too, of translation tasks that involve producing a version of a text for a particular audience and purpose (e.g. translating a section of a computer manual for use by young children; translating instructions for novices to assemble machines; translating an advertisement so that it will become persuasive to viewers in a different cultural environment).

See Cook (2010) and House (2014) for appraisals of approaches and activities that use translation in language teaching and Herrero and Yanderschelden (2019) for chapters on the creative use of translation and film.

3 Pre-teaching of Language

The pre-teaching of "new" or difficult language in texts that learners are about to read or listen to is a very popular activity, which we have seen take up a disproportionate amount of learner time in classrooms all over the world. Teachers feel that they need to make a text as comprehensible as possible for their learners before asking them to read or listen to it. Unfortunately, what we have usually observed is that the learners then micro-process the text, decoding it word by word with their main attention on the language of the text rather than its meaning and with their focus on the pretaught language in case it is tested in the subsequent "comprehension" questions. This does little to help learners to develop comprehension skills or independent learning skills, nor to achieve the engagement with the text required for it to provide a productive resource for language acquisition. We have found that readiness activities aimed to activate the learners' minds in relation to the topic, location, theme or intention of a text they are about to experience can help to make the text both comprehensible and engaging. An example of such an activity would be the learners' visualising and retelling their first day at school prior to reading a poem called First Day at School.

4 Closed Questions

Closed activities, such as multiple choice, Yes/No questions, true/false questions, matching, and filling in the blanks from a list, have usually only one correct answer and typically test learners' declarative knowledge rather than provide them with opportunities for learning. Even though these activities are often done by learners in pairs or groups, they actually inhibit peer interaction rather than stimulate it in ways that open-ended activities can do. Yet they dominate most coursebooks, probably because teachers lacking confidence in their English do not have to evaluate and respond to learner answers, and definitely because publishers say that they are responding to the teachers' need for activities that they can use as easy to administer and mark tests for their required weekly assessments. Freeman (2014) reports that a majority of the reading comprehension activities in the coursebooks she analysed were closed activities, and Tomlinson (2018b) reports the same situation for the four global coursebooks and the four Asian coursebooks he analysed. Tomlinson (2018b) also suggests easy ways in which the teacher can open up closed activities so that they match his main principles of language acquisition (the most obvious one being to ask the learners to justify their answers).

5 Controlled Practice

Controlled practice, in which the learners are given the content and the language of what they are told to say, seems to still be a common feature of language classrooms and presumably aims at the proceduralisation of learned declarative knowledge through reinforcement of the correct production of form. Unfortunately, this does not prepare learners for real-life communication, as any interaction it elicits is totally predictable, the learners do not have to retrieve, select and combine language, the process is totally linguistic, there is no pragmatic intent and there is unlikely to be any affective or cognitive engagement. The result is usually shallow processing of impoverished input, with very little prospect of valuable or durable intake.

6 Language-Focused Reading and Listening

The norm in many coursebooks is to provide reading and listening materials that have either been written or selected because of their exemplification of preselected lexis or grammar, or they have been artificially flooded with extra exemplars of the target items. The aim is to provide reading or listening practice at the same time as focusing on language-teaching points. Our experience is that this (and many other dual targets in coursebooks) results in a conflict of objectives. In most cases, the learners go against their natural inclination to focus on meaning and pay more attention to the teaching points (especially if they have been highlighted or previously introduced) because they suspect they are going to be tested on them in the post-reading/listening activities. Also, the texts are unlikely to be engaging as they have been written, selected or flooded in order to exemplify teaching points rather than in order to engage the learners or expose them to the target language in authentic use. This is evident if you analyse almost any coursebook, and also from our own experience of writing materials when constrained by a syllabus.

One way round this problem is to get the learners to read an authentic version of a text holistically, to respond to issues in the text with personal views and opinions, and then to read an altered version of the text in which a particular language feature has been enhanced through highlighting or flooding. An even better way is to use a text-driven approach, in which the core text is chosen because of its potential to stimulate affective and/or cognitive engagement, and in which language features of the text are focused on through discovery activities only after the learners have responded personally to the text and have produced a communicative text of their own. For information on and examples of the text-driven approach, see Tomlinson (2013d) and Tomlinson and Masuhara (2018b).

7 Teacher Explanations and Instructions in the L1

In most countries where we have observed lessons, we have seen teachers give explanations in the L1 of the rules and use of English structures and of the meaning of English words, as well as giving activity instructions to their learners in the L1. The teachers often say that their English is not good enough to give clear explanations and instructions in English, and that the learners find it much easier to listen in the L1. This might be true but, in using the L1 so much and so often, they are denying learners opportunities to experience English being used for communication and are therefore impoverishing their input. This is particularly damaging in those classrooms where the teacher is the learners' only source of input in the target language, and they have no exposure to the target language in use outside the classroom. This is especially so as instructions provide ideal input for acquisition. The language of instructions is significant, salient, standardised, meaningful, relevant and constantly recycled.

At the beginning of the PKG Programme in Indonesia (Tomlinson, 1990) the teachers gave explanations and instructions in Bahasa Indonesia and gave the reasons mentioned above for doing so. They were encouraged to use more English on their teacher-development courses and in their classrooms, and at first in their classrooms they used English followed by translations into Bahasa Indonesia. Unfortunately, the learners ignored the English and waited for the translations. Eventually, most of the teachers were persuaded to pluck up courage and use only English. The eventual result was much more confident and fluent teachers and far more confident learners who were comfortable operating in an English-speaking environment.

On the PKG Programme, we discouraged the teachers from giving grammatical explanations at all. It is arguable that giving grammatical explanations in the L2 is providing learners with relevant exposure to the target language in communicative use. This might be true for more advanced learners, but for the young beginners we were catering for it was almost impossible to make the input engaging and comprehensible and we knew of no evidence that such explanations facilitate acquisition of communicative competence.

All the above activities that we have not recommended are part of normal practice in classrooms around the world, not because of validation from research and observation or from obvious success in promoting language acquisition, but because they have become almost a dogmatic norm that would be very difficult for materials developers, teacher trainers and teachers to break away from. These activities also seem to make it easier for teachers to teach and learners to learn but they also seem to make the learning less effective in relation to the development of communicative competence.

We are very much aware that many people will disagree with what we have said in this section of our summary and we have no intention of discrediting or disrespecting them. Our views are genuine, and based on our research, our reading and our experience.

All we can do is to invite you to consider our views and to make your own decisions. To help you to do this, we would recommend going to Richards and Rodgers (2014) where you will find descriptions and discussion of most of the theories, approaches and activities that we have been not recommending above. We also invite you to consider your own experience as language learners, as academic students, as teachers in training, as teachers or as researchers and to evaluate our book in relation to it.

Readers' Tasks

1. What do you agree with in our summary? Say why you agree with it and suggest ways of applying it in your own situation.
2. What do you disagree with in our summary? Say why you disagree with it.
3. Select two of the approaches or activities we have recommended or not recommended in our summary that you think justify further research. Say how you would conduct such research, and how its findings could be applied in your situation.

CONCLUSION

We are well aware of the constraints that both practitioners and researchers work under. Language planners are constrained by political policy and financial restraints. Curriculum developers are constrained by language policies, by expectations, by examinations and by time allocations. Materials developers are constrained by established norms and dogmas, by the conservative instincts of the educational establishment and by publisher, teacher and learner expectations. Examiners are constrained by the need for face validity and by the priority typically accorded to achieving reliability. Teachers are constrained by traditional training, by institutional accountability, by imposed and inappropriate coursebooks, by examinations and by curricula. Researchers are constrained by the need to provide empirical substantiation of their hypotheses and often by the difficulty in obtaining ethical clearance. Everybody is constrained by fear of taking risks and losing credibility and reputation. But in our experience learners are often willing to embrace the new and new developments can be achieved within an apparent framework of established practice (Tomlinson, 2005a).

At this point we have to make a confession, which might sound surprising since we have been insisting on principled application of research supported theory throughout this book. We have found throughout our long careers that there have been teachers who have been equally successful in helping their learners to develop communicative confidence and competence and to achieve good examination marks despite using completely different and often seemingly contradictory methods and materials. In one institution, for example, three teachers achieved similar success despite one of them using very traditional grammar-centred approaches, one of them using a PPP approach and one of them using a student-centred communicative approach. All three seemed to achieve rapport with their learners, to respect and support their learners, to be empathetic, to have a sense of humour, to be patient, to be interesting, to chat with their learners inside and outside the classroom and to encourage their learners to chat with them and with each other. Perhaps it was their attitudes, their personalities, their attributes and their relationships with their learners that were responsible for their learners' success. And maybe such factors should become an important focus of SLA research in addition to how languages are taught and learned.

What we have proposed in our book is very much an unattainable goal, but we see it as a goal to aim at. Nobody has the freedom or opportunity to do everything we are proposing (certainly we do not) and nobody else is likely to have the disposition to attempt it all. However, we do believe that we all could achieve the following (providing, of course, that we believe in its value):

Ensuring that:

- all L2 learners receive as much exposure to the target language in use as possible;
- this exposure is rich in its variety of genres, text types, contexts, language features, registers, styles, strategies and communicative intentions;
- this exposure is meaningful for the learners;
- this exposure has the potential for cognitive engagement;
- this exposure has the potential for affective engagement;
- the significant features of the exposure are recycled at spaced intervals and in a variety of contexts.

Providing opportunities for learners to:

- notice how their target language is used to achieve communication;
- make discoveries about how their target language is used to achieve communication;
- make use of what they notice and discover about how their target language is used to achieve communication;
- gain help and feedback from peers and teachers when needed.

Ensuring that all learners:

- spend a large proportion of their learning time actually using the target language for purposeful communication rather than just practising it.

Encouraging learners to:

- look out for their target language outside the classroom;
- seek opportunities for meaningful interaction in their target language outside the classroom.

Being:

- realistic
- patient
- supportive
- empathetic
- positive
- interesting
- stimulating
- well-informed

We hope that you have been sufficiently informed and stimulated by our book to rethink (but not necessarily change) what you are doing. Maybe the ideal response is the one reported by an English teacher from Spain who, during a one-week workshop shouted, "Rubbish, nonsense, it wouldn't work with my students" at everything Brian said. A few weeks later she wrote to Brian, "Remember that nonsense you told us at the workshop, well I've tried it and some of it works". She had been through a natural and very useful process of rejecting the unfamiliar, recollecting the unfamiliar, selecting from the unfamiliar, applying the unfamiliar to her familiar context, evaluating her use of the unfamiliar and then incorporating some of it into her repertoire.

We very much hope you and your students do the same.

RECOMMENDED READING

Ellis, R. (2015). *Understanding second language acquisition* (2nd ed.). Oxford: Oxford University Press.

Schütze, U. (2017). *Language learning and the brain.* Cambridge: Cambridge University Press.

Tomlinson, B. (Ed.). (2016). *SLA research and materials development for language learning.* New York: Routledge.

Tomlinson, B. & Masuhara, H. (2018). *The complete guide to the theory and practice of materials development for language learning.* Hoboken, NJ: Wiley-Blackwell.

References

A guide to reflective practice for core French teachers. Module 3 – The action oriented approach. www.edugains.ca/resourcesFSL/PDF/AGuideToReflectivePractice/Module3_ActionOrientedApproach_English.pdf – retrieved 26 September 2019.

Abdel Latif, M. M. (2017). Teaching grammar using inductive and communicative materials: Exploring Egyptian EFL teachers' practice and beliefs. In H. Masuhara, F. Mishan & B. Tomlinson (Eds.), *Practice and theory for materials development in language learning* (pp. 275–289). Newcastle upon Tyne: Cambridge Scholars Publishing.

Adams, R. (2007). Do second language learners benefit from interacting with each other? In A. Mackey (Ed.), *Conversational interaction in second language acquisition* (pp. 29–51). Oxford: Oxford University Press.

Adams, R. & Oliver, R. (2019). *Teaching through peer interaction.* New York: Routledge.

Adolphs, S. & Carter, R. (2013). *Spoken corpus linguistics: from monomodal to multimodal.* New York: Routledge.

Agudo, J. M. (Ed.). (2018). *Emotions in second language teaching.* Cham, Switzerland: Springer.

Alcon, E. (1998). Input and input processing in second language acquisition. *International Review of Applied Linguistics in Language Teaching, 36*(4), 343–362. doi:10.1515/iral.1998.36.4.343

Alexander, R. (2005). *Towards dialogic teaching: Rethinking classroom talk.* Cambridge: Dialogos.

Aljaafreh, A. & Lantolf, J. (1994). Negative feedback as regulation and second language learning in the zone of proximal development. *The Modern Language Journal, I,* 465–483. Doi:10.1111/j.1540-4781.1994.tb02064.x

Allan, I. (1953). *British locomotives, 1953: Part 1.* Shepperton: Ian Allen Publishing.

Allwright, D. & Hanks, J. (2009). *The developing language learner: an introduction to exploratory practice.* Basingstoke: Palgrave Macmillan.

Altarriba, J. & Isurin, L. (2012). *Memory, language and bilingualism: Theoretical and applied approaches.* Cambridge: Cambridge University Press.

Ambridge, B. & Lieven, E. V. M. (2011). *Contrasting theoretical approaches.* Cambridge: Cambridge University Press.

(2015). A constructivist account of child language acquisition. In B. MacWhinney & W. O'Grady (Eds.), *The handbook of language emergence.* (pp. 478–510). Chichester: Wiley-Blackwell.

Andersen, R. (Ed.). (1981). *New dimensions in second language acquisition research*. Rowley, MA: Newbury House.

Anderson, J. (2017). A potted history of PPP with the help of ELT Journal. *ELT Journal, 71*(2), 218–227. https://doi.org/10.1093/elt/ccw055

Anderson, J. R. (1982). Acquisition of cognitive skill. *Psychological Review, 89*(4), 369–406.

(1993). *Rules of the mind*. Hillsdale, NJ: Lawrence Erlbaum Associates.

(2016). A unified theory of mind. In R. J. Sternberg, S. T. Fiske & D. J. Foss (Eds.), *Scientists making a difference: One hundred eminent behavioral and brain scientists talk about their most important contributions* (pp. 163–166). Cambridge: Cambridge University Press.

Andringa, S. & Dąbrowska, E. (2019). Individual differences in first and second language ultimate attainment and their causes. *Language Learning, 69*, 5–12.

Ansarian, L. & Teoh, M. L. (2018). *Problem-based language teaching and learning: An innovative approach to learn a new language*. Oxford: Springer.

Anton, M. & Dicamilla, F. J. (1999). Socio-cognitive functions of L1 collaborative interaction in the L2 classroom. *The Modern Language Journal, 83/2*, 233–247.

Arbib, M. A. (2015). Language evolution: An emergentist perspective. In B. McWhinney (Ed.), *The handbook of language emergence* (pp. 600–623). Chichester: Wiley-Blackwell.

Archer, M. S. (2003). *Structure, agency and the internal conversation*. Cambridge: Cambridge University Press.

Arnold, J. (Ed.). (1999). *Affect in language learning*. Cambridge: Cambridge University Press.

Arnold, J. & Brown, H. D. (1999). A map of the terrain. In J. Arnold (Ed.), *Affect in language learning* (pp. 1–24). Cambridge: Cambridge University Press.

Arnold, J., Dörnyei, Z. & Pugliese, C. (2015). *The principled communicative approach*. London: Helbling.

Arntzen, R., Hakansson, G., Hjelde, A. & Kefsler, J. (Eds.). (2019). *Teachability and learnability across languages*. Amsterdam: John Benjamins.

Asher, J. J. (1977). *Learning another language through actions: The complete teacher's guidebook*. Los Gatos, CA: Sky Oak Production.

(1981). The total physical response: Theory and practice. In H. Winitz (Ed.), *Native language and foreign language acquisition* (pp. 324–331). New York: New York Academy of Sciences.

Atkinson, D. (2010). Extended, embodied cognition and second language acquisition. *Applied Linguistics, 31*(5): 599–622.

(Ed.). (2011). *Alternative approaches to second language acquisition*. London: Routledge.

Auerbach, E. R. & Paxton, D. (1997). "It's not the English thing": Bringing reading research into the ESL classroom. *TESOL Quarterly, 31*(2), 237–261.

Avila, J. (2007). The value of recasts during meaning-focused communication – 2. In B. Tomlinson (Ed.), *Language acquisition and development: Studies of learners of first and other languages* (pp. 162–170). London: Continuum.

Baddeley, A. D. (2007). *Working memory, thought and action*. Oxford: Oxford University Press.

(2012). Working memory: Theories, models, and controversies. *Annual Review of Psychology*, 63, 1–29. https://doi.org/10.1146/annurev-psych-120710-100422

Badger, R. (2018). From input to intake: Researching learner cognition. *TESOL Quarterly*, 52(4), 1073–1084. doi:10.1002/tesq.448

Bailey, K., Long, M. & Peak, S. (Eds.). (1983). *Second language acquisition studies*. Rowley, MA: Newbury House.

Bailey, K. & Masuhara, H. (2013). Language testing washback: The role of materials. In B. Tomlinson (Ed.), *Applied linguistics and materials development* (pp. 466–494). London: Bloomsbury.

Bailin, A. & Grafstein, A. (2016). *Readability: Text and context*. Basingstoke: Palgrave Macmillan UK.

Baker, A., Jensen, P. J. & Kolb, D. A. (2002). *Conversational learning: An experiential approach to knowledge creation*. Westport, CT: Qurom Books.

Baldauf, R., Kaplan, R. & Kanwangamalu, M. (2011). Language planning and its problems. *Current issues in language planning*, 11, 430–438.

Baleghizadeh, S. (2017). Short stories and task-based materials. In H. Masuhara, F. Mishan & B. Tomlinson (Eds.), *Practice and theory for materials development in L2 learning* (pp. 149–163). Newcastle: Cambridge Scholars.

Baleghizadeh, S., Goldouz, E. & Mehrdad, Y. (2016). What grammar activities do ELT workbooks focus on? In B. Tomlinson (Ed.), *SLA research and materials development for language learning* (pp. 153–165). New York: Routledge.

Bao, D. (2002). *Understanding reticence: An action research project aiming at increasing verbal participation in the EFL classroom*. Unpublished PhD thesis. Leeds Metropolitan University.

(2013). Voices of the reticent: Getting inside views of Vietnamese secondary school students on learning. In M. Cortazzi & L. Jin (Eds.), *Researching cultures of learning: International perspectives on language learning and education* (pp. 136–154). Basingstoke: Palgrave Macmillan.

(2014). *Understanding silence and reticence: Ways of participating in second language acquisition*. London: Bloomsbury.

(2018). *Creativity and innovations in ELT materials: Looking beyond the current design*. Bristol: Multilingual Matters.

(2020). Silence, talk, and in-betweens: East-Asian students' responses to task challenge in an Australian university. In J. King & H. Seiko (Eds.), *East-Asian perspectives on silence in English language education*. Bristol: Multilingual Matters.

Baralt, M., Gurzynski-Weiss, L. & Kim, Y. (2016). Engagement with the language: How examining learners' affective and social engagement explains effective learner-generated attention to form. In M. Sato & S. Ballinger. *Peer interaction and second language learning: Pedagogical potential and research agenda* (pp. 209–240). Amsterdam: John Benjamins.

Barcroft, J. (2007). Effects of opportunities for word retrieval during second language vocabulary learning. *Language Learning: A Journal of Research in Language Studies. 57*(1), 35–56.

Barcroft, J. & Wong, W. (2013). Input, input processing and focus on form. In J. Hershenson & M. Young-Scholten (Eds.), *The Cambridge handbook of second language acquisition* (pp. 627–647). Cambridge: Cambridge University Press.

Bardovi-Harlig, K. & Mossman, S. (2016). Corpus-based materials development for teaching and learning pragmatic routines. In B. Tomlinson (Ed.), *SLA research and materials development for language learning* (pp. 250–267). New York: Routledge.

Barker, D. (2010a). *The potential role of unstructured learner interaction in the study of a foreign language.* Unpublished PhD thesis. Leeds Metropolitan University.

(2010b). The role of unstructured learner interaction in the study of a foreign language. In S. Menon & J. Lourdunathan (Eds.), *Readings on ELT materials IV* (pp. 50–70). Petaling Jaya, Malaysia: Pearson.

Barnard, E. S. (2007). The value of comprehension in the early stages of the acquisition and development of Bahasa Indonesia by non-native speakers. In B. Tomlinson (Ed.), *Language acquisition and development: Studies of learners of first and other languages* (pp. 187–204). London: Continuum.

Barr, D. A. (2004). Time to listen. *Annals of Internal Medicine, 140*(144), 41–44.

Barrett, L. F. (2009). The future of psychology: Connecting mind to brain. *Perspectives on Psychological Science, 4*(4), 326–339.

Batstone, R. (1996). Key concepts in ELT-noticing. *Applied Linguistics, 50*(3), 273.

Beck, I. L, McKeown, M. G. & Worthy, J. (1995). Giving a text voice can improve students' understanding. *Research Reading Quarterly, 30*(2), 220–238.

Beebe, L. B. (1985). Input: Choosing the right stuff. In S. M. Gass & C. G. Madden (Eds.), *Input in second language acquisition* (pp. 404–414). Rowley, MA: Newbury House Publishers.

Beltrán-Planques, V. & Querol-Julián, M. (2018). English language learners' spoken interaction: What a multimodal perspective reveals about pragmatic competence. *System, 77*, 80–90. doi:10.1016/j.system.2018.01.008

Benati, A. G. & Angelovska, T. (2016). *Second language acquisition: A theoretical introduction to real world applications.* London: Bloomsbury.

Benati, A. G., Laval, C. & Arche, M. (Eds.). (2013). *The grammar dimension in instructed second language acquisition.* Bloomsbury: London.

Benke, E. & Medgyes, P. (2005). Differences in teaching behaviour between native and non-native speaker teachers: As seen by the learners. In E. Llurda (Ed.), *Non-native language teachers: Perceptions, challenges and contributions to the profession* (pp. 195–215). Basel, Switzerland: Springer Science+Business Media.

Benson, P. & Reinders, H. (Eds.). (2011). *Beyond the language classroom.* London: Palgrave Macmillan.

Bentley, K. (2015). CLIL scenarios with young learners. In J. Bland (Ed.), *Teaching English to young learners: Critical issues in language teaching with 3 to 12 year olds* (pp. 91–112). London: Bloomsbury.

Berko, J. (1958). The child's learning of English morphology. *Word, 14*(2–3), 150–177.

Bernhardt, E. B. & Kamil, M. L. (1995). Interpreting relationships between L1 and L2 reading: Consolidating the linguistic threshold and the linguistic interdependence hypotheses. *Applied Linguistics, 16*(1), 15–34.

Bhatti, A., Shamsudin, S. & Said, S. (2018). Code-switching: A useful foreign language teaching tool in EFL classrooms. *English Language Teaching, 11*(6), 93. doi: 10.5539/elt.v11n6p93

Bialystok, E., Craik, F. I. M. & Luk, G. (2008). Lexical access in bilinguals: Effects of vocabulary size and executive control. *Journal of Neurolinguistics, 21*(6), 522–538. DOI: 10.1016/j.jneuroling.2007.07.001

Bland, J. (Ed.). (2015). *Teaching English to young learners: Critical issues in language teaching with 3 to 12 year olds.* London: Bloomsbury.

(Ed.). (2018). *Using literature in language education: Challenging reading for 8–18 year olds.* London: Bloomsbury.

Bock. J. K. (1982). Toward a cognitive psychology of syntax: Information processing contributions to sentence formulation. *Psychological Review, 89*, 1–47.

Bolitho, R., Carter, R., Hughes, R., Ivanic, H., Masuhara, H. & Tomlinson, B. (2003). Ten questions about language awareness. *ELT Journal, 57*(3), 251–259.

Bolitho, R. & Tomlinson, B. (1995). *Discover English.* Oxford: Macmillan.

Bolte Taylor, J. (2009). *My stroke of insight: A brain scientist's personal journey.* London: Hodder and Stoughton Ltd.

Bonilla, P. B. & Vargas, J. D. G. (2015). *"Living up the world": The materials development process of a module for fifth graders following a multi-dimensional approach.* (Unpublished PhD thesis). Pontificia Universidad Javeriana, Bogota.

Bouziri, B. (2017). Introducing curriculum authenticity. In A. Maley & B. Tomlinson (Eds.), *Authenticity in language teaching materials* (pp. 25–43). Newcastle: Cambridge Scholars.

Bowell, P. & Heap, B. (2001). *Planning process drama.* London: David Fulton Publishers.

Braine, G. (2005). A history of research on non-native speaker English teachers. In E. Llurda (Ed.), *Non-native language teachers: Perceptions, challenges and contributions to the profession* (pp. 13–32). New York: Springer Science +Business Media.

Braten, S. (Ed.). (2006). *Intersubjective communication and emotion in early ontogeny.* Cambridge: Cambridge University Press.

Bridges, P. (2018). *Bridging discourses in the ESL classroom: Students, teachers and researchers.* London: Bloomsbury.

Brinton, D. (2003). Content-based instruction. In D. Nunan (Ed.), *Practical*

English language teaching (pp. 199–224). New York: McGraw Hill.

The British Council. (2014). *Regional policy dialogues 2013–14*. London: The British Council. Retrieved from www.teachingenglish.org.uk/sites/teacheng/files/bc_regional_policy_dialogues.pdf

Broadbent, D. (1958). *Perception and communication*. London: Pergamon Press.

Broos, W. P. J., Duyck, W. & Hartsuiker, R. J. (2016). Verbal self-monitoring in the second language. *Language Learning, 66*(S2), 132–154.

Brown, G. & Yule, G. (1983). *Teaching the spoken language*. Cambridge: Cambridge University Press.

Brown, H. D. & Priyanvada, A. (2010). *Language assessment: Principles and classroom practices*. New York: Pearson Education.

Brown, R., Waring, R. & Donkaewbua, S. (2008). Incidental vocabulary acquisition from reading, reading-while-listening, and listening to stories. *Reading in a Foreign Language, 20*(2), 136–163.

Brown, S. (2020). *Language teaching materials through the critical lens*. file:///C:/Users/user/Downloads/CLER___Language_Teaching_Materials_Through_the_Critical_Lens%20(1).pdf (accessed 17 February 2020).

Buchweitz, A., Mason, R. A., Tomitch, L. M. B., & Just, M. A. (2009). Brain activation for reading and listening comprehension: An fMRI study of modality effects and individual differences in language comprehension. *Psychology & Neuroscience, 2*(2), 111–123.

Buendgens-Kosten, J. (2014). Authenticity. *ELT Journal, 68*(4), 457–459.

Bui, G. (2018). Total physical response. In J. Liontas (Ed.), *TESOL encyclopedia of English language teaching* (pp. 927–932). Hoboken, NJ: John Wiley & Sons, Inc. DOI: 10.1002/9781118784235.eelt0163

Burns, A. & Hill, D. A. (2013). Teaching speaking in a second language. In B. Tomlinson (Ed.), *Applied linguistics and materials development.* (pp. 231–248). London: Bloomsbury.

Bygate, M. (Ed.). (2018). *Learning language through task repetition*. Amsterdam: John Benjamins.

Byram, M. & Hu, A. (Eds.). (2013). *Routledge encyclopedia of language teaching and learning* (2nd ed.). Abingdon, Oxon: Routledge.

Caimi, A. (2006). Audiovisual translation and language learning: The promotion of intralingual subtitles. *The Journal of Specialised Translation, 06*, 85–98. www.jostrans.org/issue06/issue06_toc.php

Carrell, P. L., Pharis, B. G. & Liberto, J. C. (1989). Metacognitive strategy training for ESL reading. *TESOL Quarterly, 23* (4), 647–678.

Carrier, M., Damerow, R. M. & Bailey, K. M. (2017). *Digital language learning and teaching: Research, theory, and practice*. New York: Routledge and TIRF.

Carroll, J. B. (1965). The prediction of success in foreign language training. In

R. Glaser (Ed.), *Training, research and education* (pp. 87–136). New York: Wiley.

Carroll, J. B. & Sapon, S. M. (1959). *Modern language aptitude test*. New York: The Psychological Cooporation.

Carter, R. & McCarthy, M. (2006). *Cambridge grammar of English: A comprehensive guide to spoken and written English grammar and usage*. Cambridge: Cambridge University Press.

(2017). Spoken grammar: Where are we and where are we going? *Applied Linguistics*, 38(1), 1–20.

Carter, R., Hughes, R. & McCarthy, M. (2011). Telling tails: Grammar, the spoken language and materials development. In B. Tomlinson (Ed.), *Materials development in language teaching* (2nd ed., pp. 78–100). Cambridge: Cambridge University Press.

Carter, R., McCarthy, M., Mark, G. & O'Keeffe, A. (2011). *English grammar today*. Cambridge: Cambridge University Press.

Carter, R. & Nunan, D. (Eds.). (2001). *The Cambridge guide to teaching English to speakers of other languages*. Cambridge: Cambridge University Press.

Castaño Muñoz, J., Redecker, C., Vuorikari, R. & Punie, Y. (2013). Open education 2030: Planning the future of adult learning in Europe. *Open Learning*, 28(3), 171–186. doi:10.1080/02680513.2013.871199

Cazden, C., Cancino, E., Rosansky, E. & Schumenn, J. (1975). *Second language acquisition in children, adolescents and adults*. Final report. Washington. DC: National Institute of Education.

Centeno-Cortez, B. & Jimenez, B. F. (2004). Problem solving tasks in a foreign language: The importance of the L1 in private verbal thinking. *International Journal of Applied Linguistics*, 14(1), 7–35.

Chambers, B., Cheung, A. C. K. & Slavin, R. E. (2016). Review: Literacy and language outcomes of comprehensive and developmental-constructivist approaches to early childhood education: A systematic review. *Educational Research Review*, 18, 88–111.

Chapelle, C. A. & Lui, H. M. (2007). Theory and research: Investigation of "authentic" CALL tasks. In J. Egbert & E. Hanson-Smith (Eds.), *CALL environments* (2nd ed., pp. 111–130). Alexandria, VA: TESOL Publications.

Chaudron, C. (1983). Simplification of input: Topic reinstatements and their effects on L2 learners' recognition. *TESOL Quarterly*, 17(3), 437–458.

(1985). Intake: On models and methods for discovering learners' processing of input. *Studies in Second Language Acquisition*, 7(1), 1–14.

(2006). Some reflections on the development of (meta-analytic) synthesis in second language research. In J. Norris M., & L. Ortega (Eds.), *Synthesizing research on language learning and teaching* (pp. 323–339). Amsterdam: John Benjamins.

Chi, D. N. (2016). Intake in second language acquisition. Hawaii Pacific University TESOL Working Paper Series 14, 76–89.

Choi, H. & Iwashita, N. (2016). Interactional behaviours of low-proficiency learners in small group work. In M. Sato & S. Ballinger (Eds.), *Peer interaction and second language learning: Pedagogical potential and research agenda* (pp. 113–134). Amsterdam: John Benjamins.

Chomsky, N. (1955). *Logical structure of linguistic theory.* New York: MIT Humanities Library.

(1957). *Syntactic structures.* The Hague: Mouton.

(1959). Review of verbal behaviour by B. F. Skinner. *Language, 35*(1), 26–58. https://doi.org/10.2307/411334

(1965). *Aspects of the theory of syntax.* Cambridge, MA: The MIT Press.

(1965/2014). *Aspects of the theory of syntax - The 50th edition 2014.* Cambridge, MA: MIT Press.

(1976). *Reflections on language.* London: Temple Smith.

(1986). *Knowledge of language: Its nature, origin and use.* New York: Praeger.

(1995/2014). *A minimalist program for linguistic theory: The twentieth anniversary edition 2014.* Cambridge: The MIT Press.

Clandfield, L. & Benne, R. R. (2011). *Global intermediate.* Oxford: Macmillan.

Clare, A. & Wilson, J. J. (2012). *Speakout intermediate.* Harlow: Pearson.

Clark, E. V. (2015). Common ground. In B. MacWhinney, & W. O'Grady (Eds.), *The handbook of language emergence* (pp. 328–353). Chichester: Wiley-Blackwell.

(2017). *Language in children.* Oxon: Routledge.

Cohen, A. & Ishihara, N. (2013). Pragmatics. In B. Tomlinson (Ed.), *Applied linguistics and materials development* (pp. 113–126). London: Bloomsbury.

Colantoni, L., Steele, J. & Escudero, P. (2015). *Second language speech: Theory and practice.* Cambridge: Cambridge University Press.

Cook, G. (2000). *Language play, language learning.* Oxford: Oxford University Press.

(2010). *Translation in language teaching.* Oxford: Oxford University Press.

Cook, V. J. (1985). *Experimental approaches to second language acquisition.* Oxford: Pergamon.

(Ed.). (1986). *Experimental approaches to second language learning.* Oxford: Pergamon.

(1991). *Second language learning and language teaching* (2nd ed.). London: Arnold.

(1993). *Linguistics and second language acquisition.* Oxford: Macmillan.

(1994). UG and the metaphor of access. In N. Ellis (Ed.), *Implicit learning of language.* Cambridge, MA: Academic Press.

(1997). *Inside language.* London: Edward Arnold.

(1999). Going beyond the native speaker in language teaching. *TESOL Quarterly, 33*(2), 185–209.

(2001). Using the first language in the classroom. *Canadian Modern Language Review, 57*(3), 184–206.

(2003). The changing L1 in the L2 user's mind. In V. Cook (Ed.), *Effects of the second language on the first,* (pp. 1–19). Clevedon, Avon: Multilingual Matters.

(2010). *The relationship between first and second language learning revisited.*

In E. Macaro (Ed.), *The Continuum companion to second language acquisition* (pp. 137–157). London: Continuum.

(2016). *Second language learning and language teaching* (5th ed.). New York: Routledge.

Cook, V. J. & Singleton, D. (2014). *Key topics in second language acquisition.* Bristol: Multilingual Matters.

Cooker, L. (2008). Self-access materials. In B. Tomlinson (Ed.), *English language learning materials: A critical review* (pp. 110–132). London: Continuum.

(2010). Some self-access principles. *Studies in Self-Access Learning*, *1*(1), 5 9.

Coombe, C., Davidson, P., O'Sullivan, B. & Stoynoff, S. (Eds.). (2012). *The Cambridge guide to second language assessment.* Cambridge: Cambridge University Press.

Copland, F., Garton, S. & Mann, S. (Eds.). (2016). *LETs and NESTs: Voices, views and vignettes.* London: The British Council.

Costa, A. & Santesteban, M. (2004). Lexical access in bilingual speech production: Evidence from language switching in highly proficient bilinguals and L2 learners. *Journal of Memory and Language*, 50, 491–511.

Council for the Curriculum Examinations and Assessment (2019). http://ccea.org.uk/curriculum/assess_progress/types_assessment/formative/assessment_learning

Council of Europe (2001). *Common European framework of reference for languages: Learning, teaching, assessment.* Cambridge: Cambridge University Press. www.coe.int/en/web/common-european-framework-reference-languages/ (accessed 17 February 2020).

(2018). *Common European framework of reference for languages: Learning, teaching, assessment: Companion volume with new descriptors.* Strasbourg: Council of Europe. https://rm.coe.int/cefr-companion-volume-with-new-descriptors-2018/1680787989 (accessed 17 February 2020).

(2020). *Common European framework of reference for languages: Learning, teaching, assessment: Companion volume.* Strasbourg: Council of Europe Publishing. Available at: www.coe.int/lang-cefr.

Cowan, N. (2005). *Working memory capacity.* Hove, East Sussex, UK: Psychology Press.

Coyle, D., Hood, P. & Marsh, D. (2010). *CLIL: Content and language integrated learning.* Cambridge: Cambridge University Press.

Craik, F. (2002). Levels of processing: Past, present ... future. *Memory*, *10*(5-6), 305–318.

Criado, R. (2016). Insights from skill acquisition theory for grammar activity sequencing and design in foreign language teaching. *Innovation in Language Learning and Teaching.* *10*(2), 121–132.

Crystal, D. (2006). *Language and the Internet* (2nd ed.). Cambridge: Cambridge University Press.

(2011). *Internet linguistics: A student guide.* London: Routledge.

Cullen, R. & Kuo, V. (2007). Spoken grammar and ELT materials. *TESOL Quarterly*, *41*(2), 361–386.

Daelemans, W., Zabrel, J., Van der Sloot, K. & Van den Bosch, A. (2010). *TiMBL: Tilburg memory-based learner, version 6.3: Reference guide.* (No. ILK Technical Report - ILK 10-01). Tilburg: Tilburg Centre for Cognition and Communication.

Damasio, A. (1994). *Descartes' error: Emotion, reason, and the human brain.* New York: Avon.

Damasio, A. & Carvalho, G. B. (2013). The nature of feelings: Evolutionary and neurobiological origins. *Nature Reviews Neuroscience, 14*(2), 143–152.

Darici, A. & Tomlinson, B. (2016). A case study of principled materials in action. In B. Tomlinson (Ed.), *Second language acquisition research and materials development for language learning* (pp. 71–86). New York: Routledge.

Davies, C. (1995). Extensive reading: An expensive extravagance. *ELT Journal, 49*(4), 329–336.

Davis, J. McE., Norris, J., Malone, M.E., McKay, T. H. & Son, Y. (Eds.). (2018). *Useful assessment and evaluation in language education.* Georgetown: Georgetown University Press.

Davison, C. (2013). Innovation in assessment: Common misconceptions and problems. In K. Hyland & L. L. C. Wong (Eds.), *Innovation and change in English language education* (pp. 263–275). Abingdon: Routledge.

Day, R. (2003). Authenticity in the design and development of materials. In W. A. Renandya (Ed.), *Methodology and materials design in language teaching* (pp. 1–11). Singapore: SEAMEO Regional Language Centre.

Day, R. & Bamford, J. (1998). *Extensive reading in the second language classroom.* Cambridge: Cambridge University Press.

Deci, E. L. & Ryan, R. M. (1985). *Intrinsic motivation and self-determination in human behaviour.* New York: Plenum.

De Guerrero, M. C. M. (Ed.). (2005). *Inner speech: Speaking words in a second language.* New York: Springer-Verlag.

(2017). Going covert: Inner and private speech in language learning. *Language Teaching, 51*(1), 1–35. doi:10.1017/S0261444817000295

DeKeyser, R. M. (1998). Beyond focus on form: Cognitive perspectives on learning and practising second language grammar. In C. Doughty & J. Williams (Eds.), *Focus on form in second language classroom acquisition* (pp. 42–63). Cambridge: Cambridge University Press.

(Ed.). (2007a). *Practice in a second language: Perspectives from applied linguistics and cognitive psychology.* New York: Cambridge University Press.

(2007b). Skill acquisition theory. In B. Van Patten & J. Williams (Eds.), *Theories in second language acquisition. An introduction.* (pp. 94–112). London: Routledge.

(2009). Cognitive psychological processes in second language learning. In M. Long & C. Doughty (pp. 119–138). Oxford: Blackwell.

(2015). Skill acquisition theory. In B. Van Patten & J. Williams (Eds.), *Theories in second language acquisition: An introduction* (2nd ed., pp. 94–112). New York: Routledge.

DeKeyser, R. M. & Botana, G. P. (Eds.). (2019). *Doing SLA research with implications for the classroom: Reconciling methodological demands and pedagogical applicability*. Amsterdam: John Benjamins.

Dellar, H. & Walkley, A. (2010). *Intermediate outcomes*. Andover: Heinle.

Descartes, R. (1983). *Principles of philosophy* (V. R. Miller, A. R. P. Miller Trans.). Dordrecht: D. Reidel.

Deters, D., Gao, X., Miller, E. R. & Vitanova, G. (Eds.). (2015). *Theorizing and analyzing agency in second language learning*. Bristol, UK: Multilingual Matters.

Dewaele, J. (2013). Learner-internal psychological factors. In J. Hershenson & M. Young-Scholten (Eds.), *The Cambridge handbook of second language acquisition* (pp. 159-179). Cambridge: Cambridge University Press.

DiPietro, R. J. (1982). The open-ended scenario: A new approach to conversation. *TESOL Quarterly, 16*(1), 15-20.

(1987). *Strategic interaction: Learning languages through scenarios*. New York: Cambridge University Press.

Dobao, A. F. (2014). Vocabulary learning in collaborative tasks: A comparison of pair and small group work. *Language Teaching Research, 18*(4), 497-520.

Donato, R. (1994). Collective scaffolding in second language learning. In J. P. Lantolf (Ed.), *Vygotskian approaches to second language research* (pp. 33-56). London: Ablex Publishing.

Dörnyei, Z. (2009a). *The psychology of second language acquisition*. Oxford: Oxford University Press.

(2009b). The L2 motivation self system. In Z. Dornyei & E. Ushioda (Eds.), *Motivation, language identity and the L2 self* (pp. 9-42). Bristol: Multilingual Matters.

(2019). Towards a better understanding of the L2 learning experience, the Cinderella of the L2 motivational self system. *Studies in Second Language Learning and Teaching, 1*, 19.

Dörnyei, Z. & Ushioda, E. (2013). *Teaching and researching: Motivation*. (2nd ed.). New York: Routledge.

Dörnyei, Z. & Ryan, S. (2015). *The psychology of the language learner revisited*. New York: Routledge.

Dörnyei, Z., Henry, A. & Muir, C. (2015). *Motivational currents in language learning: Frameworks for focused interventions*. New York: Routledge.

Doughty, C. & Long, M. (Eds.). (2003). *The handbook of second language acquisition*. Malden: MA: Blackwell.

Doughty, C. & Varela, E. (1998). Communicative focus on form. In C. Doughty & J. Williams (Eds.), *Focus on form in classroom second language acquisition*. Cambridge: Cambridge University Press.

The Douglas Fir Group. (2016). A transdisciplinary framework for SLA in a multilingual world. *The Modern Language Journal, 100*, 19-47.

Dulay, H. C. & Burt, M. K. (1974). Errors and strategies in child second language acquisition. *TESOL Quarterly, 8*(2), 129-136.

Dulay, H. M., Burt, M. & Krashen, S. (1982). *Language two*. New York: Oxford University Press.

Dunkel, H. (1948). *Second language learning*. Boston: Gin.

Eales, F. & Oakes, S. (2012). *Speakout upper intermediate*. Harlow: Pearson.

Elley, W. B. & Mangubhai, F. (1981). *The impact of a book flood in Fiji primary schools.* N.Z. Council for Educational Research and Institute of Education, U.S.P.

Ellis, D. & Zimmerman B. J. (2001). Enhancing self-monitoring during self-regulated learning of speech. In H. J. Hartman (Ed.), *Metacognition in learning and instruction.* Neuropsychology and cognition (pp. 205–228). Dordrecht: Springer.

Ellis, N. (1994). Introduction: Implicit and explict language learning – an overview. In N. Ellis (Ed.), *Implicit and explicit learning of languages* (pp. 1–32). San Diego, CA: Academic Press.

(2005). At the interface: Dynamic interactions of explicit and implicit language knowledge. *Studies in Second Language Acquisition, 27*(2), 305–352.

(2011). Implicit and explicit SLA and their interface. In C. Sanz & R. P. Leow (Eds.), *Implicit and explicit language learning: Conditions, processes, and knowledge in SLA and bilingualism* (pp. 35–47). Washington, DC: Georgetown University Press.

(2012). Frequency-based accounts of second language acquisition. In S. Gass & A. Mackey (Eds.), *The Routledge handbook of second language acquisition* (pp. 193–210*).* New York: Routledge.

(2014). Cognitive *and* social language usage. *Studies in Second Language Acquisition, 36,* 397– 402.

(2015). Implicit *and* explicit learning: Their dynamic interface and complexity. In B. Rebuschat (Ed.), *Implicit and explicit learning of languages* (pp. 3–23). Amsterdam: John Benjamins.

(2019). Essentials of a theory of language cognition. *The Modern Language Journal, 103,* 39–60. doi: 10.1111/modl.12532

Ellis, N., O'Donnell, M. B., & Römer, U. (2015). Usage-based language learning. In B. MacWhinney & W. O'Grady (Eds.), *The handbook of language emergence* (pp. 163–180). Chichester: Wiley-Blackwell.

Ellis, R. (1985). *Understanding second language acquisition.* Oxford: Oxford University Press.

(1990). *Instructed second language acquisition.* Oxford: Blackwell.

(1994). *The study of second language acquisition.* Oxford: Oxford University Press.

(1998). The evaluation of communicative tasks. In B. Tomlinson (Ed.), *Materials development in language teaching* (pp. 217–238). Cambridge: Cambridge University Press.

(2003). *Task-based language teaching and learning.* Oxford: Oxford University Press.

(2005a). Principles of instructed language learning. *System, 33,* 209–224.

(2005b). *Instructed second language acquisition: A literature review.* Report to the Ministry of Education. Auckland: Auckland UniServices Ltd.

(2006). Current issues in the teaching of grammar: An SLA perspective. *TESOL Quarterly. 40*(1), 83–107.

(2008). *The study of second language acquisition* (2nd ed.). Oxford: Oxford University Press.

(2009). Corrective feedback and teacher development. *L2 Journal, 1,* 3–18.

(2010a). Second language acquisition research and language-teaching materials. In N. Harwood (Ed.), *English language teaching materials: Theory and practice* (pp. 33–57). Cambridge: Cambridge University Press.

(2010b). Second language acquisition, teacher education, and language pedagogy. *Language Teaching. 43*(2), 182–201.

(2011). Macro- and micro-evaluations of task-based teaching. In B. Tomlinson (Ed.), *Materials development in language teaching* (pp. 212–235). Cambridge: Cambridge University Press.

(2012). Instruction, individual differences and L2 learning. In R. Ellis (Ed.), *Language teaching research and language pedagogy* (pp. 307–335). Chichester: Wiley-Blackwell.

(2015). *Understanding second language acquisition* (2nd ed.). Oxford: Oxford University Press.

(2016a). Language teaching materials as work plans: An SLA perspective. In B., Tomlinson (Ed.), *SLA research and materials development for language learning* (pp. 203–218). New York: Routledge.

(2016b). Focus on form: A critical review. *Language Teaching Research, 20*(3), 405–428.

Ellis, R. & He, X. (1999). The roles of modified input and output in the incidental acquisition of word meanings. *Studies in Second Language Acquisition, 21*(2), 285–301.

Ellis, R., Loewen, S. & Erlam, R. (2006). Implicit and explicit corrective feedback and the acquisition of L2 grammar. *Studies in Second Language Acquisition, 28*, 339–368.

Ellis, R. & Sheen, Y. (2006). Re-examining the role of recasts in second language acquisition. *Studies in Second Language Acquisition, 28*(4), 575–600.

Ellis, R. & Shintani, N. (2013). *Exploring language pedagogy through second language acquisition research.* New York: Routledge.

Ellis, R., Skehan, P., Li, S., Shintani, N. & Lambert, C. (2019). *Task-based language teaching: Theory and practice.* Cambridge: Cambridge University Press.

Ellis, R. & Tomlinson, B. (1980). *Teaching secondary English.* Harlow: Longman.

Engle, R. W. (2002). Working memory capacity as executive attention. *Current Directions in Psychological Science, 11*, 19–23.

Erlam, R. (2012). Explicit knowledge and grammar explanation in Second Language Instruction. *Wiley Online Library.* First published: 05 November 2012 https://doi.org/10.1002/9781405198431.wbeal0404

Esrock, E. (1994). *The reader's eye.* Baltimore: The Johns Hopkins University Press.

Estes, W. K., Newell, A., Anderson, J. R., Seely Brown, J., Feigenbaum, E. A., Greeno, J., Hayes, P. J., Hunt, E., Kosslyn, S. M., Marcus, M. & Ullman, S. (1983). Report of the research briefing panel on cognitive science and artificial intelligence. *Research briefings 1983* (pp. 20–36). Washington, DC: National Academy Press.

Euromonitor International (2012). *The benefits of the English language for individuals and societies: Quantitative indicators from Algeria, Egypt, Iraq, Jordan, Lebanon, Morocco, Tunisia and Yemen.* London: Euromonitor International Ltd.

Evans, N. & Levinson, S. C. (2009). The myth of language universals: Language diversity and its importance for cognitive science. *Behavioral and Brain Sciences*, 32(5), 429-48.

Evert, S. (2007). *Corpora and collocations.* Berlin: Mouton de Gruyter.

Faneslow, J. (2019). *Small changes in teaching big success in learning: Videos, activities and essays to stimulate fresh thinking about language learning and teaching.* Independently published. https://books.google.co.uk/books/about/Small_Changes_in_Teaching_Big_Results_in.html?id=rdxmuAEACAAJ&source=kp_book_description&redir_esc=y

Felix, U. (2008). The unreasonable effectiveness of CALL: What have we learned in two decades of research? *ReCALL*, 20(2), 141-161.

Fenner, A. N. & Nordal-Pedersen, G. (1999). *Search 10.* Oslo: Gyldendal.

(2006). *Searching 8.* Oslo: Gyldendal.

Fenton-Smith, B. (2010). A debate on the desired effects of output activities for extensive reading. In B. Tomlinson & H. Masuhara (Eds.), *Research for materials development in language learning: Evidence for best practice* (pp. 50–61). London: Continuum.

Field, J. (2014). *Psycholinguistics: The key concepts.* Abingdon, Oxon: Routledge.

Finney, D. (2002). The ELT curriculum: A flexible model for a changing world. In J. C. Richards & W. A. Renandya, (Eds.), *Methodology in language teaching: An anthology of current practice.* Cambridge: Cambridge University Press.

Flesch, P. (1948). A new readability yardstick. *Journal of Applied Psychology*, 32(3), 221–233. doi:10.1037/h005753

Fletcher, P. & Garman, M. (1986). Language acquisition (2nd ed.). Cambridge: Cambridge University Press.

Floris, F. D., Renandya, W. & Bao, D. (2018). Mining on-line learning resources: From SLA principles to on-line task design. In D. Bao (Ed.), *Creativity and innovations in ELT materials development: Looking beyond the current design* (pp. 154–180). Bristol: Multilingual Matters.

Flowerdew, J. & Miller, L. (2012). Assessing listening. In C. Coombe, P. Davidson, B. O'Sullivan & S. Stoynoff (Eds.), *The Cambridge guide to second language assessment* (pp. 225–233). Cambridge: Cambridge University Press.

Foster, P. & Ohta, A. (2005). Negotiation for meaning and peer assistance in second language learning classrooms. *Applied Linguistics*, 26(3), 402–430. doi.10.1093/applin/amio14

Fotos, S. & Nassaji, H. (2007). *Form-focused instruction and teacher education: Studies in honour of Rod Ellis.* Oxford: Oxford University Press.

Foucart, A. & Frenck-Mestre, C. (2013). Language processing. In J. Hershenson & M. Young-Scholten (Eds.), *The Cambridge handbook of second language acquisition* (pp. 394–416). Cambridge: Cambridge University Press.

Fowler, Y. R. (2019). My top ten bilingual books. *The Guardian*, Wednesday 17 April, 2019 www.theguardian.com/books/2019/apr/17/top-10-bilingual-books (accessed 28 February 2020).

Fredrickson, B. L & Branigan, C. (2005). Positive emotions broaden the scope of attention and thought-action repertoires. *Cognition and Emotion, 19* (3), 313–332.

Freeman, D. (2014). Reading comprehension questions: The distribution of different types in global EFL textbooks. In N. Harwood (Ed.), *English language teaching textbooks: Content, consumption, production* (pp. 72–110). Basingstoke: Palgrave Macmillan.

Fries, C. C. (1945). *Teaching and learning English as a foreign language.* Ann Arbor: University of Michigan Press.

(1952). *The structure of English: An introduction to the structure of English sentences.* New York: Harcourt Brace.

Fromkin, V., Rodman, R. & Hyams, N. (2014). *An introduction to language* (10th ed.). Andover: Wadsworth Cengage Learning.

Frumeselu, A. D. (2019). "A friend indeed is a film indeed": Teaching colloquial expressions with subtitled television series. In C. Herrero & I. Yanderschelden (Ed.), *Using film and media in the language classroom: Reflections on research-led thinking* (pp. 92–107). Bristol: Multilingual Matters.

Fujii, A. & Mackey, A. (2009). Interactional feedback in learner-learner interactions in a task-based EFL classroom. *Internationl Review of Applied linguistics in Language Teaching, 47*, 267–301. 10.1515/iral.2009.012

Gablasova, D., Brezina, V., McEnery, T., & Boyd, E. (2015). Epistemic stance in spoken L2 English: The effect of task and speaker style. *Applied Linguistics*, Advance online publication. doi:10.1093/applin/amv055

Gablasova, D., Brezina, V. & McEnery, T. (2017). Exploring learner language through corpora: Comparing and interpreting corpus frequency information. *Language Learning, 67* (s1), 130–154.

Gabrys, D. & Bielska, J. (Eds.). (2013). *The affective dimension in second language acquisition.* Bristol: Multilingual Matters.

Galian-Lopez, G. (2018). Automaticity in second language vocabulary learning. *University of Reading Language Studies Working Papers, 9,* 26–34. www.researchgate.net/publication/325607672_Automaticity_in_Second_Language_Vocabulary_Learning

García Mayo, M. P. & Alcón Soler, E. (2013). Negotiated input and output / interaction. In J. Herschensohn, & M. Young-Scholten (Eds.), *The Cambridge handbook of second language acquisition* (pp. 209–229). New York: Cambridge University Press.

García Mayo, M. P. & Pica, T. (2000). L2 Learner interaction in a foreign language setting: Are learning needs addressed? *International Review of Applied Linguistics, 38,* 35–58.

Gardner, H. (1993). *Frames of mind: The theory of multiple intelligences* (2nd ed.). London: Fontana.

Garrett, M. F. (1988). Processes in language production. In F. J. Newmeyer (Ed.), *Linguistics: The Cambridge survey: Vol. 3 Language: Psychological and biological aspects* (pp. 69–96). Cambridge: Cambridge University Press.

Garton, S. & Graves, K. (Eds.). (2014). *International perspectives on materials in ELT*. Basingstoke: Palgrave Macmillan.

Garton, S., Copland, F. & Mann, S. (2016). Opinions and positions on native-speakerism. In F. Copland, S. Garton & S. Mann (Eds.), *LETs and NESTs: Voices, views and vignettes* (pp. 240–259). London: The British Council.

Gass, S. & Madden, C. (Eds.). (1985). *Input in second language acquisition*. Rowley, MA: Newbury House.

Gass, S. M. & Mackey, A. (Eds.), (2012). *The Routledge handbook of second language acquisition*. Oxford: Routledge.

(2015). Input, interaction, and output in second language acquisition. In B. Van Patten & J. Williams, (Eds.), *Theories in second language acquisition* (2nd ed., pp. 180–206). New York: Routledge.

Gass, S. M. & Selinker, L. (1994). *Second language acquisition: An introductory course*. New York: Routledge.

Gass, S. M. & Varonis, E. M. (1994). Input, interaction, and second language production. *Studies in Second Language Acquisition, 3*, 283.

Gazzaniga, M. S., Ivry, R. B. & Mangun, G. R. (2019). *Cognitive neuroscience: The biology of the mind* (5th ed.). New York: W. W. Norton & Company.

Geraci, L. & Rajaram, S. (2004). The distinctiveness effect in the absence of conscious recollection: Evidence from conceptual priming. *Journal of Memory and Language, 51*, 217–230.

Geraci, L., McDaniel, M. A., Miller, T. M. & Hughes, M. L. (2013). The bizarreness effect: Evidence for the critical influence of retrieval processes. *Memory & Cognition, 41*(8), 1228–1237.

Getting started with assessment (2018). https://cambridge-community.org.uk/profe development/gswafl/index.html - accessed 5 August 2018. Cambridge: University of Cambridge Assessment International Education.

Ghosn, I. (2007). Output like input: Influence of children's literature on young L2 learners' written expression. In B. Tomlinson (Ed.), *Language acquisition and development: Studies of learners of first and other languages* (pp. 171–186). London: Continuum.

(2013). *Storybridge to second language literacy: The theory, research, and practice of teaching English with children's literature*. Charlotte, NC: Information Age Publishing, INC.

(2016). No place for coursebooks in the very young learner classroom. In B. Tomlinson (Ed.), *SLA research and materials development for language learning* (pp. 50–66). New York: Routledge.

Gibbons, P. (2002). *Scaffolding language, scaffolding learning: Teaching second language learners in the mainstream classroom*. Oxford: Heinemann.

Gilmore, A. (2007). Authentic materials and authenticity in foreign language learning. *Language Teaching* 40, 97–118.

(2011). "I prefer not text": Developing Japanese learners' communicative competence with authentic materials. *Language Learning: A Journal of Research in Language Studies*, 61(3), 786–819.

(2015). Research into practice: The influence of discourse studies on language description and task design in published ELT materials. *Language Teaching: Surveys and Studies*, 48(4), 506–530.

Gingras, R. (Ed.). (1978). *Second language acquisition and foreign language teaching*. Arlington, VA.: Centre for Applied Linguistics.

Goh, C. M. & Burns, A. (2012). *Teaching speaking: A holistic approach*. New York: Cambridge University Press.

Goldstein, B. (2012). *The big picture intermediate*. Oxford: Richmond.

González-Lloret, M. & Ortega, L. (Eds.). (2014). *Technology-mediated TBLT. Researching technology and tasks*. Amsterdam: John Benjamins.

Goo, J., Granena, G., Yilmaz, Y. & Novella, M. (2015). Implicit and explicit instruction in L2 learning - Norris & Ortega (2000) revisited and updated. In P. Rebuschat (Ed.), *Implicit and explicit learning of languages* (pp. 165–182). Amsterdam: John Benjamins.

Gordon, G. N. (2019). Communication. *Encyclopedia Britannica*, www.britannica.com/topic/communication/Gestures

Grabe, W. (2009). *Reading in a second language: Moving from theory to practice*. New York: Cambridge University Press.

Granena, G. (2013). Individual differences in sequencing learner ability and second language acquisition in early childhood and adulthood. *Language Learning*, 63, 665–703.

Granena, G. & Long, M. (2013). *Sensitive periods, language aptitude, and ultimate L2 attainment*. Amsterdam: John Benjamins.

Granger, S., Gilquin, G. & Meunier, F. (Eds.). (2015). *The Cambridge handbook of learner corpus research*. Cambridge: Cambridge University Press.

Greenwood, P., Hutton, J., Dudley, J. & Horowitz-Kraus, T. (2019). Maternal reading fluency is associated with functional connectivity between the child's future reading network and regions related to executive functions and language processing in preschool-age children. *Brain & Cognition*, 131, 87–93.

Gregg, K. R. (1984). Krashen's monitor and Occam's razor. *Applied Linguistics*, 5 (2), 79–100.

Grey, S., Sanz, C., Morgan-Short, K. & Ullman, M. T. (2018). Bilingual and monolingual adults learning an additional language: ERPs reveal differences in syntactic processing. *Bilingualism-Language and Cognition*, 21(5), 970–994.

Grgurović, M., Chapelle, C. A. & Shelley, M. C. (2013). A meta-analysis of effectiveness studies on computer technology-supported language learning. *ReCALL*, 25(2), 165–198.

Griffiths, C. (Ed). (2008). *Lessons from good language learners.* Cambridge: Cambridge University Press.

Grimm, R., Cassani, G., Gillis, S. & Daelemans, W. (2019). Children probably store short rather than frequent or predictable chunks: Quantitative evidence from a corpus study. *Frontiers in Psychology, 10,* 10–80

Grundy, P. (2013). Humanistic language teaching. In M. Byram & A. Hu (Eds.), *Routledge encyclopedia of language teaching and learning* (pp. 322–325). Abingdon: Routledge.

Guerrettaz, A. M. & Johnston, B. (2013). Materials in the classroom ecology. *Modern Language Journal, 97*(3), 779–796.

Gullberg, M. & McCafferty, S. (2008). Introduction to gesture and SLA: Toward an integrated approach. *Studies in Second Language Acquisition, 30*(2), 133–146.

Gutiérrez, K. D. (2008) Developing a sociocritical literacy in the third space. *Reading Research Quarterly, 43*(2), 148–164. http://dx.doi.org/10.1598/RRQ.43.2.3

Hadley, G. (2014). Global textbooks in local contexts: An empirical investigation of effectiveness. In J. Harwood (Ed.), *English language teaching textbooks: Content, consumption, production* (pp. 205–238). Basingstoke: Palgrave Macmillan.

Haines, S. (1989). *Projects for the EFL classroom.* London: Nelson.

Halliday, M. A. K. & Webster, J. J. (Ed.). (2018). *Halliday in the 21st century, 11th edition.* London: Bloomsbury.

Han, Z. & Odlin, T. (2006). *Studies of fossilization in second language acquisition.* Clevedon: Multilingual Matters.

Han, Z., Park, E. S. & Combs, C. (2008). Textual enhancement of input: Issues and possibilities. *Applied Linguistics, 29*(4), 597–618.

Hanks, J. (2017). Integrating research and pedagogy: An exploratory practice approach. *System, 68,* 38–49.

Harlen, W. (2007). *Assessment of learning.* London: Sage.

Harley, T. A. (2008). *The psychology of language: From data to theory* (3rd ed.). Hove: Psychology Press.

Harmer, J. (2001). *The practice of English language teaching.* (3rd ed.). Harlow: Pearson.

(2007a). *How to teach English: An introduction to the practice of English language teaching* (2nd ed.). Harlow: Longman.

(2007b). *The practice of English language teaching* (4th ed.). Harlow: Longman.

Harris, B. (1979). Whatever happened to little Albert? *American Psychologist, 34*(2), 151–160.

Harwood, N. (Ed.). (2010). *English language teaching materials: Theory and practice.* Cambridge: Cambridge University Press.

(Ed.). (2014). *English language teaching textbooks: Content, consumption, production.* Basingstoke: Palgrave Macmillan.

Hatch, E. M. (1978a). Discourse analysis and second language acquisition. In E. M. Hatch (Ed.), *Second language acquisition: A book of readings* (pp. 401–435). Rowley, MA: Newbury House.

(Ed.). (1978b). *Second language acquisition: A book of readings.* Rowley, MA.: Newbury House.

(1983). *Psycholinguistics: A second language perspective.* Rowley, MA: Newbury House.

Hattie, J. (2011). *Visible learning for teachers.* Abingdon: Routledge.

Hattie, J. & Clark, S. (2018). *Visible learning: Feedback.* New York: Routledge.

Hayes, J. R. & Flower, L. S. (1986). Writing research and the writer. *American Psychologist, 41*, 1106–1113.

Hedge, T. (2000). *Teaching and learning in the English classroom.* Oxford: Oxford University Press.

Henry, A., Davydenko, S. & Dörnyei, Z. (2015). The anatomy of directed motivational currents: Exploring intense and enduring periods of L2 motivation. *The Modern Language Journal, 99*(2), 329–345.

Herrero, C. & Vanderschelden, I. (Eds.). (2019). *Using film and media in the language classroom: Reflections on research-led thinking.* Bristol: Multilingual Matters.

Herschensohn, J. & Young-Scholten, M. (Eds.). (2013). *The Cambridge handbook of second language acquisition.* Cambridge: Cambridge University Press.

Hill, J. D. & Björk, C. L. (2008). *Classroom instruction that works with English Language learners facilitator's guide.* Alexandria, VA.: ASCD. www.ascd.org/publications/books/108052/chapters/The-Stages-of-Second-Language-Acquisition.aspx - accessed 7/10/2019.

Hill, M. & Laufer, B. (2003). Type of task, time-on-task and electronic dictionaries in incidental vocabulary acquisition. *International Review of Applied Linguistics, 41*(2), 87–106.

Hinijosa, J. A., Moreno, E. M. & Ferre, P. (2019). Affective neurolinguistics: towards a framework for reconciling language and emotion. *Language, Cognition and Neuroscience, 34*(6) https://doi.org/10.1080/23273798.2019.1620957

Hinkel, E. (Ed.). (2005). *Handbook of research in second language teaching and learning.* Mawah, NJ: Laurence Earlbaum.

Hockly, N. (2013). Designer learning: The teacher as designer of mobile-based classroom learning experiences. *The International Research Foundation for English Language Education.*

Hoedemaker, R. S. & Gordon, P. C. (2014). Embodied language comprehension: Encoding-based and goal-driven processes. *Journal of Experimental Psychology: General, 143*(2), 914–929.

Hoey, M. (2005). *Lexical priming: A new theory of words and language.* London: Routledge.

Holliday, A. (2006). Native-speakerism. *ELT Journal, 60*(4), 385–387.

Holme, R. (2012). Cognitive linguistics and the second language classroom. *TESOL Quarterly. 46*(1), 6–29.

House, J. (Ed.). (2014). *Translation: A multidisciplinary approach.* London: Palgrave Macmillan.

Houssen, A. & Pierrard, M. (Eds.). (2005). *Investigations in instructed language acquisition.* Berlin: Mouton de Gruyter.

Hubbard, P. (Ed.). (2009). *Computer assisted language learning,* Vols. 1–4. New York: Routledge.

Hughes, A. (2002). *Language testing for teachers* (2nd ed.). Cambridge: Cambridge University Press.

Hummel, K. M. (2014). *Introducing second language acquisition: Perspectives and practices*. Hoboken, NJ: Wiley-Blackwell.

Hutton, J. S., Phelan, K., Horowitz-Kraus, T., Dudley, J., Altaye, M., DeWitt, T. & Holland, S. K. (2017). Shared reading quality and brain activation during story listening in preschool-age children. *The Journal of Pediatrics, 191*, 204–211.

Hyland, K. (2018). *Metadiscourse: Exploring interaction in writing*. London: Bloomsbury.

Hynninen, N. (2020). Fluency in English as a lingua franca interaction. In P. Lintunen, M. Mutta & P. Peltonen (Eds.), *Fluency in L2 learning and use* (pp. 81–95). Bristol: Multilingual Matters.

Immordino-Yang, M. H. & Damasio, A. (2007). We feel, therefore we learn: The relevance of affective and social neuroscience to education. *Mind, Brain and Education, 1*(8), 3–10.

Ishihara, N. & Paller, D. L. (2016). Research-informed materials for teaching pragmatics: The case of agreement and disagreement in English. In B. Tomlinson (Ed.), *SLA research and materials development for language learning* (pp. 87–102). New York: Routledge.

Jackson, J. O. (2016). Working memory and second language acquisition: Theory and findings. *The Journal of Kanda University of International Studies, 28*, 21–47.

Jenkins, J. (2015). *Global Englishes* (3rd ed.). Abingdon: Routledge.

Jenkins, J., Baker, W. & Dewey, M. (Eds.). (2018). *The Routledge handbook of English as a lingua franca*. Abingdon: Routledge.

Jenkins, J. & Leung, C. (2019). From mythical "standard" to standard reality: The need for alternatives to standardized English language tests. *Language Teaching, 52*(1), 86–110.

Jepson, K. (2005). Conversations – and negotiated interactions – in text and voice chat rooms. *Language Learning and Technology, 9*(3), 79–98.

Joaquin, A. D. L. & Schumann, J. H. (2014). *Exploring the interactional instinct*. New York: Oxford University Press.

Johns, T. (1997). Contexts: The background, development and trialling of a concordance based CALL program. In A. Whichmann, S. Fligelstone, T. McEnery & G. Knowles (Eds.), *Teaching and language corpora* (pp. 100–115). Harlow: Longman.

Johnson, D. (1992). *Approaches to research in second language learning*. New York: Longman.

Johnson, K. (1996). *Language teaching and skill learning*. Oxford: Blackwell.

(2001). *An introduction to foreign language learning and teaching*. Harlow: Longman.

Johnson, K. & Johnson, H. (1999). *Encyclopedic dictionary of applied linguistics*. London: Blackwell.

Johnson-Laird, P. N. (1983). *Mental models: Toward a cognitive science of language, inference and consciousness*. Cambridge, MA: Harvard University Press.

Jones, C. A. (2005). *Assessment for learning*. London: The Learning and Skills Development Agency.

Jones, C. (2017). Soap operas as models for authentic conversations: Implications for materials design. In A. Maley & B. Tomlinson (Eds.), *Authenticity in materials development for language learning* (pp.158–175). Newcastle: Cambridge Scholars.

(2019). *Literature, spoken language and speaking skills in second language learning.* Cambridge: Cambridge University Press.

Jones, G. & Rowland, C. F. (2017). Diversity not quantity in caregiver speech: Using computational modeling to isolate the effects of the quantity and the diversity of the input on vocabulary growth. *Cognitive Psychology, 98*, 1–21.

Jones, K. (1997). Simulations: A handbook for teachers and trainers (3rd ed.). London: Keagan Page.

Jones, L. C. & Plass J. L. (2002). Supporting listening comprehension and vocabulary acquisition in French with multi-media annotations. *Modern Language Journal, 86*(4), 546–561.

Jurkovič, V. (2018), Online informal learning of English through smartphones in Slovenia, *System*, 10.1016/j.system.2018.10.007

Kachru, B. B. (1985). Standards, codification, and sociolinguistic realism: The English language in the outer circle. In R. Quirk & H. Widdowson (Eds.), *English in the world: Teaching and learning the language and the literature.* Cambridge: Cambridge University Press.

(1991). Liberation linguistics and the Quirk concern. *English Today: The International Review of the English Language, 7*(1), 3–13.

Kachru, Y. (1994). Monolingual bias in SLA research. *TESOL Quarterly, 28*(4), 795–800.

Kandel, E. R. (2006). *In search of memory: The emergence of a new science of mind.* New York: W. W. Norton.

Kandylaki, K. D. & Bornkessel-Schlesewsky, I. (2019). From story comprehension to the neurobiology of language. *Language, Cognition and Neuroscience.* Published online: 21 Feb 2019. https://doi.org/10.1080/23273798.2019.1584679

Kao, S. & O'Neill, C. (1998). *Words into worlds: Learning a second language through process drama.* Stamford, CT: Ablex Publishing Corporation.

Karpicke, J. D. & Roediger, H. L. (2008). The critical importance of retrieval for learning. *Science, 319,* 966–968.

Kiddle, T. (2013). Developing digital language learning materials. In B. Tomlinson (Ed.), *Developing materials for language teaching* (2nd ed., pp. 189–206). London: Bloomsbury.

Keddie, J. *Lessonstream.* Retrieved from http://lessonstream.org/lessons/

(2009). *Images.* Oxford: Oxford University Press.

(2014). *Bringing online video into the classroom.* Oxford: Oxford University Press.

Kelly, G. (2000). *How to teach pronunciation.* Harlow: Pearson.

Kennedy, C. & Tomlinson, B. (2013). Implementing language policy and planning through materials development. In B. Tomlinson (Ed.), *Applied linguistics and materials development* (pp. 255–267). London: Continuum.

Kerr, P. (2015). *Translation and own-language activities*. Cambridge: Cambridge University Press.

Khalifa, H. & Weir, C. J. (Eds.). (2009). *Examining reading: Research and practice in assessing second language reading*. Cambridge: UCLES/Cambridge University Press.

Kim, D. & Gilman, D. (2008). Effect of text, audio, and graphic aids in multi-media instruction for vocabulary learning. *Educational Technology and Society*, *11*(3), 114–126.

Kim, H. & Krashen, S. (1997). Why don't language acquirers take advantage of the power of reading? *TESOL Journal*, *26*(9), 26–29.

King, J. & Seiko, H. (Eds.). (2020). *East-Asian perspectives on silence in English language education*. Bristol: Multilingual Matters.

King, N. (1990). Myth, metaphor, memory: Archeology of the self. *Journal of Humanistic Psychology*, *30*(2), 55–72.

Kirkpatrick, A. (Ed.). (2010). *The Routledge handbook of World Englishes*. Oxon: Routledge.

Kirkpatrick, A., & Liddicoat, A. J. (2017). Language education policy and practice in east and southeast Asia. *Language Teaching: Surveys and Studies*, *50*(2), 155–188.

Klein, W. (1998). The contribution of second language acquisition research. *Language Learning*, *48*, 527–550.

Knagg, J. (2013). EMI within a global context – Towards a British Council perspective. In *British Council regional policy dialogue 2, The role of English in higher education: Issues, policy and practice*. www.britishcouncil.org.br/sites/default/files/regionalpolicydialogue_emi.pdf (accessed 05 April 2018).

Kolb, A. & Kolb D. A. (2001). *Experiential learning theory bibliography 1971–2001*. Boston, MA: McBer and Co http://trgmcber.haygroup.com/Products/learning/bibliography.htm

Kormos, J. (2006). *Speech production and second language acquisition*. Mahwah, NJ: Lawrence Erlbaum Associates.

(2012). *Narrative tasks, individual differences, and foreign language learning*. Boston, MA: Walter de Gruyter.

(2013). New conceptualizations of language aptitude in second language attainment. In G. Granena & M. H. Long (Eds.), *Sensitive periods, language aptitude, and ultimate L2 attainment* (pp. 131–152). Amsterdam: John Benjamins.

Kosslyn, S. M. (1980). *Image and mind*. Cambridge, MA: Harvard University Press.

Krashen, S. (1979). The monitor model for second language acquisition. In R. C. Gingras (Ed.), *Second language acquisition and foreign language teaching* (pp. 1–26). Arlington, VA: Centre for Applied Linguistics.

(1981). *Second language acquisition and second language learning*. Oxford: Pergamon.

(1982). *Principles and practice in second language acquisition*. Oxford: Pergamon.

(1985). *The input hypothesis: Issues and implications*. London: Longman.

(1994). The input hypothesis and its rivals. In N. Ellis (Ed.), *Implicit and explicit learning of languages* (pp. 45–87). London: Academic Press.

(2004). *The power of reading* (2nd ed.). Littleton: Libraries Unlimited.

(2011). *Free voluntary reading.* Santa Barbara, CA: Libraries Unlimited.

Krashen, S. & Terrell, T. (1983). *The natural approach: Language acquisition in the classroom.* Oxford: Pergammon.

Kramsch, C. (1993). *Context and culture in language teaching.* Oxford: Oxford University Press.

Kuiken F. & Vedder, I. (2012). Speaking and writing tasks and their effect on second language performance. In S. Gass & A. Mackey (Eds.), *The Routledge handbook of second language acquisition* (pp. 364–377). New York: Routledge.

Kukulska-Hulme, A. & Shield, L. (2008). An overview of mobile assisted language learning: From content delivery to supported collaboration and interaction. *ReCALL*, 20, 271–289. https://doi.org/10.1017/S0958344008000335

Lagerwaard, D. (2019a). How to guide mediation in the secondary classroom. Posted on 13 March 2019. www.oxfordtefl.com/blog/through-others-we-become-ourselves-how-to-guide-mediation-in-the-secondary-classroom

(2019b). Involving emotions in the secondary classroom: Why and how? The Oxford TEFL Blog. Posted on 23 April 2019 www.oxfordtefl.com/blog/involving-emotions-in-the-secondary-classroom-why-and-how

Lado, R. (1977). *Lado English series (7 vols).* New York: Regents.

Lado, R. & Fries, C. C. (1943/1953/1957/1958). *English pattern practices: Establishing the patterns as habits.* Ann Arbor: University of Michigan Press. Retrieved from http://hdl.handle.net/2027/mdp.39015062434876

Lamb, M. (2017). The motivational dimension of language teaching. *Language Teaching, 50*(3), 301–346.

Lambert, C. & Oliver, R. (2020). *Using tasks in second language teaching: Practice in diverse contexts.* Bristol: Multilingual Matters.

Lantolf, J. (Ed.). (2001). *Sociocultural theory and second language learning.* Oxford: Oxford University Press.

Lantolf, J., Thorne, S. L., & Poehner, M. (2015). Sociocultural theory and second language development. In B. Van Patten & J. Williams (Eds.), *Theories in second language acquisition* (pp. 207–226). New York: Routledge.

Lapkin, S., Swain, M. & Psyllakis, P. (2010). The role of languaging in creating zones of proximal development: a long-term care resident interacts with a researcher. *Canadian Journal on Aging*, 29, 277–490. Doi:10.1017/S0714980810000644

Larsen-Freeman, D. (2000). *Techniques and principles in language teaching.* Oxford University Press.

(2019). On language learner agency: A complex dynamic systems theory perspective. *The Modern Language Journal, 103*(51), 61–79. https://doi.org/10.1111/modl.12536

Larsen-Freeman, D. & Long, M. (1991). *An introduction to second language acquisition research.* London: Longman.

Lasagabaster, D. & Ruiz de Zarobe, Y. (Eds.). (2010). *CLIL in Spain. Implementation, results and teacher training.* Newcastle upon Tyne: Cambridge Scholars.

Le, N. M. T. (2011). *The reception of new language materials: A case study evaluation of an EFL textbook in Vietnamese high schools.* Unpublished PhD. Macquarie University, Sydney.

(2017). Authentic materials to fulfil workplace requirements for Vietnamese graduates. In A. Maley & B. Tomlinson (Eds.), *Authenticity in materials development for language learning* (pp. 192–211). Newcastle: Cambridge Scholars.

Lech, I. B. & Harris, L. N. (2019). Language learning in the virtual wild. In M. L. Carrió-Pastor (Ed.), *Teaching language and teaching literature in virtual environments* (pp. 39–54). Singapore: Springer.

Leclercq, P., Edmonds, A. & Hilton, H. (Eds.). (2014). *Measuring L2 proficiency: Perspectives from SLA.* Clevedon: Multilingual Matters.

Lee, I. & Coniam, D. (2013). Introducing assessment for learning for EFL writing in an assessment of learning examination-driven system in Hong Kong. *Journal of Second Language Writing, 22*(1), 34–50. https://doi.org/10.1016/j.jslw.2012.11.003

Lee, J. S. (2019). EFL students' views of willingness to communicate in the extramural digitalcontext. *Computer Assisted Language Learning, 32*(7), 692–712. 10.1080/09588221.2018.1535509 (1–21).

Lee, J. S. & Hsieh, J. C. (2019). Affective variables and willingness to communicate of EFL learners in in-class, out-of-class, and digital contexts, *System, 83*, 62–73. 10.1016/j.system.2019.03.002

Lee, N., Mikesell, L., Joaquin, A. D. L., Mates, A. W. & Schumann, J. H. (2009). *The interactional instinct: The evolution and acquisition of language.* Oxford: Oxford University Press.

Lee, S. & Huang, H. (2008). Visual input enhancement and grammar learning: A meta-analytic review. *Studies in Second Language Acquisition, 30*(3), 307–331.

Leow, R. P. (1993). To simplify or not to simplify: A look at intake. *Studies in Second Language Acquisition, 15*(3), 333–355. doi:10.1017/S0272263100012146

Lessard-Clouston, M. (2018). *Second language acquisition applied to English language teaching.* Alexandria, VA: TESOL Press.

Lethaby, C. & Harries, P. (2017). Neuroscience. *IATEFL Voices, 257*, 11.

Levelt, W. J. M. (1983). Monitoring and self-repair in speech. *Cognition, 14*, 41–104.

(1989). *Speaking: From intention to articulation.* Cambridge: Cambridge University Press.

(1993). *Speaking: From intention to articulation.* Cambridge, MA: MIT.

(2001). Spoken word production: A theory of lexical access. *Proceedings of the National Academy of Sciences, 98*(23), 13464–13471.

Levinson, S. C. & Evans, N. (2010). Time for a sea-change in linguistics: Response to comments on "The myth of language universals". *Lingua, 120*(12), 2733–2758.

Lewis, M. (1993). *The lexical approach: the state of ELT and a way forward.* Hove: Language Teaching Publications.

(2000). Language in the lexical approach. In M. Lewis (Ed.), *Teaching collocation: Further developments in the Lexical Approach* (pp. 126–154). Hove: Language Teaching Publications.

Li, S. (2010). The effectiveness of corrective feedback in SLA: A meta-analysis. *Language Learning 60*, 309–365.

(2014). Oral corrective feedback. *ELT Journal, 68*(2), 196–198. https://doi.org/10.1093/elt/cct076

(2016). The construct validity of language aptitude. *Studies in Second Language Acquisition, 38*(4), 801–842.

Liddicoat, A. (2004). Language policy and methodology. *International Journal of English Studies, 41*(1), 153–171.

Liebermann, M. D. & Rosenthal, R. (2001). Why introverts can't always tell who likes them: Multi-tasking and non-verbal coding. *Journal of Personality and Social Psychology, 80*, 294–310.

Lightbown, P. M. (2000). Anniversary article: Classroom SLA research and second language teaching. *Applied Linguistics*, 21, 431–462.

Lightbown, P. M. & Spada, N. (1993). *How languages are learned*. Oxford: Oxford University Press.

(1990). Focus-on-form and corrective language teaching: effects on second language learning. *Studies in Second Language Acquisition, 12*, 429–448.

Lightfoot, D. (2006). *How new languages emerge*. Cambridge: Cambridge University Press.

Llinares, A. & Morton, T. (Eds.), (2017). *Applied linguistics perspectives on CLIL*. Amsterdam: John Benjamins. DOI 10.1075/lllt.47

Linck, J. A. & Weiss, D. J. (2015). Can working memory and inhibitory control predict second language learning in the classroom? *Sage Open*, 5(4), 1–11.

Lintunen, P., Mutta, M. & Peltonen, P. (2020). Defining fluency in L2 learning and use. In P. Lintunen, M. Mutta & P. Peltonen (Eds.), *Fluency in L2 learning and use* (pp. 1–15). Bristol: Multilingual Matters.

Littlewood, W. T. (1981). *Communicative language teaching*. Cambridge: Cambridge University Press.

Liu, C. H. & Matthews, R. (2005). Vygotsky's philosophy: Constructivism and its criticisms examined. *International Education Journal, 6*(3), 386–399.

Llinares, A. & Morton, T. (Eds.). (2017). *Applied linguistics perspectives on CLIL*. Amsterdam: John Benjamins.

Llinás, R. R. (Ed.). (1990). *The workings of the brain: Development, memory and perception*. New York: Freeman.

Llurda, E. (Ed.). (2005). *Non-native language teachers: Perceptions, challenges and contributions to the profession*. New York: Springer Science+Business Media, Inc.

Loewen, S. (2012). The role of feedback. In S. Gass & A. Mackey (Eds.), *The Routledge handbook of second language acquisition* (pp. 24–40). New York: Routledge.

(2015). *Introduction to instructed second language acquisition*. New York, NJ: Routledge.

Loewen, S. & Philp, J. (2006). Recasts in the adult English L2 classroom: Characteristics, explicitness, and effectiveness. *Modern Language Journal, 90*, 536–556.

Loewen, S. & Sato, M. (Eds.). (2017). *The Routledge handbook of instructed second language acquisition*. New York: Routledge.

Loh, J. & Renandya, W. A. (2015). Exploring adaptations of materials and methods: A case from Singapore. *The European Journal of Applied Linguistics and TEFL*, 4(2), 93–111.

Long, M. H. (1981). Input, interaction and second language acquisition, *Annals of the New York Academy of Sciences*, 379, 259–278. doi.10.1111/j.1749-6632.1981tb42014.x

(1983a). Linguistic and conversational adjustments in non-native speakers. *Studies in Second Language Acquisition*, 5(2), 177–193. Doi:10.1017/S0272263100004848

(1983b). Native speaker/non-native speaker conversation and the negotiation of comprehensible input. *Applied Linguistics*, 4(2), 126–141.

(1991). Focus on form: A design feature in language teaching methodology. In K. DeBot, R. Ginsberg & C. Kramsch (Eds.), *Foreign language research in crosscultural perspective* (pp. 39–52). Amsterdam: John Benjamins.

(1996). The role of the linguistic environment in second language acquisition. In W. C. Ritchie & T. K. Batia (Eds.), *Handbook of second language acquisition*. New York: Academic Press.

(2006). *Problems in second language acquisition*. New York: Routledge.

(Ed.). (2007a). *Problems in SLA*. Mawah, NJ: Lawrence Erlbaum.

(2007b). Recasts in SLA: The story so far. In M. Long (Ed.), *Problems in SLA* (pp. 75–118). Mawah, NJ: Lawrence Erlbaum.

(2013). Some implications of research findings on sensitive periods in language learning for educational policy and practice. In G. Granena & M. H. Long (Eds.), *Sensitive periods, language aptitude, and ultimate L2 attainment* (pp. 259–271). Amsterdam: John Benjamin Publishing Company.

(2015). *Second language acquisition and task-based language teaching*. Chichester: Wiley-Blackwell.

(2017). Instructed second language acquisition (ISLA): Geopolitics, methodological issues, and some major research questions. *ISLA*, 1(1), 7–44.

Long, M. H. & Porter, P. A. (1985). Group work, interlanguage talk, and second language acquisition. *TESOL Quarterly*, 19(2), 207–228. doi:10.2307/3586827

Lopriore, L. (2018). Reframing teaching knowledge in Content and Language Integrated Learning (CLIL): A European perspective. *Language Teaching Research*. 24(1). 94–104. https://doi.org/10.1177/1362168818777518

Lowie, W., Michel, M., Rousée-Malpat., A, Keijzer, M. & Sterinkrauss, R. (2020). *Usage-based dynamics in second language development*. Bristol: Multilingual Matters.

Lozanov, G. (1978). *Suggestology and outlines of suggestopedy*. Philadelphia: Gordon and Breach.

Lutzker, P. (2016). Beyond semantics: Moving language in foreign language learning. In B. Tomlinson (Ed.), *Applied linguistics and materials development* (pp. 31–42). London: Bloomsbury.

Lyster, R. (2004). Differential effects of prompts and recasts in form-focused instruction. *Studies in Second Language Acquisition*, 26, 399–432.

(2007). *Learning and teaching languages through content: A counterbalanced approach*. Amsterdam: John Benjamins.

Lyster, R. & Mori, H. (2006). Interactional feedback and instructional counterbalance. *Studies in Second Language Acquisition*, 28, 269–300.

Lyster, R. & Ranta, L. (1997). Corrective feedback and learner uptake: Negotiation of form in communicative classrooms. *Studies in Second Language Acquisition*, 19, 37–66.

Lyster, R., Saito, K. & Sato, M. (2013). *Language Teaching*, 46(1), 1–40. Cambridge University Press. 2012 doi:10.1017/S0261444812000365

Lyster, R. & Sato, M. (2013). Skill acquisition theory and the role of practice in L2 development. In M. Garcia-Mayo, M. J. Gutierrez-Mangado & M. Martinez-Adrian (Eds.), *Contemporary approaches to SLA* (pp. 71–91). Amsterdam: John Benjamins.

Macalister, J. & Nation, P. (Eds.). (2011). *Case studies in language curriculum design: Concepts and approaches in action around the world*. New York: Routledge.

Macaro, E. (2009). Teacher use of codeswitching in the second language classroom: Exploring "optimal" use. In M. Turnbull & J. Dailey-O'Cain (Eds.), *First language use in second and foreign language learning* (pp. 35–49). Bristol, UK: Multilingual Matters.

Mackay, J., Birello, M. & Xerri, D. (Eds.). (2018). *ELT research in action: Bridging the gap between theory and classroom practice*. Faversham: IATEFL.

Mackey, A. (2006). Feedback, noticing and instructed second language learning. *Applied Linguistics*, 27(3), 405–430.

(Ed.). (2006). *Conversational interaction in second language acquisition*. Oxford: Oxford University Press.

(2012). *Input interaction and corrective feedback in L2 learning*. Oxford: Oxford University Press.

Mackey, A., Abbuhl, R. & Gass, S. (2012). Interactionist approach. In S. Gass & A. Mackey (Eds.), *The Routledge handbook of second language acquisition* (pp. 7–24). New York: Routledge.

Mackey, A., Ziegler, N. & Bryfonski, L. (2016). From SLA research on interaction to TBLT materials. In B. Tomlinson (Ed.), *SLA research and materials development for language learning* (pp. 103–118). New York: Routledge.

MacWhinney, B. (2000). The CHILDES project: Tools for analyzing talk (third edition): Volume I: Transcription format and programs, volume II: The database. *Computational Linguistics*, 26(4), 657.

(2014). Item-based patterns in early syntactic development. In S. Faulhaber, T. Herbst & H. Schmid (Eds.), *Constructions collocations patterns* (pp. 33–69). Berlin/Boston: De Gruyter, Inc.

MacWhinney, B. & O'Grady, W. (Eds.). (2015). *The handbook of language emergence*. Chichester: Wiley-Blackwell.

Mahan, K. R., Brevik, L. M. & Odergaard, M. (2018). Characterizing CLIL teaching: New insights from a lower secondary classroom. *International Journal of Bilingual Education and Bilingualism.* Published online: 12 May 2018. https://doi.org/10.1080/13670050.2018.1472206

Maley, A. (1998). Squaring the circle: Reconciling materials as constraint with materials as empowerment. In B. Tomlinson (Ed.), *Materials development in language teaching* (pp. 279–294). Cambridge: Cambridge University Press.

(2008). Extensive reading: Maid in waiting. In B. Tomlinson (Ed.), *English language learning materials: A critical review* (pp. 133–156). London: Continuum.

(2016). "More research is needed": A Mantra too Far? *Humanising Language Teaching, Major Article*: *18*(3), June 2016. ISSN 1755-9715, www.hltmag.co.uk

Maley, A. & Duff, A. (2005). *Drama techniques: A resource book of communication activities fior language teachers.* Cambridge: Cambridge University Press.

Maley, A. & Tomlinson, B. (Eds.). (2017). *Authenticity in materials development for language learning.* Newcastle: Cambridge Scholars.

Marczak, M. (2018) Comprehension approach. *The TESOL encyclopedia of English language teaching.* Hoboken: Wiley. First published: 18 January 2018. https://doi.org/10.1002/9781118784235.eelt0599

Marsden, E., Trofimovich, P. & Ellis, N. (2019). Extending the reach of research: Introducing open accessible summaries at *Language Learning. Language Learning* (First published: 27 January 2019) https://doi.org/10.1111/lang.12337

Marsh, D., Coyle D. & Hood, P. (2010). *Content and language integrated learning.* Cambridge: Cambridge University Press.

Martin, A., Wiggs, C. L., Lalonde, F. & Mack, C. (1994). Word retrieval to letter and semantic cues: A double dissociation in normal subjects using interference tasks. *Neuropsychologia, 32*(12), 1487–1494.

Masuhara, H. (1998). *Factors influencing reading difficulties of advanced learners of English as a foreign language when reading authentic texts.* (Unpublished PhD). University of Bedfordshire, Luton.

(2000). The multi-dimensional representation model: A neural interpretation of the reading process. Proceedings in CD Rom from *AILA '99 Tokyo.*

(2005). Helping learners to achieve multi-dimensional representation in L2 reading. *Folio 9*(2), 6–9.

(2007). The role of proto-reading activities in the acquisition and development of effective reading skills. In B. Tomlinson (Ed.), *Language acquisition and development: Studies of first and other languages* (pp. 15–31). London: Continuum.

(2013). Materials for developing reading skills. In B. Tomlinson (Ed.), *Developing materials for language teaching* (2nd ed., pp. 365–389). London: Bloomsbury.

(2015). "Anything goes" in task-based language teaching materials? The need for principled materials evaluation, adaptation and development. *The European Journal of Applied Linguistics and TEFL*, *4*(2), 113–127.

(2016). Brain studies and materials for language learning. In B. Tomlinson (Ed.), *SLA research and materials development for language learning* (pp. 23–32). New York: Routledge.

Masuhara, H., Mishan, F., & Tomlinson, B. (Eds.). (2017). *Practice and theory for materials development in L2 learning*. Newcastle Upon Tyne: Cambridge Scholars Publishing.

Masuhara, H. & Tomlinson, B. (2008). Materials for General English. In B. Tomlinson (Ed.), *English language learning materials: A critical review* (pp. 17–37). London: Continuum.

Mates, A. W. & Joaquin, A. D. L. (2013) Affect and the brain. In J. Herschensohn, & M. Young-Scholten (Eds.), *The Cambridge handbook of second language acquisition* (pp. 417–435). Cambridge: Cambridge University Press.

Mauranen, A. (2012). *Exploring ELF. Academic English as shaped by non-native speakers*. Cambridge: Cambridge University Press.

(2017). Conceptualising ELF: In J. Jenkins, W. Baker & M. Dewey (Eds.), *The Routledge handbook of English as a lingua franca* (pp. 7–24). New York: Routledge.

Mauss, M. (1973). Techniques of the body. *Economy and Society*, *2*, 70–88.

McCafferty, S. G. (2004). Space for cognition: Gesture and second language learning. *International Journal of Applied Linguistics*, *14*(1), 192–203.

McCafferty, S. G. & Stam, G. (Eds.). (2008). *Gesture: Second language acquisition and classroom research*. New York: Routledge.

McCarten, J. & McCarthy, M. (2010). Bridging the gap between corpus and coursebook: The case of conversation strategies. In F. Mishan & A. Chambers (Eds.), *Perspectives on language learning materials development* (pp. 11–32). Bern: Peter Lang.

McCauley, S. M., Monaghan, P. & Christiansen, M. H. (2015). Language emergence in development: A computational perspective. In B. MacWhinney & W. O'Grady (Eds.), *The handbook of language emergence* (pp. 415–436). Chichester: Wiley-Blackwell.

McClure, G. M. (1987). Readability formulas: Useful or useless? *IEEE Transactions on Professional Communication*, *PC-30*(1). 12–15. doi:10.1109/TPC.1987.6449109

McDaniel, M. A., DeLosh, E. L. & Merritt, P. S. (2000). Order information and retrieval distinctiveness: Recall of common versus bizarre material. *Journal of Experimental Psychology: Learning, Memory, and Cognition*, *26*, 1045–1056. doi: 10.1037/0278-7393.26.4.1045

McDaniel, M. A. & Geraci, L. (2006). Distinctiveness and the mnemonic benefits of bizarre imagery. In R. R. Hunt & J. B. Worthen (Eds.), *Distinctiveness and memory* (pp. 65–88). New York: Oxford University Press.

McDonough, J., Shaw, C. & Masuhara, H. (2013). *Materials and methods in ELT: A teacher's guide* (3rd ed.). Chichester: Wiley-Blackwell.

McDonough, K. (2004). Learner-learner interaction during pair and small group activities in a Thai EFL context. *System, 32*(2), 207–224. doi: 10.1016/j.system.2004.01.003

McDonough, K., Crawford, W. J. & De Vleeschauwer, J. (2016). Thai EFL learners' interaction during collaborative writing tasks and its relationship to text quality. In M. Sato & S. Ballinger (Eds.), *Peer interaction and second language learning: Pedagogical potential and research agenda* (pp. 185–208). Amsterdam: John Benjamins.

McGrath, I. (2012). *Materials evaluation and design for language teaching.* Edinburgh: Edinburgh University Press.

(2016). *Materials evaluation and design for language teaching* (2nd ed.). Edinburgh: Edinburgh University Press.

McKee, D. (1980). *Not now, Bernard.* London: Andersen Press.

McLaughlan, B. (1987). *Theories of second language learning.* London: Edward Arnold.

McQueen, J. M. (2007). Eight questions about spoken-word recognition. In M. G. Gaskell (Ed.), *The Oxford handbook of psycholinguistics* (pp. 37–53). Oxford: Oxford University Press.

McTigue, E. M. (2010). Teaching young readers imagery in storytelling: What color is the monkey? *The Reading Teacher, 64*(1), 53–56.

Meddings, L. & Thornbury, S. (2009). *Teaching unplugged: Dogme in English language teaching.* Peaslake, UK: Delta.

Medgyes, P. (1992). Native or non-native: Who's worth more? *ELT Journal, 4,* 340.

(2017). *The non-native teacher* (Updated ed.), Richmond, UK: Swan Communication.

Mehisto, P., Marsh, D & Frigols, M. J. (2008). *Uncovering CLIL: Content and language integrated teaching in bilingual and multilingual education.* Oxford: Macmillan.

Meisel, J., Clahsen, H. & Pienemann, M. (1981). On determining developmental stages in natural language acquisition. *Studies in Second Language Acquisition, 3,* 109–135.

Menken, K. (2008). *English learners left behind: Standardized testing as language policy.* Clevedon: Multilingual Matters Ltd.

Mick, C. (2011). Learner agency. *European Educational Research Journal, 10*(4), 555–571. (www.wwwords.eu/EERJ)

(2015). Sociological approaches to second language learning and agency. In P. Deters, X. Gao, E. R. Miller, & G. Vitanova (Eds.), *Theorizing and analyzing agency in second language learning* (pp. 91–109). Bristol, UK: Multilingual Matters.

Mishan, F. (2005). *Designing authenticity into language learning materials.* Bristol: Intellect Books.

(2013a). Studies of pedagogy. In B. Tomlinson (Ed.), *Applied linguistics and materials development* (pp. 269–286). London: Bloomsbury.

(2013b). Modes of delivery. In B. Tomlinson (Ed.), *Applied linguistics and materials development* (pp. 287–302). London: Bloomsbury.

(2016). Comprehensibility and cognitive challenge in language learning materials. In B. Tomlinson (Ed.), *SLA research and materials development for language learning* (pp. 166–184). New York: Routledge.

(2017). Authenticity 2.0: Reconceptualising authenticity in the digital era. In A. Maley, & B. Tomlinson (Eds.), *Authenticity in materials development for language learning* (pp. 10–24). Newcastle upon Tyne: Cambridge Scholars Publishing.

Moore, P. J. (2018). Task-based language teaching (TBLT). In J. I. Liontas & M. DelliCarpini (Eds.), *The TESOL encyclopedia of English language teaching* (pp. 1–7). New York: Wiley online.

Morgan-Short, K. (2014). Electrophysiological approaches to understanding second language acquisition: A field reaching its potential. *Annual Review of Applied Linguistics*, 34, 15–36.

Morgan-Short, K., Faretta-Stutenberg, M., & Bartlett, L. (2015). Contributions of event-related potential research to issues in explicit and implicit second language acquisition. In P. Rebuschat (Ed.), *Implicit and explicit learning of languages*. Amsterdam: John Benjamins.

Morgan-Short, K., Faretta-Stutenberg, M., Brill-Schuetz, K. A., Carpenter, H. & Wong, P. C. M. (2014). Declarative and procedural memory as individual differences in second language acquisition. *Bilingualism*, 17(1), 56–72.

Morgan-Short, K., Steinhauer, K., Sanz, C., & Ullman, M. T. (2012). Explicit and implicit second language training differentially affect the achievement of native-like brain activation patterns. *Journal of Cognitive Neuroscience*, 24(4), 933–947.

Morgan-Short, K. & Ullman, M. T. (2012). The neurocognition of second language. In S. M. Gass & A. Mackey (Eds.), *The Routledge handbook of second language acquisition* (pp. 282–299). New York: Routledge.

Morris, F. A. (2002). Negotiation moves and recasts in relation to error types and learner repair in the foreign language classroom. *Foreign Language Annals*, 35(4), 395.

Morrow, K. (1977). Authentic texts in ESP. In S. Holden (Ed.), *English for specific purposes* (pp. 13–15). London: Modern English Publications.

Motteram, G. (2013). *Innovations in learning technologies for English language teaching*. London: British Council.

Mourão, S. (2015). The potential of picturebooks with young learners. In J. Bland (Ed.), *Teaching English to young learners: Critical issues in language teaching with 3–12 year olds* (pp. 199–217). London: Bloomsbury.

Moussu, L. & Llurda, E. (2008). Non-native English-speaking English language teachers: History and research. *Language Teaching*, 41(3), 315–348.

Mueller, J. (2018). Authentic assessment toolbox. http://jfmueller.faculty.noctrl.edu/toolbox/whatisit.htm (accessed 15/11/2020).

Muir, C. (2020). *Directed motivational currents and language education:*

Exploring implications for pedagogy. Bristol: Multilingual Matters.

Mukundan, J. & Nimehchisalem, V. (2013). Materials for writing: Was this the case of the runaway bandwagon? In B. Tomlinson (Ed.), *Applied linguistics and materials development* (pp. 213–230). London: Continuum.

Murteira, A., Sowman, P. F. & Nickels, L. (2018). Taking action in hand: Effects of gesture observation on action verb naming. *Language, Cognition and Neuroscience, 34*(3), 351–364. doi.org/10.1080/23273798.2018.1552978

Myan, K. (2010). *WWN: Language acquisition and generalization using association.* Unpublished MSc thesis Michigan State University. https://pdfs.semanticscholar.org/9f25/c9e671ec59cd7f2988225962cf31f9555cc9.pdf Retrieved 10/10/2019.

Nakata, T. (2017). Does repeated practice make perfect? The effects of within-session repeated retrieval on second language vocabulary learning. *Studies in Second Language Acquisition, 39*(4), 653–679.

Nassaji, H. & Fotos, S. (2007). Issues in form-focused instruction and teacher education. In S. Fotos & H. Nassaji. *Form-focused instruction and teacher education: Studies in honour of Rod Ellis* (pp. 7–16). Oxford: Oxford University Press.

Nassaji, H. & Kartchava, E. (2017). *Corrective feedback in second language teaching and learning: Research, theory, applications, implications.* New York: Routledge.

Nation, I. S. P. (2007). The four strands. *Innovation in Language Learning and Teaching, 1*(1), 2–13.

Nation, I. S. P. & Macalister, J. (2010). *Language curriculum design.* New York: Routledge.

Nation, I. S. P. & Waring, R. (1997). Vocabulary size, text coverage and word lists. In N. Schmitt, & M. McCarthy (Eds.), *Vocabulary: Description, acquisition and pedagogy* (pp. 6–19). New York: Cambridge University Press.

Nava, A. & Pedrazzini, L. (2018). *Second language acquisition in action.* London: Bloomsbury.

Nguyen, L. & Franken, M. (2010). Conceptions of language input in second language acquisition: A case of Vietnamese EFL teachers. *Language Education in Asia, 1,* 62–76.

Nguyen, T. P. H. (2013). A dynamic usage-based approach to second language teaching. University of Groningen/UMCG research database: www.rug.nl/research/portal/files/14424726/Nguyen_Thi_Phuong_Hong_PhD_man_1.pdf (accessed 25/11/2018).

Norris, J. M. & Ortega, L. (2000). Effectiveness of L2 instruction: A research synthesis and quantitative meta-analysis. *Language Learning, 50,* 417–528.

(Eds.). (2006). *Synthesizing research on language teaching and learning.* Amsterdam: John Benjamins.

Nunan, D. (1991). *Language teaching methodology: A handbook for teachers.* Hemel Hempstead: Prentice Hall International.

(1999). *Second language teaching and learning.* Boston: Heinle & Heinle.

(2004). *Task-based language teaching.* Cambridge: Cambridge University Press.

Nunan, D. & Richards, J. C. (Eds.). (2015). *Language learning beyond the classroom.* New York: Routledge.

Nuttall, C. (2005). *Teaching reading skills in a foreign language.* (3rd ed.). Oxford: Macmillan.

Oberg, A. & Daniels, P. (2013). Analysis of the effect a student-centred mobile learning instructional method has on language acquisition. *Computer Assisted Language Learning, 26*(2), 177–196.

O'Farrelly, C., Doyle, O., Victory, G. & Palamaro-Munsell, E. (2018). Shared reading in infancy and later development: Evidence from an early intervention. *Journal of Applied Developmental Psychology,* 54, 69–83.

O'Keefe, A. & Mark, G. (2017), The English grammar profile of learner competence: Methodology and key findings. *International Journal of Corpus Linguistics, 22*(4):457–489.

O'Keeffe, A., McCarthy, M. J. & Carter, R. A. (2007). *From corpus to classroom: Language use and language teaching.* Cambridge: Cambridge University Press.

Olive, T. (2014). Towards a parallel and cascading model of the writing system: A review of research on writing processes coordination. *Journal of Writing Research,* 6(2), 173–194.

Olkkonen, S. (2017). *Second and foreign language fluency from cognitive perspective: Inefficiency and control of attention in lexical access.* Jyvaskyla Studies in Humanities 314. Jyvaskyla: Jyvaskyla University.

O'Malley, J. M. & Chamot, A. U. (1990). *Learning strategies in second language acquisition.* Cambridge: Cambridge University Press.

On target. (1995). *Grade 10 second language learner's book.* Windhoek: Gamsberg Macmillan.

Ortega, L. (2009). *Understanding second language acquisition.* London: Hodder Education.

(2019). SLA and the study of equitable multilingualism. *The Modern Language Journal, 103,* 23–38.

Ostman, J. & Verscheuren, J. (2018). *Handbook of pragmatics: 21st annual instalment.* Amsterdam: John Benjamins.

Our favorites in brain science and how they changed our teaching. *1 MindBrained Think Tank+ V5i1,* Jan 2019.

Ovando, C., Collier, V. & Combs, M. (2003). *Bilingual and ESL classrooms: Teaching multicultural contexts* (3rd ed.). Boston: McGraw-Hill.

Oxford, R. L. (1990). *Language learning strategies: What every teacher should know.* New York: Newbury House.

(1999). Anxiety and the language learner. In J. Arnold (Ed.), *Affect in language learning.* Cambridge: Cambridge University Press.

(2011). *Teaching and researching: Language learning strategies.* Harlow: Pearson.

Padmanaban, I. (2005). Review of Van Patten, B. (2004). Processing instruction: Theory, research, and commentary. Mawah, NJ: Laurence Erlbaum Associates. *TESL-EJ, 9*(3), 1–9.

Padron, Y. N. & Waxman, H. C. (1988). The effects of EFL students' perceptions of their cognitive strategies on reading achievement. *TESOL Quarterly, 22*, 146–150.

Paivio, A. (1986). *Mental representations: Dual coding approach*. New York: Oxford University Press.

(2007). *Mind and its evolution: A dual coding theoretical approach*. Mahwah, NJ: Lawrence Erlbaum.

Pan, P. C. (2015). The interleaving effect: Mixing it up boosts learning. *Scientific American*, www.scientificamerican.com/article/the-interleaving-effect-mixing-it-up-boosts-learning/ – retrieved 24 October 2019.

Papafragu, A. & Grigoroglu, M. (2019). The role of conceptualization during language production: Evidence from event encoding. *Language, Cognition and Neuroscience*. Published online: 24 Apr 2019. https://doi.org/10.1080/23273798.2019.1589540

Paradowski, M. B. (2014). Storytelling in language teaching: Re-evaluating the weight of kinaesthetic modality for brain-compatible pedagogy. *Storytelling: An Interdisciplinary Journal. 1*(2): 13–52.

Paran, A. & Robinson, P. (2015). *Literature*. Oxford: Oxford University Press.

Partanen, E., Kujala, T., Näätänen, R., Liitola, A., Sambeth, A. & Huotilainen, M. (2013). Learning-induced neural plasticity of speech processing before birth. *Paper presented at the Proceedings of the National Academy of Sciences of the United States of America, 37*, 15145–15150.

Park, H. (2010). Process drama in the EFL classroom: A case study of Korean middle school classrooms. In B. Tomlinson & H. Masuhara (Eds.), *Research for materials development in language learning: Evidence for best practice* (pp. 155–171). London: Continuum.

Pavlenko, A. (2005). *Emotions and multilingualism*. Cambridge: Cambridge University Press.

(2013). The affective turn in SLA: From "Affective factors" to "Language desire" and to "Commodification of affect". In D. Gabryś-Barker, & J. Bielska (Eds.), *The affective dimension in second language acquisition* (pp. 3–8). Bristol: Channel View Publications.

Pavlov, I. P. (1904). Retrieved from www.nobelprize.org/prizes/medicine/1904/pavlov/lecture/

(1927/1960/2003). *Conditioned reflexes: An investigation of the physiological activity of the cerebral cortex* (G. V. Anrep Trans.). New York: Dover Publishing.

(1928). In W. H. Gantt (Ed.), *Lectures on conditioned reflexes: Twenty-five years of objective study of the higher nervous activity (behaviour) of animals*. New York: Liveright Publishing Corporation.

Peccei, J. S. (2002). *Child language*. Retrieved from https://ebookcentral.proquest.com

Pegrum, M. (2014). *Mobile learning. Languages, literacies and cultures*. Basingstoke: Palgrave Macmillan.

Peltonen, P. (2020). Gestures as fluency-enhancing resources in L2 interaction: A case study on multimodal fluency. In

P. Lintunen, M. Mutta & P. Peltonen (Eds.), *Fluency in L2 learning and use* (pp. 111-128). Bristol: Multilingual Matters.

Pennycook, A. (2010). The future of Englishes: One, many or none? In A. Kirkpatrick (Ed.), *The Routledge handbook of World Englishes* (pp. 673-687). Oxon: Routledge.

Perdue, C. (Ed.). (1993). *Adult language acquisition: Crosslinguistic perspectives.* Cambridge: Cambridge University Press.

Pérez, K. F. P. (2018). English Open Doors programme: The results of a public policy for English language teaching in Chile. In J. Hernandez-Ferenandez & J. Rojas (Eds.), *English public policies in Latin America: Looking for innovation and systemic improvement in quality English language teaching.* Mexico City: British Council.

Philp, P., Adams, R. & Iwashita, N. (2014). *Peer interaction and second language learning.* New York: Routledge.

Piazzoli, E. (2018). *Embodying language in action: The artistry of process drama in second language education.* Oxford: Springer.

Pica, T., Lincoln-Porter, F., Paninos, D. & Linnell, J. (1996). Language learners' interaction: How does it address the input, output, and feedback needs of L2 learners? *TESOL Quarterly, 1,* 59. doi:10.2307/3587607

Piccardo, E. & North, B. (2019). *The action-oriented approach: A dynamic vision of language education.* Bristol: Multilingual Matters.

Pickering, L. (2012). Second language speech production. In S. M. Gass & A. Mackey (Eds.), *The Routledge handbook of second language acquisition* (pp. 335-348). Abingdon, Oxon: Routledge.

Pienemann, M. (1985). Learnability and syllabus construction. In K. Hyltenstam (Ed.), *Modeling and assessing second language acquisition* (pp. 23-75). Clevedon, Avon: Multilingual Matters.

(1998). *Language processing and second language development: Processability theory.* Amsterdam: John Benjamins Publishing Company.

Pinnard, L. (2016). Looking outward: Using learning materials to help learners harness out-of-class learning opportunities. *Innovation in Language Learning and Teaching, 10*(2), 133-143.

Polio, C. (2012). The acquisition of second language writing. In S. M. Gass & A. Mackey (Eds.), *The Routledge handbook of second language acquisition* (pp. 319-334). Abingdon, Oxon: Routledge.

Prabhu, N. S. (1987). *Second language pedagogy.* Oxford: Oxford University Press.

Prior, M. T. (2019). Elephants in the room: An "affective turn," or just feeling our way? *The Modern Language Journal, 103*(2), 516-527.

Puchta, H. & Rinvolucri, M. (2007). *Multiple intelligences and EFL: Exercises for secondary and adult students.* Cambridge: Cambridge University Press.

Pyc, M. A. & Rawson, K. A. (2009). Testing the retrieval effort hypothesis: Does greater difficulty correctly recalling information lead to higher levels of memory? *Journal of Memory and Language, 60,* 437-447.

Quirk, R. (1990). Language varieties and standard language. *English Today, 6*(1), 3-10.

Rahman, R. A. & Melinger, A. (2019). Language processing during language production: An update of the swinging lexical network. *Language, Cognition and Neuroscience.* Published online: 16 Apr 2019. https://doi.org/10.1080/23273798.2019.1599970

Rebuschat, P. (Ed.). (2015) *Implicit and explicit learning of languages.* Amsterdam: John Benjamins.

Redecker, C. (2014). The future of learning is lifelong, lifewide and open. *Lifewide Magazine, 9,* 12–17.

Reimann, A. (2018). Behaviorist learning theory. *The TESOL Encyclopedia of English Language Teaching.* (pp. 1–6). doi:10.1002/9781118784235.eelt0155

Reinders, H. W. (2012). Towards a definition of intake in second language acquisition. *Applied Research on English Language, 1*(2), 15–36.

Renandya, W. A., & Farrell, T. S. (2011). "Teacher, the tape is too fast!": Extensive listening in ELT. *ELT Journal, 65*(1), 52–59.

Revell, J. & Norman, S. (1997). *In your hands: NLP in ELT.* London: Sapphire Press.

Revesz, A. (2012). Working memory and the observed effect of recasts on different L2 outcome measures. *Language Learning 62,* 93–132.

Richards, J. C. (Ed.). (1978). *Understanding second and foreign language learning: issues and approaches.* Rowley, MA; Newbury House.

(1985). *The context of language teaching.* Cambridge: Cambridge University Press.

(2001). *Curriculum development in language teaching.* Cambridge: Cambridge University Press.

(2017). *Curriculum development in language teaching* (2nd ed.). Cambridge: Cambridge University Press.

(2018). What is CBLT? The Official Website of Educator and Arts Patron Professor Jack C. Richards. www.professorjackrichards.com/cblt/ (accessed 18/11/2018).

Richards, J. & Rodgers, T. (2001). *Approaches and methods in language teaching.* New York: Cambridge University Press.

(2014). *Approaches and methods in language teaching* (3rd ed.). Cambridge: Cambridge University Press.

Richards, J. C. & Schmidt, R. (2010). *Longman dictionary of language teaching and applied linguistics* (4th ed.). Harlow: Pearson.

Richman, C. L. (1994). The bizarreness effect with complex sentences: Temporal effects. *The Canadian Journal of Experimental Psychology, 48*(3), 444–450.

Rilling, S. & Dantas-Whitney, M. (Eds.). (2009). *Authenticity in the language classroom and beyond: adult learners.* Alexandria, VA: TESOL.

Rinvolucri, M. (2002). *Humanising your coursebook.* Peaslake: Delta Publishing.

Ritchie, W. C. & Batia, T. K. (Eds.). (1996). *Handbook of second language acquisition.* New York: Academic Press.

Rivers, W. M. (1981). *Teaching foreign language skills* (2nd ed.). Chicago: University of Chicago Press.

Roberts, R. (2020). Avoiding burnout. *IATEFL Voices, 273,* 7–8.

Robinson, P. (1995). Attention, memory and the "noticing" hypothesis. *Language Learning, 45,* 283–331.

(2002). *Individual differences and instructed second language learning.* Amsterdam: J. Benjamins.

(2005a). Cognitive complexity and task sequencing: A review of studies in a Componential Framework for second language task design. *International Review of Applied Linguistics in Language Teaching, 43,* 1, 1–33.

(2005b). Aptitude and second language acquisition. *Annual Review of Applied Linguistics, 25,* 45–73.

Robinson, P., Mackey, A., Gass, S. & Schmidt, R. (2012). Attention and awareness in second language acquisition. In S. M. Gass & A. Mackey (Eds.), *The Routledge handbook of second language acquisition* (pp. 247–267). New York: Routledge.

Roediger, H. L. & Pyc, M. A. (2012). Inexpensive techniques to improve education: Applying cognitive psychology to enhance educational practice. *Journal of Applied Research in Memory and Cognition, 1*(4), 242–248.

Rohrer, D. (2009). The effects of spacing and mixing practice problems. *Journal for Research in Mathematics Education, 40* (1), 4–17.

Rokita-Jaskow, J. & Ellis, M. (2019). *Early instructed second language acquisition: Pathways to competence.* Bristol: Multilingual Matters.

Rosborough, A. (2014). Gesture, meaning-making, and embodiment: Second language learning in an elementary classroom. *Journal of Pedagogy, 5*(2), 227–250.

Rose, R. R. & Kasper, G. (2001). *Pragmatics in language education.* Cambridge: Cambridge University Press.

Roth, G. & Dicke, U. (2005). Evolution of the brain and intelligence. *Trends in Cognitive Sciences, 9*(5), 250–257.

Rumelhart, D. E., McClelland, J. L. & PDP Research Group (Eds.). (1986). *Parallel distributed processing: Explorations in the microstructure of cognition.* Cambridge, MA: MIT Press.

Rydland, V., Aukrust, V. G. & Fulland, H. (2012). How word decoding, vocabulary and prior topic knowledge predict reading comprehension. A study of language-minority students in Norwegian fifth grade classrooms. *Reading and Writing, 25*(2), 465–482. Published online 2010 Nov 3. doi: 10.1007/s11145-010-9279-2 (accessed Aug 27 2018).

Sachs, M. E., Habibi, A., Damasio, A. & Kaplan, J. T. (2018). Decoding the neural signatures of emotions expressed through sound. *Neuroimage, 174,* 1–10.

Sadoski, M. (1985). Commentary: The natural use of imagery in story comprehension and recall: Replication and extension. *Reading Research Quarterly, 20*(5), 658–667.

Sadoski, M. & Paivio, A. (1994). A dual coding theory of imagery and verbal processes in reading comprehension. In R. B. Ruddell, M. R. Ruddell & H. Singer (Eds.), *Theoretical models and processes of reading* (4th ed., pp. 582–601). Newark, DE: International Reading Association.

(2001). *Imagery and text: A dual coding theory of reading and writing.* Mahwah, NJ: Lawrence Erlbaum Associates Publishers.

Saito, Y. & Wales, K. (Eds.). (2015). *Literature and language learning in the EFL classroom.* Oxford: Palgrave Macmillan.

Samuda, V., Van den Branden, K. & Bygate, M. (Eds.). (2018). *TBLT as a researched pedagogy.* Amsterdam: John Benjamins.

Samur, Y. (2012). Redundancy effect on retention of vocabulary words using multimedia presentation. *British Journal of Educational Technology, 43*(6), E166–E170 doi:10.1111/j.1467-8535.2012.01320

Sánchez, C. R. (2016). Insights from skill acquisition theory for grammar activity sequencing and design in foreign language teaching. *Innovation in Language Learning and Teaching, 10*(2), 121–132.

Saraceni, M. (2015). *World Englishes: A critical analysis.* London: Bloomsbury Academic.

Sato, C. J. (1986). Conversation and interlanguage development: Rethinking the connection. In R. Day (Ed.), *Talking to learn,* (pp. 23–51), Rowley, MA: Newbury House Publishers.

(1988). Origins of complex syntax in interlanguage development. *Studies in Second Language Acquisition, 10,* 371–395.

Sato, M. (2015). Density and complexity of oral production in interaction: The interactionist approach and an alternative. *International Review of Applied Linguistics in Language Teaching, 53*(3), 307–329. doi:10.1515/iral-2015-001

Sato, M. & Ballinger, S. (Eds.). (2016a). *Peer interaction and second language learning: Pedagogical potential and research agenda.* Amsterdam: John Benjamins.

(2016b). Understanding peer interaction: Research synthesis and directions. In M. Sato & S. Ballinger. *Peer interaction and second language learning: Pedagogical potential and research agenda* (pp. 1–32). Amsterdam: John Benjamins.

Sato, M. & Loewen, S. (Eds.). (2019). *Evidence-based second language pedagogy: A collection of instructed second language acquisition studies.* New York: Routledge.

Sato, M. & Lyster, R. (2007). Modified output of Japanese learners: Variable effects of interlocutor v feedback types. In A. Mackey (Ed.), *Conversational interaction in second language acquisition: A collection of empirical studies* (pp. 123–142). Oxford: Oxford University Press.

Sato, M. & Viveros, P. (2016). Interaction or collaboration? Group dynamics in the foreign classroom. In M. Sato & S. Ballinger (Eds.), *Peer interaction and second language learning: Pedagogical potential and research agenda* (pp. 91–112). Amsterdam: John Benjamins.

Saville-Troike, M. (1988). Private speech: Evidence for second language learning strategies during the "silent" period. *Journal of Child Language, 15*(3), 567–590.

Saville-Troike, M. & Barto, K. (2017). *Introducing second language acquisition* (3rd ed.). Cambridge: Cambridge University Press.

Schmidt, A. (2017). What is more effective: explicit or implicit grammar instruction? www.eltresearchbites.com/201705-what-is-more-effective-explicit-or-implicit-grammar-instruction/ 8 May 2017 – accessed 10 August 2017.

Schmidt, R. W. (1983). Interaction, acculturation, and the acquisition of communicative competence. In N. Wolfson, & E. Judd (Eds.), *Sociolinguistics and language acquisition* (pp. 137–174). Rowley, MA: Newbury House.

(1990). The role of consciousness in second language learning. *Applied Linguistics, 11*(2), 129–158.

(1994). Deconstructing consciousness in search of useful definitions for applied linguistics. *AILA Review 11*, 11–26.

(2001). Attention. In Robinson, P. (Ed.), *Cognition and second language instruction.* Cambridge: Cambridge University Press.

(2010). Attention, awareness, and individual differences in language learning. In W. M. Chan, S. Chi, K. N. Cin, J. Istanto, M. Nagami, J. W. Sew, T. Suthiwan & I. Walker, Proceedings of CLaSIC 2010, Singapore, December 2–4 (721–737). Singapore: National University of Singapore, Centre for Language Studies.

(2012). Attention, awareness, and individual differences in language learning. In W. M. Chan, K. N. Chin, S. K. Bhatt & I. Walker (Eds.), (pp. 27–50). Berlin, Germany: de Gruyter Mouton.

Schmidt, R. & Frota, S. (1986). Developing basic conversational ability in a second language: A case-study of an adult learner. In R. Day (Ed.), *Talking to learn.* Rowley, MA: Newbury House.

Schmitt, N. (2008). Instructed second language research vocabulary learning. (Review article) *Language Teaching Research, 12*, 329.

Schmitt, N. & Schmitt, D. (2014). A reassessment of frequency and vocabulary size in L2 vocabulary teaching. *Language Teaching, 47*(4), 484–503.

Schüler, A. (2019). The integration of information in a digital, multi-modal learning environment. *Learning and Instruction, 59*, 76–87.

Schumann, J. H. (1976). Social distance as a factor in second language acquisition. *Language Learning, 26*(2), 135–143.

(1978) *The pidginization process: A model for second language acquisition.* Rowley, MA: Newbury House.

(1997). *The neurobiology of affect in language learning.* Boston: Blackwell.

Schumann, J. H., Crowell, S. E., Jones, N. E., Lee, N., & Schuchert, S. A. (2004). *The neurobiology of learning: Perspectives from second language acquisition.* New York: Routledge.

Schütze, U. (2015). Spacing techniques in second language vocabulary acquisition: Short term gains v long-term memory. *Language Teaching Research, 19*(1), 28–42.

(2017). *Language learning and the brain.* Cambridge: Cambridge University Press.

Selinker, L. & Han, Z.-H. (2001). Fossilization: Moving the concept into empirical longitudinal study. In C. Elder, A. Brown, E. Grove, K. Hill, N. Iwashita, T. Lumpley, T. McNamara and K. O'Loughlin (Eds.), *Studies in language testing: Experimenting with uncertainty* (pp. 276–291). Cambridge: Cambridge University Press.

Serrano, R. & Huang, H. Y. (2018). Learning vocabulary through assisted repeated reading: How much time should there be between repetitions of the same text? *TESOL Quarterly, 52*(4), 971–994. doi: 10.1002/tesq.445

Selvi, A. F. (2011). The non-native speaker teacher. *ELT Journal, 65*(2), 187–189.

Selvi, A. F. & Rudolph, N. (Eds.). (2018). *Conceptual shifts and contextualized practices in education for glocal interaction Issues and implications.* Singapore: Springer Nature Singapore pte Ltd.

Shannon, C. (1948). A mathematical theory of communication. *Bell System Technical Journal, 27*, 379–423.

Shannon, C. & Weaver, W. (1949). *The mathematical theory of communication.* Urbana: The University of Illinois Press.

Sharwood Smith, M. (1981). Consciousness-raising and the second language learner. *Applied Linguistics, 2*, 159–168.

(1993). Input enhancement in instructed SLA: Theoretical bases. *Studies in Second Language Acquisition, 15*(2), 165–179 doi:10.1017/S0272263100011943.

Shatz, M. & Wilkinson, L. C. (Eds.). (2010). *The education of English language learners.* New York: Guilford Press.

Sheen, Y. & Ellis, R. (2011). Corrective feedback in language teaching. In E. Hinkel (Ed.), *Handbook of research in second language teaching and learning II* (pp. 593–610). New York: Routledge.

Shepherd, G. M. & Shepherd-Barr, K. (2009). Proust effect. In M. D. Binder, N. Hirokawa & U. Windhorst (Eds.), *Encyclopedia of neuroscience* (pp. 3333–3335). Berlin, Heidelberg: Springer Berlin Heidelberg. https://doi.org/10.1007/978-3-540-29678-2_4852

Shintani, N. (2016). *Input-based tasks in foreign language instruction for young learners.* Amsterdam: John Benjamins.

Shoba, K. N. (2017). Can wordwalls enhance vocabulary at the tertiary level?: An experimental study. In Tomlinson, B. (Ed.), *Explorations: Teaching and learning English in India, Issue 3.* Kolkata: British Council. www.britishcouncil.in/programmes/english-partnerships/research-policy-dialogues/eltrep-papers

Shooshtaria, Z. G. & Mirb, F. (2014). Peer scaffolding: Sociocultural theory in writing strategies application. *Procedia – Social and Behavioural Sciences, 98*, 1771–1776. doi: 10.1016/j.sbspro.2014.03.605

Simpson, A. (2017). The misdirection of public policy: Comparing and combining standardised effect sizes. *Journal of Education Policy, 32*(4), 450–466.

Sinclair, J., McHardy, J. & Carter, R. (Eds.). (2004). *Trust the text: Language, corpus and discourse.* New York: Routledge.

Skehan, P. (1989). *Individual differences in second language learning.* London: Edward Arnold.

(1998). *A cognitive approach to language learning.* Oxford: Oxford University Press.

(2002). Theorising and updating aptitude. In P. Robinson (Ed.), *Individual differences and instructed language learning* (pp. 69–93). Amsterdam: John Benjamins.

(2012). Language aptitude. In S. M. Gass & A. Mackey (Eds.), *The Routledge handbook of second language acquisition* (pp. 381–395). New York: Routledge.

(2015). Foreign language aptitude and its relationship with grammar: A critical overview. *Applied Linguistics, 36*(3), 367–384.

Skinner, B. F. (1938). *The behavior of organisms: An experimental analysis.* Oxford: Appleton-Century.

(1953). *Science and human behavior.* New York: Free Press.

(1957). *Verbal behavior.* New York: Appleton-Century-Crofts.

(1958). Teaching machines. *Science, 128* (3330), 969–977.

(1976). *About behaviorism.* New York: Vintage Books.

(1985). Cognitive science and behaviourism. *British Journal of Psychology, 76*(3), 291–301.

Snow, M. A. & Brinton, D. M. (2017) *Content based instruction: New perspectives on integrating language and content* (2nd ed). Ann Arbor, MI: University of Michigan Press.

Soars, J. & Soars, L. (2012). *Headway pre-intermediate student's book* (4th ed.). Oxford: Oxford University Press.

Sockett, G. (2014). *The online informal learning of English.* Basingstoke: Palgrave Macmillan.

Sonbul, S. & Schmitt, N. (2010). Direct teaching of vocabulary after reading: Is it worth the effort? *ELT Journal, 64*(3), 253–260.

Sorell, T. (1987). *Descartes.* Oxford: Oxford University Press.

Spada, N. & Tomita, Y. (2010). Interactions between type of instruction and type of language feature: A meta-analysis. *Language Learning, 60*, 263–308.

Staddon, J. (2014). *The new behaviourism.* (2nd ed.). Philadelphia: Psychology Press.

Stanely, G. (2013). *Language learning with technology: Ideas for integrating technology in the classroom.* Cambridge: Cambridge University Press.

Stent, G. S. (1975). Limits to the scientific understanding of man. *Science, 187*, 1052–1057.

Stern, H. H. (1983). *Fundamental concepts of language teaching.* Oxford: Oxford University Press.

Sternberg, R., Fiske, S., & Foss, D. (Eds.). (2016). *Scientists making a difference: One hundred eminent behavioral and brain scientists talk about their most important contributions.* Cambridge: Cambridge University Press.

Stetsenko, A. (2017). *The transformative mind: Expanding Vygotsky's approach to development and education.* New York: Cambridge University Press.

Stevick, E. W. (1982). *Teaching and learning languages.* Cambridge: Cambridge University Press.

Stewart, R. D. (1996). Using mythic-archetypal approaches in the language arts. *ERIC* Clearinghouse on Reading English and Communication. Bloomington, IN.

Stoller, F. (2002). Project work: A means to promote language and content. In J. C. Richards & W. A. Renandya (Eds.), *Methodology in language teaching: an anthology of current practice* (pp. 107–120). Cambridge: Cambridge University Press.

(2006). Establishing a theoretical foundation for project-based learning in second and foreign language contexts. In G. H. Beckett & P. C. Miller (Eds.), *Project-based second and foreign language education: past, present, and future* (pp. 19–40). Greenwich, CT: Information Age Publishing.

Storch, N. & Wigglesworth, G. (2003). Is there a place for the use of the L1 in an L2 setting? *TESOL Quarterly, 37*(4), 760–770.

Sultana, S. (2018). Role of first language in second language development. *Academia*: www.academia.edu/40737388/Role_of_First_Language_in_Second_Language_Development

Swain, M. (1985). Communicative competence: Some roles of comprehensible input and comprehensible output in its development. In S. Gass & C. Madden (Eds.), *Input in second language acquisition* (pp. 235–253). Rowley, MA: Newbury House.

(1995). Three functions of output in second language learning. In G. Cook & B. Seidlhofer (Eds.), *Principle and practice in applied linguistics: Studies in honour of H. G. Widdowson* (pp. 125–144). Oxford: Oxford University Press.

(1996). Integrating language and content in immersion classrooms: Research perspectives. *The Canadian Modern Language Review, 52*, 529–548.

(1998). Focus on form through conscious reflection. In C. Doughty & J. Williams (Eds.), *Focus on form in second language acquisition* (pp. 64–82). Cambridge: Cambridge University Press.

(2005). The output hypothesis: Theory and research. In E. Hinkel (Ed.), *Handbook of research in second language learning* (pp. 471–485). Mawah, NJ: Lawrence Erlbaum.

(2013). The inseparability of cognition and emotion in second language learning. *Language Teaching, 46*(2), 195–207.

Swain, M., Kinnear, P. & Steinmann, L. (2015). *Socio-cultural theory in second language education: An introduction through narratives* (2nd ed.). Bristol: Multilingual Matters.

Swain, M. & Lapkin, S. (1995). Problems in output and the cognitive processes they generate: A step towards second language learning. *Applied Linguistics, 16*(3), 371–391.

Syerett, K. & Arunachalam, S, (Eds.). (2018). *Semantics in language acquisition.* Amsterdam: John Benjamins.

Sylven, L. K. (Ed.). (2019). *Investigating content and language integrated learning: Insights from Swedish high schools.* Bristol: Multilingual Matters.

Taguchi, N. & Kim, Y. (2018). *Task-based approaches to teaching and assessing pragmatics.* Amsterdam: John Benjamins.

Tallal, P. (2003). Neuroscience, phonology and reading: The oral to written language continuum. Retrieved from www.childrenofthecode.org/interviews/tallal.htm

Tan, K. (2011). Assessment for learning in Singapore: Unpacking its meanings and identifying some areas for improvement. *Educational Research for Policy and Practice. 10*(2), 91–103.

Tarone, E. (1988). *Variation in interlanguage.* London: Edward Arnold.

(2005). Impact of literacy on oral language processing: Implications for second language acquisition research. *Annual Review of Applied Linguistics, 25,* 77–97. doi: 10.1017/S0267190505000048

Tasseron, M. (2017). How teachers use global ELT coursebooks. In H. Masuhara, B. Tomlinson & F. Mishan (Eds.), *Practice and theory of materials development in language learning* (pp. 290–311). Newcastle upon Tyne: Cambridge Scholars Publishing.

Tatsuki, D. (2006). What is authenticity? In *Proceedings of the 5th annual JALT Pan-SIG conference* (pp. 1–15). Shizuoka, Japan: Tokai University College of Marine Science.

Tatsumi, T., Ambridge, B. & Pine, J. M. (2018). Disentangling effects of input frequency and morphophonological complexity on children's acquisition of verb inflection: An elicited production study of Japanese. *Cognitive Science, 42,* 555–577.

The Mind Brain Ed Think Tanks (ISSN 2434-1002) Place of Publication: Kyoto, Japan.

Thomas, M. (Ed.). (2010). *Handbook of research on Web 2.0 and second language learning.* Hershey, PA: IGI Global.

Thomas, M. & Reinders, H. (2015). *Contemporary task-based language teaching in Asia.* London: Bloomsbury.

Thomas, M., Reinders, H. & Warschauer, M. (2013). *Contemporary computer-assisted language learning.* London: Bloomsbury Academic.

Thornbury, S. (2002). *How to teach vocabulary.* Harlow: Pearson.

(2005). *How to teach speaking.* Harlow: Pearson.

(2011). *Language teaching methodology.* In J. Simpson (Ed.), *The Routledge handbook of applied linguistics.* London: Routledge.

Thorndike, E. L. (1898/1956). *Animal intelligence: An experimental study of the associative processes in animals.* The Psychological Review. Series of Monograph Supplements, vol. 2, no. 4 (whole no. 8). New York: Macmillan.

Timmis, I. (2013). Spoken language research: The applied linguistics challenge. In B. Tomlinson (Ed.), *Applied linguistics and materials development* (pp. 79–94). London: Continuum.

Todes, D. P. (2014). *Ivan Pavlov: A Russian life in science.* New York: Oxford University Press.

Tollefson, J. & Miguel Pérez-Milans, M. (Eds.). (2018). *The Oxford handbook of* language policy and planning. Oxford: Oxford University Press.

Tomlinson, B. (Ed.). (1981). *Talking to learn*. Port Vila: Ministry of Education of Vanuatu.

(1990). Managing change in Indonesian high schools. *ELT Journal* 44(1), 25–27.

(1994a). *Openings*. London: Penguin.

(1994b). Materials for TPR. *Folio. 1*(2), 8–10.

(1994c). Pragmatic awareness activities. *Language Awareness, 3*(3/4), 119–129.

(1995). Work in progress. *Folio. 2*(2), 26–30.

(1997). *The role of visualisation in the reading of literature by learners of a foreign language*. Unpublished PhD thesis. University of Nottingham.

(Ed.). (1998a). *Materials development in language teaching*. Cambridge: Cambridge University Press.

(1998b). Introduction. In B. Tomlinson (Ed.), *Materials development in language teaching* (pp. 1–24). Cambridge: Cambridge University Press.

(1998c). Seeing what they mean: Helping L2 learners to visualize. In B. Tomlinson (Ed.), *Materials development in language teaching* (pp. 265–278). Cambridge: Cambridge University Press.

(2000a). A multi-dimensional approach. *The Language Teacher, 24(7)*, 1–6.

(2000b). Talking to yourself: The role of the inner voice in language learning. *Applied Language Learning, 11*(1), 123–124.

(2001). *They came from the sea*. In Watcyn-Jones, P. (Ed.), *Top class activities 2*. London: Penguin.

(Ed.). (2003). *Developing materials for language teaching*. London: Continuum.

(Ed.). (2004). *Improve your English*. Addis Ababa: Ministry of Education.

(2005a). English as a Foreign Language: Matching procedures to the context of learning. In E. Hinkel (Ed.), *Handbook of research in second language teaching and learning* (pp. 137–154). Mawah, NJ: Lawrence Erlbaum.

(2005b). Testing to learn. *ELT Journal, 59* (1), 39–46.

(2007a). Introduction: some similarities and differences between L1 and L2 acquisition and development. In B. Tomlinson (Ed.), *Language acquisition and development: Studies of learners of first and other languages* (pp. 1–12). London: Continuum.

(2007b). The value of recasts during meaning-focused communication – 1. In B. Tomlinson (Ed.), *Language acquisition and development: Studies of learners of first and other languages* (pp. 141–161). London: Continuum.

(2007c). Using form-focused discovery approaches. In S. Fotos & H. Nassaji (Eds.), *Form-focused instruction and teacher education: Studies in honour of Rod Ellis* (pp. 177–192). Oxford, England: Oxford University Press.

(Ed.). (2008a). *English language teaching materials: A critical review*. London: Continuum.

(2008b). Language acquisition and language learning materials. In B. Tomlinson (Ed.), *English language teaching materials: A critical review* (pp. 3–14). London: Continuum.

(2010a). Helping learners to fill the gaps in their learning. In F. Mishan & A. Chambers (Eds.), *Developing language learning materials to meet needs and wants* (pp. 87–108). Oxford: Peter Lang.

(2010b). Principles and procedures of materials development. In N. Harwood (Ed.), *Materials in ELT: Theory and practice* (pp. 81–108). Cambridge: Cambridge University Press.

(2010c). Principles and procedures for self-access materials. *Studies in Self-Access Learning Journal*, *1*(2), 72–86.

(2010d). Which test of English and why? A. Kirkpatrick (Ed.), *The Routledge handbook of world Englishes* (1st ed., pp. 599–617). New York: Routledge.

(Ed.). (2011a). *Materials development in language teaching* (2nd ed.). Cambridge: Cambridge University Press.

(2011b). Introduction: Principles and procedures of materials development. In B. Tomlinson (Ed.), *Materials development in language teaching* (2nd ed., pp. 1–34). Cambridge: Cambridge University Press.

(2011c). Access-self materials. In B. Tomlinson (Ed.), *Materials development in language teaching* (2nd ed., pp. 414–432). Cambridge: Cambridge University Press.

(2011d). Seeing what they mean: Helping learners to visualise. In B. Tomlinson (Ed.), *Materials development in language teaching* (2nd ed., pp. 257–278). Cambridge: Cambridge University Press.

(2012). Materials development for language learning and teaching. *Language Teaching*, *45*(2), 1–37.

(Ed.). (2013a). *Developing materials for language teaching* (2nd ed.). London: Bloomsbury.

(Ed.). (2013b). *Applied linguistics and materials development*. London: Bloomsbury.

(2013c). Language acquisition research and materials development. In B. Tomlinson (Ed.), *Applied linguistics and materials development* (pp. 11–30). London: Bloomsbury.

(2013d). Developing principled frameworks for materials development. In B. Tomlinson (Ed.), *Developing materials for language teaching* (2nd ed., pp. 95–118). London: Bloomsbury.

(2013e). Humanising the coursebook. In B. Tomlinson (Ed.), *Developing materials for language teaching* (pp. 140–155). London: Bloomsbury.

(2014a). Looking out for English. *Folio*, *16*(1), 5–8.

(2014b). Let the teacher speak. In Pattinson, T. (Ed.), *IATEFL 2013: Liverpool conference selections* (pp. 70–72). Faversham: IATEFL.

(2015). TBLT materials and curricula: From theory to practice. In M. Thomas & H. Reinders (Eds.), *Contemporary task-based language teaching in Asia* (pp. 328–340). London: Bloomsbury.

(2016a). Achieving a match between SLA research and materials development. In B. Tomlinson (Ed.), *SLA research and materials development for language* learning (pp. 3–22). New York: Routledge.

(2016b). Applying SLA principles to whole class activities. In B. Tomlinson (Ed.), *SLA research and materials development for language learning* (pp. 33–49). New York: Routledge.

(2017). Introduction. In A. Maley & B. Tomlinson (Eds.), *Authenticity in materials development for language learning* (pp. 1–9). Newcastle: Cambridge Scholars.

(2018a). Discovery-based instruction. In J. I. Liontas (Ed.), *TESOL encyclopedia*. Hoboken, NJ: Wiley.

(2018b). Making typical coursebook activities more beneficial for the learner. In D. Bao (Ed.), *Creativity and innovations in ELT materials development: Looking beyond the current design* (pp. 21–34). Bristol: Multilingual Matters.

(2018c). Text-driven approaches to task-based language teaching. *Folio, 18*(2), 4–7.

(2019a). Using literature in text-driven materials to help learners to develop spoken pragmatic awareness. In C. Jones (Ed.), *Literature, spoken language and speaking skills in second language learning* (pp. 38–65). Cambridge: Cambridge University Press.

(2019b). Developing intercultural awareness through reflected experience of films and other visual media. In C. Herrere & I. Yanderschelden (Eds.), *Using film and media in the language classroom: Reflections on research-led thinking* (pp. 19–29). Bristol: Multilingual Matters.

(2020a). Assisting learners in orchestrating their inner voice for L2 learning. Pathways to the successful teaching and learning of an L2. *Language Teaching Research Quarterly. Special Issue in Honour of Andrew Cohen's Contribution to L2 Teaching and Learning Research.* 19, 32–47. doi: 10.32038/ltrq.2020.19.03

(2020b). Is materials development progressing? *Language Teaching Research Quarterly. Special Issue in Honour of Brian Tomlinson's Contribution to Language Materials Research, 15*, 1–20. doi: 10.32038/ltrq.2020.15.01

(2020c). Which test of English and why? A. Kirkpatrick (Ed.), *The Routledge handbook of World Englishes* (2nd ed.), New York: Routledge.

Tomlinson, B. & Avila, J. (2007a). Seeing and saying for yourself: The role of audio-visual mental aids in language learning and use. In B. Tomlinson (Ed.), *Language acquisition and development: Studies of learners of first and other languages* (pp. 61–81), London: Continuum.

(2007b). Applications of the research into the roles of audio-visual mental aids for language teaching pedagogy. In B. Tomlinson (Ed.), *Language acquisition and development: Studies of learners of first and other languages* (pp. 82–89), London: Continuum.

Tomlinson, B., Hill, D. A. & Masuhara, H. (2000). *English for life 1*. Singapore: Marshall Cavendish.

Tomlinson, B. & Keedwell, A. (Eds.). (2017). *Explorations: Teaching and learning*

English in India. Kolkata: British Council. www.britishcouncil.in/ programmes/english-partnerships/ research-policy-dialogues/eltrep-papers

Tomlinson, B. & Masuhara, H. (1994). *Use your English*. Tokyo: Asahi Press.

(Eds.), (2010). *Research for materials development in language learning: Evidence for best practice*. London: Continuum.

(2013). Review of adult ELT textbooks. *ELT Journal, 67*(2), 233–249.

(2018a). Materials adaptation. In B. Tomlinson & H. Masuhara, *The complete guide to the theory and practice of materials development for language learning* (pp. 82–116). Hoboken, NJ: Wiley-Blackwell.

(2018b). *The complete guide to the theory and practice of materials development for language learning*. Hoboken, NJ: Wiley-Blackwell.

(2018c). Issues in materials development. In *The complete guide to the theory and practice of materials development for language learning* (pp. 1–51). Hoboken, NJ: Wiley-Blackwell.

Tomlinson, B. & Whittaker, C. (Eds.), (2013). *Blended learning in English language teaching: Course design and implementation*. London: The British Council. Retrieved from www.britishcouncil.org

Tono, Y. & Díez-Bedmar, M. B. (2014). Focus on learner writing at the beginning and intermediate stages: The ICCI corpus. *International Journal of Corpus Linguistics, 19*(2), 163–177.

Torday, P. (2007). *Salmon fishing in the Yemen*. London: Weidenfeld and Nicolson.

Trabelsi, S. (2010). Developing and trialling authentic materials for business English students at a Tunisian university. In B. Tomlinson & H. Masuhara (Eds.), *Research for materials development in language learning: Evidence for best practice* (pp. 103–120). London: Continuum.

Tranel, D. & Damasio, A. R. (2002). Neurobiological foundations of human memory. In A. D. Baddeley, M. D. Koppelman, & B. A. Wilson (Eds.), *Handbook of memory disorders* (2nd ed., pp. 17–56), Chichester: Wiley.

Tschichold, C. (2012). French vocabulary in Encore Tricolore: Do pupils have a chance? *Language Learning Journal, 40*(1), 7–19.

Turnbull, M. (2001). There is a role for the L1 in second and foreign language teaching, but . . . . *Canadian Modern Language Review, 57*(4), 150–163.

Twomey, K. E., Ranson, S. L. & Horst, J. S. (2014). That's more like it: Multiple exemplars facilitate word learning. *Infant and Child Development, 23*(2), 105–122.

Tyler, A. E. (2010). Usage-based approaches to language and their applications to second language learning. *Annual Review of Applied Linguistics, 30*, 270–291.

Tyler, A. E., Ortega, L., Uno, M. & Park, H. I. (Eds.). (2018). *Usage-inspired L2 instruction: Researched pedagogy*. Amsterdam: John Benjamins.

Uden, J. (2013). The extensive reading foundation's guide to extensive reading. *ELT Journal, 67*(2), 270–272.

Ünlü, A. (2015). How alert should I be to learn a language? The noticing hypothesis and its implications for language teaching. *Procedia – Social and Behavioral Sciences, 199*, 261–267.

Ur, P. (1996). *A course in language teaching.* Cambridge: Cambridge University Press.

Van den Branden, K. (2006). *Task-based language education: From theory to practice.* Cambridge: Cambridge University Press.

Van den Branden, K., Bygate, M. & Norris, J. (2009). Task-based language teaching: Introducing the reader. In K. Van den Branden, M. Bygate & J. Norris (Eds.), *Task-based language teaching: A reader* (pp. 1–19). Amsterdam: John Benjamin Publishing Company.

Van der Veer, R. & Valsiner, J. (1991). *Understanding Vygotsky. A quest for synthesis.* Oxford: Basil Blackwell.

Van Deursen, A. J. & Van Dijk, J. A. (2014). The digital divide shifts to differences in usage. New Media & Society, *16*(3), 507–526.

Van Kestern, M. T. R., Rijpkema, M., Rutter, D. J., Morris, R. G. M. & Fernandez, G. (2014). Building on prior knowledge: Schema-dependent encoding processes relate to academic performance. *Journal of Cognitive Neuroscience, 26* (10), 250–261.

Van Leeuwen, T. (2015). Multimodality in education: Some directions and some questions. *TESOL Quarterly /Teachers of English to Speakers of Other Languages, 49*(3), 582–589.

Van Lier, L. (2014). *Interaction in the language curriculum: Awareness, autonomy and authenticity.* New York: Routledge.

Van Patten. B. (2002). Processing instruction: An update. *Language Learning, 54*(2), 755–803. doi: 10.1111/1467-9922.00203

(2004). Processing instruction: Theory, research, and commentary. Mawah, NJ: Laurence Erlbaum Associates.

(2012). Input processing. In S. M. Gass & A. Mackey (Eds.), *The Routledge handbook of second language acquisition* (pp. 268–281). New York: Routledge.

Van Patten, B. & Cadieno, T. (1993). Input processing and second language acquisition: A role for instruction. *The Modern Language Journal, 77*(1), 45–57.

Van Patten, B. & Lee, J. (Eds.). (1990). *Second language acquisition: Foreign language learning.* Clevedon, Avon: Multilingual Matters.

Van Patten, B. & Williams, J. (Eds.). (2007). *Theories in second language acquisition.* Mahwah, NJ: Lawrence Erlbaum.

Vrikki, M. (2017). Investigating task repetition with feedback as a package for materials aiming towards L2 fluency development: The case of primary EFL schools in Cyprus. In H. Masuhara, F. Mishan & B. Tomlinson (Eds.), *Practice and theory for materials development in L2 learning* (pp. 110–130). Newcastle: Cambridge Scholars.

Vygotsky, L. S. (1962/1986/2012). Kozulin A. (Ed.), *Thought and language* (E. Hanfmann, G. Vakar Trans.) (revised and expanded ed.) MIT Press.

(1978). *Mind in society: The development of higher psychological processes.* Cambridge, MA: Harvard University Press.

(1987) The genesis of higher mental functions. In R. Reiber (Ed.), *The history of the development of higher mental functions* (Vol. 4, pp. 97–120). New York: Plenum.

Walkinshaw, I., Fenton-Smith, B. & Humphreys, P. (2017). EMI issues and challenges in Asia-Pacific higher education: An introduction. In B. Fenton-Smith, P. Humphreys & I. Walkinshaw (Eds.), *English medium instruction in higher education in Asia-Pacific: From policy to pedagogy* (pp. 1–18). Cham, Switzerland: Springer International Publishing.

Wang, L., Miller, M. J., Schmitt, M. R. & Wen, F. K. (2013). Assessing readability formula differences with written health information materials: Application, results and implications. *Research in Social and Administrative Pharmacy, 9*(5), 503–516.

Warschauer, M. & Healey, D. (1998). Computers and language learning: An overview. *Language Teaching, 31*, 57–71.

Watson, J. B. (1913). Psychology as the behaviorist views it. *Psychological Review, 20*(2), 158–177.

(1924/1998/2017). *Behaviorism.* Oxon: Routledge.

Watson, J. B., & Rayner, R. (1920/2000). Conditioned emotional reactions. *American Psychologist, 55*(3), 313–317.

Webb, C. (1963). *The graduate.* New York: Signet.

Weber, A. & Broersma, M. (2012). Spoken word recognition in second language acquisition. In C. A. Chapelle (Ed.), *The Encyclopedia of Applied Linguistics.* Bognor Regis: Wiley Online. doi: 10.1002/9781405198431

Wen, Z., Biedron, A. & Skehan, P. (2017). Foreign language aptitude theory: Yesterday, today and tomorrow. *Language Teaching, 50*(1), 1–31.

Weiskopf, D. (2010). Embodied cognition and linguistic comprehension. *Studies in History and Philosophy of Science, 41*, 294–304.

Wenden, A. (1991). *Learner strategies for learner autonomy.* New York: Prentis Hall.

Whitney, C., Huber, W., Klann, J., Weis, S., Krach, S. & Kircher, T. (2009). Neural correlates of narrative shifts during auditory story comprehension. *Neuroimage, 47*(1), 360–366.

Wicks. M. (2000). *Imaginative projects.* Cambridge: Cambridge University Press.

Widdowson, H. G. (1978). *Teaching language as communication.* Oxford: Oxford University Press.

(1979). *Explorations in applied linguistics.* Oxford: Oxford University Press.

(2001). Interpretations and correlations: A reply to Stubbs. *Applied Linguistics, 22*(4), 531–538.

Widodo, H. P., Wood, A. & Gupta, D. P. (2018). *Asian English language classrooms: Where theory and practice meet.* Abingdon: Routledge.

Widyalankara, R. C. (2012). *The judicious integration of L1 in ESL learning contexts*. London: Blackwell.

Willis, D. (1990). *The lexical syllabus: A new approach to language teaching*. London: Collins.

Willis, J. (2010). *A framework for task-based learning*. Harlow: Longman.

Willis, J. & Willis, D. (Eds.). 1996. *Challenge and change in language teaching*. Oxford: Macmillan Heinemann.

Wilson, K. (2008). *Drama and improvisation*. Oxford: Oxford University Press.

Winitz, H. (Ed.). (1981). *The comprehension approach to foreign language instruction*. Rowley, MA: Newbury House.

Wolf, M. K. & Butler, Y. G. (2017). *English language proficiency assessments for young learners*. New York: Routledge.

Wong, B., Yin, B. & O'Brien, B. (2016). Neurolinguistics: Structure, function, and connectivity in the bilingual brain. *BioMed Research International*, Vol. 2016, http://dx.doi.org/10.1155/2016/7069274

Wu, S. (2016). *The use of L1 cognitive resources in L2 reading by Chinese EFL learners*. New York: Routledge.

Yano, Y., Long, M. H. & Ross, S. (1994). The effects of simplified and elaborated texts on foreign language reading comprehension. *Language Learning*, 44(2), 189–219.

Yasnitsky, A. (2012). The complete works of L. S. Vygotsky: PsyAnima complete Vygotsky project. *PsyAnima, Dubna Psychological Journal*, 5(3), 144–148.

Yevtushenko, Y. (1962). Schoolmaster. In *Selected Poems by Yevgengy Yevtushenko*. London: Penguin.

Ying, H. (1995). What sort of input is needed for intake? *International Review of Applied Linguistics*, 33(3), 175–194. doi: 10.1515/iral.1995.33.3.175

Young, A. & Tedik. D. J. (2016). Collaborative dialogue in a two way Spanish/English immersion classroom: Does heterogeneous grouping promote peer linguistic scaffolding? In M. Sato & S. Ballinger, *Peer interaction and second language learning: Pedagogical potential and research agenda* (pp. 135–162). Amsterdam: John Benjamins.

Zheng, X. & Borg, S. (2014). Task-based learning and teaching in China: Secondary school teachers' beliefs and practices. *Language Teaching Research*, 18(2), 205–221.

Zhisheng, W., Skehan, P., Biedron, A., Li, S. & Sparks, R. L. (Eds.). (2019). *Language aptitude: Advancing theory, testing, research and practice*. New York: Routledge.

Zou, B. & Thomas, M. (2018). *Handbook of research on integrating technology into the contemporary teaching and learning of languages*. Hershey, PA: IGI Global.

Zulfıkar, Z. (2018). Rethinking the use of L1 in L2 classroom. *Englisia*, 6(1), 43–51.

Zwaan, R. A. & Madden, C. J. (2005). Embodied sentence comprehension. In D. Pecher & R. A. Zwaan (Eds), *Grounded cognition* (pp. 224–245). Cambridge: Cambridge University Press.

Index

acquisition, 148–180
  achievement of acquisition, 178–180
  definition, 148
  LAD (Language Acquisition Device), 151–153
  L1 acquisition, 150–151
  psychological studies, 151–168
  SLA studies, 168–172
affect, 328–331
  affective engagement, 91
Alcon, E., 67, 68
Alexander, R., 293
Allen, I., 194
Ambridge, B. and Lieven, E., 154
Anderson, J. R., 135, 318
Anton, M. and Dicamiila, F. J., 300
aptitude, 89–90
Arbib, M. A., 152, 156
Arnold, J., Dornyei, Z. and Pugliese, C., 135
Arnold, J. and Brown, H. D., 328
assessment, 62–64, 188, 215–217, 242–244, 278–281, 296
attention (see consciousness and attention)
Auerbach, E. R. and Paxton, D., 225
authenticity, 87, 121, 332–339
  curriculum authenticity, 121
auto-input, 45, 282–297
  research, 288–289
  the value of auto-input, 283–284
  types of auto-input, 285

Badger, R., 82–83
Baldauf, R., Kaplan, R. and Kamwangamalu, M., 115
Barcroft, J. and Wong, W., 71
Barker, D., 99
Batstone, R., 68

Bao, D., 144, 200
Beebe, L. B., 67
Behaviourism, 157–161, 345–346
bizarreness, 88
Bock, J. K., 263
Bouziri, B., 121
brain studies, 3, 8
Bridges, P., 273
Brown, S., 140
Buendgens-Kosten, J., 332, 333

Carroll, J. B., 90
Carroll, J. B. and Sapon, S. M., 324
Carter, R., Hughes, R. and McCarthy, M., 33
Chaudron, C., 67, 68
Chi, D. N., 67–69
Choi, H. and Iwashjta, N., 265
Chomsky, N., 15–16, 26, 39, 151, 345, 346
Clandfield, L. and Robb Benne, R., 60, 241, 275
Clare, A. and Wilson, J. J., 137–138, 269
Clark, E. V., 153
classical conditioning, 154–157
classroom activities, 294–295, 303–304
CLIL (Content and Language Integrated Learning), 54, 119, 129–130, 270, 290, 344
closed questions, 351–352
code-switching, 302–303
Cohen, A., 34, 35, 70, 282
cognitive engagement, 91–92
cognitive science, 162–165
Colantoni, L., Steele, J. and Escudero, P., 71, 81
Competency Based Language Teaching (CBLT), 270
comprehensibility, 16–19, 83
comprehension, 219–232
  mental representation in comprehension, 223–227

  the roles of comprehension in language acquisition, 227–232
connecting, 102–103
connecting theory and practice, 1–5
  post-graduate courses, 4–5
consciousness and attention, 89, 314
consciousness raising, 127–128
Content Based Instruction (CBI)/ Content and Language-Based Teaching, 54, 119, 129–130, 270, 290, 344
contextual awareness, 103–104
cotextual awareness, 103
Cook, V., 9, 26–27, 299–300
correction (see feedback and correction)
Council for the Curriculum, Examinations and Assessment, 296
coursebooks, 182, 274–278
Craik, F., 92
Criado, R., 123, 135, 347
curriculum development, 49–51, 117–121, 180–181, 209–211, 235–236, 268–269

Damasio, A. and Carvalho, G. B., 329
data-driven learning, 128–129
Davison, C., 279
DeKeyser, R. M., 107, 109, 205, 319
declarative knowledge, 109
Dellar, H. and Walkley, A., 137–138, 274, 275
development, 148–180
  definition, 149
developmental readiness, 94
discovery approaches, 127–128
Dörnyei, Z., 326
drama-based approaches, 131, 272, 292, 344

electrophysiology, 66
Ellis, N., 107, 176, 313, 337
Ellis, R., 8, 14, 19, 23, 26, 35, 42, 45, 69, 72, 100, 108, 109, 257, 282, 283, 300, 307, 308, 318
Ellis, R. and Shintani, N., vii, 9
English as a Lingua Franca (ELF), 258
Evans, N. and Levinson, F. C., 152
explicit learning and explicit knowledge, 107, 313–314, 314–318, 319, 320–323
explicit teaching, 106–107, 320–323
extensive reading/listening/viewing, 55, 133, 209, 270, 293, 344

Faneslow, J., 278–279
Farrell, T. S. C., 331
feedback and correction, 272, 304–312
  auto-input, 310
  corrective feedback, 108, 266
  explicit teacher correction, 305–306
  input feedback, 311
  peer feedback, 309–310
  recasts, 17, 266–267, 306–8
  remediation, 308–309
  responsive teaching, 58, 141, 272, 305
  situational feedback, 310–311
films in language teaching, 272, 293
Flesch, R., 41
form-focused, 110
forms-focused, 109
form-focused in meaning-focused, 110
fossilisation, 175–176
Foster, P., 35, 70, 282
Foucart, A. and Frenk-Mestre, C., 71
functional magnetic resonance imaging, 66
further processing, 148–180
  definition, 148

Garcia Mayo, M. P. and Alcón Soler, E., 69
Gass, S. and Mackey, A., 23

Geraci, L., McDaniel, M. A., Miller, T. M., and Hughes, M. L., 88
Ghosn, I., 44
Gilmore, A., 59
global Englishes, 28–29
Goldstein, B., 60

Hadley, G., 134
Han, Z., and Odlin, T., 175
Han, Z., Park, E. S. and Combs, C., 42
Harley, T. A., 258–259
Hattie, J. and Clark, S., 145
Hayes, J. R. and Flower, L. S., 259
Herschenchsohn, J. and Young-Scholten, M., 23, 69, 71, 72
Hinijosa, J. A., Moreno, E. M. and Ferre, P., 91
Hoedemaker, R. S. and Gordon, P. C., 102
Holliday, A., 234
humanistic approaches, 130–131, 294
Hyland, K., 274
hypothesis testing, 176

imaging, 101–102 (see also visualisation)
immersion, 19
Immordino-Yang, M. H. and Damasio, A., 329
implicit learning and implicit knowledge, 108–109, 313, 314–318, 319, 320–323
information processing (IP), 162–165
inner voice/inner speech, 57–58, 78, 102, 191, 212–213, 247–255, 260–262, 286–287, 290–296
input, 15–55
  comprehensible input, 16–19
  constituents of input, 29–36
  definitions of input, 22–24, 38–39
  input and the language acquisition device, 15–16
  input and interaction, 19–22
  input as interaction, 19–22, 45
  input in materials development, 59–62
  input in assessment, 62–64
  input providers, 24–29

kinds of input, 40
multi-modality of input, 34
significance in SLA, 39–40
supplementary input, 58–59
teachers' perceptions of input, 36
instructed second language acquisition (ISLA), 9–10, 315
intake, 56–147
  application of theory, 114–147
  characteristics of intake, 76–81
  definitions of intake, 67–76
  determiners of intake, 81
  environmental determiners, 98–99
  experiential determiners, 99–106
  extra-linguistic intake, 78–7
  intake in assessment, 144–145
  intake in curriculum development, 117–121
  intake in language policy and planning, 114–117
  intake in materials development, 137–141
  intake in methodology, 121–137
  intake in teacher development, 146
  linguistic determiners, 82–89
  non-linguistic intake, 78–79
  neurolinguistic definitions of intake, 73–74
  pedagogical determiners, 106–111
  psycholinguistic determiners, 89–95
  sociolinguistic determiners of intake, 96–106
  summary of determiners, 111
  theory, 56–113
intelligibility, 82–83
interaction, 19–22, 45, 96–97, 141–143, 249, 251, 257–258, 294

Jackson, J. O., 72–73

Keddie, J., 237
Kennedy, C. and Tomlinson, B., 114, 115, 117, 139

King, J. and Seiko, H., 144
Kirkpatrick, A., 28, 169
Knagg, J., 48
Kormos, J., 12
Krashen, S., 16–19, 23, 25, 26, 39, 44, 93, 168, 246, 299, 314–315
Kuiken, F. and Vedder, I., 256–257, 264

LAD (Language Acquisition Device), 151–153
Lagerwaard, D., 293
Lamb, M., 326
language anxiety, 93–94
language aptitude, 324–325
language courses, 183–188
  proposal for a course, 183–188
language learners, 37–38
  learners as agents, 6, 70, 285, 290, 340
Language Policy and Planning (PPL), 47–49, 114–117, 180–181, 208–209, 233–235, 268
language production, 247–282
  interaction, 249, 251
  planned discourse, 248, 250–251
  the mental process of production, 247–255, 258–259
  the roles of language production in language acquisition, 255
  speech, 248–249
  unplanned discourse, 247, 250
  writing, 250
Language Through Literature, 270–271, 293
language use, 104
Le, N. M. T., 115
learner agency, 6, 70, 285, 293, 340
learner differences, 323–232
Lech, I. B. and Harris, L. N., 143
Lee, J. S. and Hsieh, J. C., 143
Lee, J. S. and Huang, H., 42
Leow, R. P., 67
Letharby, C. and Harries, P., 136
Levelt, W. J. M., 255, 263
Li, S., 308, 324
Liebermann, M. D. and Rosenthal, R., 94

Lightfoot, D., 39, 151, 154
Linck, J. A. and Weiss, D. J., 89
Lintunen, P., Mutta, M. and Peltonen, P. 259–260
literature on computer assisted language learning (CALL), 10–11
literature on digital learning, 10–11
literature on second language acquisition (SLA), 6–8
literature on materials development, 10
literature on the application of SLA theory to language learning, 8–14
literature on the learning of languages, 5–6
literature on the teaching of languages, 5–6
Llinás, R. R., 224
Loewen, S., 136, 266, 307, 325
Loh, J. and Renandya, W. A., 233, 235
Long, M. 19–20, 23, 44, 71, 124, 169, 249, 299, 316
Long, M. and Porter, P. A., 21–22
looking out for the L2/out of class activities, 57, 133–134, 295–296, 344

Maley, A., 25, 26
Masuhara, H., 136, 224, 329–330
materials adaptation, 238–242, 276–278
materials analysis, 60, 214
materials development, 59–62, 127–140, 181–188, 214–215, 237–242, 274–278
  a language acquisition and development course, 183–188
materials evaluation, 238–242
MATSDA, 138–139, 146
McGrath, I., 10
McTigue, E. M., 223
meaning-focused, 110
meaning-form connections, 32
meaningfulness, 92
meaning negotiation, 22
Medgyes, P., 27
memorising, 105, 350

methodology, 51–59, 121–137, 181–188, 211–214, 269–274, 290–296, 343–345, 347–354, 236–237, 343–344
Mishan, F., 51, 123, 126–127, 127–128, 129, 130, 334
monitoring, 260–267
  self-monitoring, 260–265
  peer monitoring, 265–266
  teacher monitoring, 266–267
Morgan-Short, K., 66, 166
Morgan-Short, K. and Ullman, M. T., 121–123
Morrow, K., 333
motivation, 90
Muir, C., 327
multi-dimensional approaches, 133

Nation, P., 105
Nation, P. and McCallister, J., 86
Nava, A. and Pedrazzini, L., 12
neurolinguistics and neuroscience, 73–74, 136, 165–167, 317–318
Nguyen, L., 271
Nguyen, L. and Franken, M., 36, 49
non-native speakers of English, 27–28
Norris, J. and Ortega, L., 315
noticing, 19, 100–101, 263–264
noting, 106

On Target, 119–121
operant conditioning, 159–160
Ortega, L., 20, 23, 27–28
Ovando, C., Collier, V. and Combs, M., 97

Pan, P. C., 322
Papafragu, A. and Grigoroglu, M., 253
parallel distributed processing, 162–165
Pavlov, I. P., 154–155
Peccei, J. S., 150
peer feedback, 309–310
peer input, 96
Peltonen, P., 260
Pérez. K. F. P., 302
Piccardo, E. and North, B., 132
Pienemann, M., 95, 176

pre-teaching, 351
processing, 176–177
psychological distance, 93
psychological readiness, 94–95
positive learning environment, 144
Presentation, Practice, Production (PPP), 4, 13, 134–136, 229, 272–273, 349
Problem-Based Teaching (PBT), 52–53, 126–127, 344
procedural knowledge, 109
processing, 75–76
project-based approaches, 50, 54–55, 119, 131–132, 272, 292–293, 344

Rahman, R. A. and Melinger, A., 253
readability formulae, 41
recall, 197–200, 207
recasts, 17, 266–267, 306–308
recognition, 191–197, 207
recycling, 86–87
Redecker, C., 38
redundancy, 85
rehearsal, 201–203, 207
Reinders, H., 67, 68
responsive teaching, 58, 141, 272, 305
retrieval, 104, 203–206, 207–208
Richards, J., 274
Richards, J. and Rodgers, T., 161, 274
Richards, J. and Schmidt, R., 222
richness, 87
Robinson, P., 92
Rohrer, D., 322
roles of the teacher, 6

salience, 82
Samur, Y., 85
Sato, M. and Ballinger, S., 24, 25, 96, 249, 257, 258
Sato, M. and Viveros, P., 264
Saville-Troike, M. and Barto, K., 70–71, 90, 96, 97, 250
scaffolding, 97
Scenario Approaches, 271–272, 291
Schmidt, R., 21, 100, 101, 135, 169, 263–264

Schmidt, R. and Frota., 313–314
Schütze, U., 73, 78, 103, 176, 201, 202, 205, 213, 248, 259
sensory imaging, 93
Serrano, R. and Huang, H. Y., 213
Sharwood-Smith, M., 67
significance, 84, 101
silence, 144
simplicity, 85–86
Simpson, A., 317
Simulation Approaches, 271, 290–291, 344
skill acquisition theory, 198, 205, 318–319, 346–347
Skinner, B. F., 159–160, 162, 164, 345
Sockett, G., 143
sociological distance, 97–98
Spada, N. and Tomada, Y., 135
spoken grammar, 33
Stent, G., 164
Stern, H. H., 26
Stetsenko, A., 293
Storch, N. and Wigglesworth, G., 300
Sultana, S., 300
supplementary input, 141
Swain, M. 21, 169, 257, 288, 299, 328–329
Swain, M., Kinnear, P. and Steinmann, L., 300

Tallal, P., 227
Tarone, E., 256
Task-Based Language Teaching (TBLT), 50–52, 119, 124–126, 271, 343
Task-Free Activities, 56–57, 141, 344
teacher development, 188, 217–218, 244–245, 279–280
teacher talk, 56, 108, 141, 245
Text-Driven Approach (TDA), 50, 53, 119–121, 124–126, 127, 238, 271, 290, 343, 352–353
The Action-Oriented Approach (AoA), 132, 344
The Audio-Lingual Method, 161–162, 348–349

The Common European Framework, 118, 132
The Communicative Approach, 123–124
The Direct Method, 348
The Douglas Fir Group, 170, 171, 180, 181
The Lexical Approach, 129
The Stellar Programme in Singapore, 233, 235
Thomas, M. and Reinders, H, 117
tolerating ambiguity, 103
Tomlinson, B., 10, 11, 50, 83, 84, 91, 93, 95, 99, 117, 124–126, 130–131, 140, 149, 203, 213, 223, 231, 235, 238, 267, 271, 279, 333–334, 353
Tomlinson, B. and Avila, J., 93, 101, 102, 213
Tomlinson, B. and Masuhara, H., 10, 14, 50, 87, 133, 140, 335
TPR Plus, 55–56, 271, 291–292, 344
translation, 104–105, 350–351

Universal Grammar (UG), 151–153, 346
Usage Based Approaches, 271, 337
using the L1 in L2 acquisition, 105, 298–304, 353

Van Patten, B., 67, 75, 80, 176
Vanuatu, 193–194
visualisation, 101–102, 205–206, 212–213, 247–255 (see also imaging)
Vygostsky, L. S., 153

Watson, J. B., 157–159
Weber, A. and Broersma, M., 194
Widdowson, H. G., 332–333
Widodo, H. P., Wood, D. and Gupta, G. P., 12
Wong, B., Yin, B. and O'Brien, B., 66
working memory, 72–74

Ying, H., 67

Zone of proximal development (ZPD), 18

Made in the USA
Monee, IL
28 April 2026

49136488R00232